PERSPECTIVES ON EARLY AMERICAN HISTORY

A 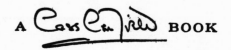 BOOK

PERSPECTIVES ON EARLY AMERICAN HISTORY

Essays in Honor of Richard B. Morris

EDITED BY ALDEN T. VAUGHAN

AND GEORGE ATHAN BILLIAS

HARPER & ROW, PUBLISHERS

New York, Evanston, San Francisco, London

1817

FIRST EDITION

STANDARD BOOK NUMBER: 06-014504-8

LIBRARY OF CONGRESS CATALOG CARD NUMBER: 78-181651

Designed by Sidney Feinberg

Contents

Editors' Preface

FROM 1946 TO 1973 Richard B. Morris prodded scores of doctoral candidates over the hurdles of Columbia University's graduate program. We are now scattered across the country in a wide variety of academic and nonacademic institutions. Some of us have never met; others have long since lost close contact with fellow Columbia graduates and with the institution itself. Yet we all bear the stamp of Richard Brandon Morris. This volume is the tangible tribute of his students to the intangible heritage he gave to us.

Professor Morris knew the art of teaching. He planned his courses well, but never let them become rigid or routine. He lectured with enthusiasm—and machine-gun tempo—but never too intensely to exclude student participation. He led discussions with good humor and a loose rein, but never lost sight of the educational value of a serious exchange of ideas. And he befriended his students sincerely but never —well, almost never—allowed them to waste their time or his own by confusing idle chatter with intellectual growth. Rather, Professor Morris quickly sensed which of his students needed close scrutiny and frequent help and which needed to go their own ways. On the former he lavished his attention and wisdom; on the latter he invoked his blessing to get on with their work and let him know when it was completed. The finished product invariably benefited from RBM's unexcelled substantive and stylistic critique.

All this we learned later. What initially drew most of us to Richard B. Morris was not his teaching skill but his reputation as a productive scholar. By the time of his appointment to the Columbia faculty, Professor Morris had a national reputation for meticulous research and lucid writing. He was clearly one of the most energetic and perceptive scholars in his field, and few graduate students could miss the excitement of becoming historians under his tutelage. And while he guided us in the classroom he continued that amazingly versatile literary productivity—to which several parts of this volume bear testimony.

In planning a book of essays in honor of Richard B. Morris, we have tried to reflect to some extent his versatility—the whole of early American history and beyond—and at the same time to produce a book with unity and coherence. Hence we offer these historiographical essays. They range in focus from the early seventeenth century through the early nineteenth; they cover geographical areas as diverse as New England and Virginia, and they treat topics as heterogeneous as Puritanism, Loyalism, and the emergence of American political parties. The essays have in common, however, a concern with how Americans interpreted their formative years, how historians from the time of John Smith to Richard B. Morris himself have sought to understand and explain the variegated experiences that culminated in the American Revolution. In sum, this is a book about historians and their perspectives on early America.

All of the contributors to this volume save one earned their doctoral degrees under Richard B. Morris's sponsorship. Michael Kraus, a fellow graduate student at Columbia and longtime colleague at City College of New York and Columbia, has written an introduction in which he assesses the contributions of Dr. Morris's major writings, and in a bibliography at the end of the volume there is an extensive listing of the principal Morris publications. In between there are eleven historiographical essays, including one by the master himself. Its inclusion here is unconventional but, we believe, not inappropriate. Richard B. Morris served as our example and helped to shape our careers. We think it right and proper that a sample of his scholarship —in this case an affectionate and perceptive assessment of another great colonialist—be reprinted here. Because the recipient of a *festschrift* is not presumed to know of its existence until publication, we surreptitiously acquired permission to reprint an essay Dr. Morris had published a few years ago. We trust he will forgive us. We trust, too, that he will forgive the absence of contributions from some of his ablest students. Space precluded all but a handful of the many Morris-trained scholars who would gladly have joined this enterprise. The authors of the following essays should be considered simply as representatives of the Morris legion.

A. T. V.

G. A. B.

Cos Cob, Connecticut
Worcester, Massachusetts
July 1972

"How few have the talents, the patient diligence,
and the love of truth which history requires."

—John Jay to Jedediah Morse
1 January 1813

MICHAEL KRAUS

Richard B. Morris: An Assessment

WHEN RICHARD B. MORRIS left his post at City College, New York, to join Columbia's staff, his colleagues toasted him at luncheon and reminisced about their years together. Professor Nelson P. Mead, then chairman of the history department, reminded the group that Dick, as a student, had been largely responsible for the introduction of the honors program at City College. His achievements as an undergraduate were so advanced that a new standard had to be created in recognition of such superiority. It is a tribute to sustained excellence that his students now offer him. As teacher, scholar, archivist, and administrator he has poured his undiminished energy into a host of activities.

The range of his scholarly interests is exceedingly broad. Legal, economic, political, and diplomatic history have all been enriched by his researches. So too have the tools of historical research: in collaboration with his mentor, Evarts B. Greene, Morris brought out, in 1929, *A Guide to the Principal Sources for Early American History (1600–1800) in the City of New York*. The volume was a stimulus to similar publications elsewhere and made possible more soundly based investigations into local history.

Out of dusty archives in New York and other states, this country's legal development in the colonial period was traced in Morris's *Studies in the History of American Law* (1930). With justification he noted

1

then that "the investigator of early American law . . . has to plot his own course virtually unaided. No general treatise deals at any length with the seventeenth and eighteenth centuries in American law." Morris's findings prompted him to write that "certain common tendencies and certain common characteristics appearing in the law of the British colonies in America are in some respects without parallel in the history of the common law in the seventeenth and eighteenth centuries." Their existence justifies the term "American law."

Morris continued his legal studies, editing a volume of *Select Cases of the Mayor's Court of New York City, 1674–1784* (American Legal Records, 1935). In his earlier *Studies,* Morris had written that "the extent to which the common law was adopted in the colonies must be actually determined in each specific situation." Early American law was, in many respects, "indigenous." But the "indigenous" characteristics of the law in colonial America, said Morris, "have gained little recognition in the modern courts." The Supreme Court did something to rectify that neglect when it quoted the Morris study in one of its decisions.

In the 1930's Morris was secretary of the Committee on Legal History of the American Historical Association. In this capacity he retraced the steps of Jared Sparks, who, a century earlier, had searched the archives of the Atlantic coastal states. Morris surveyed archives from Maine to Florida to uncover materials for projected volumes of American Legal Records. "The field of American legal history," said the scholarly F. S. Philbrick, "is vast and almost untilled." Out of Morris's survey came his *Early American Court Records: A Publication Program* (1941, Anglo-American Legal History Series), which laid the groundwork for later studies.

Richard Morris's researches in the law, as well as history, were the foundation for his pioneering study *Government and Labor in Early America* (1946). A massive contribution to a neglected area of American life during the colonial and Revolutionary periods, its findings were supported by an examination of some twenty thousand cases, most of them unpublished. Other scholars had dealt with slavery and some aspects of the free labor and indentured servant systems, but none had analyzed so closely the legal and social position of free and bound labor. We are reminded of the relevance to later practice of earlier concerns and procedures: "The experience of government with labor in the first two centuries of American history holds numerous clues to later developments and provides significant parallels to current patterns. Wage- and price-fixing and economic stabilization, the right of workers to take concerted action for their own advancement, child labor, absenteeism in industry, pirating of workers, restrictions on admission to a trade, restraints upon dismissals . . . constitute the core of the master-servant relations that were supervised by colonial and Revolutionary governments."

In after years, fourteen prominent criminal cases, from Anne Hutchinson to Alger Hiss, were examined in Morris's *Fair Trial* (1952). Written for a broad audience, it raised important questions about justice in America. "Glaring deficiencies in the conduct and procedure of American criminal trials" have not yet "been eradicated." The practice of courts in England, says Morris, has much to teach us.

While the history of labor, especially in the nineteenth century, continued to engage Professor Morris (he published articles on this theme), the American Revolutionary era came to be of more absorbing interest. In 1957 he edited a volume of Hamilton's writings, *Alexander Hamilton and the Founding of the Nation.* The stress is on Hamilton's intense nationalism, urging the young nation to "think continentally." His advocacy, along with that of Madison, of a strong national government in the Confederation period "was profoundly radical." Hamilton was "an administrative genius," envisioning America as a great industrial power. Justly paying tribute to Hamilton's virtues and adherence to basic principles, Morris does not ignore his limitations. His failures as a statesman stemmed from personality defects and tactical blunders; he lacked "the art of compromise."

Another Federalist, John Jay, formerly underrated by many historians, has won a vigorous champion in Professor Morris. Well over a century ago, Richard Hildreth, describing Federalist leadership as superb, bracketed Jay with Washington and Hamilton in "a trio not to be matched, in fact, not to be approached in our history, if indeed, in any other." Morris, as editor of the Jay Papers, is more familiar with his career than anyone else and gives the evidence endorsing Hildreth's praise. In *John Jay, the Nation, and the Court* (1967), Morris differs sharply with earlier historians who had downgraded the Federalist's achievements in diplomacy, state constitution-making in New York, and his role in the Supreme Court. In the events leading up to the Revolution Jay was "a prudent revolutionary"; in drawing up the first constitution of New York State, 1777, he played a central part. When it came time for New York to ratify the United States Constitution, the most influential of the Federalists in winning over the "antis" was Jay.

Jay's nationalism was exceedingly strong. As Chief Justice in the Supreme Court he expounded the Constitution as a powerful instrument of nationalism. "In bringing the States into subordination to the federal government, in asserting the supremacy of treaties, and in laying the foundation for the later exercise by the Supreme Court of power to declare acts of Congress unconstitutional, Jay gave bold directions to the new constitutional regime."

In articles and in his volume *The American Revolution Reconsidered* (1967), Professor Morris dissented from the view that the Revolution was a "conservative movement" and that Antifederalists were the progressive element in the Confederation period. The Revolutionary era, he argued, was not defined by simplistic explanations. Those who asserted that the period was marked by conservatism or who maintained that progressivism was the hallmark of Antifederalists had both oversimplified.

In its origins, the American Revolution was an "anticolonial war," but marked by "liberative currents, class conflicts, and equalitarian urges." Morris listed political reforms stemming *directly* from the Revolution: "government resting on consent of the people, constitution making and republican institutions . . . were truly revolutionary notions." The social and economic changes that came were "not part of the avowed objectives of the war." Having in mind the upheaval created by other revolutions since the eighteenth century, Morris said,

"The most remarkable fact about the American Revolution was not that there was social change but that it was relatively so modest."

Consensus historians—Hartz, Rossiter, Boorstin—who saw a "homogenized" American society in the eighteenth century, are answered by Morris, who undermined the view that America skipped the feudal age. Differing with Beard and Jensen, Morris denied that the new Constitution was "effected by a conspiracy of speculators and counter-revolutionaries." As for assigning labels, he asserted that the Federalists, not the Antifederalists, "were the real radicals of their day."

In his volume *The Emerging Nations and the American Revolution* (1970), Morris examined the repercussions of the Revolution around the world. As against other writers, he argued that the American Revolution has been more influential than the French Revolution in Europe, Latin America, Africa, and Asia. "The American Revolution has meaning and message for our own age, not only for the enduring political and constitutional change that it effected but also because the profound transformation of American society that it sparked has touched the lives of all peoples everywhere."

That transformation, as already mentioned, owed much to John Jay. The New Yorker's special contribution as a diplomat was given full measure in Morris's brilliant *The Peacemakers: The Great Powers and American Independence.* The author's gifts of organization, dramatic narration, and acute analysis stamp it as authoritative. Whatever remained of the myth of French support of the American Revolution and Vergennes's alleged friendliness to America's independence was exploded by Morris. Franklin's importance in making the treaty was downgraded, Jay's enhanced. Morris threaded his way through a labyrinthine intrigue which failed to entrap Jay. It was Jay, perhaps more than his fellow American negotiators, who was responsible for winning the prized concessions in making the peace. The peacemaking "began as an encounter between innocence and guile, but the Americans rapidly acquired a measure of sophistication sufficient for the task at hand." John Adams gleefully spoke of himself and his fellow commissioners as "undisciplined marines," but "we were better tacticians than was imagined." *The Peacemakers* has been justly acclaimed as a work of fundamental importance. It goes beyond previous studies in its wide coverage and in its reassessment of the roles of the many participants in making the peace. It has earned for its author Julian P. Boyd's accolade, a "master historian."

This evaluation of necessity must close on an incomplete note because Richard Morris continues to be a productive scholar. We can look forward to future contributions through the Jay Papers, the New American Nation Series, and further writings on topics that have been of lifelong interest to him and to the historical profession.

Added to his mastery as a scholar has been his masterful teaching. From his classes have come the writings of able students who have refashioned the history of colonial New York, provided support for ethnic studies, and rescued from obscurity the once-prominent. Quick to recognize talent, Morris's contribution lies in the spur given to the neophyte and in the magisterial quality of his own scholarship.

COLONIAL PERSPECTIVES

ALDEN T. VAUGHAN

The Evolution of Virginia History: Early
Historians of the First Colony

AMERICANS, it has often been observed, take particular delight in recounting their early history, a trait that is as old as the American people themselves. During the colonial period, amateur historians abounded—so much so that analyses of early American literature have been predominantly the story of chroniclers and narrative historians. And much of that historical literature continues to be highly regarded: while America's early poetry and fictional prose are notably sparse and uninspiring, its historical efforts are abundant and on the whole vigorous. The works of John Smith, William Bradford, Cotton Mather, and Thomas Hutchinson come readily to mind. Other colonial historians have enjoyed less acclaim but illustrate almost as clearly the pervasiveness of historical consciousness in British America.

Early Virginians shared that consciousness but expressed it in ways significantly different from the contemporaneous Massachusetts writers with whom they vied, at least in the modern mind, for priority of settlement and primacy in literary production. In the century and a half between the founding of the colonies and the American Revolution, Massachusetts produced William Bradford, John Winthrop, Edward Johnson, William Hubbard, Increase and Cotton Mather, Thomas Prince, and Thomas Hutchinson (to name only the major figures). Virginians could point only to John Smith, Robert Beverley, and William Stith as writers who set forth the colony's history in a

9

comprehensive synthesis. The point here is neither to demean Virginia's historians nor to laud New England's, but rather to suggest that the distinctive ethos of each area shaped the character, and to some extent the quantity, of its historical writing. For the Virginians, almost as much as the New Englanders, took pleasure in writing about their part of the New World. But unlike their countrymen to the north, the settlers of the oldest British outpost cared less for narratives of the colony's origin and growth and more for two other forms of historical literature: chronicles of recent events, and descriptions of "the present state" of the colony. Both genre have much in common with each other and with historical synthesis; they nonetheless can be approached as separate literary categories.

In chronicles of exploration and discovery Virginia's literature undoubtedly exceeds that of any other colony, both in quantity and in quality. The vast quantity is in part explained by Virginia's greater longevity, but only in part. Equally important were the circumstances of the colony's founding—its search for precious metals, for a passage to the Pacific, for survivors of the Roanoke colonies. Exploration had been from the first a part of the mission of the Jamestown colony; reports of discoveries and daily events were therefore less a conscious literary effort than a requirement placed on the leaders of colonization by the parent organization in London. And the very existence of the London Company—regardless of its interest in exploration—made inevitable a flow of reports to the mother country. Unlike the New England settlements with their supreme governing bodies in the colonies themselves, or the proprietorships in which the principal political authority or his representative resided in America, the Virginia colony for almost two decades took its orders from a large and unwieldy joint-stock company from whose headquarters in London came an insatiable demand for information. In response the company received, and subsequently published, the detailed chronicles of George Percy, John Pory, Ralph Hamor, and others.

Long before they set foot on Virginia's soil, the leaders of the Jamestown colony had models of New World reportage on which to draw. In 1588 Thomas Hariot, an Oxford mathematician, had described the Roanoke colony's experiences in *A brefe and true report of the new found land of Virginia.* (Theodore DeBry's fusion of Hariot's text with John White's drawings was for its time an inspired conjunction of verbal and visual reporting which unfortunately had few imitators. High printing costs and a paucity of artists conspired to leave most early chronicles without illustrations.)[1] At about the same time appeared the voluminous collections of Richard Hakluyt the younger; his *Principal Navigations, Voyages, Traffiques and Discoveries of the English Nation made by Sea or over Land to the most remote and farthest distant quarters of the earth, at any time within the compass of these 1500 years* came off the presses in 1589 and an expanded edition appeared in 1598–1600.[2] Hakluyt's material stretched from the days of King Arthur to those of Walter Raleigh and presented exploration as a noble and exciting national mission. The clergyman-anthologist-imperialist has accordingly been credited with a major role in prodding England into the race for empire. But Hakluyt's influence was literary as well. Englishmen now had abundant examples of how to write about discoveries; they also had a fair prospect that their reports would be broadcast to the world by Hakluyt or his self-appointed successor, Samuel Purchas.

All of which is merely to say that the adventurers—in the modern sense of the word—to Virginia could hardly have escaped the then current fascination with tales from exotic parts of the world. And the needs of the London Company added whatever impetus the lure of literary fashion did not provide. So too did the chaotic conditions of

1. David B. Quinn has collated the original London edition of 1588 with those of Hakluyt (*Principal Navigations* [1589]), and DeBry (*America* [1590]), in *The Roanoke Voyages, 1584–1590,* 2 vols. (London, 1955). In Robert E. Spiller et al., eds., *The Literary History of the United States,* 3 vols. (New York, 1948), I, 31, Hariot's work is described as "a slim volume which must ever be 'Number One' in the literary history of the British colonies which form the present United States." DeBry's illustrated edition first appeared in 1590 and was reprinted at least nineteen times in the next thirty-five years. *Ibid.,* 32.

2. Innumerable later versions have been published. The most accessible complete edition was issued in 1907 as Richard Hakluyt, *Voyages,* Everyman's Library, 8 vols. (London and New York).

Virginia's early years. Among the score or more chronicles that survive from seventeenth-century Virginia, a significant portion—perhaps
half or two-thirds—have as their major theme a partisan view of
events in the colony.[3] The very first chronicles to come back from Virginia—the anonymous "Relayton" in 1607[4] and parts of George
Percy's "Discourse" printed in *Purchas His Pilgrimes*[5]—contain little
of a contentious quality, but beginning with Captain Smith's *True
Relation* of 1608,[6] controversy crept into much of the literature that
emanated from English America.

Other chroniclers, contentious or not, deserve mention because they
added importantly to Virginia's corpus of historical works. Among
them were Alexander Whitaker, whose *Good Newes from Virginia*
(London, 1613)[7] is perhaps most notable for its distinctively Puritan

3. "Chronicles" is here used in the sense of a basically chronological account
of a brief period or episode.
4. "A relayton of the Discovery of our River, from *Iames Forte* into the
Maine . . . writen and observed by a gent: of the Colony." Printed in Ameri-
can Antiquarian Society, *Archaeologia Americana*, IV (1860), 40–65; in
Edward Arber and A. G. Bradley, eds., *Travels and Works of Captain John
Smith*, 2 vols. (Edinburgh, 1910), I, xl–lv; in Philip Barbour, ed., *The Jamestown Voyages under the First Charter, 1606–1609*, 2 vols., Hakluyt Society
Publications, ser. II, vols. CXXXVI–CXXXVII, I, 80–98.
5. "Observations gathered out of a Discourse of the Plantation of the
Southerne Colonie in Virginia by the English, 1606." First published by
Samuel Purchas, *Hakluytus posthumus or Purchas His Pilgrimes*, 4 vols. (London, 1625), IV, 1685–1690; reprinted in Samuel Purchas, *Hakluytus posthumus
or Purchas His Pilgrimes*, 20 vols. (Glasgow, 1905–7), XVIII, 403–419; Arber
and Bradley, *Works of John Smith*, I, lvii–lxxiii; and Barbour, *Jamestown
Voyages*, I, 129–146. Percy's later "A Trewe Relacyon" (written sometime
after 1625) may have been an indirect rebuttal to Smith's *Generall Historie*.
But because Percy's work was not published until 1922 it is not discussed in
this essay. It remains, however, a highly important document for the understanding of early Virginia. It is, as Howard Mumford Jones has noted, "a
masterpiece of disagreeable details." (*The Literature of Seventeenth Century
Virginia*, 2d ed. [1968], 19). Similarly, I have not discussed here Edward Maria
Wingfield's "Discourse" because it did not appear in print until 1845. Both
the Percy and the Wingfield pieces may have enjoyed a limited circulation in
manuscript, but their impact on the historical consciousness of Jacobean
England must have been slight.
6. *A True Relation of such occurences and accidents of noate as hath
hapned in Virginia since the first planting of that Collony . . .* (London,
1608). Reprinted in Arber and Bradley, *Works of John Smith*, I, 1–40; and in
Barbour, *Jamestown Voyages*, I, 165–208.
7. Reprinted in facsimile, New York, 1936.

flavor; much of his fund-raising tract sounds like a sermon on "right-giving"—highly moralistic, highly biblical, and conspicuously Ramean in its logic. By contrast, Ralph Hamor's *True Discourse* (London, 1615)[8] is known less for its rather pedestrian text than for its appendix, which includes John Rolfe's letter to Governor Thomas Dale requesting permission to marry Pocahontas. Important too were William Strachey's "True reportory of the Wracke and redemption of Sir Thomas Gates Knight . . . his coming to Virginia and the estate of that Colonie then and after . . ." (London, 1625),[9] a vivid description of the wreck of the *Sea Venture* on Bermuda Island. Scholars have long believed, and on apparently solid grounds, that this narrative provided the setting for Shakespeare's *Tempest*.

The full title of Strachey's account of the shipwreck on Bermuda and the years immediately following give the clue to the second main type of Virginia historical writing—those stressing "the present state of" Virginia. Many of the earliest tracts straddle the gap between the two genres, being at once chronicles of events and descriptions of the colony's condition. Strachey's history is a case in point, for it includes a fairly detailed description of Virginia in 1610. Similarly, Ralph Hamor's title reads in part: *A True Discourse of the Present State of Virginia, and the Successe of the Affaires There till the 18 of June, 1614. Together with a Relation of the Severall English Townes and forts. . . .* Hamor, like Strachey, sought to tell readers in Europe what Virginia was at that time, as well as the events that had recently transpired.

As the colonial period wore on, the blend of chronicle and description became less common. The earliest chroniclers had had good reason to include description—readers back home wanted to know what the country's flora, fauna, and climate were, how its natives looked and acted, where its principal rivers and harbors and mountains lay. Similarly, the descriptive historians often incorporated reports of

8. *A True Discourse of the Present State of Virginia.* Reprinted in facsimile, Richmond, Va., 1957.
9. "A True Reportory of the Wracke, and redemption of Sir Thomas Gates, Knight . . . ," in *Purchas His Pilgrimes* (1906 ed.), XIX, 5–72. Reprinted in Louis B. Wright, ed., *A Voyage to Virginia in 1609* (Charlottesville, Va., 1964), 1–101.

recent events to satisfy their readers' appetites for news from the colony. The distinction, then, between chroniclers and descriptive historians has relatively little meaning for the first decades. That situation altered perceptibly by the middle of the seventeenth century.

Then began a spate of works that stressed the current structure of the colony's political and economic life, with, in some instances, a description of some unusual aspect of the area's geography. A prime example is an anonymous tract of 1649 immodestly titled *A Perfect Description of Virginia*.[10] Through fifty-seven numbered sections, varying from a sentence to several paragraphs in length, the reader is introduced to the present and prospective commodities of Virginia; only in an appended letter of about three pages is any notice given of human events. The next year appeared a pamphlet by one E. Williams entitled *Virginia: More especially the South part thereof, Richly and truly valued* which focused on the economic potential of the area later known as North Carolina but did not ignore Virginia proper.[11] Near the end of the century three of Virginia's officials penned what may be the most interesting and coherent of the descriptive accounts of Virginia: Henry Hartwell, James Blair, and Edward Chilton, *The Present State of Virginia, and the College*.[12] For reasons still obscure it did not appear in print until 1727, three years after Hugh Jones's *The Present State of Virginia*.[13] Between them the Hartwell-Blair-Chilton volume and the Jones volume brought to full maturity the descriptive genre. (It would later gain its most illustrious exemplar in Thomas Jefferson's *Notes on Virginia* [1785].) The two publications of the 1720's revealed not only stylistic but substantive superiority: whereas the focus

10. Reprinted in Peter Force, ed., *Tracts and Other Papers, Relating Principally to the Origin, Settlement, and Progress of the Colonies in North America . . .*, 4 vols. (Washington, D.C., 1836; repr. Gloucester, Mass., 1963), II, No. 8.
11. Reprinted in *ibid.*, III, No. 9.
12. Reissued Williamsburg, Va., 1940, ed. by Hunter Dickinson Farish. For a thorough review of the circumstances of the book's authorship and the possible reasons for publication see Robert A. Bain, "The Composition and Publication of *The Present State of Virginia and the College*," *Early American Literature*, VI (1971), 31–54.
13. London, 1724. Reissued Chapel Hill, 1956, ed. by Richard L. Morton. See also Spiller et al., *Literary History*, 47.

of "present state" works of the seventeenth century had been almost exclusively economic and occasionally political, those of the eighteenth century rested on a far broader concept of society. The contents of the 1727 book, for example, included information on the militia, the church, dissenting sects, and education. The colony's economic opportunities did not fade from view, but they now shared center stage with less materialistic aspects of colonial Virginia. Similarly, Hugh Jones, professor of mathematics at the College of William and Mary, in 1724 presented his readers with information on, among other things, "the Habits, Customs, Parts, Imployments, Trade, etc. of the Virginians; and of the Weather, Coin, Sickness, Liquors, Servants, Poor, Pitch, Tar, Oar, etc."[14]

The shift in emphasis in the descriptive accounts, and the frequent presence of descriptive material in the early chronicles, stems from the purpose of the "present state" genre. For both chronicles and descriptions must be considered as elements in the promotional campaign to attract immigrants to the colony, and before 1624 to entice investors in the London Company of Virginia. As Hugh T. Lefler has observed, Virginia had the most abundant, most varied, and most exaggerated promotional literature of any British colony.[15] Almost all of the published literature that originated in Virginia during its first seventy-five years, and much of its later literature, sought to convince Englishmen that Virginia fell little short of being an earthly paradise.

The promotional nature of Virginia's literature showed in a variety of ways. Much of it indulged in shamelessly inflated descriptions of the flora and fauna: the New World's plants were always larger, the fruit sweeter, the animals more abundant and prolific, the weather more salubrious. And those who still dreamed of the riches of the Orient need not despair: until well past mid-seventeenth century, most accounts—whether chronicles or descriptions or a mixture of both—insisted that the day would soon arrive when a route through Virginia to the Pacific Ocean would bring a boom to the colony's economy.

14. Jones, *Present State of Va.*, table of contents.
15. Hugh T. Lefler, "Promotional Literature of the Southern Colonies," *Journal of Southern History*, XXXIII (1967), 4.

The chimera of trade between Europe and the Orient, with Virginia as the critical depot and point of transshipment, clung with unbelievable tenacity in the minds of seventeenth-century Virginians. Another technique often used by the promoters was a flattering comparison of Virginia with nations of similar climates. E. Williams, for example, in his *Virginia . . . Richly and truly Valued* (1650), compared "this felicity-teeming Virginia" with Persia: the latter is proclaimed to be wonderfully productive, and inferior only to this "Virgin Countrey, so preserved by Nature out of a desire to show mankinde . . . what a brow of fertility and beauty she was adorned with when the world was vigorous and youthfull. . . ."[16] Still another tactic employed by Williams and typical of promotional literature was inclusion of a list of Virginia's commodities and their values—sure to look appealing to the relatively depressed economy of England.[17]

It would be stretching a definition past the breaking point to include all promotional literature in the category of history. Much of English promotional writing came from men who had never set foot in America and made no effort either to narrate colonial events or to describe the current condition of the colony; their intent, rather, was to defend the actions of the company or Crown, praise the colony's prospects for the future, and urge further investment and settlement. Such were Robert Johnson's *Nova Britannia: Offering Most Excellent fruites by Planting in Virginia. Exciting all such as be well affected to further the same* (1609),[18] perhaps the earliest piece of purely promotional writing aimed at an existing colony, and William Symonds's *Virginia: A sermon preached at White-Chapel in the presence of . . . the adventurers and planters for Virginia* (1609),[19] published under the sponsorship of the London Company. These and similar works are of great historical interest but are not, on the basis of the authors' "nationality" and the substance of the writing—at least in the terms of this essay—products of early Virginia historians. But it is nonetheless true, and significant, that the promotional necessities of early Vir-

16. Force, *Tracts*, III, No. 11, 19.
17. *Ibid.*, 51–53.
18. Reprinted in Force, *Tracts*, I, No. 6, and in facsimile from the original edition, New York, 1969.
19. Reprinted in facsimile, New York, 1968.

ginia helped to determine the tone of the early chronicles and descriptive histories. And in both categories Virginia produced widely and well.

Of comprehensive historians, however, colonial Virginia could boast only three. John Smith, chronicler and descriptive historian in his earliest writings, in 1624 turned to historical synthesis. More than seventy-five years later, Robert Beverley wrote the second comprehensive history of the colony, though he too had one foot in another genre: his *History and Present State of Virginia* is as significant for its descriptions of early eighteenth-century Virginia as it is for his narration of the events of the preceding century. Only with the appearance in 1747 of William Stith's *The History of the First Discovery and Settlement of Virginia* did the colony have an attempt at pure historical synthesis.

There is little doubt that Captain John Smith excelled among the early seventeenth-century historians of Virginia. What is in doubt is whether he can be considered an American writer. He spent barely two and a half years in Virginia, far less than in eastern or western Europe or, of course, in England. Born and raised an Englishman, he died one too, far from the embryonic nation that has long insisted on making him its earliest and—in the eyes of some—its most representative hero.

And yet a good case can be made for John Smith, American historian. Despite the drama of his adventures in Hungary and Turkey, the American episode seems to have been his most meaningful personal experience, and he spent the better part of his life between his departure from Virginia in 1609 and his death in 1631 trying unsuccessfully to get back to America, at first to Jamestown, later to New England. His most lasting contributions remain on this side of the Atlantic too: his naming of New England and many of its localities; his explorations and appellations in Virginia; his advice and assistance to prospective settlers in both areas; and his vigorous championing of an expanded British America. More importantly, Smith's historical writings are overwhelmingly American in theme and content. He wrote his first historical account in and of Virginia, and he devoted most of his subsequent historical writing to British America. (His *True Travels,* which deals primarily with his Hungarian adventures, is autobiography rather than history.) And throughout his historical writing he focused on Indians, the American wilderness, hardships of settlement, the necessity and advantage of hard work in a frontier environment, and the priority of merit over family status in the building of a new society. Smith, in short, saw in America the very themes that would later become hallmarks of American literature.

In recent years John Smith's reputation as a historian has risen to a new high. It had been substantial from Smith's own day until the mid-nineteenth century when Henry Adams, convinced by John Gorham Palfrey that an attack on Smith's veracity "would attract as much attention, and probably break as much glass, as any other stone that could be thrown by a beginner," launched his own impressive career as a historian by deprecating John Smith's.[20] Before long it became *de rigueur* to put Smith down, in part as inaccurate, in part as excessively vain—two characteristics that seemed to undermine the value of Smith's history and make it border on fiction. Most damaging to the Captain's reputation were highly unfavorable assessments by two late nineteenth-century authorities on early Virginia, Edward D. Neill in *The Virginia Company of London* (1869) and *The English Colonization of America* (1871), and Alexander Brown in his extremely influential *Genesis of the United States* (1890).[21] As recently as 1964 Samuel Eliot Morison observed that "John Smith was a liar, if you will, but a thoroughly cheerful and generally harmless liar . . . ," a trait that Admiral Morison attributed to Smith's "matching stories on long sea-voyages and telling tales around Virginia camp-fires, [until] he became unable to distinguish the true from the false."[22]

20. Henry Adams, *The Education of Henry Adams* (Boston, 1918; reissued New York, 1931), 222. Henry Adams, *Historical Essays* (New York, 1891), 42–79; reprinted from *North American Review,* CIV (1867), 1–30.
21. Neill's works were influential in their time but gained little attention in the twentieth century. Brown, on the other hand, continues to be read, largely because his two-volume *Genesis of the United States* is primarily a collection of source material that has yet to be supplanted. A reprint edition appeared in 1964. Brown also wrote critically of Smith in *The First Republic in America* (Boston, 1898).
22. Samuel Eliot Morison, *Builders of the Bay Colony* (Boston, 1930; rev. ed., Boston, 1964), 8.

Because Smith remains the only source for much of Virginia's earliest history, the question of his veracity takes on considerable historiographical importance. If Smith prevaricated, his history cannot be trusted. Either he told the truth and his works can therefore be accepted as valid historical sources, or he twisted the facts to suit himself and must therefore largely be rejected as a guide to early Virginia. Jarvis M. Morse's contention does not wash that we could believe Smith on Virginia even if he proved fictitious on Transylvania.[23] This makes sense in principle but not in practice: with no means of verification we could hardly trust the reporter of one event if he is known to have lied on another.

The three most persistent doubts about Smith's historical accuracy have recently been put to rest, not definitively perhaps, but convincingly. First, the dramatic and often bizarre adventures in eastern Europe. It almost takes an act of faith to believe that one man could have lived through so many hazardous situations: attacked by brigands, cast overboard by religious fanatics, robbed, engaged in hand-to-hand combat at sea—all this en route to Hungary. And once there, to have lived through battle after battle, to have beheaded three Turks in spectacular single combats, to have been captured and enslaved, to have slain his brutal owner and escaped on the master's horse into Russia, and finally to have served briefly aboard a pirate ship before at last returning to his native land—it is more than the credible mind could bear. And so, beginning with Thomas Fuller's caustic *Worthies of England* (1662), continuing through Hungarian Lewis L. Kropf's judgments that Smith had fabricated the entire eastern European story, to S. E. Morison's persistent suspicions, historians—and through them the general public—have raised a doubting eyebrow at John Smith's story of superhuman exploits.[24]

Implausible, yes; improbable, no, is the current verdict on Smith's *True Travels*. Largely through the efforts of Laura Polanyi Striker and

23. "John Smith and His Critics: A Chapter in Colonial Historiography," *Journal of Southern History,* I (1935), 130.
24. Thomas Fuller, *The Worthies of England,* ed. by John Freeman (London, 1952); Lewis L. Kropf, "Captain John Smith of Virginia," *Notes and Queries,* 7th ser., IX (1890), 1–2, 41–43, 102–104, 161–162, 223–224, 281–282; Morison, *Builders,* 8.

Philip Barbour, both of whom combine linguistic and historical talents, the places and events in Smith's account have been shown to be substantially accurate.[25] Perhaps Smith exaggerated his importance or his bravery or his fortitude, but wherever his story can be verified as to people, places, and events, it stands up well. His two most recent biographers and the editors of two recent anthologies of his writings unite in proclaiming Smith reliable on his exploits in Eastern Europe.[26]

The Captain has long been suspected of distorting his American adventures, too, but here again recent scholarship appears to vindicate him. Suspicion had long lingered on Smith's several versions of the Pocahontas episode. It had been assumed by many that the absence of the Pocahontas rescue scene from the *True Relation* (1608) and its appearance in the *Generall Historie* (1624) pointed inexorably at literary invention. Why leave the rescue out in the first book but include it in the second unless it was a figment of his later imagination? But defenders of Smith now contend that (1) Smith had no control over the publication of his *True Relation*. Someone in England edited the original version, now lost, and may well have deleted the story if, in fact, Smith included it. (2) Smith had good reason *not* to tell the story then. In large part a promotional tract, his *Relation* soft-pedaled the Indians' hostility; either Smith or his editor would want as little as possible on the Captain's capture and close escape from death. But in 1624 the story could be told. Smith now had control over the contents

25. Laura Polanyi Striker, "Captain John Smith's Hungary and Transylvania," in Bradford Smith, *Captain John Smith* (Philadelphia, 1953), Appendix I; Striker, "The Hungarian Historian, Lewis L. Kropf, on Captain John Smith's *True Travels*," *Virginia Magazine of History and Biography*, LXVI (1958), 22–43; Striker and Bradford Smith, "The Rehabilitation of Captain John Smith," *Journal of Southern History*, XXVIII (1962), 474–481; Philip L. Barbour, "Captain John Smith's Route Through Turkey and Russia," *William and Mary Quarterly*, 3d ser., XIV (1957), 358–369; Barbour, "Captain John Smith's Observations of Life in Tartary," *Virginia Magazine of History and Biography*, LXVIII (1960), 271–283; Barbour, "Fact and Fiction in Captain John Smith's *True Travels*," in Warner G. Rice, ed., *Literature as a Mode of Travel* (New York, 1963).

26. B. Smith, *Captain John Smith;* Philip L. Barbour, *The Three Worlds of Captain John Smith* (Boston, 1964); John Lankford, ed., *Captain John Smith's America* (New York, 1967); David Freeman Hawke, ed., *Captain John Smith's History of Virginia* (Indianapolis, 1970).

of his book, had the time and space to tell whatever he wished, and because he had long since ceased to feel kindly toward the London Company he felt no compunction against revealing the seamier side of Virginia's early years. And (3) for a man whose vanity might well cause him to underplay rescue by a ten-year-old girl, Pocahontas's subsequent fame could well have changed the Captain's perspective: in 1624 rescue by a forest princess who later became a Christian, married an Englishman, and visited the Queen of England must have seemed downright romantic. Finally, adoption into a tribe on the plea of an Indian chief's daughter comports with current knowledge about the customs of Algonquian tribes. In sum, the story, as well as the reasons for the delay in its telling, now appears plausible.[27]

So do the numerous alterations in Smith's other passages from the *True Relation* to the *Generall Historie*. In 1935 Jarvis Morse reported on his analysis of Smith's changes: half of them had no effect on Smith's reputation, some diminished his role, and some others clearly enhanced it.[28] A more recent and more thorough comparison by Everett H. Emerson strengthens the point.[29] All in all, Smith in the *Generall Historie* expanded his narrative to provide more detail and corrected earlier passages in the light of new evidence. The thrust of his alterations was toward better history, not self-aggrandizement.

Lastly, modern scholars make perhaps their most convincing point when they note the acceptance of Smith's veracity by his contemporaries. Some differences of opinion appeared over the interpretation of events in early Virginia, but none seems to have arisen over basic facts.

27. This reassessment appears most extensively in the Bradford Smith and Philip Barbour biographies. Earlier contributions had been made by Arber and Bradley, *Works of Captain John Smith,* especially I, cxv–cxviii; Morse, "John Smith and His Critics"; Jay B. Hubbell, "The Smith-Pocahontas Story in Literature," *Virginia Magazine of History and Biography,* LXV (1957), 275–300. See also James P. C. Southall, "Captain John Smith (1580–1631) and Pocahontas (1595?–1617)," *Tyler's Quarterly Historical and Genealogical Magazine,* XXVIII (1946–47), 209–225; and Everett H. Emerson, "Captain John Smith as Editor: *The Generall Historie," Virginia Magazine of History and Biography,* LXXV (1967), 143–156.
28. Morse, "John Smith and His Critics," 131.
29. Everett H. Emerson, *Captain John Smith,* Twayne's United States Authors Series (New York, 1971), 78–87.

Two men in England could testify to Smith's adventures in Transylvania and any number to events in Virginia.[30] None challenged him, at least in print. And it may be true, as some authorities insist, that Smith would not have dared to tell lies in a book dedicated to the Duchess of Richmond and Lenox, England's ranking noblewoman, and including testimonial poems to the author from several distinguished men of the times, among them John Donne and Samuel Purchas, or, in the case of *True Travels,* dedicated to three of the most prominent men in England, including his own manor lord.[31] (That failed to impress Thomas Fuller, who was in some sense a contemporary of Smith's, but Fuller's own credentials as an impartial observer leave much to be desired, and his brief critical remarks on Smith—about thirty lines altogether—can hardly be taken as a significant refutation.) Everyone who wrote during Smith's lifetime seems to have upheld him. By 1685 he had become the subject of a short biography in Latin by Henry Wharton, a distinguished cleric and scholar, who may have had access to a manuscript, since lost, that corroborated Smith's account. Wharton believed Smith's story and insisted on the accuracy of his own biographical treatment.[32] Since then Smith has had more supporters than detractors.

Much of what we usually dub "John Smith's history," is not, in the strict sense, his writing at all. Smith did compose some history, both from personal recollection and from written and verbal reports gleaned from others. But the bulk of his compilations, as he freely admitted, were just that—compilations of accounts written by participants in the events. Smith's most important book, *The Generall Historie of Virginia, New-England and the Summer Isles,* was a collaborative effort in the Hakluyt-Purchas tradition, with Smith providing some of the text but more importantly serving as compiler

30. Arber and Bradley, *Works of John Smith,* I, viii.

31. Charles Poindexter, *Captain John Smith and His Critics* (Richmond, 1893), 54–58; B. Smith, *Captain John Smith,* 58; John Gould Fletcher, ed., *The True Travels* (New York, 1930), vii–viii, and "The Credibility of the Narrative," by Lawrence C. Wroth, in *ibid.,* 76–78.

32. Henry Wharton, *The Life of John Smith, English Soldier,* trans. by Laura Polanyi Striker (Chapel Hill, 1957).

and editor of the writings of others.[33] Smith claimed to have "such a number of variable Relations, that would make a Volume of at least a thousand sheets"—i.e., 4,000 pages.[34] From that mass Smith culled the best (we trust) and wove them into a fairly concise and coherent story. Today's standards of scholarship would insist that Smith be acknowledged as "editor" or perhaps "editor and contributor"; in 1624 the title page could read "By Captaine John Smith." But Smith made no pretense to sole authorship of the book itself. Time and again large passages are identified in the running heads and section titles as "A relation from Master John Rolfe," or "The observations of Master John Pory," or "Captaine Huses Relation." At times Smith got careless with credit lines, but not, it seems clear, from intent to deceive. Rather, Smith as editor leaves something to be desired by today's canons. He cut and pasted, often radically condensing the originals, and as a rule he gave credit where it was due. But he provided little connecting material, and often he worked with more haste than proficiency. The most recent and perceptive analyst of Smith's writings faults the *Generall Historie* for not being "a coherent and satisfying book."[35] It remains, however, a landmark in the emergence of American historianship and an exciting story in its own right.

Had Smith not compiled his *Generall Historie,* he would stand nonetheless as an important historian of early Virginia for three other contributions: the *True Relation* (1608), the *Map of Virginia* (1612), and the concluding section of *True Travels* (1630). The first of these, *A True Relation of such occurences and accidents of noate as hath hapned in Virginia since the first planting of that Collony . . .,* is generally considered the first published book to be written in America about America.[36] It was also Smith's only entirely original work— assuming that his editor did not add to Smith's account. We know that the editor subtracted; he admits to that in his preface where he acknowledges that "somewhat more was by him [Smith] written, which being

33. Emerson, *Captain John Smith,* 87.
34. Arber and Bradley, *Works of John Smith,* I, 279.
35. Emerson, "Captain John Smith as Editor," 156.
36. Emerson, *Captain John Smith,* 45.

as I thought (fit to be private) I would not adventure to make it publicke."[37] Some modern authorities have argued that Smith did not intend to have any of his relation made public.[38] That seems improbable. In the seventeenth century it was widely assumed that reports of travel and description would begin as private letters but would end as public tracts if interest in them sufficed. John Smith could hardly have been surprised that his letter "to a worshipfull friend of his in England" soon appeared in print. In any event, *A True Relation* was more reportage than historical narrative and places Smith at the outset of his literary career among the chroniclers of early America. His reputation as a true historian would have to wait until he returned to England and there assembled his *Map of Virginia* and other books.

To his own generation, and perhaps to ours too, *A Map of Virginia* may well have been Smith's most important work. It included the oft reprinted and amazingly accurate map of the eastern part of the Jamestown colony that Smith had drawn while still there—a major source of information on the location of Indian tribes, rivers, and other geographical data.[39] It contained too his fascinating observations on Indian life and institutions (Smith here proved his skill as a descriptive historian). And it closed with a quasi-synthetic account of "the Proceedings of the English Colonies in Virginia since their first beginning from England in the yeare of our Lord 1606 till this present 1612. . . ." This, like much of the *Generall Historie,* is compilation rather than synthesis, for as the title page makes clear, the contents are "taken faithfully as they were written out of the writings of Thomas Studley . . . , Anas Todkill, Walter Russell," and others.[40] But unlike the *Generall Historie,* Smith seems to have had no hand in constructing the narrative part of the volume, "the Proceedings," either as author or as editor. The title page attributes the latter office to "W. S." —probably William Symonds. *A Map of Virginia* thus represents the three principal types of colonial historiography—chronicles, descrip-

37. Arber and Bradley, eds., *Works of John Smith,* I, 4.
38. For example, Emerson, *Captain John Smith,* 32.
39. Coolie Verner, "The First Maps of Virginia, 1590–1673," *Virginia Magazine of History and Biography,* LVIII (1950), 8–12.
40. Arber and Bradley, *Works of John Smith,* I, 85.

tion, and synthesis—but only the first two can be credited to Captain Smith.

Smith's first attempt at historical synthesis—in this case consisting of little more than extracts from a few letters—appeared in the second edition of *New England Trials* (1622), to which he appended a brief account of the Plymouth colony's first two years. Smith's first synthetic account of Virginia came two years later in the *Generall Historie*. There, in Books III and IV, he fused a variety of accounts into a comprehensive if awkward narrative of Virginia's history from 1607 to 1624. Much of the material Smith culled from previous publications—the "Proceedings" in Book III, Ralph Hamor's *True Discourse* and Edward Waterhouse's *Declaration* in Book IV—but in both sections Smith added new material, deleted some old material, and modified wherever recent information clashed with the original versions. The result is not graceful, nor is it always convincing; it nonetheless stands as the first effort by Smith at a consecutive history of Virginia from its beginnings to the time of publication. And because of Smith's close knowledge of events, his access to Purchas's materials, and the wide range of sources on which he drew, Books III and IV of the *Generall Historie* remain to this day the most important single source on early Virginia.

In a recent analysis of Books III and IV, Everett Emerson has found that Smith made about ninety-six changes of more than a word or two in the "Proceedings" that had appeared first in the *Map of Virginia* and now reappeared in the *Generall Historie,* this time with Smith rather than Symonds serving as editor of other men's accounts. Most important are ten new passages which constitute Smith's principal original contributions. They include an expanded account of his captivity by the Indians and rescue by Pocahontas, an account of battles with the Rappahanocks, and another passage in which Pocahontas is credited with saving the colony from attack by Powhatan. Professor Emerson is undoubtedly correct in concluding that the thrust of Smith's additions and emendations is an attempt to persuade his readers, and especially the Virginia Company, to adopt a harsh policy toward the Indians. But, as Emerson also notes, other changes reflect an objective historian at work: corrections of minor errors, new geographical information, new biographical details. Book IV, less synthetic than Book III, presents much important though ill-digested material, including the only known versions of several letters and other documents, and a considerable amount of Smith's own judgments on events in Virginia and on policies of the London Company. Again, Smith made corrections, additions, and deletions in the materials he reprinted from earlier publications.[41]

Of John Smith's later writings only the final section of *True Travels* can be considered Virginia history, but here again the Captain resorted to synthesis rather than chronicles or description, and again the material is partly a reprint of others' works, partly alterations and additions by Smith based on "discoursing with those returned thence."[42] But this appendage to the *True Travels* covers five years of the colony's history (1624–1629) in less than half a dozen pages in the modern edition of Smith's *Works* and is thus more of a snippet of history than a work in its own right.

What in the end makes John Smith prominent, and representative, in the historiography of colonial Virginia is his versatility. He gave us our first significant report written in America, he gave us the first and best description of the area and its inhabitants, and he gave us the first —though certainly not the best—published narrative of the colony's history based on a wide range of personal observations, documents, and interviews. It is easy to disparage the Captain for what he did not do, and easy to belittle him for what he did poorly. It is only fair, however, to remember with some appreciation the very considerable contribution to historical literature made by a man whose life and inclinations impelled him to action rather than contemplation, to the sword rather than the pen.

Almost a century elapsed between the first book on the founding of Virginia, Smith's *True Relation,* and the second, Robert Beverley's *The History and Present State of Virginia* (1705). Beverley's work—

41. Emerson, *Captain John Smith,* chs. 4 and 5.
42. Arber and Bradley, *Works of John Smith,* II, 884.

part history, part promotional description—enjoyed some popularity in its day on both sides of the Atlantic. The book appears to have sold well in Virginia; in England, where it was published, it earned the contempt of historian John Oldmixon, but nonetheless was translated into two French editions, published simultaneously at Orléans and Amsterdam.[43] A second English edition came out in 1722, the year of Beverley's death.

For the next two centuries and more, the Beverley history suffered undeserved neglect. It seldom gained notice in histories of American literature, and when on occasion it did, it was only to be damned with faint praise. Recently Louis B. Wright has almost single-handedly revived Beverley's literary reputation, initially by giving it good notice in *The First Gentlemen of Virginia,* then praising it in a scholarly article, and finally by bringing the *History* back into circulation through a new edition.[44] Wright contends that Beverley produced a minor classic, "an ornament to colonial American literature and a document of genuine importance." Not a great book, not a major historical contribution, but in the context of its times a very worthy piece, deserving far more attention than it has received. According to Wright, "Many a reader, choking on some indigestible chunk of Cotton Mather's *Magnalia Christi Americana,* has cursed the quality of colonial letters without realizing that the age offered any tastier fare. As a historian and stylist, Beverley, it is true, is no forgotten Gibbon or Macaulay, but measured by the standard of colonial America, his *History* deserves high rank for its simplicity, clarity, and interest."[45]

Less than half of Beverley's work is synthetic history. He labeled the

43. Louis B. Wright, "Beverley's History . . . of Virginia (1705), a Neglected Classic," *William and Mary Quarterly,* 3d ser., I (1944), 49–51.
44. Louis B. Wright, *The First Gentlemen of Virginia: Intellectual Qualities of the Early Colonial Ruling Class* (San Marino, Calif., 1940), 295–299 and passim; Wright, "Beverley's History," 49–64; Robert Beverley, *The History of the Present State of Virginia,* ed. by Louis B. Wright (Chapel Hill, 1947). Wright also discussed Beverley's history in *The Cultural Life of the American Colonies, 1607–1763* (New York, 1957), 166f. For a biographical sketch of Beverley see Fairfax Harrison, "Robert Beverley, the Historian of Virginia," *Virginia Magazine of History and Biography,* XXXVI (1928), 333–344.
45. Wright, "Beverley's History," 49.

first of the four parts of his volume "Book I. The History of the First
Settlement of Virginia, and the Government thereof to the present
Time"; the remaining three parts treat the "present state" of the
colony. In total space they comprise almost twice as many pages as
the section on history. But as the first effort since Smith's to offer a
coherent narrative of the history of the colony, and the first including
Smith's to fully synthesize its material, Beverley's work is a landmark
in American historiography.

He might never have written it had the London bookseller Richard
Parker not asked him to read and correct a segment of John Oldmixon's manuscript on British America. Beverley had already prepared some notes on the current state of Virginia, probably for use
in luring French Huguenots to the colony. Appalled by the inaccura-
cies of Oldmixon's account (drawn largely, in fact, from a draft by
Beverley's brother-in-law, William Byrd), Beverley composed a historical introduction to his descriptive account and published the whole
in 1705, three years before Oldmixon's book appeared. There followed a running battle between the Virginian and the Englishman.[46]
In *The British Empire in America,* Oldmixon took advantage of his
later publication date to praise his own account of the colony, which
he admits to having drawn largely from an earlier history, "written
with a great deal of Spirit and Judgment by a Gentleman of the
Province to whom this Historian confesses he is very much indebted;
but in some Places he was forc'd to leave him, to follow other Guides;
and whosoever compares the one History with the other, will see
enough Difference to give that which is now published the Title of
New." Beverley assumed that the comparison was to his own work,
though in fact Oldmixon, as he pointed out in the second edition of
British Empire, meant a manuscript by "Col. Bird."[47] In any event
Beverley in turn castigated Oldmixon in the revised edition of his
History (1722). "He nowhere," charged the Virginian, "varies from

46. *Ibid.,* 51f.
47. John Oldmixon, *The British Empire in America, Containing the History
of the Discovery, Settlement, Progress and present State of all the British
Colonies on the Continent and Islands of America* (London, 1708), x; 2d ed.
(London, 1741), x.

the Account that I gave, nor advances any thing new of his own, but he commits so many Errors and imposes so many Falsities upon the World."[48] Because Oldmixon outlived the Virginian by twenty years, he had a chance to say the last word; he used it in the preface to his 1741 edition to cast gentle aspersions on "another *History of Virginia,* written by one R. B. . . ."[49]

Beverley, like Smith, reflects American themes. In fact, as Louis Wright has noted, the *History* "is self-consciously American."[50] Beverley chides Virginians for too heavy reliance on England, and he speaks out often in defense of American liberties. And, as much as if not more than Smith, he places the American Indian near the center of the New World stage. With this difference: whereas Smith saw the Indians largely as potential enemies and barriers to English colonization, Beverley saw them as an integral part of the colonial scene—almost a symbol of America. Smith had attributed the crudeness of his "rough Pen" to being a soldier; Beverley, on the other hand, insisted that "I am an *Indian,* and don't pretend to be exact in any Language. . . ."[51] Both, of course, exaggerated. By 1624 Smith had written several books and had long since sheathed his sword; while Beverley, the epitome of early eighteenth-century Virginia aristocracy, could hardly be considered an unlettered aborigine. Yet both metaphors had some validity. Smith, an Englishman with strong ties to America, had been succeeded in historiographical sequence by Beverley, an American with deep loyalty to England.

In content and style, the progression from Smith to Beverley reflects the gap between a seventeenth-century explorer-soldier of fortune, of yeoman stock, and an eighteenth-century planter of moderately patrician origins. Smith's *Historie* stressed the almost daily crises of early colonization, for that had been his world, and he sought less to be a "Compiler of hearsay" than a recounter of events in which he had

48. Beverley, *History and Present State of Virginia,* 2d ed. (London, 1722), preface.

49. Oldmixon, *British Empire* (1741 ed.), x.

50. Wright, "Beverley's History," 52.

51. Arber and Bradley, *Works of John Smith,* I, 275; Beverley, *History and Present State of Virginia* (Wright ed.), 9.

been "a reall Actor."[52] Beverley recounted events too, but from the detached perspective of a later day and without personal rancor— except in his version of Bacon's Rebellion, which may well have reflected his father's involvement in the episode. Yet both historians of early Virginia shared simplicity of style and a general forthrightness of presentation. Not surprisingly, Beverley had a better technical command of language and a better resistance to the rhetorical flourishes that the self-conscious Smith succumbed to; otherwise the two men shared much the same manner.

In accuracy, Beverley, like Smith, holds up well under scrutiny. Because he perforce relied heavily on Smith for the period of discovery and initial settlement, Beverley's accuracy often in fact depends on Smith's. In a few instances Beverley modified the Captain's explanation of events on the basis of Purchas or other early authorities, but most of his facts and quotations come straight from Smith. Apparently Beverley's contemporaries found few if any errors in the historical part of the Virginian's book. The 1722 edition preserves almost verbatim the historical text of the first edition; the changes Beverley made came in the descriptive rather than the narrative section.

Beverley also shared with the Captain a candor that overcame the customary deference to men in high position. In his first edition Beverley wrote critically of royal governors and anyone else whose actions he disapproved. For reasons unknown—perhaps a mellowing with age, perhaps a closer regard to the propagandistic value of his book—in the edition of 1722 Beverley confessed that he had "retrench'd such Particulars as related only to private Transaction and Characters . . . without Reflection on the private Conduct of any Person."[53] He had removed most of the biting attacks on royal officials. The rancor had been excised.

In his references to Indians and Negroes, Beverley reflects how far ethnic relations had changed since Smith's day. While not an "Indian-hater" of the sort familiar to the American frontier, Smith had not al-

---

52. Arber and Bradley, *Works of John Smith*, I, 275.
53. Beverley, *History and Present State of Virginia,* 2d ed., preface.

ways been charitable in his descriptions of the natives, and seldom in his dealings with them. Beverley is fairer and more perceptive, and for his day unusually generous. Much of his information he lifted from Smith and other chroniclers; his interpretations differ, however, when he interjects his own judgments of Indian behavior and assigns responsibility for Indian-white friction. He regretted, for example, that the Rolfe-Pocahontas marriage had not been followed by further miscegenation. The English, Beverley opined, should have seized upon intermarriage with the natives as beneficial to both peoples and an almost certain guarantee of racial harmony.[54] Beverley's portrayal of the Virginia Indians in the descriptive part of his book is also highly favorable to the natives. No similar attitude marks his discussion of Negroes, however. As owner of a large plantation worked by black bondsmen, Beverley saw no need to describe or praise the Africans. In the historical portion of his book he mentions the arrival of the first Negroes in 1619 (he misdated it 1620); in the descriptive portion he explained the difference between the servants and slaves: "Slaves are the Negroes, and their Posterity, following the condition of the Mother, according to the Maxim, *partus sequitur ventrem*. They are call'd Slaves, in respect of the time of their Servitude, because it is for Life."[55] Several pages follow on the fair treatment accorded to white servants.

Partly because Beverley so thoroughly reflected the mores and perspectives of his time and class, his *History* continues to be read, but for its traditional descriptive sections rather than its more unique attempt at historical synthesis. At the same time, Beverley serves as an important transition in Virginia historiography, standing midway between the earlier "present state" writers and the later comprehensive historians.

Not until 1747 when William Stith published *The History of the First Discovery and Settlement of Virginia* did a work appear that attempted simply to tell the story, based on primary sources, of the

54. *Ibid.* (Wright ed.), 38f.
55. *Ibid.*, 48, 271.

history of Virginia. Stith adhered exclusively to the synthetic genre; neither chronicles nor descriptive sections intrude on his narrative. But unfortunately for his contemporaries and for posterity, Stith failed to produce the grand history of the colony that he set out to write. So doggedly did he search for source materials and so conscientiously did he apply himself to the task of "conning over our old musty Records, and of studying, connecting and reconciling the jarring and disjointed Writings and Relations of different men and different Parties," that in 331 printed pages his story reached only to 1624.[56] That is only as far as John Smith had carried the story in his *Generall Historie* and not as far as he had taken it in the closing sections of his *True Travels*. Stith wanted to extend his coverage in subsequent volumes, but the apathy that greeted his initial effort left him too discouraged to continue. Although he lived for eight more years he published nothing further. Nor did any of Stith's fellow colonists pick up his lead. The first comprehensive history of colonial Virginia would not be written until John Daly Burk's three volumes appeared early in the nineteenth century.

Few men of Stith's day were better equipped to fashion a comprehensive history of Virginia.[57] His education at Queen's College, Oxford, and his long affiliation with the College of William and Mary—where he served as master of its grammar school and during the last three years of his life as president of the college—reflect his considerable academic achievement. His chaplaincy of the House of Burgesses and his rectorship of Henrico Parish placed him close to the top echelons of colonial government. So too did his family tree. He was related to many of the most influential Virginia families and, like Robert

56. William Stith, *The History of the First Discovery and Settlement of Virginia: Being an Essay towards a General History of the Colony* (Williamsburg, 1747, reprinted in facsimile, New York, 1969). The quotation appears on iii–iv.
57. For biographies and critical information see Jarvis M. Morse, *American Beginnings: Highlights and Sidelights of the Birth of the New World* (Washington, D.C., 1952), 218–220; Moses Coit Tyler, *History of American Literature, 1607–1765*, 2 vols. (New York, 1878; reprinted in 1 vol., New York, 1962), 493–496; Spiller et al., *Literary History of the United States*, I, 31–33; Darrett B. Rutman, introduction to Stith, *History of . . . Virginia* (1969 ed.); and Allen Johnson and Dumas Malone, eds., *Dictionary of American Biography*, 22 vols. (New York, 1928–58), XVIII, 34–35.

Beverley, could be counted among the colony's aristocracy, with all that implied in the way of access to private papers, connections in Williamsburg and London, and the wealth that ensured "perfect Leisure and Retirement . . . not burthened with any publick Post or Office."[58]

Stith made good use of his advantages. More persistently and successfully than John Smith or Robert Beverley he gathered the documentary evidence that had survived the ravages of more than a century. Some of the documents came readily. His uncle, Sir John Randolph (grandfather of the statesman and historian Edmund Randolph), had intended to write a history of Virginia as a preface to an extensive collection of "useful Papers and Records" collected by William Byrd II and housed in Byrd's library at Westover. But Stith went beyond that collection. When John Randolph died before starting his historical preface, Stith not only took over the documents at Westover but added to them substantially by scouring official depositories at Williamsburg and elsewhere. Before his search ended he had amassed a highly impressive array. Although we have no detailed list of its contents, the Byrd-Randolph-Stith papers probably included more than half the manuscripts that exist today for the study of early Virginia.[59] In the twentieth century Susan Myra Kingsbury made a meticulous search in both England and America for materials relating to the Virginia Company of London; she uncovered many important sources unavailable to Stith, and other scholars in the nineteenth and twentieth centuries have discovered additional items. But for his time William Stith proved remarkably adept as a collector of documents on colonial Virginia.

The use Stith made of his materials also deserves respect, for he applied a healthy skepticism to manuscripts and published works alike. Of necessity, he drew heavily on John Smith for the period from 1607 to 1619, and he held high regard for the Captain, "a very honest Man, and a strenuous Lover of Truth," whose works Stith considered "ex-

58. Stith, *History of . . . Virginia* (1969 ed.), iv.
59. *Ibid.*, Rutman's introduction, ix.

cellent but confused."[60] But he recognized the difference between Smith's treatment of the colony's first two years, for which Smith is the "unquestionable Authority," and the later years when the Captain no longer reported from his own experience. His works then became "liable to some just Suspicion" because of Smith's friendship with Sir Thomas Smythe and Samuel Argall, whose accounts he drew on, and from the bitterness against the company for slighting Smith and his accomplishments in the colony. ". . . [S]uch Prejudices and Partialities do silently and unperceptibly slide into the best and honestest Minds; and ought therefore to be carefully watched and guarded against by all Men, but especially by Historians."[61]

Aware that Captain Smith had an ax of his own to grind, Stith sought corroboration in other sources. His principal help came from a copy of the London Company's records, provided by William Byrd II, whose father had purchased them in England, consisting of the proceedings of the company from 1619 to 1624. Stith also drew on the published works of Samuel Purchas, Thomas Hariot, and a collection of visual records described somewhat cryptically as "With's *Cuts and Maps,*" as well as on the extensive Randolph collection of manuscripts and the public documents at Williamsburg.[62]

From his varied sources Stith fashioned a highly detailed and largely chronological narrative. Unlike Beverley he revealed little interest in economic issues—except to decry the colony's early dependence on tobacco and to vent his own contempt for the "stinking, nauseous, and unpalatable Weed."[63] Stith's distaste for tobacco marks his sole area of agreement with James I; to the extent that a villain emerges from Stith's story it is the Stuart monarch who abolished the London Company of Virginia. Stith had failed to carry his critical use of sources far enough to realize that his reliance on the company's records for 1619–1624 exposed him to only one side of the story. Hence Stith concluded, with remarkable candor and perhaps a smattering of incipient American nationalism, that King James "was at

60. *Ibid.,* Stith's preface, iii–iv.
61. *Ibid.,* iv.
62. *Ibid.,* iv–viii.
63. *Ibid.,* 182f.

best, . . . very simple and unjudicious, without any steady Principle of Justice and Honour. . . . I have ever had, from my first Acquaintance with History, a most contemptible Opinion of this Monarch; which has perhaps been much heightened and increased, by my long studying and conning over the materials of this History."[64]

Other men, besides "that silly Monarch," incurred the wrath of the Virginia parson. The Earl of Warwick, for his role in conspiring to break up the company, Sir Thomas Smythe for his shortsighted administration of the organization, and the avaricious early settlers who almost wrecked the colony at the outset, all became objects of Stith's scorn. But there were heroes too, some of them unlikely ones. Thomas Dale, the harsh governor of the second decade, emerges in Stith's account as "among the first and best of our Governors";[65] and Captain Samuel Argall, whose stock among modern authorities has been low, fared almost as well as Dale in Stith's hands. He heaped praises too on Sir Edwin Sandys for rescuing the company from the maladministration of Smyth and for putting up a noble fight for its survival against the machinations of Warwick and King James. Modern scholars, led by Wesley Frank Craven, have significantly revised the traditional picture of Sandys, but here again the limited nature of Stith's sources and his naïve confidence in the company's records led him to see the Sandys-Southampton administration through company-colored glasses.[66] In sum, Stith produced a highly personal and largely political narrative, yet one that had the merits of thoroughness, frankness, and documentation.

Stith's labors have been both damned and praised. Thomas Jefferson put Stith's writing down as "of no taste in style. He is inelegant, therefore, and his details often too minute to be tolerable, even to a native of the country whose history he writes."[67] Moses Coit Tyler took issue with Jefferson but concluded that Stith had committed "a sin against

64. *Ibid.*, vii.
65. *Ibid.*, 139.
66. See especially Wesley Frank Craven, *Dissolution of the Virginia Company: The Failure of a Colonial Experiment* (New York, 1932; reprinted Gloucester, Mass., 1964).
67. Thomas Jefferson, *Notes on the State of Virginia*, ed. by William Peden (Chapel Hill, 1955), 177.

artistic proportions and the limits of human life" in devoting so much space to such trivial detail.[68] Had Stith continued his narrative in the same proportions, he would have needed, Tyler implies, innumerable volumes and another lifetime. And yet Stith, for all his flaws, has been recognized by many recent authorities as having accomplished more than he has usually been given credit for: extensive research, modern canons of historical skepticism, a readable narrative, and a refreshing candor. Jarvis Morse called him "colonial Virginia's greatest historian," and Darrett B. Rutman, in a perceptive introduction to a modern reprint of Stith's *History*, praises him as a charming narrator as well as a tentative pioneer in methodology.[69] And if for nothing else, he deserves acknowledgment as the author of colonial Virginia's only volume of truly comprehensive history. What he started he could not finish, but he at least attempted history in the fullest sense.

It has long been recognized that the Puritans who settled New England felt a special need to convince the world, and themselves, that they were God's chosen people and that He watched with special concern their experiment in Christian living. Hence New England's outpouring of historical treatises that served a function for the mass of Puritan society much the same as diaries and other introspective writings did for the individual. Of synthetic histories New England held almost a monopoly in colonial America.

Because Virginians did not share the Puritan colonists' sense of divine mission, the settlers of the southern colony seldom tried to broadcast their achievements, at least in the same manner. Instead, Virginia's writers focused on the more proximate needs of reporting the discoveries and events of the immediate past and describing to prospective colonists the advantages of the present and future of the colony. The net result is somewhat different in quantity (in the combined categories of descriptive and historical writers Moses Coit Tyler lists nine Virginians and twenty-two New Englanders),[70] partly, per-

68. Tyler, *History of American Literature*, 494.
69. Morse, *American Beginnings*, 220; Stith, *History of . . . Virginia*, Rutman introduction, xix.
70. Tyler, *History of American Literature*, 34, 266–268.

haps, different in quality, but most conspicuously different in character. As Kenneth Murdock and others have made abundantly clear, the Puritans used all their writings—histories, sermons, and private correspondence—as vehicles to transmit the message they wanted to hear: God had chosen New England for His new Zion. With both Puritan and Virginian writers, the title pages tell almost the whole story. New England produced *Wonder-Working Providence of Sions Saviour in New England, New England's Memoriall,* and *Magnalia Christi Americana;* Virginians wrote *The History and Present State of Virginia, The History of the Dividing Line betwixt Virginia and North Carolina,*[71] and *The History of the First Discovery and Settlement of Virginia.* Not surprisingly, most New England authors came from the clergy or were laymen of a strongly religious bent—in the latter category William Bradford, John Winthrop, and Edward Johnson are obvious examples—in contrast to the more secular and mundane Virginians—Robert Beverley, William Byrd, and of course, John Smith. The New Englanders, in sum, wrote ecclesiastical history, the Virginians natural history; the Puritans wrote of Canaan, the Anglicans of Eden.

Not all of the difference between the form and character of Virginia and New England historical writing can be attributed to religion, however. Granted that lukewarm Anglicans viewed history in a different light from impassioned Puritans, the *facts* of colonization also affected historical forms. Virginia's early history had been marked by bitter dissension among the settlers, famine (including the infamous case of cannibalism), Indian massacre, collapse of the Virginia Company, rampant materialism (especially in the mania over tobacco), and the failure to discover the expected gold mines and a passage to the Orient.

71. William Byrd, II, *The History of the Dividing Line betwixt Virginia and North Carolina* (1841; reprinted in Louis B. Wright, ed., *The Prose Works of William Byrd of Westover* [Cambridge, Mass., 1966]). I have not included Byrd in this essay because he was not, in my opinion, a historian in any sense of the word. He was a diarist, pure and simple, and such a good one that he well deserves a prominent position among the writers of his time. I cite his *History of the Dividing Line* here because he is sometimes referred to as a historian and because he used the word "history" in the title of his journal of a surveying expedition—which tells us something about the Virginians' view of history.

Heroes were few and far between. Even John Smith, a bona fide hero, failed in Virginia, as later did both Governor Berkeley and Nathaniel Bacon. It was not a beginning to admire or immortalize in historical narrative. (Not surprisingly, much of the best writing on Virginia has focused on the era of Washington, Jefferson, and Madison, or on that of Robert E. Lee.) It made far more sense—it was imperative, in fact —to downplay the early failures and concentrate instead on Virginia's potentialities. Hence the prevalence in Virginia historiography of reportage and description and the relative absence of historical synthesis.

New England, on the other hand, learned from the trials and errors of the Jamestown venture. The Puritans went better prepared, had their supervisory authority in their midst, guarded against massacre (they had read with care the accounts of 1622), and they for the most part avoided internecine quarrels. More immigrants therefore flocked to the Puritan colonies and for nearly a generation economic prosperity accompanied the population boom. Word of mouth carried the good news back to England; propaganda literature became unnecessary if not redundant, especially in light of the Puritans' almost phobic animosity toward strangers. As a result the New England historians with only slight distortion of the truth could concentrate on synthetic history that reveled in the achievements of New England's early years. If a society needs to find comfort in its own roots, Puritan New England could not avoid gloating on its auspicious beginnings.

Virginians, in the meantime, developed to a high pitch the promotional tracts that in one guise or another formed so important a part of early American literature. While Puritan historians acted like preachers in disguise, Virginia's historians put on the mantle of the press agent. Less concerned with the *why* of Virginia's settlement, they cared deeply about *what* had emerged. Thus Virginia's historiographical output during the colonial period can be considered abundant only in the broadest sense of "history"; in the narrow sense of synthetic history the colony did not need or want anything more extensive than John Smith's *Generall Historie*. In the middle of the eighteenth century William Stith thought the time ripe for a comprehensive narrative, "For I need not say, how empty and unsatisfactory every thing, yet published upon the Subject, is; excepting the excellent but confused Materials, left us in Captain *Smith*'s History."[72] But Stith misjudged; the colony had yet to experience a golden age of which its citizens and heirs would yearn to read.

That day was fast approaching, however: Washington was already fifteen years old when Stith's book appeared, and Jefferson was five. When the great age of Virginia at last arrived it speedily gave birth to a new breed of Virginia historians. In the early years of the nineteenth century readers anxious to learn about the origins and growth of the Old Dominion could consult John Daly Burk's *History of Virginia* (3 vols., 1804–1805; his death in a duel prevented completion of a fourth volume), or John Marshall's *Life of George Washington* (5 vols., 1804–1807), the first volume of which gave a fairly thorough recitation of Virginia's past. Eventually the national historians who emerged in the middle of the nineteenth century, in particular George Bancroft and Richard Hildreth, incorporated the history of the oldest American colony and of all other colonies into truly comprehensive treatments of the nation's past. But in so doing, they and their successors have of necessity drawn much of their knowledge of colonial Virginia from the early writers of chronicles and descriptions, who passed on a richer legacy than they could have imagined.

72. Stith, *History of . . . Virginia,* preface, iii.

HARRY M. WARD

The Search for American Identity: Early
Historians of New England

THREE SEPARATE STAGES—an "inspired invention of Western thought,"[1] actual discovery, and the process of settlement—brought into being the new entity called "America." But time was required for the peoples inhabiting the New World to acquire an identity not only spatially, but culturally and institutionally, from Europe. Settlers on the Atlantic frontier had to recognize their own unique qualities, and to perceive of themselves in a new perspective before they could become "Americans." The process of achieving identity takes generations, centuries, or even ages when there is a complex mingling of peoples and cultures, as was the case in the shaping of European nations. In America, isolated and distant from the Old World, the process was quickened.

New Englanders, in the last quarter of the seventeenth century, were caught up in the anxiety of a changing society. Appropriately enough, they turned to the past to discover whether or not they had kept the faith of the founders, what they had become, and what the prospects were of the future. Life had proceeded far beyond the primitive communities that had marked their beginnings. An indigenous sectionalism had emerged out of which would grow a conceptualiza-

1. Edmundo O'Gorman, *The Invention of America: An Inquiry into the Historical Nature of the New World and the Meaning of Its History* (Bloomington, Ind., 1961), particularly the Introduction and pt. IV.

tion of what it meant to be an American. To the historian fell the task of delineating the common heritage, tradition, and traits.

The five colonial historians selected for discussion—William Hubbard, Cotton Mather, Thomas Prince, Thomas Hutchinson, and Jeremy Belknap—each represented a succeeding generation from 1670 to 1790.[2] This span stretched from the first stirrings for a quest of identity to the eve of the idealization of America's past. Four of the five were clergymen; the other carved out a career as a professional civil servant. Three traced their ancestry to New England founders, while Prince's father migrated to America and Hubbard's came over as a child. To compare these writers in terms of their construction of a usable past, it has been necessary to establish a cutoff date in the Hutchinson and Belknap histories at around 1730—even though both men reached the era of the American Revolution in their works.

Writing of New England's past, they all felt, could be instructive and provide new insights into the character of the people in the region. History could "be of use to Posterity, as well as those of the present Generation," to "carry along the Memory of such eminent Deliverances, and special Preservations granted by divine Favour to the People here."[3] Mather and Prince, in particular, had as their prime

2. William Hubbard (1621–1704), minister at Ipswich; Cotton Mather (1662/3–1728), minister at the Second (North) Church in Boston; Thomas Prince (1687–1758), co-pastor at the South Church in Boston; Thomas Hutchinson (1711–1780), chief justice and governor of Massachusetts; Jeremy Belknap (1744–1798), minister at Dover, New Hampshire, and after 1786 at the Federal Street Church in Boston. The chief works are as follows: William Hubbard, *A General History of New England from the Discovery to 1680*, 1st ed. (Boston, 1815); William Hubbard, *The History of the Indian Wars in New England*, orig. pub. 1677, ed. by Samuel G. Drake, 2 vols. (Boston, 1865); Cotton Mather, *Magnalia Christi Americana*, orig. pub. 1702, 2 vols. (Hartford, 1820); Thomas Prince, *A Chronological History of New-England*, originally published 1736 (Boston, 1826)—this edition contains the *Annals* (1630–33), orig. pub. 1755; Thomas Hutchinson, *The History of the Colony and Province of Massachusetts-Bay*, orig. pub.: I (1764), II (1767), and III (1828), ed. by Lawrence S. Mayo, 3 vols. (Cambridge, 1936); Jeremy Belknap, *The History of New-Hampshire*, orig. pub.: I (1784), II (1791), and III (1792) (Boston, 1813).

3. Hubbard, *Indian Wars*, The Epistle Dedicatory, I, 12. "Foundation and corner stones, though buried . . . ought not to be out of mind; seeing they support and bear up the weight of the whole building." Hubbard, *General History*, 100.

motivation the recapturing of the purity and simplicity of the first communities. "Certainly one good way to save that loss," wrote Mather, "would be to do something that the memory of the great thing done for us by God may not be lost, and that the story of the circumstances attending the foundation and formation of this country and of its preservation hitherto, may be impartially handed unto posterity."[4] What our forefathers "hath seen done by the most High" was "well worth bequeathing" in order that the descendants "may set their hope in God."[5] New Englanders ought to remember their founding forefathers, "to treat their Names with Veneration as the worthy FATHERS of this Countrey" and to follow their examples and goals.[6] Next to the history of the church, a history of the early experiences in America provided a guide for the further perfection of society which would usher in the new golden age. "To *Prize* what we have, is the way for us to *Gain* what we have not," wrote Prince.[7]

An awareness of the past also contributed to the formation of individual identity. Hutchinson noted: "We are fond of prolonging our lives to the utmost length. Going back to so familiar an acquaintance with those who have lived before us, approaches the nearest to it of any thing we are capable of, and is in some sort, living with them."[8] Belknap had a more romantic interest. He felt that there was an unfolding adventure in his New Hampshire, which had hitherto been told only in "fugitive pieces." Hence, he sought "to delineate the characters, the passions, the interests and tempers of the persons" who

4. Mather, *Magnalia*, I, 40.

5. Cotton Mather, *The Wonderful Works of God* . . . (Boston, 1690), 19.

6. Thomas Prince, *The People of New England Put in mind of the Righteous Acts of the LORD to Them and their Fathers, and Reasoned with concerning them*, Election Sermon (Boston, 1730), 34. Prince's extant published sermons and many of his manuscript notes and letters have been issued as a microfilm publication of the University of Washington. For the collateral published writings of all the historians the Evans microcard collection (American Antiquarian Society) is also used.

7. Prince, *Chronological History*, Preface, xi; Cotton Mather, *A Recapitulation of Wonderful Passages which have Occur'd* . . . [upon] *New-England* (Boston, 1694), 16. "Sad Events should rather be improved to our own Instruction, than the condemning of others." Hubbard, *Indian Wars*, ed. Drake, II, 249.

8. Hutchinson, *History of Massachusetts-Bay*, ed. Mayo, II, ix.

contributed to the shaping of the colony and "to describe the most striking features of the times. . . ."[9]

New England's history was a connecting link between the history of the Western world and the future realization of God's master plan for the whole human race. Prince spelled out in detail the evolution of a providential history from the beginning of time to demonstrate that the world was now prepared for New England's perfectionism, which represented the highest stage in the development of man. In America, God had elected an entire society rather than an individual. Cotton Mather likewise emphasized the conspicuous setting of the New England experiment in the eyes of the world; only in this region had world reformation been advanced.[10] Though there was hardship and suffering, no people were more blessed with advantages of the land and sea, and freedom of religion and civil government.[11]

All five historians appealed to the Old Testament and classical symbols of antiquity in their efforts to place America within the context of world history. Puritan historians drew parallels between past and present history, wrote in allegorical terms, and, in the case of Prince, established a line of ancestry that went back to antiquity. As Kenneth Murdock pointed out, they indicated "a desire to define and preserve a tradition . . . so that their people might not be children vainly seeking for fathers."[12] To Prince the settlement of New England represented a restaging of the Old Testament experience:

> There never was any People on Earth, so parallel in their general History to that of the ancient Israelites as this of NEW-ENGLAND. To no

9. Belknap, *History of New-Hampshire*, I, iv–vi.
10. E.g., Mather, *Wonderful Works*, 23. See Richard S. Dunn, "Seventeenth-Century English Historians of America," in James M. Smith, ed., *Seventeenth-Century America: Essays in Colonial History* (Chapel Hill, 1959), 218–219, and Peter H. Smith, "Politics and Sainthood: Biography by Cotton Mather," *William and Mary Quarterly*, 3d ser., XX (1963), 186–206.
11. Prince, *The People of New England*, 34–35.
12. Kenneth B. Murdock, "Clio in the Wilderness: History and Biography in Puritan New England," *Church History*, XXIV (1955), 233–234. Murdock contends that the loneliness in a "howling desert"—the anxiety of feeling the need to belong—heightened the urge to search out parallels and allegories from the Bible and classical literature. Through tropology and typology, New England could claim a great tradition as well as expectations for the future.

other Country of People cou'd there ever be so directly applied a Multitude of Scripture Passages in the literal sense, as to this particular Country.
That excepting *Miracles,* and changing *Names,* one wou'd be ready to
think, the greater Part of the OLD TESTAMENT were written about *us;*
or that *we,* tho' in a lower Degree, were the particular Antitypes of that
primitive People.[13]

Belknap, like Mather, tentatively subscribed to the idea that American discovery reached back to "the remotest antiquity" of the Phoeni-
cians.[14] In his grandiose *American Biography,* begun on the eve of his
death, he included entries of no fewer than fifty explorers and dis-
coverers. To most Puritan historians, the founding of New England was
largely a religious fulfillment; to Hutchinson it was an extension of the
English experience; but to Belknap America's settlement marked a
new age which commenced with the freeing of the European mind.
America's discovery was a convergence of enthusiasm and technical
advance of all European nations.

It is happy for America that its discovery and settlement by the
Europeans happened at a time when they were emerging from a long
period of ignorance and darkness. The discovery of the magnetic needle,
the invention of printing, the revival of literature and the reformation of
religion, had caused a vast alteration of their views, and taught them the
true use of their rational and active powers. To this concurrence of
favourable causes we are indebted for the precision with which we are able
to fix the beginning of this great American empire; An advantage of which
the historians of other countries almost universally are destitute; their first
areas being either disguised by fiction and romance, or involved in im-
penetrable obscurity.[15]

None of these historians—not even Hutchinson, who slanted his
history from an imperial view—was willing to remove the marrow out
of the providential destiny of early America. The idea of divine inter-

13. Prince, *The People of New England,* 21.
14. Mather, *Magnalia,* I, 41; Jeremy Belknap, *American Biography: An
Historical Account of Those Persons Who Have Been Distinguished in
America,* I (Boston, 1794), Introduction; Jeremy Belknap, *The Foresters, an
American Tale* (Boston, 1792), 62. To Mather, God concealed the discovery
of America until the "fulness of time was Come" for rediscovery.
15. Hutchinson, *History of Massachusetts-Bay,* I, xxix; Belknap, *History
of New-Hampshire,* I, 9; Sidney Kaplan, "The *History of New-Hampshire:*
Jeremy Belknap as Literary Craftsman," *William and Mary Quarterly,* 3d
ser., XXI (1964), 22.

vention in the affairs of man, as expressed by Puritan historians, is all too familiar. God had granted His people a promised land, where they could approach the Invisible City, where "their conversation might have been said to be in heaven."[16] The region would have to be conquered to test the zeal of God's people, but in persevering they would inherit a land of milk and honey. The heathen would be driven before them: "a land of darkness" and a "wilderness" would become "a country capable with good improvement to maintayne a nation of people."[17] To Prince "the omniscient and sovereign GOD had espied and chosen this Land for our Fathers, for a Refuge and Heritage for them and their Children." God directed the voyages of the Pilgrims and Puritans to a location suitable to their mission.[18] Afflictions that were visited upon New England evidenced God's concern for His people to keep their covenant with Him.[19]

Hubbard and Mather saw everywhere "special providences" in the life of the colonists, but Hubbard—especially in his *Indian Wars*—considered the natural causes as well as the supernatural.[20] Even the

16. William Hubbard, *The Benefit of a Well-Ordered Conversation* (Boston, 1684), 102.

17. Hubbard, *General History*, 22, 60, 83, 376–377, 577. Hubbard divided his history in short periods of "lustres"—each indicating that God's providence shone on New England. God punished in remarkable ways those who thwarted the mission into the promised land (e.g., *ibid.*, 580–581). See also Mather, *Magnalia*, I, 49. For an election sermon-as-history on the city-on-a-hill theme, see William Hubbard, *The Happiness of a People* (Boston, 1676), 49–61.

18. Prince, *Chronological History*, 170, 280; Prince, *The People of New England*, 24; Thomas Prince, *Civil Rulers Raised up by God to Feed His People* (Boston, 1728), 14; John Van de Wetering, "Thomas Prince: Puritan Polemicist" (unpubl. Ph.D. dissertation, University of Washington, 1959), 246–248. For Prince's relation of science to providence, see Theodore Hornberger, "The Science of Thomas Prince," *New England Quarterly*, IX (1936), 26–42.

19. E.g., "God has had, in some Countrey or other, a peculiar People owning his Revelation and their covenant Engagement to him, so he has sometimes brought them into the most threatening Dangers, to humble them for their Sins, awaken them to Repentence, make them sensible of their Dependance on him, excite their Cries to him and Hope and Trust in him. . . . Then he has made them *stand still* and *see it* with Wonder. . . ." Thomas Prince, *The Salvation of God in 1746* (Boston, 1746), 10.

20. Hubbard, *General History*, 620; R. E. Watters, "Biographical Technique in Cotton Mather's *Magnalia*," *William and Mary Quarterly*, 3d ser., II (1945), 157–163. Kenneth B. Murdock contends that Hubbard meant by his

secular-minded Hutchinson discerned that God provided His people "favourable seasons" for their harvest.[21] He and Belknap both recorded remarkable "providences" well into the eighteenth century when some misfortune befell the colonists' French foe. Yet Hutchinson cautioned that "the best use to be made by posterity" of "remarkable incidents" was "not to depend upon special interpositions of providence because their ancestors have experienced them, but to avoid imminent dangers and to weigh the probability and improbability of succeeding in the ordinary course of events."[22] Each of the historians put the providential theory to special use: Hubbard to blend the workings of God and nature; Mather and Prince to recover the Puritan mission; Hutchinson to capture, more as a literary device, the spirit of the founding fathers; and Belknap to justify a national destiny.

The overall significance of the providential theory was threefold. As Howard Mumford Jones noted, the transition from "the illogical union of providence and natural causes" in Hubbard and other early historians to a "cyclical theory of history that simultaneously commanded the Americans to avoid the luxury of the ancient world and to progress as Christians and republicans" was not a difficult one.[23] Americans were considered as citizens of a new society under the auspices of God, and therefore they were not merely transplanted Englishmen. Implicit in the theory was the idea of progress. America was the dawn of a new civilization. New England historians were conscious that they were writing of the morn of a new age, and that future progress would depend substantially on a correct evaluation of what had already been accomplished.

All five historians agreed that a primary motive for early migra-

---

frequent reference to divine dispensations to extol the industriousness of the settlers. "William Hubbard and the Providential Interpretation of History," *American Antiquarian Society, Proceedings,* LII (1942), 24–37. See also Anne K. Nelsen, "King Philip's War and the Hubbard Mather Rivalry," *William and Mary Quarterly,* 3d ser., XXVII (1970), 627–628.

21. Hutchinson, *History of Massachusetts-Bay,* ed. Mayo, I, 25.

22. *Ibid.,* II, 321–322; Belknap, *History of New-Hampshire,* II, 180. Also on the capture of Louisbourg (1745) see Thomas Prince, *Extraordinary Events the Doings of GOD, and marvellous in pious Eyes* (Boston, 1745), 17, 32, 34–35.

23. Howard Mumford Jones, *O Strange New World* (New York, 1964), 242–243.

tion to New England had been to secure purity of worship. In England men were "persecuted for their desire to see, and seek a reformation of the church," and they had to keep their principles "inwardly retained."[24] But in America they were free to follow their pristine faith, which demanded discipline and incessant devotion. Perfection was always elusive, and the rising generation soon wearied of the cause. Thus, Puritan historians were especially concerned with the declension of religious life in their own time. The great bulk of their historical writing was ecclesiastical in nature. Indeed, for New Englanders to waver from the goal of religious purity would be "to pull down with our hand" the "house . . . which our fathers have built."[25] Hutchinson and Belknap, writing in a more modern temper than earlier historians, emphasized the same desire for religious liberty. Although they did not discount as a motivation the quest for purity, the attentiveness of the Massachusetts state to doctrinal purity was justified, in part, because of a real danger of infiltration of corrupting influences from the Church of England.[26]

Only in New England, of all the world, was there a "real and vital Religion,"[27] a "richer Storehouse" of "Christian Charity" than in "all the Spanish Mines or Banks of Venice, or Amsterdam."[28] New England's expansion witnessed the "visible Kingdom of CHRIST enlarged" against the "Antichristian Power" of France.[29] The baneful influence of a French popish power in America was considered by all the historians as a just cause for making war. Even Hutchinson, who was more cautious in evaluating the motivation of New Englanders, constantly denigrated Catholicism when compared with the superiority of New England's religious and civil institutions.

That freedom of conscience grew with the passing of time and was

24. Hubbard, *General History*, 42; Mather, *Magnalia*, I, 227; Prince, *Chronological History*, 173–175, 293; Hutchinson, *History of Massachusetts-Bay*, ed. Mayo, I, 352.

25. Mather, *Magnalia*, II, 59.

26. Hutchinson, *History of Massachusetts-Bay*, ed. Mayo, I, 179–188, 193, 274, 358–359; Belknap, *History of New-Hampshire*, I, 42–53.

27. Worthington C. Ford, ed., *Diary of Cotton Mather*, I (1911), Massachusetts Historical Society *Collections*, 7th ser., VII, 410.

28. Hubbard, *The Happiness of a People*, 62.

29. Prince, *Extraordinary Events*, 34.

impressed upon the character of New Englanders was a point stressed by all the later historians. But they all believed that religious freedom had to be balanced with the interests of legitimate authority. Hutchinson gave short shrift to his own ancestor of Antinomian fame as a disrupter of the social order.[30] Quaker subversion rightly merited repression, but none of the historians, including Mather, condoned the extreme penalties inflicted upon members of that sect by the Bay Colony. In the end, it was acknowledged that the Quakers provided a leaven toward greater religious freedom. To Hutchinson and Belknap, the seventeenth century both in Europe and in America was an age of persecution. New Englanders had to learn to live with one another's views—and out of the "blind zeal" of people eventually resulted an appreciation for toleration. The growing pluralism of the population and the Glorious Revolution also contributed to the legacy of freedom of conscience.[31]

New Englanders developed into a distinct and virtuous people, not so much because of a pervading consciousness of their removal from England or a sense of mission, but because of environmental circumstances. The wilderness was a challenge that called forth energies that transformed the people. As Roderick Nash noted, "wilderness was the basic ingredient of American civilization."[32] Although the region was a "desert" and "waste" devoid of Edenic quality, yet it was a sanctuary[33] where men were freed from the corruptions of the Old World.

30. Hutchinson, *History of Massachusetts-Bay*, ed. Mayo, I, 50–51, 59, 62–67; cf. Hubbard, *General History*, 285–297; Belknap, *History of New-Hampshire*, I, 76.

31. Hubbard, *General History*, 571–574; Mather, *Magnalia*, II, 440–449; Hutchinson, *History of Massachusetts-Bay*, ed. Mayo, I, 3, 162, 167, 169, 196, 270; II, 8, 51–52; Belknap, *History of New-Hampshire*, I, 69; Belknap to Ebenezer Hazard, Oct. 23, 1783, and April 20, 1789, *The Belknap Papers*, Massachusetts Historical Society *Collections*, 5th ser., II (1877), 267–268, and III (1877), 118. In reflecting on his *History of New-Hampshire*, Belknap thought he could have gone further in presenting the Quaker side fairly. Had Prince continued his history, he would also probably have criticized the Massachusetts severity. See Thomas Prince, *The Case of HEMAN Considered* (Boston, 1756), 29.

32. Roderick Nash, *Wilderness and the American Mind* (New Haven, 1967), vii.

33. For the Puritan conception of wilderness deriving from medieval

In the wilderness one battled the devil, and one's wits were sharpened by the conflict. The perils of the environment afforded a unifying experience, and brought about a personality that blended with the landscape,[34] thus building a common identity and strengthening the sense of community. Although Puritan historians regarded the wilderness primarily as a test of the soul and took pride in its conquest, they did pay heed to the formative influences of the environment.

To Belknap the environment was the all-important factor. The land made a vigorous people. One could not understand New Englanders without visiting the region to see "how much human industry and ingenuity can perform in a short time, when nature has already done her part toward making a good country and a happy people."[35] Belknap devoted his entire third volume to the natural environment of New Hampshire. In one of his chapters, for example, he treated the "effect of the climate and other causes on the human constitution."[36]

New England was won primarily by those who tilled the soil. Among the early settlers, those who came to fish and trade did not succeed.[37] Agriculture was the main pursuit of a virtuous people whom God had chosen to move to a new land. The "treasures of the rich cabinets of nature wayted a long time for *an expert and* skilful hand, better acquainted with their worth than the natives. . . . the great Husbandman is *not pleased* to send forth labourers, where he hath no harvest to bee *gathered in,* or work for them to accomplish."[38]

Christianity, see *ibid.,* chs. 1 and 2 and for the use of "wilderness" as a metaphor of a spiritualization of the community, see Cecilia Tichi, "Spiritual Biography and the 'Lords Remembrances,'" *William and Mary Quarterly,* 3d ser., XXVIII (1971), 73–74.

34. See Perry Miller, "Shaping of American Character," *New England Quarterly,* XXVIII (1955), 445, 450; Hans Kohn, *American Nationalism* (New York, 1957), 22.

35. Belknap, *History of New-Hampshire,* III, 102, 172; Belknap, *Foresters,* 210–212.

36. Belknap, *History of New-Hampshire,* III, 171–190.

37. Hubbard, *General History,* I, 334, 524, 555; Mather, *Magnalia,* I, 79; Belknap, *History of New-Hampshire,* I, 31, 155–156, and III, 197. The mischief of selling arms and ammunition to the Indians was due to foreign neighbors pursuing commerce and quick riches instead of planting colonies as did New England settlers. Hubbard, *Indian Wars,* ed. Drake, II, 249–251.

38. Hubbard, *General History,* 7–8, 195.

Although New England had a "rougher Surface, a farrener Soil, a
more inclement Air" than the South, wrote Prince, perseverance and
hard work made the wilderness "a fruitful field."[39] The agrarian life
was a symbol of a sturdy and self-reliant people. Hence, Mather mentioned an incident in 1630 in which sailors threw overboard "malignant
papers against the Country" in hope of abating a storm: "the *corn-
fields* in *New*-England, still stood undisturbed, notwithstanding the
various *names* affixed unto the *tailes* of *petitions* against their
liberties."[40]

America's expansiveness continually nourished the growing freedom. Men moved to the frontier to obtain their own freeholds.[41] All
historians regarded space as an elemental dimension of American
liberty. Geographical mobility was indispensable to a free people; not
only could persons improve themselves by moving to less inhabited
regions, but the availability of land served as a safety valve to enable
malcontents to depart from settled society and to find new homes
where they could express themselves as they pleased.[42] Belknap romanticized the idea of refugees searching to become whole men in
some "barre part" of the forest. To Mather the "spacious country"
was the "most charming part of New-England." Yet along the frontier
communities quickly appeared, as pioneers in the lonely wilderness
discovered that "company is good."[43] A man lured into the forest and
surmounting the odds of nature became a new man. He cherished
what he had wrought by his own labors, and freedom and privileges,
he insisted, went hand in hand with his material accomplishments.

In the search for essential attributes of American character, the
Indian emerged as a depraved antagonist instead of becoming a

39. Prince, *The People of New England*, 24.
40. Mather, *Magnalia*, I, 258.
41. Hutchinson, *History of Massachusetts-Bay*, ed. Mayo, I, 406–407. "A
fondness for freeholds to transmit to posterity . . . excited so many of the
first planters of America to hard labor, and supported them under hard fare.
. . . The same passion still continues, and affords a prospect of the like happy
effect for ages yet to come."
42. *Ibid.*, I, 363–364; II, 251.
43. Mather, *Magnalia*, II, 573; Belknap, *Foresters*, 22–29. Because of the
openness of the wilderness, proprietary plantations were doomed. Belknap,
American Biography, I, 379.

symbol of external naturalization with which the colonists could identify. The idea of creating the Indian as a noble child of nature in the
primeval forests of America was never fully realized by these New
England historians. In the earliest histories, the Indian was seen as a
savage animal given to violence and rapine. He did not have a human
and cultural identity of his own, and was of interest solely as an ob-
stacle to expansion. He was incapable of living in a social order and
was viewed as a member of a subcommunity that was to be tolerated
on the fringes of the frontier or else destroyed. To Hubbard, writing
during King Philip's War, the Indian "was a Murderer from the Beginning," a "Cannibal," a "Miscreant with Envy and Malice against
the English," a "bloody and deceitful" monster,[44] and "very stupid
and blockish" to immediate danger.[45] Mather, who outdid Hubbard's
vilification, dismissed the Indians as devil worshipers, aliens, and a
treacherous people.[46] Yet Hubbard grudgingly admitted their can-
niness and that as "wild Creatures" they "ordinarily love the Liberty
of the Woods, better than the Restraint of a Cage." He had only disgust for Uncas, chief of the Mohegans, who sold his birthright to gain
advantage with the English.[47] It was to Hubbard's credit that he criticized the Puritan authorities for underestimating the prowess of the
Indian, which resulted in wars and in high casualties.[48]

Although Hutchinson and Belknap also looked upon the Indian as
an antagonist and carefully noted atrocities, both sympathized with
his plight. Most of the responsibility for the Indian wars in the East
was charged to the hated French. The Indian himself reacted only to
the examples of "treachery and infidelity" set by Europeans.[49] He was

44. Hubbard, *Indian Wars,* ed. Drake, I, 52, 121, 170.
45. Hubbard, *General History,* 629–630.
46. Mather, *Magnalia,* I, 479; Cotton Mather, *A Discourse Delivered unto
some part of the Forces Engaged in the Just War of New-England Against
the Northern and Eastern Indians* (Boston, 1689), 26.
47. Hubbard, *Indian Wars,* ed. Drake, I, 287–288.
48. *Ibid.,* 178; II, 259–260; Nelsen, "King Philip's War and the Hubbard-
Mather Rivalry," *William and Mary Quarterly,* 3d ser., XXVII (1970), 621–
622.
49. Hutchinson, *History of Massachusetts-Bay,* ed. Mayo, II, 198–199,
238–240, and passim; Belknap, *History of New-Hampshire,* I, 11, 196, 199–
225, contains many instances of the French being responsible for Indian
atrocities during King William's War.

no more barbarous than the English in treating captives, and was guilty of no crimes and cruelties that could not be found among other ancient or modern countries.[50] The Indian was no longer to be treated with disdain as had been the case of earlier historians. "It ill becomes us to cherish an inveterate hatred of the unhappy natives . . . ," wrote Belknap. "We should therefore proceed with calmness in recollecting their past injuries, and forming our judgment of their character."[51] Hutchinson made an even greater effort to describe Indian culture. Even though he was repulsed by their filthiness—"cracking lice between teeth" and "never so clean and sweet as when they were well greased"—he concluded the Indians were not dissimilar in religious beliefs from the English.[52] In Belknap's writings, the Indian was already beginning to take the shape of the noble savage, even though he still succumbed to the wiles and impositions of the white man. The treatment of the Indian wars by both Belknap and Hutchinson suggested more the theme of a conflict between civilizations than that of ridding the land of savages.

A people in search of their identity in the past require heroes. What better source was there than the valor of those New Englanders who matched the fury of the Indians? None of these historians, however, felt the need to develop a folklore of exaggerated exploits of some super frontier culture hero. Nor does the veteran Indian fighter, such as Benjamin Church, or any other military commander come alive in a full-scale sketch. Mather's lengthy and flattering biography of William Phips, whose alleged daring deeds were obvious inventions by the author, presented Phips in rather stodgy terms.[53] The hero that emerges from their pages instead was the representative New Englander who displayed fortitude and resourcefulness during times of

50. Hutchinson, *History of Massachusetts-Bay*, ed. Mayo, I, 70–71; II, 104, 122; Belknap, *History of New-Hampshire*, I, 100–113; II, 37. See Belknap, *History of New-Hampshire*, I, 225–230, 263–285, and II, 37–67, on Indian conduct in three Indian wars.
51. Belknap, *History of New-Hampshire*, I, 103.
52. Hutchinson, *History of Massachusetts-Bay*, ed. Mayo, I, 394–395. Ch. vi gives a human portrayal of the Indians—their customs, sports, and beliefs.
53. E.g., Mather, *Magnalia*, I, 159, 171.

crisis. The undaunted pioneer housewife, in particular, stood forth, fighting savages single-handedly and braving the perils of captivity.[54]

Of the five historians, two showed some flair for the dramatic in writing about heroes in the Indian wars. Mather's contrived portraits of exemplary Puritans, out of "a stock of heroes," who do "nothing but what is heroical," performing exemplary deeds for the instruction of posterity,[55] were no match, however, for his simple flesh-and-blood yeomen who bore the brunt of Indian violence.[56] But of all the historians, Hubbard demonstrated the greatest fervor in describing the tribulations of the common folk, the bloodletting, the details of battle, and the moments of decision of young militia officers during the periods of Indian fighting.[57] The courage of the people, though sustained by God, was of their own mettle:[58] King Philip's War was fought without outside help; "fighting made soldiers"; and the victory was New England's and not of the mother country.[59]

Although all the historians celebrated the pioneer spirit and heroism of the early settlers, it took perspective to single out those men of stature whose names should be etched in the cornerstone of American

54. Hubbard was personally acquainted with Mrs. Rowlandson and apparently received information on her captivity first hand. Hannah Dustin was the leading heroine among many others escaping from Indian captivity during King William's War. Hutchinson, *History of Massachusetts-Bay*, ed. Mayo, II, 80–81. See particularly Cotton Mather, *Decennium Luctuosum . . .* (1699) in Charles H. Lincoln, ed., *Narratives of the Indian Wars* (New York, reprint 1959), 193–199, 210–213. This account is also included in Mather, *Magnalia*, 502–572. For a minister-hero (Rev. John Wilson) during the Pequot War, see Mather, *Magnalia*, I, 286.

55. Mather, *Magnalia*, I, 108–109. For Mather's "formula" in setting parallels of his "Lives" with Israelite heroes, the stereotyped virtues, the repeated similarities in the rise to distinction, and his misrepresentations, see Watters, "Biographical Technique," *William and Mary Quarterly*, 3d ser., II (1945), 154–162; for an appreciation of the polemical and informative qualities of Mather's biographical technique, see Peter Gay, *A Loss of Mastery: Puritan Historians in Colonial America* (Berkeley, 1966), 59–70. Mather believed that New England had produced its own heroes, and hence the purpose of his writing biography. Mather, *Magnalia*, II, 94, 128.

56. See Mather, *Magnalia*, II, 480–501, 505, 558.

57. E.g., Hubbard, *Indian Wars*, ed. Drake, I, 70–99, 211–212; II, 218–224.

58. E.g., the town of Bridgewater. *Ibid.*, I, 184–192; Murdock, "William Hubbard," American Antiquarian Society *Proceedings*, VII (1942), 25.

59. Hutchinson, *History of Massachusetts-Bay*, ed. Mayo, I, 262–263.

liberty. Puritan historians invariably followed one general rule: they indiscriminately honored all those in authority in church and state. Prince and Mather put such leaders within the context of the Old Testament. John Winthrop, for example, was a Moses who led "a colony of chosen people into an American wilderness."[60] Dissenters, on the other hand, were treated as troublemakers. Roger Williams was a case in point. Although Hubbard and Mather expressed admiration for Williams's determination, they regarded him as an irresponsible radical in religion and politics who was unstable of mind.[61] Hutchinson, however, found Williams a true worker for the cause of freedom of conscience.[62] Hutchinson also praised, though sparingly, other men who stood against the majority, like Daniel Gookin, who attempted in vain to obtain humane treatment for displaced Indians.[63] Belknap, with his Federalist bias in evidence, viewed the dissenters in New Hampshire as a cantankerous lot; he credited them, nevertheless, for making religious freedom a reality.[64]

There were villains as well as heroes. One who was held in unanimous opprobrium was Sir Edmund Andros, governor of the Dominion of New England. Because he trampled the colonists' freedoms, even the most imperial-minded historians saw him as an arbitrary dictator furthering Stuart despotism.[65]

To Hutchinson and Belknap, the parochial leaders of early New England were seen in terms of their frailties: they were children of their age escaping persecution but, in turn, becoming persecutors themselves. Nevertheless, their greatness was not denied.[66] Hutchinson

60. Prince, *Chronological History*, 330. Cf. Mather on Bradford and Winthrop. Mather, *Magnalia*, I, 108–111.
61. Hubbard, *General History*, 205–207, 213.
62. Hutchinson, *History of Massachusetts-Bay*, ed. Mayo, I, 34–35.
63. *Ibid.*, 280.
64. E.g., John Underhill. Belknap, *History of New-Hampshire*, I, 38–46. Surprisingly John Wheelwright gets only passing mention. A just man, to Belknap, was one who recognized that he was "only a secondary instrument of bringing to pass God's great designs." Belknap to Hazard, March 8, 1781, *Belknap Papers*, Massachusetts Historical Society *Collections*, 5th ser., II (1877), 87.
65. Hutchinson, *History of Massachusetts-Bay*, ed. Mayo, I, 300–311.
66. E.g., John Winthrop. Belknap, *American Biography*, II, 344–356.

saw both good and bad traits in the Massachusetts governors under the new charter,[67] but factional leaders earned his disfavor.[68]

Belknap, however, was searching for heroes who contributed to the larger sphere of constitutional liberty that emerged in a new nation. Unfortunately, he admitted, the scattered New Hampshire frontier offered little opportunity for men to loom large in politics and government. He singled out one Crown official for unqualified praise—the Earl of Bellomont, who had that combination of aristocratic character and sympathy for the rights of the people that Belknap admired.[69] With New Hampshire and New England as a microcosm for a broader vision of national destiny,[70] Belknap, unlike his predecessors, played down the role of ecclesiastical history. Belknap also resorted to satire in picturing the colonial experience with England.[71] The American hero lost much of his chronological significance and was seen as part of a total experience. Although in the *History of New-Hampshire,* the Indian wars had an "anonymous stream of heroism" and the "plethora of names makes it not less anonymous,"[72] in his *American Biography* Belknap began a configuration essential for a national consciousness. On the Pilgrims—Robinson, Carver, Bradford, Brewster, Cushman, and Winslow—he conferred laurels for their zeal for liberty. Even Captain Miles Standish was the "intrepid soldier, the hero of New-England, as [was] John Smith of Virginia. . . ."[73]

67. E.g., Joseph Dudley. Hutchinson, *History of Massachusetts-Bay,* ed. Mayo, II, 159–162.

68. Especially the Vane-Hutchinson group of 1636–1637, the theocratic party headed by the Mathers, opponents of the administrations of Governors Shute and Belcher, and the faction of merchants in general. *Ibid.,* 59–59n., 99, 160–304.

69. Belknap, *History of New-Hampshire,* I, 248. Similarly in the Revolutionary period, Governor John Wentworth, Jr., *ibid.,* III, 265–273. On the lateness of the people of New Hampshire "in political improvement," see *ibid.,* 193–194.

70. See Charles W. Cole, "Jeremy Belknap: Pioneer Nationalist," *New England Quarterly,* X (1937), 743–751.

71. Belknap, *Foresters.* Not only do the characters (e.g., George [Washington], son of Walter Pipeweed) bring a successful lawsuit against Mr. Bull [England], but they also demonstrate their need for unity.

72. Kaplan, "Belknap as Literary Craftsman," *William and Mary Quarterly,* 3d ser., xxi (1964), 27–30.

73. Belknap, *American Biography,* I–II; on Standish, II, 310.

Americans were considered the freest of men by these historians. They enjoyed the liberties of freeborn Englishmen and yet were not restrained in creating their governments out of a state of nature.[74] The civil compact originating from plantation agreements contributed to the uniqueness of the American experiment. Interestingly enough, the first and last historians—Hubbard[75] and Belknap[76]—made the most of this point. Hubbard stressed that the lack of guidance from England necessitated forming of local governments by convention. Belknap saw in the plantation covenants, though he recognized them as expedients, an exercise in freedom for men coming to the New Hampshire frontier. Mather and Prince, seeking to justify a unitary Puritan society and the historic role of the church of New England, treated the propensity to form into a civil body politic as a working out of the Congregational way.[77] Hutchinson recognized the significance of the social compacts, but concluded that they were no more than outcroppings of English liberty.[78] All writers agreed, however, that the founders of New England left an important legacy: the idea that men make governments and that authority derives from the body of freemen.[79]

The viability of New England institutions, it was stressed, depended upon the character of the people. Members of a community had to be willing to work together for the general good; they had to possess the "inward" virtues of a "valiant minde": magnanimity (courage), con-

74. Thus the Massachusetts government resembled an English model, but government in the colony was more democratic and laws less severe than in England. Hubbard, *General History*, 114, 158–159.

75. E.g., *ibid.*, 173–174, 219–223, 335.

76. E.g., Belknap, *History of New-Hampshire*, I, 47–49 (planting of Dover and Portsmouth). For Belknap taking issue with Hutchinson's assertion (Hutchinson, *History of Massachusetts-Bay*, ed. Mayo, II, 354) that the Plymouth colony did not establish a distinct code of laws, see Belknap, *American Biography*, II, 242n.

77. E.g., Mather, *Magnalia*, I, 76. See Van de Wetering, "Thomas Prince," 162–163.

78. Hutchinson, *History of Massachusetts-Bay*, ed. Mayo, I, 34, 39, 88–89, 215–217, 272–273; Catherine B. Mayo, ed., "Additions to Thomas Hutchinson's 'History of Massachusetts Bay,'" American Antiquarian Society *Proceedings*, LIX (1950), 39, 52.

79. Hubbard, *General History*, 147, 333; Prince, *Chronological History*, 390; Mather, *Magnalia*, I, 112, 113, 182; Hutchinson, *History of Massachusetts-Bay*, ed. Mayo, I, 33–34; Belknap, *History of New-Hampshire*, I, 95–97.

fidence, patience, and benevolence.[80] There was an elitist tone running through all the writings of these historians—the people had to be careful to elevate to positions of authority only those with proven abilities. It was better to cultivate experienced leaders than "to put the helm into the hands of an unexperiencd Pilot in a tempestuous or stormy season."[81] This theme fit Mather's view that God had made manifest in America a few men with great talents for political rule. Governance was not for the sake of power but for the common good. Although Hubbard, Mather, and Prince subscribed to the theory of providential election of magistrates, they felt that all citizens were equal under the law and the sovereignty of God. Later historians did not contest these views, but placed greater emphasis on the distinction between the state (rather than wise rulers) and the individual citizens. They believed also that liberty was sacrificed when there was an equality of condition, as had been the case in early Massachusetts.[82] Not every person was equally qualified by position or stake in society to exercise the same degree of responsibility. Yet men ought to be free to change their status, to rise or fall according to their own merit, as long as they did not affect the general interest of the society as a whole. Belknap believed that in America the principle of inequality of condition had to be retained in order for each person to have equality of opportunity. A collective responsibility through education ought to be promoted to safeguard liberty, he concluded, and to ensure the pursuit of happiness for each individual.

Now, if there is *in fact* such an inequality among us, why all this pother about reducing every thing to equality by metaphysical rules? If Providence has placed us in a mountainous country, why should we reduce it to a plain? Let it stand as a principle that government originates from the people; but let the people be taught (and they will learn it by experi-

---

80. Hubbard, *The Happiness of a People*, 21–23.
81. *Ibid.*, 26. Because New England had wise magistrates, they should have been given broader discretionary powers. Hubbard, *General History*, 413.
82. Hutchinson, *History of Massachusetts-Bay*, ed. Mayo, I, 48, 370; Gov. Hutchinson to ———, Jan. 22, 1771, Massachusetts Historical Society *Proceedings*, XIX (1882), 129. Cf. William Bradford's passage on the equality of condition in the primitive community as strengthening the power of the majority to isolate and crush dissent. *History of Plymouth Plantation, 1620–1647,* ed. by Worthington C. Ford et al., II (1912), 309–310.

ence, if no other way) that they are not able to govern themselves. Let us take care to improve the advantages arising from our situation, and not miscall those inequalities which *necessarily* spring up among us by the name of disadvantages. Let *literature* be duly cultivated, and liberty will not be in danger without sufficient sentinels to give the alarm. Should even a limited monarchy be erected, our liberties may be as safe as if every man had the keeping of them solely in his own power.[83]

The position on civil liberty of the historians writing after Hubbard, generally speaking, was a complete endorsement of the Glorious Revolution. That Revolution had fixed liberties already affirmed by the colonists. To Mather and Prince, the Revolution and the subsequent privileges granted to New England by the new charter were a victory against the "general tyranny, both in church and state," that had existed in England. The colonists were now safe in "all *English* liberties, and can be touched by no law, by no tax, but of their own making."[84]

Hutchinson likewise approved of the Revolution as a means of escaping Stuart tyranny, and praised New England's role in it. But he saw the measure of freedom conferred by the charter in a different light from that of Mather. Although the clergy had been instrumental in bringing on the uprising, they "turned the scale for the last time."[85] The acquiescence of the people to the liberal charter of 1691 set an example of religious toleration for other colonies.[86] Politically, the principles of the Revolution and the Massachusetts charter had not made Massachusetts any more independent from the mother country. The colony had always been subordinate to British authority, Hutchinson concluded, and this fact had been unquestioned in the colony since 1640.[87] Until 1760 there had been no awareness of the diverging

83. Belknap to Hazard, March 3, 1784, *Belknap Papers,* Massachusetts Historical Society *Collections,* 5th ser., II (1877), 315; Belknap, *History of New-Hampshire,* III, 193–194.

84. Prince, *Chronological History,* Dedication, viii; Mather, *Magnalia,* I, 182; II, 438. See also Van de Wetering, "Thomas Prince," 204–206.

85. Hutchinson, *History of Massachusetts-Bay,* ed. Mayo, I, 285.

86. *Ibid.,* 317, 321–324, 326n., 330, 351; II, 111.

87. *Ibid.,* I, 179. Even the earliest of the historians, Hubbard, considered Massachusetts as willingly supporting the Restoration. Hubbard, *General History,* 575.

and conflicting aims of England and America. The final subjugation of the French and the pressure of population expansion at mid-century, which brought about the vision of "an American empire" and a "higher sense of the grandeur and importance of the colonies," paved the way for an independence movement.[88]

Belknap, on the other hand, discerned a continual independent spirit in New England from the time of its founding. This trend had evoked "jealousy" in England, and was "strengthened by age."[89] The settlers acted as if ownership of land gave them a sovereignty separate from that of England. They came at their own expense, made laws and institutions to their own liking, conducted Indian policy separate from England, treated any semblance of royal authority with disrespect (particularly the king's commissioners at Dover and Portsmouth), and circumvented the acts of trade and navigation.[90] The uprising of 1689 had been inevitable. There were "many instances of tyranny and oppression which the country suffered"—among them being the denial of rights of speech, press, and representation. Moreover, imaginary fears played a part in provoking New Englanders to rebellion. Although Belknap dismissed as an outrageous calumny the rumor that Andros was a papist intending to betray the country to the French, the patience of the people "was worn out, and their native love of freedom kindled at the prospect of deliverance."[91] It was in this same context that Belknap treated the dissension of 1693–1698 against John Usher's administration, which favored the proprietary interests above the will of the people.[92] Even the boundary dispute between New Hampshire and New York at a later date conditioned the colonists to assert their rights against England. The controversy "was carried on with a degree of virulence, unfriendly to the progress of civilization and humanity . . . it called into action, a spirit of vigorous self defence, and hardy enterprise, which prepared the nerves

88. Hutchinson, *History of Massachusetts-Bay*, ed. Mayo, III, 62.
89. Belknap, *History of New-Hampshire*, II, 173, 245.
90. *Ibid.*, I, 64, 91, 94, 130–131, 143–148.
91. *Ibid.*, 188–190.
92. *Ibid.*, 231–247.

of that people for encountering the dangers of a revolution, more extensive and beneficial."[93]

If the historians differed in their interpretations as to the exact time this spirit of independence emerged, they all agreed it was regional in character. The guiding influence of Massachusetts, however, as might be expected of four of the writers, was emphasized. In Belknap's *New-Hampshire* there was likewise a consciousness of the hovering presence of the Bay Colony. All the New England colonies owed their settlement, culture, and institutions to the wellsprings of their larger neighbor. For the New Hampshire settlements and other colonies, "a long and intimate connexion with Massachusetts, both in peace and war, kept alive a democratic principle."[94]

Suffice it to say that all the historians (except Prince, of course) viewed the New England Confederation as an example of an awareness of the need for unity both internally and externally in the region. Hubbard highlighted the Confederation as an integral role in New England affairs—at least while he relied on Winthrop's *Journal* as his chief source.[95] Hutchinson, however, discovered little of constitutional importance in the Confederation: "all the colonies [simply] found a union or confederacy necessary for their defence, not only against the Indians but against the French and Dutch; and there could be no encouragement for small bodies of men to sit down any where independant and unconnected."[96] Mather and Hutchinson noted the continued unity in military affairs,[97] but like Belknap emphasized the

93. *Ibid.,* II, 244.

94. Ibid., III, 191–192. Cf. Hubbard, *General History,* 319–320 (on New Haven).

95. Hubbard actually favored a consolidation, instead of confederation, of the Puritan colonies. For the Puritan view of the New England Confederation as an extension of the organic community, see Peter W. Carroll, *Puritanism and Wilderness: The Intellectual Significance of the New England Frontier, 1629–1700* (New York, 1969), 3, 127–132, 177–179.

96. Hutchinson, *History of Massachusetts-Bay,* ed. Mayo, I, 79.

97. E.g., *ibid.,* 79–80; II, 142, 154; Mather, *Magnalia,* I, 167–169. Mather's constant reference to New England, when in most instances he means Massachusetts, was to show that the colonists were first of all Englishmen, and thereby Mather hoped to gain favor for the Puritan church establishment of New England. Hutchinson tended to exaggerate the unity and patriotism of New England in Queen Anne's War.

miscellaneous and isolated frontier actions of the colonial wars rather than the organization of intercolonial participation.[98] Belknap, who had the advantage of having witnessed the culmination of nationhood, made the point that a gathering of precedents, from the New England Confederation through the intercolonial war congresses, had paved the way for an American union.[99]

In summary, the roots of an American identity lay in the shared experiences of the past, in the building of a free and industrious society, and in the consciousness of a dream to turn the hostile land into the world's best hope. Whatever their motives were for writing—the recovery of a loss of mastery through panegyrics and filial patriotism by the Puritan historians, Hutchinson's sober recounting of the history of one English colony, or the quest for the roots of national character as sought by Belknap—all the historians revealed a nostalgia for the ideals of the past. New Englanders had a vast heritage with which to identify. To the determination of the founding fathers, wrote Prince:

we firstly owe our pleasant houses, our fruitful fields, our growing towns and churches, our wholesome laws, our precious privileges, our grammar schools and colleges, our pious and learned ministers and magistrates, our good government and order, the public restraints of vices, the general knowledge of our common people, the strict observation of the Christian sabbath, with those remains of public modesty, sobriety, social virtues, and religion; for which this country is distinguished among the British colonies, and in which we are as happy as any on earth.[100]

The legacy of the founding fathers left "native and essential characteristics," a "firmness of nerve, patience in fatigue, intrepidity in danger and alertness in action."[101] The most "happy society" in the world was the New England town of the earliest ancestors: "consisting of a due mixture of hills, valleys and streams of water . . . the land

---

98. "The history of a war on the frontiers can be little else than a recital of the exploits, the sufferings, the escapes and deliverances of individuals, of single families or small parties." Belknap, *History of New-Hampshire*, II, 186.

99. *Ibid.*, 284–285.

100. Prince, *Chronological History*, Dedication, vi.

101. Belknap, *History of New-Hampshire*, III, 194.

well fenced and cultivated . . . a decent inn . . . the inhabitants
mostly husbandmen . . . a suitable proportion of handicraft work-
men and two or three traders . . . a clergyman of any denomination
. . . agreeable to the majority . . . . a school master . . . a social
library . . . . a club of sensible men . . . a decent musical society.
No intriguing politician, horse jockey, gambler or sot. . . ."[102] This
idealized community of the past provided a model for the present and
future.

New Englanders felt home was America, not England. Thus, Hutchinson could write that Joseph Dudley sought the governorship of
Massachusetts because "he had a passion for laying his bones there,
which equalled that of the antient Athenians."[103] If the connotative
and generic meaning of the American as a "new man" was still elusive, it was because he was making history begun on a tabula rasa.
Societal realization came through the freedom of the individual,
abetted by the beneficence and open-endedness of nature. These historians saw early America, as did Alexis de Tocqueville, as a "great
experiment"—an experiment, which since the initial success of the
founders, was cumulative in patterns of life and culture.

From the discovery of the roots of the past in the special quality
and separateness of the American experience, these New England
historians brought an awareness of a self-consciousness that would
become a chief ingredient of a national identity. The American was
a man wrought by the hardships, and by the fierce dedication of forefathers who had come to a strange land and left to posterity a worthy
patrimony. New England's early historians succeeded in assembling a
rich heritage in their region which gave greater meaning to the whole
of America.

102. *Ibid.*, 251.
103. Hutchinson, *History of Massachusetts-Bay,* ed. Mayo, II, 91. Cf.
Mather, *Magnalia,* I, 128.

PATRICIA U. BONOMI

The Middle Colonies: Embryo of the New Political Order

DID SUCH A REGION as the "middle colonies" ever really exist, other than for the convenience of historians? Can any kind of logical unity be claimed for the provinces of New York, New Jersey, and Pennsylvania, or were they simply "what was left over between New England and the South"?[1] Does the term "middle-colony culture" carry any real meaning? For the other two sections of the mainland colonies, such questions can generally evoke a dependable similarity of response. For all the qualifications and exceptions, there remain certain peculiar configurations of "southern" and "New England" features that are generally recognized and taken as real. The colonial South may mean a great many things, but central among them are

This essay is not in the form a historiographical study normally takes, being more an effort to discern the central character of a region, as revealed in early writings about it, than a discussion of the writers themselves. The diversity and variety of life in the middle colonies has tended to discourage modern writers from dealing with the section as a unit. The author of the present essay, however, believes that it was this very diversity that created a style of politics distinctive of the region, one which in certain ways more closely resembled modern political practices than did that of either the southern or New England colonies. Each of the early historians herein mentioned had some inkling of this. But they would have needed the perspective of time, and to see the political innovations of the nineteenth century, before they could have been expected to grasp the full significance of what they were witnessing.

1. Frederick B. Tolles, "Historians of the Middle Colonies," in *The Reinterpretation of Early American History*, ed. by Ray Allen Billington (New York, 1968), 65. Delaware will be treated as part of Pennsylvania in this essay.

somehow plantation agriculture, slavery, and a patrician gentry; as for colonial New England, the Congregational Church and township government can serve as common notation for a wide range of elements. And both regions, of course, were indisputably English. But for the middle colonies, a collective personality and a distinguishing unity are not so obvious. They may be there, but they do not naturally suggest themselves—as do those of the South and New England—through free association.

For instance, the middle region can certainly not be defined by its Englishness. In no other part of the colonies was there such a diversity of cultures and nationalities, the English often being outnumbered by Dutch, German, Scotch-Irish, French, or Swedes. Nor does religion provide a unifying theme. No single creed could dominate in a society where Presbyterian, Dutch Reformed, Anglican, Quaker, and German Reformed churches all contended for influence, and where a variety of small pietistic sects flourished in the unregulated atmosphere that resulted from the stand-off. Economic interests were equally varied, as the twin blessings of rich soil and deep natural harbors led to the development of agricultural and commercial enterprises of relatively equal importance. Furs, grains, meats, and dairy and wood products were all exported from the mid-Atlantic region, thereby stimulating the rapid growth of the ports of Philadelphia and New York, as well as the development of numerous specialized trades connected with the increasingly commercial character of those two cities. Nor were the middle colonies defined by any special geographical unity, segmented as the region was by rivers and mountain ranges. So were the others, to be sure; but in the middle colonies these natural divisions were reinforced by the tendency of ethnic and religious groups to settle with their own kind in well-defined pockets. The swarming of German pietists to Lancaster County in Pennsylvania is one example; the concentration of Dutch in the upper Hudson Valley is another. The result was a localism, or subsectionalism, that was often rooted in cultural distinctions, and that added even further to the atomized character of middle-colony society. It may well be, in short, that if the middle colonies did have a special style and character of their own, it could only have been as a consequence of this very diversity.

One way to take the measure of these provinces is to reexamine what contemporaries had to say about them. A number of eighteenth-century observers wrote histories of New York, New Jersey, and Pennsylvania. These accounts were often highly personal and parochial; sometimes they were undisguised polemics. But if they fall short of modern historical standards, they nonetheless contain certain common and recurrent themes that have much to tell us about middle-colony ways. They all tell of a pluralistic and competitive people who fought to obtain, and then to protect, the liberties and privileges each group valued most. They reveal a bewildering variety of individual and group interests, each contended for with a remarkable persistence. There were endless squabbles and bickerings; parallel with them went bargains, compromises, and accommodations. No single group or belief could dominate, and in discovering this, a heterogeneous people learned not necessarily to "cherish" their differences—which is a great deal to ask of any society—but at least to tolerate and live with them. Contention was inevitable, and bound to be more or less chronic; the question seems to have been one not of stopping it but of carrying it on in ways that would not tear the society to pieces.

The process whereby this occurred cannot adequately be covered by the "melting pot" metaphor. Nor does the formation of a "composite nationality"—to use Turner's phrase[2]—seem the most accurate way to note the result. It is not so much a social phenomenon as a political one. Reread, the old chronicles suggest that the principal contribution of the middle colonies was not—as with the South and New England—to our cultural heritage, but to the formation of our political habits.

A brief accounting of the diverse elements present in the middle colonies will suggest the complex character of that society. In no other part of the English colonies did the mélange of nationalities approach

2. Everett E. Edwards, comp., *The Early Writings of Frederick Jackson Turner* (Madison, Wis., 1938), 79.

that found in New York, New Jersey, and Pennsylvania. William Smith, Jr., perhaps the best-known contemporary historian of New York Colony, asserted in 1757 that the inhabitants of the province were "a mixed people, but mostly descended from the original Dutch planters." The Dutch were indeed numerous in the Hudson Valley counties; at the end of the seventeenth century they constituted from two-thirds to more than nine-tenths of the white population there. Even by the late colonial era, the Dutch language predominated over English in many areas.[3] In the seaboard sections, however, the Dutch were soon equaled and then outnumbered by other nationalities— English mainly, supplemented by smaller infusions of French Huguenots, Germans, and Scotch-Irish.[4] This mixture was further enhanced by the presence of smaller enclaves of Jews, Swedes, Highland Scots, occasional Irish, and a larger number of blacks than could be found in any of the other northern colonies. By the Revolution, people of English stock may have constituted almost 50 percent of the population of New York, but other elements, particularly the Dutch, maintained a strong influence over the culture and politics of the colony.[5]

Pennsylvania's ethnic variety was also wide, with the principal groups being somewhat more equally balanced than in New York. The English and Germans each made up about one-third of the population by the late colonial period; the remaining third consisted of many Scotch-Irish, a number of Welsh, and a scattering of Highland Scots, Dutch, French, and Swedes. People of English stock tended to con-

3. William Smith, Jr., *The History of the Province of New-York,* ed. by Michael Kammen, I (Cambridge, Mass., 1972), 203. Smith noted that Dutch was "still so much used in some counties, that the sheriffs find it difficult to obtain persons, sufficiently acquainted with the English tongue, to serve as jurors in the courts of law." *Ibid.,* 226. Orange, Ulster, and Dutchess counties had from 66 to 75 percent Dutch population; 93 percent of Albany County's people were of Dutch descent. American Council of Learned Societies Report of Committee on Linguistic and National Stocks in the Population of the United States, *Annual Report* of the American Historical Association for the Year 1931 (Washington, D.C., 1932), 120.

4. A major exception was Kings County, which was 88 percent Dutch in 1698 and remained the southern stronghold of that group. Staten Island contained strong elements of both Dutch and French Huguenots. American Council of Learned Societies, *Report,* 120; Smith, *History of New-York,* I, 220.

5. American Council of Learned Societies, *Report,* 124; Maldwyn A. Jones, *American Immigration* (Chicago, 1960), 16–17, 20.

centrate more heavily in those lower counties which later became the state of Delaware, constituting perhaps as much as 60 percent of the population there. Swedes also were more numerous in that section, being a cultural remnant of that brief period in the seventeenth century when the region at the mouth of the Delaware was known as New Sweden.[6] The Germans were diffused throughout the colony, settling most densely—according to Pennsylvania's leading eighteenth-century historian, Robert Proud—in the counties of Lancaster, York, Berks, and Northampton.[7]

Such a potpourri of cultures and languages did not always make for a harmonious coexistence. Some early Pennsylvania historians saw the large influx of Germans in the eighteenth century as a distinct threat to English ways. The Reverend William Smith expressed such a view in his 1755 treatise, *A Brief State of the Province of Pennsylvania*. It had become essential "to open the Eyes of the *Germans* to their true Interests," declared Smith. "Faithful Protestant Ministers, and School-masters, should be sent and supported among them . . . to teach them sound Principles of Government, and instruct their Children in the *English* Tongue, and the Value of those Privileges to which they are born among us." Until that was done, Smith recommended that the province "suspend the Right of Voting for Members of Assembly, from the *Germans*."[8] Robert Proud also commented on the flood of Germans entering Pennsylvania in the eighteenth century, noting that they constituted "near one-third, at least, of the inhabitants." In the summer of 1749, twenty-five ships filled with Germans had arrived, adding some "twelve thousand souls . . . and in some years near as many annually from Ireland."[9]

New Jersey, too, became the home of a heterogeneous people, the

6. American Council of Learned Societies, *Report*, 124; Jones, *American Immigration*, ch. 1. In the census of 1790, the English made up 60 percent and the Swedes 8.9 percent of the population of Delaware.

7. Robert Proud, *The History of Pennsylvania in North America* . . ., II (Philadelphia, 1797–98), 273. Proud noted that Cumberland County was settled mostly by Scotch-Irish, "who abound through the whole Province" (274). A detailed discussion of Pennsylvania's cultural pluralism will be found in Frederick B. Tolles, "The Culture of Early Pennsylvania," *Pennsylvania Magazine of History and Biography*, LXXXI (1957), 119–137.

8. (London, 1755), 33–34, 40.

9. Proud, *History of Pennsylvania*, II, 273.

earliest settlers in that colony being mainly Dutch and a few Scandinavians. To these were soon added—according to the eighteenth-century New Jersey historian Samuel Smith—New Englanders and "the Scotch, of whom there came a great many, such settlers as came from England, those of the Dutch that remained, and those from the neighboring colonies."[10] By the Revolution, citizens of English ancestry composed slightly less than half the population. The rest were made up of a large contingent of Dutch, substantial numbers of Germans, Highland Scots, and Scotch-Irish, and smaller elements of French and Swedes.[11]

The great variety of national strains that were attracted to the middle English colonies gave rise to another striking feature of the region's character—its religious diversity. Pennsylvania represents the best example: after it was established in part as a haven for the outcast Quaker sect, Pennsylvania's reputation for religious tolerance attracted other persecuted dissidents. These "plain people," as they were called—part of the flotsam thrown up in the wake of the Protestant Reformation and the religious wars of the sixteenth and seventeenth centuries—were seeking both religious freedom and economic opportunity. Such groups as the Mennonites, Amish, Dunkers, Schwenkfelders, and later the Moravians added a picturesqueness to Pennsylvania's religious heterodoxy, but since most of these small sects preferred to remain apart their impact on political and social life was limited. The most influential religious groups in Pennsylvania, besides the Quakers, were the large congregations of Presbyterians, German Reformed, Lutherans, and Anglicans. There were, in addition, a few Roman Catholics and a few Jews.[12]

In rural New York, as in Pennsylvania, religious patterns reflected

10. Samuel Smith, *The History of the Colony of Nova-Caesaria, or New-Jersey* (Burlington, N.J., 1765, 1877), 62.

11. American Council of Learned Societies, *Report*, 124.

12. In 1776 there were, according to one count, 106 German Reformed congregations, 68 Presbyterian, 63 Lutheran, 61 Quaker, 33 Episcopalian, 27 Baptist, 14 Moravian, 13 Mennonite, 13 Dunker, 9 Catholic, and 1 Dutch Reformed. W. W. Sweet, *Religion in Colonial America* (New York, 1942), 163, 210–229.

the ethnic makeup of the community. Thus, in the upper Hudson Valley the Dutch Reformed Church predominated. In the town of Kingston in Ulster County, where the citizens were mainly of Dutch extraction, the Dutch Reformed congregation met in "a large stone church," while the Anglicans were "so inconsiderable that their church is only a mean log-house." The Anglican church at Albany, "the only one in this large county," was made of stone, but the congregation was "small, almost all the inhabitants resorting to the Dutch church." Suffolk County was settled by New Englanders, and "except [for] one small episcopal congregation, consists entirely of English presbyterians."[13] And so it went in all the rural counties of New York. New York City's religious picture, however, was another matter. The variety of affiliations was listed by William Smith, Jr., in 1757, and reflects the cosmopolitan nature of that capital town. There were two Anglican churches (Trinity and St. George's), one Dutch Reformed, one Presbyterian, two Lutheran, one small Huguenot congregation, one Quaker meeting, and one Moravian church. Smith noted also that "the anabaptists assemble at a small meeting house, but have as yet no regular settled congregation. The jews, who are not inconsiderable for their numbers, worship in a synagogue erected in a very private part of the town, plain without, but very neat within."[14] It is difficult to determine the strength of the several congregations in the city. Because of the semiofficial status of the Anglican Church, as well as the political and social prominence of many of its parishioners, Anglican influence was greater than mere numbers would imply. The Dutch Reformed was another influential church, and in the later colonial years the Presbyterians were increasing in numbers and power. Religious rivalries often found expression in New York City politics; the King's College controversy of the 1750's, for example, was described by the New York historian Thomas Jones as something close to a Presbyterian conspiracy.[15]

13. Smith, *History of New-York,* I, 212, 215, 221.
14. *Ibid.,* 203–208.
15. Thomas Jones, *History of New York During the Revolutionary War,* I (New York, 1879), 12–16. Another example of the connection between re-

That the religious spectrum in New Jersey was equally comprehensive is shown by an informal county-by-county church census taken by Samuel Smith in 1765. The numbers of active congregations were found to be: Presbyterian, 55; Quaker, 39; Episcopalian, 21; Dutch Reformed, 21; Baptist, 19; Dutch Lutheran, 4; Seventh Day Baptists, 2; German Reformed, 2; and one each for the Swedish Lutheran, Moravian, Lutheran, Anabaptist, Separatist, and Rogereens churches.[16] The Quakers had settled very early in New Jersey and, having greatly increased in numbers, especially in West Jersey, came to have a marked influence on all aspects of the colony's affairs. Their importance was further strengthened by the ties they developed with other Quakers of the region, especially those in Pennsylvania. Similar bonds were formed by middle-colony Presbyterians, as William Smith of New York, himself a staunch Presbyterian, tells us. Members of that church "inhabiting New-York, New-Jersey, Pennsylvania, and the three Delaware counties, are regularly formed, after the manner of the church of Scotland, into consistories or kirk sessions, presbyteries and synods, and will probably soon join in erecting a general assembly."[17] The increasing sense of solidarity within religious sects strengthened their ability to bring pressure on government for desired reforms— such as the right of Quakers to affirm rather than take oaths, or the Presbyterians' insistence on recognition and full religious liberty in New York City. Moreover, as William Smith, Jr., explains, whenever the Anglicans tried to claim a privileged position based on their official status at home, "the presbyterians, independents, congregationalists, anabaptists, quakers, and all those among us, who in England would fall under the general denomination of dissenters, are warm in the negative."[18]

---

ligion and politics can be found in the New York Assembly election of 1769, when the "Anglican party" squared off against the "Presbyterian party." Patricia U. Bonomi, *A Factious People: Politics and Society in Colonial New York* (New York, 1971), 248–254.

16. Smith, *History of New-Jersey*, ch. 24.
17. Smith, *History of New-York,* I, 234; Rufus M. Jones, *The Quakers in the American Colonies,* 2d ed. (New York, 1966), 377, 391–393.
18. Smith, *History of New-York,* I, 235.

That such jars and jealousies would be a regular feature of middle-colony life was made inevitable by the region's ethnic and religious multiplicity. Few visitors failed to comment on this. Dr. Alexander Hamilton, whose "Itinerarium" took him to Philadelphia in 1744, recorded that he "dined att a tavern with a very mixed company of different nations and religions." Among the twenty-five men at table were "Scots, English, Dutch, Germans, and Irish; there were Roman Catholics, Church men, Presbyterians, Quakers, Newlightmen, Methodists, Seventh day men, Moravians, Anabaptists, and one Jew."[19]

Ethnic and religious divisions were not the only forces that served to fragment mid-Atlantic society. The sectionalism that was present to some degree in all the mainland colonies found perhaps its sharpest expression in New York, New Jersey, and Pennsylvania. From its beginnings New Jersey was a somewhat artificial domain, composed as it was of the two separate proprietaries of East and West Jersey. Each half of the province had its own unofficial capital, and each was oriented outward to a neighboring colony. West Jersey, a Quaker stronghold that looked to Burlington as its chief seat, faced south and west to the Delaware River and Pennsylvania. Because the section bordering the Atlantic Ocean consisted of "a great extent of salt meadows, swamps and marshes," adjoined by "barrens or poor land, [which] generally continues from the sea up into the province thirty miles or more," settlement occurred mainly along the Delaware River, while trade, following the natural drainage of creeks and streams, flowed toward the port at Philadelphia.[20] East Jersey, on the other hand, settled principally by Dutch, Scots, and English, considered its governmental seat to be Perth Amboy. Throughout the late seventeenth and early eighteenth centuries, East Jersey leaders dreamed of developing "Amboy" into a commercial port. As Samuel Smith explains, the location was ideal, "lying open to Sandy-Hook, whence vessels may arrive almost any weather in one tide . . . and find a

19. Carl Bridenbaugh, ed., *Gentleman's Progress: The Itinerarium of Dr. Alexander Hamilton, 1744* (Chapel Hill, 1948), 20.

20. Smith, *History of New-Jersey*, 487; John E. Pomfret, *The Province of West New Jersey, 1609–1702* (Princeton, 1956), 118.

safe commodious harbour, capacious enough to contain many large ships. . . ." Yet East Jerseymen found the project "up-hill work," largely because New Yorkers resented any effort to develop a competing port and used all their connections in London to discourage it. The result was "a fatality attending almost every attempt for trade in the province," and a dependence on the port of New York that threatened, at times, to reduce East Jersey to the position of a minor satellite.[21]

The divisive influence of these geographic and economic forces was such that the two Jersies retained fairly separate identities throughout much of the colonial era. Moreover, the split was institutionalized in politics, for it became the rule to hold sessions of the New Jersey legislature alternately in each sectional "capital." When Governor Robert Hunter, caught in a factional broil with West Jersey leaders in 1716, defied tradition and called the Assembly to meet in Perth Amboy when it was Burlington's turn, the West Jersey legislators flatly refused to attend.[22]

The province of New York had two major sections, the division being in part a reflection of localized economic interests. The upriver-Albany region was centered on the fur trade in the early years; but by the eighteenth century the production of grains and other foods had taken precedence and made the Hudson Valley one of the major staple-producing centers of colonial America. To the south, the counties bordering the roadways of New York harbor were bound together by a common concern with the export trade. By the mid-eighteenth century, according to William Smith, Jr., flour was being exported in the amount of "80,000 barrels per annum," and it was in the seaboard merchants' interest to maintain the high quality of the product. Thus, "to preserve the credit of this important branch of our staple, we have

21. Smith, *History of New-Jersey*, 489–490; John E. Pomfret, *The Province of East New Jersey, 1609–1702* (Princeton, 1962), ch. 9. The story of New York's resistance to the port at Perth Amboy and its efforts to force all ships to enter and clear only at New York is related in Pomfret, *East New Jersey*, 311–324.

22. Smith, *History of New-Jersey*, 405–409; Donald L. Kemmerer, *Path to Freedom: The Struggle for Self-Government in Colonial New Jersey, 1703–1776* (Princeton, 1940), 101–104.

a good law, appointing officers to inspect and brand every cask before its exportation." The centralization of inspection procedures, as well as various metropolitan efforts to place controls on other Hudson Valley products, led to resentment and strong feelings of sectional competition.[23] A geographical form of sectionalism was reflected in the division of Orange County, on the west bank of the Hudson, by a range of mountains. As Smith notes: "On the north side the lands are very broken but fertile, and inhabited by Scotch, Irish, and English presbyterians. . . . The people on the south side of the mountains are all Dutch." As for Dutchess County, the "inhabitants on the banks of the [Hudson] river are Dutch, but those more easterly Englishmen, and for the most part, emigrants from Connecticut and Long Island."[24]

The sharpest sectional division of Pennsylvania's early years was that which pitted Quaker leaders in the counties around Philadelphia against the older settlers of Swedish, Dutch, and English origins in the three "lower counties" of New Castle, Kent, and Sussex. William Penn in 1685 decried the growth of factions produced by that split in his well-known letter to the Pennsylvania Council: "For the love of God, me and the poor country, be not so governmentish, so noisy and open in your dissatisfactions." Yet by 1690 tension had reached such a pitch that the lower counties actually seceded from the central government, forcing Penn to appoint a deputy governor for that section in order to maintain some degree of authority over it. In 1701, according to Robert Proud, friction between the two sections had come to occupy so much attention that "not much other public business of importance appears to have been transacted in the affairs of government." In order to break the stalemate, Penn finally agreed to grant

23. Smith, *History of New-York,* I, 229; Bonomi, *A Factious People,* 101–102, 177–178. A third center of specialized economic interest was Suffolk County at the eastern end of Long Island, where proximity to New England caused most "East End" products to be "carried to markets in Boston and Rhode-Island." The imperial government's efforts to enforce exclusive customs jurisdiction for New York City created hostility between the two seaboard sections until 1721, when a customs inspector was located at Montauk Point and direct trade allowed. Smith, *History of New-York,* I, 221; Bonomi, *A Factious People,* 82n., 100.
24. Smith, *History of New-York,* I, 211, 216.

the lower counties their own separate legislature.²⁵ An east-west tension developed in the later years, as problems arose between the central government and the frontier settlers, many of whom were of Scotch-Irish and German descent. Demands for greater protection from marauding Indians and more equal representation in the provincial assembly led to such challenges as the march of the Paxton Boys in 1763 and the growth of a popular faction that would assume a leading role at the time of the Revolution.²⁶ Thus sectionalism and sectional fragmentation took many forms in the middle colonies, particularly where economic and ethnic interests became identified with a regional center.

All the eighteenth-century chroniclers describe middle-colony politics as turbulent and competitive, qualities which they saw as direct reflections of the society's very pluralism. Robert Proud declared that Pennsylvania "appears to have been never entirely without a discontented and murmuring party in it," and he noted an "increase of party" as more and more "persons of very different principles and manners" from those of the original settlers arrived in the course of the eighteenth century. Others observed that the citizens of Pennsylvania were "factious, contentious," and "the People at Variance, and distrustful of each other!"²⁷ Samuel Smith of New Jersey, for all his Quaker benevolence, could not close his eyes to the party quarrels that beset his colony in the eighteenth century. Indeed, Smith himself was denied

25. Penn to Council, Aug. 19, 1685, quoted in Gary B. Nash, *Quakers and Politics, Pennsylvania, 1681–1726* (Princeton, 1968), 49; Proud, *History of Pennsylvania*, I, 454–455. See also Nash, *Quakers and Politics,* 67–70, 131–133, 236. The "lower counties" later split off entirely from Pennsylvania to become the state of Delaware.
26. Theodore Thayer, *Pennsylvania Politics and the Growth of Democracy, 1740–1776* (Harrisburg, Pa., 1953), chs. 7, 13. Not all historians are agreed on the sectional nature of the later division. See David Hawke, *In the Midst of a Revolution* (Philadelphia, 1961), 62–63; Joseph E. Illick, "The Writing of Colonial Pennsylvania History," *Pennsylvania Magazine of History and Biography*, XCIV (1970), 18–22.
27. Proud, *History of Pennsylvania,* II, 228–229; [Rev.] William Smith, *A Brief State of the Province of Pennsylvania* (London, 1755; New York, 1865), 15, 26.

a seat on the New Jersey Council in 1751 when he was charged with being "a Wellwisher to the [land] Rioters and his Family active in that Faction."[28] William Smith, Jr., of New York was also directly involved in the political contests of his time. Though Smith tried to preserve some measure of detachment in his *History,* a barely controlled passion vibrates through his account of the almost continuous squabbles that kept New York politics in turmoil from the late seventeenth century to the Revolution. Thomas Jones, New York's other major historian, made no effort at all to be objective. The introductory section of his work is a philippic against the "Presbyterian" or "republican" faction, which in his view embroiled New York in continuous party debate throughout the pre-Revolutionary era.[29]

Perhaps the most revealing passages of these early histories, however, are those that describe how middle-colony political leaders learned to manipulate interest groups to achieve particular political ends. At election time they might be found shamelessly currying favor with one group or stirring up prejudices against another. Candidates realized very early, for example, that they could gain credit with the Quakers by upholding their privilege of affirmation—an issue of some consequence since it involved the Quakers' right to vote, to hold office, and to sit on juries. In New Jersey, a party that controlled the provincial Council in the early eighteenth century had for years denied the right of affirmation—which was a good way of excluding certain Quaker rivals from office. When an opposition group of Assembly leaders finally took up the Quakers' cause, achieving success in 1713 when Governor Hunter signed a bill confirming the right, the New Jersey Friends naturally became solid adherents of the faction that had supported their interests.[30] Affirmation was a political issue in New

28. Lords of Trade to Gov. Jonathan Belcher, March 27, 1751, *New Jersey Archives,* 1st ser., VII, 586, quoted in Carl E. Prince, "Samuel Smith's *History of Nova-Caesaria," The Colonial Legacy,* ed. by Lawrence H. Leder, II (New York, 1971), 168. Though Smith later won appointment to the Council, his alienation from the Crown and strong support for the Revolution may in part be accounted for by the earlier rebuff. *Ibid.,* 169.

29. Jones, *History of New York During the Revolutionary War,* I, ch. 1.

30. Smith, *History of New-Jersey,* 306–308, 334, 372–373, 393, 402–403; Kemmerer, *Path to Freedom,* 50–51.

York as well. Of Frederick Philipse, one of the candidates in the 1729 Assembly election in Westchester, it was reported that the "Quakers to a man will vote against" him. "Some of the Principals of them on Long Island have been over and acquainted their brethren how much Phillipse is in [Lieutenant Governor] George Clarkes Interest who intends to abridge them of their Priviledges."[31] Even in Pennsylvania the Quakers needed to maintain their vigilance. In the 1720's a controversy arose over the Friends' keeping their heads covered in courts of law. The Philadelphia Meeting "appointed a committee to wait on the Governor," to press for continuation of the privilege. The governor, Sir William Keith, supported the Quakers, and as a result was "very popular" among them.[32]

An even balder example of group manipulation occurred in New York in connection with an Assembly election in 1737. In a brawling contest that apparently stimulated new peaks of participation, Adolph Philipse, a wealthy New York City merchant, won his seat by a mere 15 votes. So close an election was always vulnerable to challenge, and in this case Philipse's opponent, Cornelius Van Horne, demanded a scrutiny of the votes by the Assembly. Speaking for Van Horne, William Smith (father of the New York historian) raised the question "whether Jews were qualified for electors, some of them having voted for Mr. Philipse." Smith, whose Christian fervor seems to have been somewhat heightened by the occasion, "so pathetically described the bloody tragedy at Mount Calvary that a member cried out with agony and in tears, beseeching him to desist, and declaring his conviction. Many others wept; and the unfortunate Israelites were content to lose their votes, could they escape with their lives."[33]

The Quakers themselves were not above manipulating ethnic blocs.

31. Lewis Morris, Jr., to James Alexander, Morrisania, Jan., 1729, Rutherfurd Collection, I, 105, New-York Historical Society. In the 1733 Westchester County election for assemblyman, the sheriff tried to effect the defeat of Lewis Morris, Sr., by refusing to accept 38 Quaker votes cast for him by affirmation. The Morrisites denounced this as "a violent attempt on the Liberties of the People," thereby winning the praise and support of Quakers throughout the colony. Bonomi, *A Factious People*, 115.
32. Proud, *History of Pennsylvania*, II, 196–201.
33. Smith, *History of New-York*, II, 33–34.

They managed to retain political influence in Pennsylvania, despite their proportionately decreasing numbers, both through purposeful organization and by the forming of alliances with the Germans. The Quakers, according to one critic, "entered into Cabals in their yearly Meeting, which is convened just before the Election, and being composed of Deputies from all the monthly Meetings in the Province, is the finest Scheme that could possibly be projected, for conducting political Intrigues, under the Mask of Religion." Employing a printer named Christopher Sauer, whose German-language newspaper was "universally read and believed by the Germans in this Province," the Quaker party had apparently convinced the Germans in 1754 that both their liberties and their tax rates were in danger if the governor's party won a majority in the forthcoming Assembly election. "In consequence of this, the *Germans,* who had hitherto continued peaceful, without meddling in Elections, came down in Shoals, and carried all before them. Near 1800 of them voted in the County of *Philadelphia,* which threw the Balance on the Side of the *Quakers,* though their Opponents, in that grand Struggle, voted near 500 more than ever lost an Election before." In 1764, however, the Germans deserted the "Quaker" party, then led by Benjamin Franklin, and sided instead with the "Proprietary party." Franklin himself was defeated by 26 votes, a loss he ascribed to the proprietary party's tactics: "They carried (would you think it!) above 1000 Dutch [German] from me, by printing part of my Paper . . . where I speak of the Palatine *Boors herding* together, which they explain'd that I call'd them a *Herd of Hogs.*"[34]

Nor was such opportunism unique to Pennsylvania. In the upper Hudson Valley, political offices were largely monopolized by the Dutch until the mid-1740's when the population became more diverse

34. Smith, *Brief State of Province of Pennsylvania,* 28–30. Nor was this the first time the German vote had come to the notice of politicians. See Thayer, *Pennsylvania Politics,* 17–19, 37. For Franklin's remark see his letter to Richard Jackson, Philadelphia, Sept. 25, 1764, *The Papers of Benjamin Franklin,* ed. by Leonard Labaree, XI (New Haven, 1959-), 397. See also Norman S. Cohen, "The Philadelphia Election Riots of 1742," *Pennsylvania Magazine of History and Biography,* XCII (1968), 306–319; and Philip Gleason, "A Scurrilous Colonial Election and Franklin's Reputation," *William and Mary Quarterly,* 3d ser., XVIII (1961), 68–84.

and new groups began to challenge the original settlers' predominance. New York governors looking to reduce the power of entrenched Dutch leaders did so by appointing New Englanders or Englishmen to office. Thus they played off one part of the community against the other, with consequences both for ethnic self-awareness and for group tensions. In Dutch strongholds such as Albany, Schenectady, and Kingston, suspicion of newcomers, "whom the Dutch look on as intruders into their patrimony," was a major factor in both local and provincial political alignments.[35] Similar rivalries appeared in New Jersey, where Scotch, Quaker, and Anglican factions were added to the east-west division already mentioned.[36]

Pressures from economic and sectional interests, as well as from ethnic and religious ones, contributed to the growing responsiveness of political leaders. Men engaged in the Philadelphia shipbuilding trades, including an association known as the White Oaks, constituted at times a significant weight in that city's political balance. The White Oaks played an important role, and may have provided the margin of victory for the Quaker party, in the election of October, 1766. By the 1770 election, the tide had shifted the other way. "We are all in Confusion," wrote Joseph Galloway to Benjamin Franklin, "the White Oaks and Mechanicks or many of them have left the old Ticket and 'tis feared will go over to the Presbyterians"—as indeed they did. One historian has recently suggested that this turnabout was prompted by economic self-interest. The White Oaks favored nonimportation as retaliation against the Townshend Acts because it reduced foreign competition with their own products, and by the same token they very much disliked Galloway's equivocal stand on the issue.[37] Instances of

35. Cadwallader Colden to Gov. Clinton, copy, New York, Aug. 8, 1751, *The Letters and Papers of Cadwallader Colden* (New-York Historical Society, *Collections*, LIII [New York, 1921]), IV, 273; Bonomi, *A Factious People*, 26–28, 48–52.

36. For factions in New Jersey see Smith, *History of New-Jersey*, 302ff., ch. 20; Kemmerer, *Path to Freedom*, 48–50, 53–55, 79–81.

37. James H. Hutson, "An Investigation of the Inarticulate: Philadelphia's White Oaks," *William and Mary Quarterly*, 3d ser., XXVIII (1971), 22. A question has been raised about what economic level the White Oaks actually represented in Philadelphia's shipbuilding industry. See the discussion among

group awareness in the crafts and trades, and readiness to exert various kinds of pressure on behalf of group interests, appear again and again in the pages of Richard B. Morris's *Government and Labor in Early America.*[38] Such groups, in New York City as in Philadelphia, took active roles in the political contests of the 1760's and 1770's.[39]

In the course of time, a body of political practice grew up throughout the American colonies which contained elements special enough to distinguish it from the practice of any other country in the world. There were, nonetheless, wide internal variations. And it may not be too much to suggest that there was a direct connection between that pluralism and diversity of interest just noted, present to a more advanced degree in the middle colonies than in the others, and a peculiar mode of political partisanship, also more highly developed in the middle colonies than anywhere else.

One of the welcome contributions of recent years to American colonial history has been a body of scholarship which examines provincial politics in its larger Anglo-American setting.[40] The sheer

---

Jesse Lemisch, John K. Alexander, Simeon J. Crowther, and James H. Hutson in *William and Mary Quarterly,* 3d ser., XXIX (1972), 109–142. For the purposes of this essay, the important point is that the White Oaks were a cohesive group that could, on occasion, act as a concerted force in Philadelphia affairs.

38. (New York, 1946), especially 136–166.

39. Carl Lotus Becker, *The History of Political Parties in the Province of New York, 1760–1776* (Madison, Wis., 1909), 120–128; Staughton Lynd, "The Mechanics in New York City Politics, 1774–1788," *Labor History,* V (1964), 225–246; Bonomi, *A Factious People,* 254–255; Roger J. Champagne, "Liberty Boys and Mechanics of New York City, 1764–1774," *Labor History,* VIII (1967), 115–135.

40. Bernard Bailyn, *The Origins of American Politics* (New York, 1968); Jack P. Greene, *The Quest for Power: The Lower Houses of Assembly in the Southern Royal Colonies, 1689–1776* (Chapel Hill, 1963); Stanley N. Katz, "The Origins of American Constitutional Thought," *Perspectives in American History,* III (1969), 474–490; J. R. Pole, *Political Representation in England and the Origins of the American Republic* (New York, 1966); Jack P. Greene, "Political Mimesis: A Consideration of the Historical and Cultural Roots of Legislative Behavior in the British Colonies in the Eighteenth Century, with A Comment by Bernard Bailyn, and A Reply by Jack P. Greene," *American Historical Review,* LXXV (1969), 337–367; Paul Lucas, "A Note on the Comparative Study of the Structure of Politics in Mid-Eighteenth-Century Britain

broadening of vision which this work has effected is immensely beneficial. But now that it is well on its way to full absorption into the
historiography of early America, there may be reason to look at the
ground once more from a provincial—perhaps even parochial—point
of view. There were regional variations. Yet this hardly means that the
politics of each individual colony was so idiosyncratic that generalizations cannot be made; quite the contrary. The details of local squabbles
may constitute more of a pattern than we thought. Quite beyond the
broad principles which governed political responses throughout the
colonies as a whole, local and regional conditions, as well as variations
in them, may tell us a great deal about the critical ways in which
Anglo-American practice developed into a purely American practice.

Whatever the differences among students of Anglo-American politics, there are certain broad areas of accord. All agree, for example,
that the one thing eighteenth-century political man feared most—in
the colonies and elsewhere—was the tendency of power to encroach
on liberty. "The antinomy of power and liberty was accepted as the
central fact of politics, and with it the belief that power was aggressive,
liberty passive, and that the duty of free men was to protect the
latter and constrain the former."[41] Whether the threat came from an
overpowerful executive, a corrupt ministry, or a self-serving faction,
the remedy was always the same. Militant power had to be checked,
controlled, balanced, and headed off, for if the internal equilibrium of
the state were upset the way would be open to anarchy, chaos, and
eventually to the loss of all liberty when a tyrant arose to restore
order. Most eighteenth-century Englishmen believed that in their own
government they had found the best of all formulas for preserving both
order and liberty. Their mixed constitution blended in near-perfect
proportions the three basic interests of the state—monarchy, aristocracy, and commons—with the aristocracy so poised as always to
preserve the balance between the other two. While this ideal balance
may have existed more in theory than in reality, the reverential regard

---

and Its American Colonies," *William and Mary Quarterly,* 3d ser., XXVIII
(1971), 301–309.
41. Bailyn, *Origins of American Politics,* 56.

in which the British constitution was held nonetheless "colored all aspects of political and constitutional thought."[42]

The colonists, being Englishmen, were thoroughly familiar with these ideas, and in the early years they seemed to believe they were reproducing that happy combination in their own provincial governors, councils, and assemblies. In time, however, it became apparent that with no provincial nobility to supply the critical equipoise between governor and assembly, something was missing from the model of the mixed constitution. Thus, uniquely local circumstances—a social structure that contained no institutionally defined aristocracy—gave particular impetus to a colonial politics that was balanced between two centers of power, executive and legislative, rather than the traditional three. Moreover, the ambiguities that developed in the relationship between England and her colonies during the age of Walpole meant a shifting and ill-defined connection throughout most of the eighteenth century. Provincial suspicions of encroaching power could have lively play in such an atmosphere, and the colonists could imagine that their anomalous constitutional position exposed them to the most capricious shifts of the political winds at home. They sent agents to lobby in London for whatever enhanced their constitutional footing, while business associates and family connections were forever looking out for a variety of colonial interests.[43] And the symbol of prerogative power which the provincials saw as most immediate and potentially encroaching was, of course, the colonial governor. Thus, with the arrival of each new governor they found themselves, almost by instinct, developing their own checks on that power. The forms such checks would take were determined largely by local conditions and institu-

42. *Ibid.*, 23. See also Jack P. Greene's discussion of these ideas in "Changing Interpretations of Early American Politics," *The Reinterpretation of Early American History*, ed. by Ray Allen Billington (New York, 1968), especially 173–175. For an interesting examination of the mixed constitutional system, see the pamphlet by New York royal officeholder Archibald Kennedy, *An Essay on the Government of the Colonies* (New York, 1752).

43. Michael Kammen, *A Rope of Sand: The Colonial Agents, British Politics and the American Revolution* (Ithaca, 1968); Stanley N. Katz, *Newcastle's New York: Anglo-American Politics, 1732–1753* (Cambridge, Mass., 1968).

tions, and therefore they evolved a little differently in the southern, the New England, and the middle colonies.

The southern colonies, whose patrician gentry came as close to being an "aristocracy" as any group in America, also came closest to achieving the English constitutional ideal. With the lower houses of assembly as their main theater of activity in the eighteenth century, the southern elites, each bound together by a homogeneity of interests and outlook, formed consolidated units of power that could be brought to bear in government. At times they might speak for the people, defending provincial liberties and privileges. At other times, when the governors made reasonable requests of them, the lower houses would support the executive. In either case, the southern assemblies maintained sufficient internal cohesion and authority to act as a truly independent force in government.[44] Thus the mixed constitutional form came nearest to being approximated in the southern colonies. This may be one way of explaining the relative tranquillity of that section's politics, for the colonial South had found a way to limit power that was not only effective but that operated within the approved boundaries of the theoretical ideal.

The New England colonies were also concerned with the checking of power; they, like the others, had had direct experience with its abuses in the seventeenth century. Yet the New England legislatures, while often showing a talent for orderly procedures, rarely developed the same sense of internal solidarity that is evident in the South. This may be accounted for in part by the greater complexity of northern society. Despite the relative homogeneity of the New England population, it nonetheless reflected a broader range of cultural, economic, and sectional viewpoints, and these were not easily subordinated to the goal of legislative unity. Although this made their assemblies less de-

44. Outstanding recent studies of southern colonial politics include Greene, *Quest for Power;* M. Eugene Sirmans, *Colonial South Carolina: A Political History, 1663–1763* (Chapel Hill, 1966); Charles S. Sydnor, *Gentlemen Free-holders* (Chapel Hill, 1952); Robert M. Weir, "'The Harmony We Were Famous For': An Interpretation of Pre-Revolutionary South Carolina Politics," *William and Mary Quarterly,* 3d ser., XXVI (1969), 473–501. North Carolina may represent an exception to the southern pattern discerned here, as group conflict was spirited throughout that colony in the eighteenth century.

pendable as a check and counterweight, New Englanders were not without resources when it came to resisting their governors. For New England's political structure harbored a built-in mechanism for obstructing higher authority of any sort—its townships—and it was upon these that assembly representation was based and to which annually elected representatives were responsible.[45] The decentralized character of power in Massachusetts distressed the administration of more than one royal official. Thomas Hutchinson observed in the 1760's that holding "each representative to vote according to the opinion of his town is unconstitutional and contradicts the very idea of a parliament. . . ." Earlier, Governor Shirley had tried to deny "representation to newly created townships in order to preserve his precarious majority in the House." One recent historian has called the Massachusetts House of Representatives a mere "congress of communities," and a "creature of the towns."[46]

In a number of cases, New England towns simply ignored their central governments, either refusing to send deputies to the lower houses or disregarding laws that were contrary to local practices and preferences. Such, it seems, was the situation in New Hampshire, where elected representatives "customarily felt more responsible to their local constituents than to imperial interests. . . ."[47] In any case,

45. At times the townships feared that governors might succeed in corrupting some ambitious legislators by showering them with honors and offices. "In such a situation . . . the legislature could no longer be trusted to safeguard the constitution. That responsibility then fell directly upon the people, who were urged to bind their representatives by positive and inflexible instructions to prevent them from selling their constituents' liberty for pelf or position." Jack P. Greene, "Political Mimesis," 358. For more on the "attorneyship" form of representation and the instructing of legislators, see Bernard Bailyn, *The Ideological Origins of the American Revolution* (Cambridge, Mass., 1967), 164ff.; Michael Zuckerman, *Peaceable Kingdoms: New England Towns in the Eighteenth Century* (New York, 1970), 21–24.

46. Hutchinson to William Bollan, Nov. 22, 1766, quoted in J. R. Pole, *Political Representation*, 53; Bailyn, *Origins of American Politics*, 117; Zuckerman, *Peaceable Kingdoms*, 20.

47. Jere R. Daniell, *Experiment in Republicanism: New Hampshire Politics and the American Revolution, 1741–1794* (Cambridge, Mass., 1970), 22. One eighteenth-century observer described Rhode Island government as "downright democracy" and anarchy. David Lovejoy suggests that local issues were indeed important in Rhode Island, but he also sees two fairly well-defined factions

it is well known that when local power was challenged head on—as it was so dramatically in Massachusetts by the 1774 "Intolerable Acts" which in effect suspended the town meetings—the final showdown between power and liberty was at hand.

Thus it was that the southern and New England colonies fashioned at least partial checks on executive power, checks that became associated with their assemblies and their institutions of local government. But what restraints were placed on power in the middle colonies? Neither of the mechanisms just noted seems to have been present there, and for reasons that may have much to do with the "character" of that region as set forth earlier. The eighteenth-century histories make it abundantly clear that competition and conflict were the dominant impulses in the public life of New York, New Jersey, and Pennsylvania. The diversity of cultures, the clash of opinions, and the emerging legitimacy of group self-interest as a motivating force in politics[48] seem to have inhibited the growth of cohesive provincial elites. It is hard to think of a time in the pre-Revolutionary history of those colonies when the political leadership drew together as a unified force to resist executive power. Nor were institutions of local

---

contending for power in the immediate pre-Revolutionary era. David S. Lovejoy, *Rhode Island Politics and the American Revolution, 1760–1776* (Providence, 1958), 2–3, 14–15. The role of localism in Connecticut politics is also difficult to assess, for no one has examined the colony from that point of view. The most comprehensive studies of colonial Connecticut are Richard L. Bushman, *From Puritan to Yankee: Character and the Social Order in Connecticut, 1690–1765* (Cambridge, Mass., 1967), and Oscar Zeichner, *Connecticut's Years of Controversy, 1750–1776* (Williamsburg, 1949).

The sectional characteristics I have thus far associated with southern and New England politics should be regarded more as tendencies or probable orientations than as rigid typologies. I have already suggested that North Carolina may represent an exception to the southern pattern, and similar exceptions may be found among the New England colonies. Rhode Island, for example, seems at times to conform more closely to what I shall describe as the middle-colony norm than to that of New England. Still, the sectional paradigm offered here may, it is hoped, be of some value in highlighting the most obvious differences among the colonies, and thus of suggesting another way of thinking about early American politics.

48. On the matter of self-interest as a theme in colonial politics, see Bernard Friedman, "The Shaping of the Radical Consciousness in Provincial New York," *Journal of American History,* LVI (1970), 781–801; Bonomi, *A Factious People,* 281–283.

government sufficiently strong and articulate to constitute an effective rein on central authority.[49]

Since they had so little practice in pulling together, it is hardly surprising that middle-colony leaders should find themselves at odds on most political issues.[50] Nor is it difficult to understand why governors so regularly exploited these divisions within the province as they strove to organize sufficient power to rule their factious subjects. "A Governor is no sooner appointed," declared Archibald Kennedy of New York, "than the first Question is, Into whose Hands shall I throw myself? the Answer is ready, Into whose but such as can best manage the Assembly. Hence Prime Ministers and Courtiers are established; and, of Course, Anticourtiers. Hence Parties are formed. . . . And what is all this for? . . . [but] to shew how dexterously the one Side can manage the Assembly for [the governor] and the other against him?"[51] In Pennsylvania and New Jersey too, groups of "rival gentleman leaders" ranged themselves on the "court" or "country" side of all the major issues.[52] It was in this way that middle-colony politics became an incessant grapple between a governor's party and an opposition, between—one might almost say—a set of "ins" and a set of "outs." The arrival of each new governor brought a fresh opportunity to rebalance the political scales, as contending elites jostled each other for patronage and preference.

This movement in and out of power came to be more and more

49. Though instruction of representatives and the petitioning of legislatures were not unknown in the middle colonies, these assertions of local interest were made no more than spasmodically; they did not occur on a regular basis.

50. Discussing Philadelphia politics, David Hawke says, "Rarely did an event occur that overrode racial, religious, and economic differences and united the people to act as one." *Midst of a Revolution,* 87.

51. [Archibald Kennedy], *An Essay on the Government of the Colonies* (New York, 1752), 34. As early as 1702, Robert Livingston of New York noted that the people of that colony "are not unanimous, and doe not stick to one another." Governors capitalized on this by "Striking in with one Party and they assist him to destroy the other. . . ." Quoted in Lawrence H. Leder, "The Politics of Upheaval in New York, 1689–1709," *New-York Historical Society Quarterly,* XLIV (1960), 426.

52. William S. Hanna, *Benjamin Franklin and Pennsylvania Politics* (Stanford, 1964), 52; Kemmerer, *Path to Freedom,* 48–53; Richard P. McCormick, *New Jersey from Colony to State* (Princeton, 1964), 63–72.

regularized in the middle colonies during the eighteenth century. Nor would it be quite right to think of this polarization as necessarily occurring about issues of class, family, principle, or even interest. It could conceivably be any one of these, or several, or all: but never quite directly, because the thing always at stake was power—or rather access to power. And the struggle for that access was, in turn, peculiarly shaped in its tone and character by the pluralism, heterogeneity, and diversity of the society itself.

The sources of strength in the governor's faction were clear enough. The governor's own powers, though under erosion in the course of the eighteenth century,[53] still made his office and person a nucleus of attraction for the ambitious. For the opposition, on the other hand, it was not so simple. Their platform was the assembly; it was from there that they did what they could to strike back, concert measures, and undermine the governor's support. Yet they could seldom count on an assembly which moved as a unit, as was the case in the southern colonies; it was not the assembly as a whole that they were organizing but a faction within it. Access to the assembly itself, moreover, depended on an electorate whose temper and inclinations could never be taken for granted. Thus, candidates found themselves going to the people, appealing to their interests, playing on their prejudices, and dramatizing any threats, real or suspected, to their rights and liberties. It was thus that politicians of the middle colonies developed the arts of what they themselves termed "political management": the building of "coalitions," the courting of self-interest groups, the balancing of "tickets," and the fashioning of propaganda.[54]

53. Bailyn, *Origins of American Politics,* 66–80; Hanna, *Benjamin Franklin,* 20; Katz, *Newcastle's New York,* 44.

54. A 1764 Pennsylvania election pamphlet declared: "As there are two Parties, we find that each of them, to gain your Votes and Interest, profess a zealous Concern for the preservation of the Rights and Privileges of the good People of this Province." *To the FREEHOLDERS and other ELECTORS for the City and County of Philadelphia, and Counties of Chester and Bucks* [1764], *Papers of Benjamin Franklin,* XI, 377. Pennsylvanians voted either Old Party or New Party "Tickets" in 1764, and New Yorkers chose between two full slates of candidates in 1769. In 1776, one Frederick Kuhl was placed on a Pennsylvania ticket "to attract the German vote." Hanna, *Benjamin Franklin,* ch. 10; Bonomi, *A Factious People,* 251–252; Hawke, *Midst of a Revolution,* 26.

Another way to think about this polarizing process, this ongoing division of "ins" and "outs," is to view it as a preliminary stage in the development of political parties. And it was without question in the middle colonies that notions about parties received their most advanced and elaborate testing. This is hardly to say that "parties," of the systematic sort now known, existed in colonial America. These would not develop until at least the late 1820's, although it is worth noting that when they did, they had their first flowering in the middle-Atlantic region.[55] But what *was* happening in the eighteenth century is not without interest. The incidence of faction and party in middle-colony political life is too obtrusive to be ignored, nor did men ignore it then. In their efforts to reconcile what they saw all about them with a theoretical frame that defined parties as "symptoms of disease in the body politic,"[56] middle-colony leaders were forced to think about the unthinkable.

Thus, in 1734, at the height of the Morris-Cosby-Zenger episode in New York, an essay appeared in the *New-York Gazette* that asserted the inevitability of *"Parties, Cabals* and *Intrigues"* in government. The writer goes on: "Some Opposition, tho' it proceed not entirely from a public Spirit, is not only necessary in free Governments, but of great Service to the Public. Parties are a Check upon one another, and by keeping the Ambition of one another within Bounds, serve to maintain the public Liberty . . . and instead of clogging, [party] regulates and keeps in their just and proper Motion the Wheels of Government."[57]

That the colonists upon occasion explored the possible benefits of parties has been noted before, though it has generally been assumed

55. Michael Wallace, "Changing Concepts of Party in the United States: New York, 1815–1828," *American Historical Review* (1968), LXXIV, 453–491. Discussing the controversy over ratification of the U.S. Constitution, Richard Hofstadter notes that in New York and Pennsylvania the issue "became involved with well-developed struggles between leading political factions, struggles which in Pennsylvania were so systematic and continuous as to foreshadow the two-party system." *The Progressive Historians* (New York, 1969), 241; Hofstadter, *The Idea of a Party System* (Berkeley, 1970), 45. In *Federalist* Number Fifty, James Madison mentions "the parties which pre-existed in the State" of Pennsylvania.

56. Bailyn, *Origins of American Politics,* 125.

57. March 11–18, 1733/34. This major essay on parties covers three columns in the *Gazette*.

that such thoughts "trailed away" too fast to represent more than random conjectures.[58] Yet it is possible that this early probing of the two-party idea may not have been quite so ephemeral as we have supposed. The comment of 1734 noted above, for example, was part of an extended inquiry into the whole question of organized opposition to constituted authority. John Peter Zenger's paper, the *New-York Weekly Journal,* had been founded to provide a voice for the Morrisite opposition to Governor William Cosby, and the *Journal* and the *New-York Gazette* were the vehicles for a debate that lasted over many months. In the course of that debate, the Morrisites wrote a number of essays supporting their right to resist what they saw as executive tyranny, "especially in an Age of Liberty in which *the slavish Doctrine of passive Obedience* is out of Fashion." While unjust criticism of those in power continued to be seen as destructive of the common good, "JUST CLAMOUR [one writer claimed] is the Right of all Freemen to make, when Cause is given for it." A correspondent to the *Journal* asked "leave to call my self a Party Man," noting that he would have been so labeled anyway for defending Zenger's paper.[59] In the course of this debate, the frequency with which the words "Opposition" and "Party" appear in a positive context gives more than a hint that attitudes were undergoing some sort of alteration.[60]

The thought did not end there. A Pennsylvanian averred in 1738 that "there can be no liberty without faction; for the latter cannot be suppressed without introducing slavery in the place of the former." And in 1739, an essayist saw positive benefits in having two newspapers with different viewpoints in New York City, as they represented

58. Bailyn, *Origins of American Politics,* 127.
59. *New-York Weekly Journal,* Jan. 21, Feb. 4, Feb. 18, 1733/34. See also the issues of April 1 and May 20, 1734, and the *New-York Gazette* for Mar. 18–25, April 8–15, and April 15–22, 1734; as well as James Alexander, *A Brief Narrative of the Case and Trial of John Peter Zenger* . . ., ed. by Stanley N. Katz (Cambridge, Mass., 1963).
60. Colonial Americans "were becoming conscious of the healthy plurality of interests and sects that prevailed among them, and were growing increasingly aware of the necessity for mutual tolerance that this imposed—two elements of consciousness that provided the intellectual and moral prerequisites of an understanding of the party system." Hofstadter, *Idea of a Party System,* 35.

"Weight[s], in the opposite Scale of the Balance of Parties . . . [and] will tend to keep the Ballance even. . . . [Thus] Injuries on either Side are either prevented or redressed. . . . [and] we find the Province and City has flourished . . . each [party] being such a Check and Ballance to the other, that neither dared to do oppressive Things. . . ." Again, in 1749, parties were depicted by one "Tuphonicus" "as so many Spies upon one another," which defended "the Public against the Incroachments of Power and Tyranny." The writer noted, to be sure, that "Party Spirit" in New York had lately grown "wild," and that this could lead to anarchy and loss of liberty. Two weeks later, nonetheless, we learn that "Tuphonicus is, and ever will be a Friend to Party, as long as Party keeps itself within Bounds, and answers the Purpose for which it ought to be supported." Similar comments continue to appear in middle-colony newspapers and pamphlets down to the start of the Revolution.[61]

In considering why these notions about opposition should have found their most advanced expression in colonial America, we might listen to the words of the Reverend William Smith of Pennsylvania. The year was 1764, and Benjamin Franklin and the "Quaker party" were attempting to have Pennsylvania's proprietary charter replaced by a royal charter. To demonstrate that the Assembly did not unanimously support a royal charter, Smith and other "Proprietary party" men had drawn up a "Protest" against the plan. Franklin disapproved of such a mode of dissent, noting that this was not the way things

61. *Pennsylvania Gazette*, Mar. 21–30, 1737/8; *New-York Weekly Journal*, Mar. 12, 1738/39; *New-York Gazette Revived in the Weekly Post-Boy*, Jan. 9, Jan. 29, 1748/49. In 1752, New York printer James Parker pleaded with the two parties in New York City not to hold him responsible for the aspersions cast by their opponents, for if a printer "will not print for both Sides, he must shut up Shop, and starve." Moreover, Parker stated, "all *Englishmen* have a Right to speak their Sentiments . . . if one Side only is to be served, then adieu to . . . Liberty. . . ." *New-York Gazette Revived in the Weekly Post-Boy*, Feb. 24, 1752. See also William Livingston and Others, *The Independent Reflector, or Weekly Essays on Sundry Important Subjects More Particularly adapted to the Province of New-York*, ed. by Milton M. Klein (Cambridge, Mass., 1963), 147–148, 195, 208–209, 261; *Pennsylvania Journal*, Supplement, Sept. 27, 1764; *New-York Gazette; or, The Weekly Post-Boy*, Feb. 29, 1768; *New-York Journal; or, The General Advertiser*, Mar. 3, 1768.

were done in the House of Commons. In response, Smith pointed out that "when cases and emergencies arise which are new and unprecedented in their nature, a new and unprecedented mode of proceeding against them, may become indispensably necessary." Those who disagreed with majority policies should consider it "both a publick and private duty . . . to oppose them by every means in their power." The broad acceptance that such a view had gained by the end of the colonial era is reflected by a passage in Robert Proud's history— hardly a radical work—which declared that it was "the extreme alone of party design, which, in reality, is so pernicious to human society; while its moderate exertion excites a stricter attention to men's real interests, and under proper management and direction, becomes subservient to the more effectual security of the public good."[62] Thus "party" had become a recognized device, in the middle colonies at least, for safeguarding liberty against the encroachments of power.

Resistance to the policies of Crown and Parliament in the 1770's gave the practice of organized opposition another long push in the direction of legitimacy. But once the war began, this emergent tendency was again subordinated to the more orthodox and familiar side of the question, that which stressed the viciousness of faction and party. Dissent and opposition were, of course, now seen as treasonable, and were everywhere suppressed—as they probably had to be if the Revolution were to succeed. Nor did the early years of the Republic bring an immediate loosening of the idea that faction should not be allowed to produce any fissures in the newly created arrangements of government. The leaders of new nations, fashioned as such nations usually are in revolutionary circumstances, do not as a rule believe they can afford the luxury of an opposition. Those of the United States—the first extended republic in history, whose survival nobody could predict with much assurance—were no exception. Yet all of this tends to obscure, rather than illuminate, the extent to which the idea of party had been tested already in America.

62. [William Smith], *An Answer to Mr. Franklin's Remarks, on a Late Protest* (Philadelphia, 1764), *Papers of Benjamin Franklin*, XI, 489; Proud, *History of Pennsylvania*, I, 479–480.

For the Republic was barely a dozen years old when, as Richard Hofstadter has pointed out,[63] there occurred an extraordinary event in the history of the party idea. The inauguration of Thomas Jefferson on March 4, 1801, and with it the peaceful transfer of power from one party to another, would have been a phenomenon hardly conceivable in a society that did not already possess a substantial fund of experience in political accommodation. That experience had its beginnings well back in the colonial phase of America's history.

It is, moreover, in the middle colonies of New York, New Jersey, and Pennsylvania that we can see this development at its clearest. It was there that the techniques of political management and party building first took on those more genial, and even gamelike, aspects which would in turn make politics something less than a life-and-death struggle. Robert Proud perceived that though Pennsylvania's "parties were very free with each other's conduct, yet, they are said mostly to have kept within the rules of decency and order. . . ." David Hawke, a recent scholar, also referring to Pennsylvania, has written that by 1776 "the tradition had already developed that regardless of the bitterness of any campaign, regardless of how wide the split between contending factions, the results of any election were accepted by both sides. This did not mean that the loser ceased to oppose. It did mean he carried on his opposition within the accepted political framework and did not threaten, because he had lost, to overthrow the government."[64] In such circumstances, whether a Franklin or a Galloway could have looked so different from an Allen or a Dickinson may be mostly a question of degree—and the same might be said of a Philipse or a DeLancey, on the one hand, and a Morris or a Livingston on the other.[65] The public had accustomed itself to seeing all such men move

63. *Idea of a Party System,* 128.

64. Proud, *History of Pennsylvania,* I, 484; Hawke, *Midst of a Revolution,* 130. Richard Hofstadter calls this "comity." "The basic humanity of the opposition is not forgotten; civility is not abandoned . . . [;] an awareness that the opposition will someday be the government is always present." *The Progressive Historians,* 454.

65. The best brief summary of factional groupings in New Jersey is in McCormick, *New Jersey from Colony to State,* ch. 4.

in and out of power with a certain regularity. The question of access to power, then, and the activities that went with it, may tell us as much as ideology, or interest, or indeed anything else, about why men and groups behaved as they did. Even the question of whether or not a man became a Loyalist had a great deal more to do with the groupings of provincial politics than we once thought—and it is surely not by mere chance that the incidence of loyalism was higher in the middle colonies than in either of the other sections.[66] But the main thing, to repeat, was movement in and out of power: this and its eventual consequences for an ethic of party competition was the true innovative element in middle-colony politics.

Thus the transition in 1801 from an Adams to a Jefferson, though a wrench in more ways than one, meant something less than total upheaval. Things not dissimilar had occurred before. And when the legitimacy of the party idea was fully established, as it came to be in the 1820's and 1830's, it flourished first and best in the middle-Atlantic region, where the soil had been long prepared. Middle-colony politicians of the eighteenth century—and perhaps a few early historians—might have found some sly satisfaction in this.

66. William H. Nelson, *The American Tory* (New York, 1961), 87ff.

TWENTIETH-CENTURY
PERSPECTIVES

PHILIP L. WHITE

Herbert Levi Osgood: An Intellectual Tragedy

THE PROFESSIONAL CAREER of Herbert Levi Osgood suggests three major observations. First, Osgood's deep commitment to the dogmas of scientific history caused him to minimize explicit analysis, despite the fact that the keenness of his intellect and the vastness of his research qualified him to interpret American colonial history extremely well. Second, despite this deficiency and the age of his volumes, they still hold rewards for the analytical historian searching for better understanding of the preconditions of the American Revolution. Third, the traditional association of Osgood with the imperial school of colonial historians appears to need qualification in recognition of his differences with others in that school and his largely unnoticed links to the Whig, or patriot, school of the much maligned George Bancroft.

Before considering these three themes, a brief summary of Osgood's career and an appraisal of his professional reputation appear warranted. Unlike so many of the gentlemen amateurs who dominated American historical writing until his own generation, Osgood had no inherited fortune to subsidize his education, research, and writing. His father was a farmer of modest means in Canton, Maine, where Osgood was born in 1855. What his parents gave Osgood, at considerable sacrifice, was "broad exemption from the usual farm boy's chores so that he might apply himself to books."[1] He did so with the utmost seriousness, establishing a work pattern which in his mature years kept his nose to the grindstone usually about eleven hours a day.[2] Osgood's parents managed also to send him to Amherst College, where he became in some measure the protégé of John W. Burgess, a promising young scholar who had just finished a period of prestigious training in Germany.

Osgood's professional apprenticeship lasted from his graduation at Amherst in 1877 until 1890 when, at the age of thirty-five, he secured an appointment at Columbia. During his apprentice years, Osgood taught in secondary schools (Worcester Academy, 1877–1879; Brooklyn High School, 1883–1889) and did graduate study at Amherst, Yale, and Columbia. He managed somehow to spend the required year in Germany at the University of Berlin (1882–1883) plus another in England (1889–1890). In Germany Osgood studied under a battery of outstanding scholars—Wagner, Schmoller, and Gneist—but it was the ideas of the aged Leopold von Ranke which fixed themselves most firmly in his mind.

The budding American historical profession in general had committed itself to Ranke's beliefs that historical writing must, above all else, be meticulously accurate in detail and absolutely free of partiality in interpretation. To Osgood, however, the commitment became almost complete. He dedicated himself also to a concomitant principle: that the historian should avoid interpretation for the most part and let the facts speak for themselves. In this spirit, Osgood at the outset of his professional career began archival research in England on American colonial history. He did so at the suggestion of Burgess, whom he had followed to Columbia as a graduate student and to whom he owed his Columbia appointment.[3]

Judged by the narrowly specialized standards of today, Osgood's

---

1. Dixon Ryan Fox, *Herbert Levi Osgood: An American Scholar* (New York, 1924), 18. Fox was Osgood's son-in-law and colleague at Columbia. His sensitive biographical memoir is the basic source on Osgood's life.

2. *Ibid.*, 109.

3. *Ibid.*, passim; Herbert L. Osgood, *American Colonies in the Seventeenth Century*, 3 vols. (New York, 1904–07), I, preface.

teaching experience in his first years at Columbia was remarkably broad. He taught graduate-level courses on political economy, European history from Rome to his own time, English constitutional history, and of course the "Political History of the Colonies and the American Revolution." Dixon Ryan Fox noted that the manuscripts from which he read his lectures were of massive proportions and that behind each manuscript lay "piles of rough notes, digests, and analyses, almost appalling in the labor they represent."[4] Thus, in meeting his responsibilities as a teacher, Osgood secured an enormous range of erudition and qualified himself in a manner inconceivable to most modern scholars to study the political history of the American colonies in a remarkably broad context.

Osgood's early journal articles, in contrast to the essentially factual emphasis in his books, are brilliantly interpretive. They abound in generalizations, some of them clearly anticipating conclusions subsequently set forth in monographs of distinction by other scholars. When he was only thirty-two and still a high school teacher, Osgood published in 1887 an essay on "England and the Colonies." The society which had evolved gradually in America, Osgood affirmed,

was far different from anything which existed in the mother country. It was democratic rather than aristocratic; it was also extremely particularistic and too remote from England to feel much interest in the general concerns of empire. In this divergence of social organization and interests . . . lay the germ which might develop into resistance on the part of the plantations if at any time England should attempt to enforce her rightful supremacy over them.[5]

This insight was considerably more sophisticated than the famous observation by John Adams that the Revolution was in the "Minds and Hearts of the People" and "was effected before the War commenced."[6] Equally significant, it preceded by a full generation the well-known affirmation of Charles M. Andrews that a "silent revolu-

4. Fox, *Osgood*, 47.
5. Herbert L. Osgood, "England and the Colonies," *Political Science Quarterly*, II (1887), 440–469.
6. Lester J. Cappon, ed., *The Adams-Jefferson Letters*, 2 vols. (Chapel Hill, 1959), II, 445.

tion" had prepared the way for independence by differentiating American from British society.[7]

    In the same essay Osgood stated that the "political character and tendencies of Puritanism" had the strongest bearing on the "alienation and final separation of the colonies from the crown. . . ." "Here [in America]," he declared, "was played the last act of the great historic drama which absorbed the attention of England during the seventeenth century."[8] Four years later in a two-part article on "The Political Ideas of the Puritans,"[9] he elaborated on the same theme and related the English Levellers to New England Puritans. In these affirmations he anticipated in considerable measure the thesis of Caroline Robbins's superb study, *The Eighteenth-Century Commonwealthman*.

    Osgood published next a series of articles analyzing the major forms of colonial government.[10] With reference to the government of the corporate colonies—Massachusetts, Connecticut, and Rhode Island—he stressed the extent to which the "actual settlers" assumed power, and he contrasted that political system with European practices and those practices in the colonies of nations other than England. He also linked the corporate form of organization to the "burgher class and the incipient democracy of the European cities."[11]

    Discussing proprietary provinces in the same series of articles, Osgood showed still more clearly the evolutionary connection between European and American institutions. "The history of the American provinces," he wrote, "is emphatically the history of the adaptation of

    7. Charles M. Andrews, *The Colonial Background of the American Revolution* (New Haven, 1924), 181.
    8. Osgood, "England and the Colonies," 446.
    9. Herbert L. Osgood, "Political Ideas of the Puritans," *Political Science Quarterly*, VI (1891).
    10. Herbert L. Osgood, "The Classification of American Colonial Governments," American Historical Association *Annual Report* (1895), 617–627; "The Colonial Corporation," *Political Science Quarterly*, XI (1896), pt. I, 259–297; pt. II, 502–533; pt. III, 694–715; "The Proprietary Province as a Form of Colonial Government," pt. 1, *American Historical Review*, II (1896–1897), 644–664; pt. 2, III (1897–1898), 31–55; pt. 3, III (1897–1898), 244–265; "Connecticut as a Corporate Colony," *Political Science Quarterly*, XIV (1899), 251–280.
    11. "The Colonial Corporation," pt. III, 694–695.

English institutions to the conditions of life on a newly settled continent. There the tendencies favorable to the democratic element in the constitution of the provinces were stronger than they were in England prior to the close of the eighteenth century, while the obstacles to its development were less powerful than in the mother country."[12] In accounting for such differences, Osgood noted: "Those who became colonists came largely from the classes which were least wedded to the aristocratic and monarchical institutions of the Old World."[13] Thus, factors in both the European heritage and the American environment "facilitated the democratizing of the American province" and "made the process shorter and more certain of ultimate success than in the European kingdom."[14]

Colonial history in general and the American Revolution in particular were his subjects for another series of articles published between 1898 and 1902. In a review article on Moses Coit Tyler's *Literary History of the American Revolution,* Osgood praised Tyler's objectivity in treating the Loyalists, but censured him severely for echoing Bancroft's characterization of George III as tyrannical.[15] Parliament, Osgood insisted, was the real source of danger to the American people; only when Parliament supported the king did Americans have any reason to fear royal power. Anticipating those who would later dismiss as propaganda the charges against George III in the Declaration of Independence, Osgood noted that it would be difficult to justify the accusations. His principal observation on that score, however, was that "until the eighteenth century shall be studied much more thoroughly than it ever has been," on both the British and the American sides, no final judgment could be rendered.[16] Osgood also caught Tyler in a logical inconsistency. Tyler had argued that "virtual representation" was constitutional but that Parliamentary taxation of the Americans

---

12. "The Proprietary Province as a Form of Colonial Government," pt. I, 653.
13. *Ibid.*
14. *Ibid.*
15. Herbert L. Osgood, "The American Revolution," *Political Science Quarterly,* XIII (1898), 41–59.
16. *Ibid.,* 59.

for revenue was not. Osgood observed that if virtual representation was constitutional, then taxation was also—a conclusion which he himself found no difficulty in accepting.

Osgood's major message for future scholars appeared in his essay of 1898 on "The Study of American Colonial History."[17] His chief aim in writing the essay was to call for more work on the period between 1690 and 1760. "The simple fact of the case," he wrote, "is that we have in print scarcely an approximation to a satisfactory treatment of American history in the early eighteenth century."[18] "How can we hope to understand 'our' revolution adequately," he complained, "if we know so little of the seventy years which preceded it? The scholar who takes up the secondary literature on the subject," he continued, "will find himself contemplating a multitude of events, many of them petty, none apparently of very great importance, some occurring on one side of the Atlantic and some on the other, and between them all he will often fail to discern any clear connection."[19] "In the interest of American history in general, the greatest need today is the critical investigation and exposition of the colonial period as a whole and with a view to the ascertainment of its position in the general history of the world."[20] He had discerned, even at that early date, not only the neglect of a major chronological segment of American history, but also the pernicious tendency of scientific historians to produce atomistic if not merely antiquarian reports. While he could not have foreseen the intellectual chaos which such atomistic tendencies would later produce in disciplines such as social psychology,[21] he saw clearly that historians were in danger of losing the cosmic perspective which had characterized the work of early giants such as Bancroft. "Only by keeping well in view the essential unity of English development and that of her American colonies," he concluded, "and by treating the

17. Herbert L. Osgood, "The Study of American Colonial History," American Historical Association *Annual Report* (1898), 63–76.
18. *Ibid.,* 64.
19. *Ibid.,* 65.
20. *Ibid.*
21. See Gordon W. Allport, "The Historical Background of Modern Social Psychology," in Gardner Lindzey and Elliott Aronson, *Handbook of Social Psychology,* 2d ed., 5 vols. (Reading, Mass., 1968–9), I, 1–80.

history of the colonies broadly and comparatively, can the obscurities of the period be removed and its true interest and meaning be revealed."[22] Thus, six years before the appearance of the first of his volumes on the seventeenth century and a full quarter of a century before the appearance of his volumes on the eighteenth century, Osgood put his finger on the major historiographical problems and marked out tasks which would occupy him the rest of his life.

Within a few years after the turn of the century Osgood ceased almost entirely to write journal articles and reviews or even to attend meetings of the American Historical Association. Instead, as his colleague E. R. A. Seligman noted, "he resolutely refrained from all extraneous tasks and potboiling in order to devote himself wholeheartedly to his supreme object."[23] The "supreme object" was, of course, the completion of his multivolume history of the American colonies in the seventeenth and eighteenth centuries. Volumes I and II of *The American Colonies in the Seventeenth Century* appeared in 1904, Volume III in 1907. The four volumes of *The American Colonies in the Eighteenth Century* were not quite finished at his death in 1918. He had planned to write one chapter on slavery and another comparing institutional development in the American colonies with that in Ireland and the West Indies plus a conclusion.[24] Dixon Ryan Fox completed preparation of the manuscript for publication and, with the financial aid of Dwight Morrow, an appreciative former student of Osgood's, brought the volumes into print in 1923.

After 1904 Osgood had only two important publications in addition to his great work and a few reviews. He agreed reluctantly to do an essay on American history from the beginning to 1785 for the eleventh edition of the *Encyclopaedia Britannica.*[25] There, in a relatively few pages, he summed up brilliantly his life's work. Writing in remarkably broad perspective, he made a superbly comprehensive synthesis of the evolutionary growth of American political institutions and of the anti-colonial revolution which was its nearly inevitable consequence. At the

22. "The Study of American Colonial History," 73.
23. Fox, *Osgood,* 146.
24. *Ibid.,* 102.
25. *Ibid.,* 89–90.

other end of the historiographical spectrum, he edited with meticulous accuracy, but without commentary, the *Minutes of the Common Council of the City of New York, 1675–1776,* published in six volumes in 1906. He also tried with some success to prod state officials into a more respectful and professional regard for archival material.[26]

Osgood's last years were tinged with tragedy. His own health was failing relatively early; one son was an invalid requiring institutional care; the other died as a victim of poison gas in World War I. Osgood himself deplored the anti-German and pro-Allied sentiment which dominated American public opinion. The supreme tragedy, however, was his early death. Osgood was just sixty-three when he died. At that age Gipson had reached only about the halfway point in his great series. Andrews was seventy-one when his first volume of *The Colonial Period of American History* appeared.

Osgood's contemporaries ranked him as one of the greatest historians of his generation, if not of all time. Charles M. Andrews perceived in reviewing the first of Osgood's volumes that remarkable combination of features which would characterize the entire series. The author, he noted, displayed "a wide and deep knowledge of the documentary evidence for colonial history and rare powers of analysis and interpretation." He predicted that when complete the series would "occupy a place of first importance in the literature of American history."[27] Reviewing the eighteenth-century volumes in 1926, Andrews tempered his enthusiasm somewhat, but despite his criticisms he still concluded that they constituted "a really great work."[28] In the *English Historical Review,* H. E. Egerton praised the eighteenth-century volumes as a "high water mark of learning and luminous judgment which will secure a place among the classics of American history."[29] Osgood's colleague Harry Elmer Barnes compared Osgood favorably to some of the great historians of the past.[30]

    26. *Ibid.,* ch. VII.
    27. *American Historical Review,* XI (1905–6), 397–403.
    28. *Ibid.,* XXXI (1925–26), 533–538. Andrews also reviewed the third of the seventeenth-century volumes, *ibid.,* XIII (1907–8), 605–609.
    29. *English Historical Review,* XXII (1907), 804–807.
    30. Harry Elmer Barnes, ed., *The History and Prospects of the Social Sciences* (New York, 1925), 29, 49.

Within a few years after the appearance of his eighteenth-century volumes, however, Osgood's reputation began to decline noticeably. Homer J. Coppock, a former student of Osgood's, published in 1933 the first major reassessment of Osgood's career. Although he included quotations of high praise from reviewers, Coppock added no such praise of his own except to note that Osgood showed "marked ability in generalizing." On the other hand, he criticized Osgood's organization and accused him of bias against Quakers.[31] E. C. O. Beatty's thorough but largely objective article on Osgood in the *Jernegan Essays in American Historiography* (1937) concluded that his "fame has not diminished," but Beatty himself employed no such words of praise as had reviewers in the previous decade.[32] In the same year Michael Kraus, in *A History of American History,* characterized Osgood moderately as a "pioneer in the modern study of the political origins of the United States," one whose work enabled others "to walk more easily over the path he had so laboriously hewn."[33] Unlike most others who have written on Osgood, Kraus quoted extensively and appreciatively from Osgood's often brilliant generalizations concerning the evolution of American political institutions. More typical of the attitude which soon became prevalent were the brief references to Osgood in Allan Nevins's *Gateway to History* (1938). His volumes, wrote Nevins in his only references to Osgood, were "minutely detailed," a "laborious array of marshalled facts."[34]

During the 1940's and the 1950's Osgood attracted very little attention from American historians, but H. Hale Bellot, a British scholar, showed high appreciation of his work. In his *American History and American Historians* (1952), Bellot categorized Osgood as a member of the "Columbia School" of institutional historians in which he included W. A. Dunning and John W. Burgess. The work of the Columbia School, Bellot noted, "had all the merits of German scholarship

---

31. Homer J. Coppock, "Herbert Levi Osgood," *Mississippi Valley Historical Review,* XIX (1932–33), 394–403.

32. E. C. O. Beatty, "Herbert Levi Osgood," in William T. Hutchinson, ed., *The Marcus W. Jernegan Essays in American Historiography* (Chicago, 1937), 291.

33. Michael Kraus, *A History of American History* (New York, 1937), 423.

34. Allan Nevins, *Gateway to History* (New York, 1938), 42, 60.

and was firmly based upon the records; it was concerned primarily with the history of political institutions; and it was European in outlook." His only major criticism of Osgood was that he confined his attention "too closely to the development of governmental institutions and public policy" and "took too little account of what the governed were meanwhile doing."[35] Bellot's summary of colonial history seemed to draw very largely upon Osgood, and he explicitly endorsed Osgood's conclusions without specifying very clearly what they were.

Since the late 1940's historians in the United States have tended to write about Osgood primarily within the context of the imperial school. In doing so they have relied very largely upon his early articles and ignored for the most part his magnum opus. Max Savelle, in writing sympathetically of "The Imperial School of American Colonial Historians" (1949),[36] identified Osgood as the founder of the movement —the first to renounce the partisan spirit so evident in Bancroft. Unlike some later writers, Savelle did keep the seven volumes in view and noted also that Osgood was not entirely in agreement with the imperial school on all matters.

In 1955 Abraham S. Eisenstadt's brilliant biography of Charles McLean Andrews honored Osgood as the founder of "the new colonial history"—Eisenstadt's term for what most historians have preferred to call the imperial school. Osgood's concern with institutional history, as usual, drew relatively little attention, but Eisenstadt did mention Osgood's differences with Andrews over the proper perspective in which to view American colonial history. He took notice also of Osgood's feeling that Beer had gone too far in rejecting the "American way of interpreting colonial history."[37]

Harvey Wish, in *The American Historian: A Social-Intellectual History of the Writing of the American Past* (1960), titled the chapter in which he discussed Osgood "From Fiske to Gipson: The Rise of

35. H. Hale Bellot, *American History and American Historians* (London, 1952), 41–42.

36. Max Savelle, "The Imperial School of American Colonial Historians," *Indiana Magazine of History,* VI (1949), 123–134.

37. Abraham S. Eisenstadt, *Charles McLean Andrews: A Study in American Historical Writing* (New York, 1956), 179, 189.

Colonial Institutional History." Like most of his predecessors, however, Wish made little effort to identify Osgood's contribution to an understanding of the evolution of American political institutions in the colonial period. He stressed instead Osgood's role in initiating the imperial school. "For all his stylistic drawbacks and woodenness of organization," Wish wrote, "Osgood had a creative influence among the rising generation of colonial historians, particularly George Louis Beer, Charles Andrews, and Lawrence H. Gipson. . . ."[38]

Lawrence Henry Gipson, dean of the imperial school in the 1960's, identified Beer's master's thesis as the first work of "any scholar beyond the Loyalist generation . . . to deal with the history of the British Empire." Gipson did note, however, that "Beer was undoubtedly deeply influenced by Herbert Levi Osgood under whom he studied at Columbia."[39] He pointed out as well that Osgood's essay of 1887 on "England and the Colonies" supported "the eighteenth-century" British interpretation of the powers of Parliament and also took the position that the limitations which American colonials placed on these powers were revolutionary in nature."[40] Gipson concurred of course with Osgood's assertion that any adequate interpretation of the American Revolution had to take into account the various forces which had led to the creation and the growth of the British Empire. He noted with approval that Osgood's seventeenth-century volumes had been "written from the imperial approach," but he observed a little sorrowfully that in the eighteenth-century volumes "imperial relations are not stressed as forcibly as one was led to believe they would be. . . ."[41]

Jack P. Greene tended to view Osgood primarily within the context of the imperial school. In his long essay "The Reappraisal of the American Revolution in Recent Historical Literature" (1966), Greene devoted only a paragraph to Osgood because his writings

38. Harvey Wish, *The American Historian: A Social-Intellectual History of the Writing of the American Past* (New York, 1960), 119, passim.
39. Lawrence Henry Gipson, "The Imperial Approach to Early American History," in Ray Allen Billington, ed., *The Reinterpretation of Early American History* (San Marino, Calif., 1966), 193, 195.
40. *Ibid.*, 195.
41. *Ibid.*, 195–196.

could hardly qualify as "recent." Greene characterized Osgood as "one of the most prominent of the imperial historians." Of Osgood's numerous works the one which Greene singled out was the review essay of 1898 on Tyler. He noted in particular Osgood's denial that the British were "guilty of intentional tyranny toward the colonies" and his sharp criticism of unpatriotic American conduct during the Seven Years' War.[42]

George Athan Billias agreed with the traditional point of view in describing Osgood as "one of the founders of the Imperial School." Unlike Gipson, Billias chose to name Osgood's essay of 1887 on "England and the Colonies" as "the first to propose that the history of the colonial past be viewed from the imperial as well as the colonial side." "Considering himself a 'scientific historian,' " Billias continued, "Osgood steeped himself in British primary sources in order to view colonial affairs in the proper perspective and to achieve objectivity in the Rankean tradition." Citing Osgood's denial of tyrannical intent in British policy, Billias depicted the essay of 1887 as "a revisionist attack upon the patriotic school of Bancroft and Fiske."[43]

From the foregoing observations it appears obvious that recent historians have largely lost sight of Osgood's monumental volumes and remember him instead mainly for his earlier essays. It is clear also that these early essays seem worthy of notice to such scholars primarily as support for their observation that Osgood pioneered in the interpretive emphasis which culminated in the imperial school. By looking closely at both the early essays and the later volumes it may be possible to determine more precisely where Osgood stood in relation to both the Whig and the imperial schools.

To deal with the problem within this context, it will be useful to delineate the central features of both schools. Fundamental to the Whig interpretation was the belief that representative government was evolving more rapidly in the American colonies than in Britain itself, and that following the accession of George III a conservative turn in

42. Jack P. Greene, ed., *The Reinterpretation of the American Revolution, 1763–1789* (New York, 1968), 4–5.

43. George Athan Billias, "The Revolutionary Era: Reinterpretations and Revisions," in George Athan Billias and Gerald N. Grob, eds., *American History: Retrospect and Prospect* (New York, 1971), 42.

Britain accentuated the conflict between the two societies, culminating in revolution. Whig historians for the most part wrote within a broad international perspective and dealt with long spans of time. They were not at all reluctant to generalize. They were generally liberal in the political contests of their own times. Most were gentlemen amateurs who reached maturity before the professionalization of the field of history had taken place. They wrote chiefly for other amateurs and in so doing catered to a public taste by depicting dramatic confrontations between the forces of good and evil. They tended also to blacken their villains and to glorify their heroes with great rhetorical exaggeration. Some did remarkably extensive research, but none approached the professional criteria for historical investigation set by the "scientific" ideal which was coming into vogue in the late nineteenth century.[44]

How did the imperial school differ from the Whig? In the first place the imperial writers tried very hard to be objective; they disdained the partisanship which characterized the Whig school. Unlike the Whig historians, those of the imperial school were professionals, trained in graduate schools, and they wrote primarily for other historians rather than for the general public. On the whole, they had higher standards for exhaustiveness in research and accuracy in detail. Like Ranke, they tended to carry their dedication to objectivity to the point of eschewing interpretation almost entirely in the expectation that a detailed and accurate rendition of the facts would convey to the reader whatever conclusions, if any, were warranted.

With objectivity as their goal, historians of the imperial school attemped to neutralize the partisanship of their Whig predecessors. George Louis Beer, studying commercial regulation meticulously, concluded that Britain's efforts to channel colonial trade were mutually beneficial rather than exploitive as Bancroft had argued.[45]

44. Probably no other historian would agree fully with this characterization, but see Herbert Butterfield, *The Whig Interpretation of History* (New York, 1951); Merrill Jensen, "Historians and the Nature of American Revolution," in Billington, ed., *The Reinterpretation of Early American History*, 101–127; Jack P. Greene, "The Flight from Determinism," *South Atlantic Quarterly*, LXI (1962), 235–259.

45. George Louis Beer apparently never used the phrase "mutually beneficial." Like his mentor, he preferred to allow the facts to convey their own message. He did write, however, that British regulation of American commerce

Andrews added the assertion that the proper perspective in which to view the history of colonial America was that of the imperial administrators. He did not state explicitly that it was improper to write the history of the colonies from an American perspective, but he implied strongly that it was.[46] Finally, Gipson affirmed that Parliamentary taxation of the Americans for revenue was not only constitutional but fair. In making this point, Gipson noted the benefits which accrued to the Americans from the Seven Years' War, the lightness of their own tax burdens in comparison with those of the British, and the relative prosperity and hence ability to pay which characterized American society.[47]

How in fact did Osgood's views relate to those of the two opposing schools? Without any question, Osgood, as noted above, was the first to attack the Whig historians on the score of objectivity. He differed from them in other respects as well. He had more professional training; he insisted more on exhaustive research; he wrote for his fellow professionals rather than for amateurs. But where did he stand on the other points of view identified with the imperial school and on the fundamental Whig concern with the evolution of representative government?

First of all, how did Osgood react to the conclusion set forth in the master's thesis which Beer did under his direction that the acts of trade aimed to benefit both Britain and America? Six years before the publication of Beer's thesis, Osgood had expressed surprise that "the worst grievance of all, viz. the laws of trade, was scarcely mentioned in the controversy" preceding the Revolution.[48] Thus, on the one

---

"was based on the idea of reciprocity," and aimed to be "mutually complementary." "The Colonial Policy of Great Britain, 1760–1765," in American Historical Association *Annual Report* (1906), I, 179–190 (quote on p. 180). Oliver M. Dickerson, *Navigation Acts and the American Revolution* (Philadelphia, 1951), similarly denies at length that the system was exploitive without asserting that it was mutually beneficial. See ch. II, "Were the Navigation Acts Oppressive?"

46. See Eisenstadt, *Andrews*, 222.

47. Lawrence Henry Gipson, *The Coming of the Revolution, 1763–1775* (New York, 1954), 84, 128–129, 135–141, 149–150, 170–172.

48. "England and the Colonies," *Political Science Quarterly*, II (1887), 467.

hand, Osgood endorsed Bancroft's position that the Navigation Acts had been oppressive and, on the other hand, anticipated the assertion of both Beer and Oliver M. Dickerson (*The Navigation Acts and the American Revolution*) in noting how little commercial regulations figured in the revolutionary debates. Five years after the publication of Beer's thesis, Osgood denied that the acts of trade were a "badge of servitude" as Bancroft had branded them, and argued instead that they were "a natural and necessary phase in the development of colonization. . . ."[49] By 1902 Osgood had arrived at a characteristically balanced judgment—that "to a considerable extent the commercial policy was consistent with the economic condition of the colonies as it then was, but in some respects and to varying degrees it crossed their interests."[50] When he reviewed Beer's *Origins of the British Colonial System* (1908), Osgood was similarly ambivalent. The work was "satisfying in its conclusions," he wrote, but, he added, Beer was "looking at events almost wholly from the imperialist point of view. . . ."[51] His last statement of consequence on the subject appeared in the first volume of the *American Colonies in the Eighteenth Century:* "In a certain sense," he wrote, "the colonists were an imperial estate, a source of revenue, an object of exploitation. They were not exclusively so, but received benefits in return."[52] Thus, Beer's thesis fell considerably short of winning Osgood's unqualified endorsement. In the end he may even have been a little closer on this issue to Bancroft than to Beer.

Andrews's insistence that historians should write the history of colonial America from the perspective of imperial administrators apparently was derived, at least in some measure, from Osgood, but Andrews pushed the thesis to extremes which Osgood never countenanced. As Eisenstadt concluded in his biography, the imperial focus became to Andrews *the* avenue by which to approach American colonial history rather than merely *an* avenue.[53]

49. "The Study of American Colonial History," 68.
50. "England and the American Colonies in the Seventeenth Century," *Political Science Quarterly,* XVII (1902), 217.
51. *Political Science Quarterly,* XXIV (1909), 127–130.
52. *American Colonies in the Eighteenth Century, I,* 186.
53. See Eisenstadt, *Andrews,* 174, 179, 222.

What specifically did Osgood say on the subject? In 1898 he had affirmed that the student of colonial American history must not only pursue research in London "but in imagination too frequently establish himself there that he may thus view colonial affairs in their proper perspective." Preceding that affirmation, however, was a more characteristic assertion: "we must look at the colonial period . . . not only from the colonial but from the British standpoint; full justice must be done to both sides."[54] In the preface to the first volume of the eighteenth-century series, Osgood bemoaned the neglect of the British or imperial aspects of American colonial history. A little later, however, he noted that one could legitimately choose either the British or the American viewpoint in writing colonial history. He preferred the American vantage point, he wrote, because his interests were in this country's land and people.[55] Still more specifically he noted that "though a substratum of British law and precedent lay at the foundation of our colonial system, at the same time physical, social and political conditions in America from the first differed to such an extent from those in Great Britain as to lead to the early development of a distinct type of society and government."[56] These American innovations, rather than the vagaries of British imperial policy and administration, were the subjects of real interest to him. On this score, therefore, Osgood clearly rejected a major contention of the imperial school with which historians so often identify him.

On the other hand, Osgood came very close to justifying British taxation in much the same way that Gipson would many years after Osgood's death. Although the chronological span of Osgood's volumes did not encompass the rise of the taxation issue after 1763, Osgood never doubted Britain's constitutional authority to tax Americans for revenue. Beyond that, however, he argued along the same lines as Gipson that in view of the failure of the requisition system to secure supporting revenue from the colonies during the colonial wars, Brit-

54. "The Study of American Colonial History," 63–76.
55. *American Colonies in the Eighteenth Century,* I, xiii, 40.
56. *Ibid.,* 41.

ain's resort to imperial taxation seemed "worthy of fair consideration."[57] He did not fix his attention clearly on the implications of such
a policy for colonial self-government, but he thought that "clear-
headed" Americans might well have concluded—as in fact many did
conclude—that the "British king and Parliament could be trusted to
carry through this policy without imperilling the essential political
privileges of the colonists."[58] Thus, on the final point of comparison
of Osgood's views with those of the imperial school, Osgood in 1898
agreed essentially with a position which Gipson was to take a generation later.

Osgood's differences with the Whig school were clearly evident and
recognized from the outset, but the points of similarity have been less
widely recognized. Osgood never defined clearly what he meant by
"institutional history," but the nature of his volumes suggests strongly
that what interested him was the evolution of representative government in the American colonies. Perhaps the closest he ever came to
stating a thesis was in the third volume of the seventeenth-century
series. Speaking of the New England colonies at first, but broadening
his focus as he went on, Osgood stated that the colonies

had existed under a system of separatism and *de facto* self-government
which was inconsistent with the main trend of events in England subsequent to the Restoration. Had they been colonies of the Greek city type
they could hardly have been more self-centered or independent of the
metropolis. But in reality the British system was Roman and feudal, that
is provincial, in character, and with the Restoration the forces which were
moulding it after this model came permanently into operation. They came
necessarily and at once into conflict with the democratic and separatist
tendencies which were inherent in colonial life. The central thread of our
colonial history is to be found in the record of that conflict. It did not
occasion a resort to arms until the final stage was reached. But it was
nonetheless a struggle fought out . . . through all the twists and turns
of executive and legislative action, prolonged through a century and
repeated in nearly twenty jurisdictions.[59]

57. "The American Revolution," 56–58.
58. *Ibid.*
59. *American Colonies in the Seventeenth Century,* III, 314.

Thus it appears that although Osgood wrote with none of the romantic rhetoric and exaggeration which Bancroft employed, his central theme was essentially the same.

Bancroft and Osgood shared also an essentially Darwinian approach to American colonial history. Despite the fact that Bancroft was well along in his great work before the publication of Darwin's study, his cast of thought was evolutionary in character, although he did convey his ideas with little of the Darwinian terminology. Osgood has both the Darwinian terms and an evolutionary pattern of thought. Beer and Andrews wrote with an evolutionary emphasis too, but they focused more on imperial administration and less on the evolution of representative government.

To recapitulate, it appears that Osgood, as befitted a truly objective scholar, had a foot in both the Whig and the imperial camps. He accepted the basic theme of the Whig historians, but he supported it with more detailed research and stated it with a far greater measure of professional objectivity and restraint. His criticism of the partisan presentation rendered by the Whig historians represented the opening blast of the imperial school, but he clearly rejected Andrews's contention that scholars should write American colonial history from the perspective of British imperial administration. On the issue of whether or not the acts of trade were exploitive, Osgood straddled. Only in his belief that Parliamentary taxation of the Americans for revenue was fair as well as constitutional did he take a firm stand in support of another of the major contentions of the imperial school. Thus, Osgood ought not to be placed in the imperial school without qualification. He could, with considerable justice, be classified as an objective or a scientific Whig.

Many recent scholars, as noted previously, have overlooked this ambiguity in Osgood's position, but Andrews and Gipson did not. In reviewing Osgood's eighteenth-century volumes, Andrews observed a "disrelish—I would not call it prejudice for the British system and all who upheld it." Andrews denied that there was any basis for believing that the British imperial system violated "fundamental principles of political liberty," but he thought Osgood assumed at times that it did. Andrews noted also that the volumes were "more American than

British and growing more and more American with every decade that passes."[60] Gipson, as already noted, chose to identify Beer rather than Osgood as the founder of the imperial school and complained as well that the eighteenth-century volumes were not written from an imperial point of view. Richard B. Morris had also declined to place Osgood in the imperial school, but categorized him instead as an institutional historian.[61]

Contemporary American historians seem largely to ignore Osgood's many volumes, or if they remember them at all, do so chiefly to criticize them. They do offer a splendid target. Osgood's most conspicuous weakness was his writing style. His essays demonstrate that he could write in a clear and even forceful expository vein, but in his seven volumes it is painfully obvious that he did not take the trouble to do so. Many of his sentences in the early volumes read like literal translations from German. He also found the passive voice particularly appealing; he used it so often as to make his pages particularly lifeless. His sentences were rarely of inordinate length, but paragraphs running a page and a half quite frequently tax the reader's patience.

Osgood's organization represented another major deficiency. With his avowed interest in institutional history he should have employed a topical organization such as that which distinguishes Jack P. Greene's *Quest for Power.* Instead he used mainly a conventional chronological narrative. He did generally treat each colony separately, but his time periods were usually quite brief and were set arbitrarily within the context of military history. Osgood himself complained that the history of Europe appeared invariably as "bundles of national histories" rather than being integrated in some form,[62] but his own history of colonial America consisted largely of bundles of provincial histories. Topical chapters covering several or all of the colonies were rare.

Osgood's organizational deficiencies stemmed in some measure from his failure to define what he meant by institutional history. Because he

60. *American Historical Review,* XXXI (1925–26), 533–538.
61. Richard B. Morris, *The American Revolution Reconsidered* (New York, 1967), 26.
62. *American Colonies in the Seventeenth Century,* I, x.

never set forth a clear-cut definition, Osgood lacked satisfactory criteria by which to judge what was relevant to his central thesis. As a result, he often included material which was tangential at best.

Many critics have chastised Osgood for omitting or slighting topics such as social, economic, or intellectual history. In view of the bulk of his work and of his stated concern with institutional history, such criticism seems unfair. Nevertheless, it is true that a modern analyst studying the evolution of American political institutions in the colonial period would probably write in a much broader context than did Osgood.

Deficiencies in documentation appear with frequency that is surprising in view of Osgood's very obvious dedication to the highest standards of professionalism. Statements which by present standards clearly require footnote citations appear often without such references. Quite often a vague "we hear that" introduces a statement for which the reader longs for a specific citation. References to secondary authorities with whom Osgood disagreed simply do not appear. References to those upon whom he relied were relatively few. Such deficiencies have of course made it difficult for other scholars to use his work as fully as they might have otherwise.

Bias is by no means absent from Osgood's pages even though he had a strong commitment to objectivity. Despite strong Congregational influence in his early years, Osgood was no conventional believer. As Fox put it, the "Apostle's Creed did not take firm hold upon his mind . . . and he was not counted among the admirers of revivalist religion, as his chapter on the Great Awakening may reveal." "Orthodoxies wearied him," Fox added, whether they were in politics or in religion.[63]

Osgood's attitude toward religion in colonial America, reflecting these preconceptions, was less than eulogistic. All Protestant groups in the colonies, he stated, had an essentially medieval attitude which "implied intellectual and moral stagnation and in many quarters actually resulted in that." Congregationalism's Saybrook Platform, he declared, "aided the formation of a crust of dead orthodoxy under

63. Fox, *Osgood*, 21, 153.

which the churches slumbered until the rude awakening of the White-field revival." Puritanism in the eighteenth century had become so worldly, he believed, that the impression was "one sometimes of intolerable hypocrisy." Jonathan Edwards aroused Osgood's admiration, but also his pity. That so powerful a mind should have been "imprisoned within the stone walls and the iron gates of late New England Puritanism," he lamented, "makes his career a tragedy." One of his last observations on the subject was that New England's Congregationalists provided "one of the most finished examples of intolerance, both in theory and in practice, which the world has ever seen."[64]

Puritanism's contribution to the evolution of democracy, on the other hand, won unstinting praise in the article cited earlier on Puritan political ideas. Despite the oligarchic character of early New England government, he contended (oversimplifying somewhat), the Puritans had "put into operation a democratic ecclesiastical policy. As religion lost force, the restrictions it imposed on political equality and freedom necessarily disappeared and an approximation was made toward a perfect democracy."[65]

Homer Coppock acquitted Osgood of favoring New England's Puritans unduly, but did accuse him of unfairness to Quakers. To support his charges, however, Coppock cited only statements which now seem quite accurate as generalizations: that Quakers were "decidedly plebeian in origin" and that "their views reflected well the character of the social class whence they came." Osgood's characterization of George Fox as possessing a "towering conceit born largely of simplicity and ignorance" was perhaps somewhat more prejudicial but not entirely unfounded. Coppock failed to mention that in his last volume when Osgood compared Quaker ideals to those of the Puritans, the Friends came off very well indeed.[66]

Despite Osgood's basic sympathy with the American colonial legis-

---

64. *American Colonies in the Eighteenth Century,* III, 85, 298, 319, 411–412, 460.
65. "Political Ideas of the Puritans," *Political Science Quarterly,* VI (1891), 16.
66. Homer Coppock, "Herbert Levi Osgood," *Mississippi Valley Historical Review,* XIX (1932–33); Osgood, *American Colonies in the Eighteenth Century,* IV, 49.

latures in their perennial battles with the governors, there is evident an undercurrent of appreciation for the beleaguered executives. Influenced perhaps by the temper of the Progressive era in which he lived, Osgood was clearly on the side of the governors when it came to goading niggardly legislatures to provide money needed for various public purposes, most often for warfare against the French. Even when only effective administration rather than military security seemed to be the issue, Osgood showed impatience with the hamstringing assemblies and clearly wished that they had showed more disposition to help rather than hinder the governors. Like Andrews and Beer, he may to some extent have absorbed the bias of his sources on this point. Executive correspondence, after all, comprised the bulk of the official documentation available to him.

For all his deficiencies, Osgood still has much to offer the modern analytical historian seeking better understanding of the preconditions of the American Revolution. No one before or since has combined such extensive research with both geographic and chronological breadth. What other historian has ever informed himself so thoroughly on the political history of *all* the colonies which became the United States? What other historian has encompassed *all* of American colonial history prior to 1763? Andrews knew the seventeenth century and the British administrative system better, but he was not as well informed as Osgood on eighteenth-century developments within the colonies. Gipson's volumes far exceed Osgood's in geographic breadth as well as in bulk, but they cover only the generation immediately preceding the Revolution and show far more understanding of the British than of the American point of view. Recent scholars have adduced more data and, at times, new points of view on just about every issue which Osgood considered, but their very specialization has tended to impede, if not to preclude, the kind of broad-based understanding that distinguishes the work of the Columbia historian.

Even if one grants that Osgood's efforts had prepared him to understand the evolution of American political institutions and the relation of those developments to the American Revolution, there still remains a fundamental question. How much understanding does Osgood, in fact, impart to his readers? The answer must be that by way of explicit thesis or conclusion he conveys relatively little. He might have conveyed more had he lived longer. One suspects, however, that his commitment to Rankean ideals would have continued to prevent him from considering seriously interpretive theses or conclusions of significant breadth. As Eisenstadt has observed, it was characteristic of the profession in general in the period of Osgood's life to state generalized conclusions quite casually, almost as *obiter dicta* or "in the interstices," if at all.[67]

Can the modern reader interested in the preconditions of revolution extract meaningful conclusions of his own from Osgood's work? For purposes of this essay, such preconditions might be defined as "long-run, underlying causes . . . which create a potentially explosive situation."[68] Preconditions of course contrast with "precipitants" which trigger or set off a revolution. Drawing selectively upon a number of authorities, it is possible, even if somewhat arbitrarily, to identify several factors which are likely to constitute preconditions of revolution:[69] (1) an unrepresentative and, in particular, an incompetent government holding stubbornly to a fixed but decidedly unpopular course; (2) grave anomalies or inconsistencies in status within the social structure, as, for example, when many men of high economic standing have relatively low status in terms of political power and

67. Eisenstadt, *Andrews,* 175. See also David M. Potter, "Explicit Data and Implicit Assumptions in Historical Study," in Louis Gottschalk, ed., *Generalization in the Writing of History* (Chicago, 1963), 178–194.

68. Lawrence Stone, "Theories of Revolution," *World Politics,* XVII (1966), 159–176.

69. *Ibid.;* Robert Forster and Jack P. Greene, eds., *Preconditions of Revolution in Early Modern Europe* (Baltimore, 1970); Bruce Mazlish, ed., *Revolution: A Reader* (New York, 1971); James Chowning Davies, ed., *When Men Revolt and Why* (New York, 1971); Chalmers Johnson, *Revolutionary Change* (Boston, 1966); Ernest Barker, ed. and trans., *The Politics of Aristotle* (Oxford, 1946); Crane Brinton, *Anatomy of Revolution,* rev. ed. (New York, 1952); Walter Laquer, "Revolution," in *International Encyclopedia of the Social Sciences* (1968); Hannah Arendt, *On Revolution* (New York, 1963); Irving L. Janis, "Group Identification Under Conditions of External Danger," *British Journal of Medical Psychology,* XXVI (1963), 227–238; Chalmers Johnson, *Revolution and the Social System* (Stanford, 1964); Harry Eckstein, ed., *Internal War: Problems and Approaches* (New York, 1964).

social prestige ("The more frequently acute status inconsistencies occur within a population," runs the hypothesis, "the greater would be the proportion of that population willing to support programs of social change"[70]); and (3) an ideology which affords moral justification for the overthrow of the old regime.

What has Osgood to offer on the first of these points—the incompetence and intransigence of the British government? Clearly he is less pointed than such recent scholars as Thomas Barrow in *Trade and Empire* or Jack P. Greene in *Quest for Power,* but Osgood did pile up evidence over a wider range, either topically or geographically, than either of these authors. He does show long-term incompetence and intransigence in support of unpopular courses of action.

Status inconsistencies are also made evident throughout Osgood's works. His most insightful observation on that score was the following:

To them [top colonial administrators in London] the colonists stood on the level of the lower trading and agricultural classes at home. . . . The magistrates and clergymen of New England, the traders and landed proprietors of the middle colonies, the officials and planters of the south might lord it over their dependents and play the aristocrat in their little provincial capitals or on their estates, but in London they sank to the common level of colonials and all alike were objects of a more or less supercillious patronage.[71]

Ideological considerations did not figure appreciably in Osgood's work, but in occasional interstices he did note ideological differences between the British and the Americans. In recounting the struggle over revocation of the Massachusetts charter, for example, Osgood broke from his factual narrative long enough to observe: "the forces which determined the course of American colonial history appear [here] in unusually clear relief. On the one side we have a community of religious non-conformists whose natural tendency was toward the largest degree of self-government which was consistent with any

70. Gerhard E. Lenski, "Status Crystallization: A Non-Vertical Dimension of Social Status," *American Sociological Review,* XIX (1954), 405–413.
71. *American Colonies in the Eighteenth Century,* I, 118.

recognition whatever of the supremacy of the mother state." "On the other side," he continued, "appears an assertion of imperial authority and restraint over the colonies . . . almost unlimited in scope."[72] However infrequently he was willing to point it out explicitly, such ideological differences clearly underlay a high proportion of the political disputes with which his volumes are so largely concerned.

A diligent reader can secure insight on the preconditions of revolution from Osgood's writings. The mature professional who works his way carefully through Osgood's seven volumes must concede, however grudgingly, that scientific historians such as Osgood were not entirely wrong in their assumption that interpretation was unnecessary. All those facts do convey a message of their own. The problem is that what any one reader perceives to be the message is likely to depend in some degree upon his own preconceptions.

In conclusion, three points concerning Osgood's career seem most important. Despite the fact that he led off the attack upon Bancroft's patriotic bias, Osgood by no means qualified fully for inclusion in the imperial school. He flatly rejected Andrews's contention that one should write the history of colonial America from the perspective of British administrators. He was at best ambivalent concerning Beer's thesis that the Navigation Acts were not exploitive. Among major contentions of the imperial school, only Gipson's view that Parliamentary taxation for revenue was justified won his wholehearted endorsement. On the other hand, Osgood's basic concern was the same as Bancroft's—the evolution of representative government. He differed from Bancroft in treating the theme objectively and by declining, in keeping with the dogmas of scientific history, to draw explicit conclusions. Finally, in reviewing Osgood's achievement it seems most appropriate to paraphrase his own lament over Jonathan Edwards: That his powerful mind and great endowment should have been imprisoned within the stone walls and the iron gates of scientific history makes his career a tragedy, a tragedy not only for him but for all those who still strive for clearer understanding of how the American Revolution came about.

72. *American Colonies in the Seventeenth Century,* III, 378.

MILTON M. KLEIN

Detachment and the Writing of American History: The Dilemma of Carl Becker

CARL BECKER is by all odds one of the most intriguing and elusive of American historians. That he was and still is regarded as one of the most influential members of the profession, helping to recast its view both of itself and of the American past, is unquestioned; but the reasons for his importance are not so easily determined. He was a leading figure of Progressive historiography, but when Richard Hofstadter set out to study the major expositors of that school of historians, he omitted Becker. Acknowledging that Becker had a "subtler mind" and a "better prose" than Turner, Beard, or Parrington, Hofstadter was compelled to admit that Becker had little influence on his own professional training or on that of American historians of his generation.[1] It is no discredit to Becker to concede, with Hofstadter, that Becker's writings in American history did not arouse

I am indebted to Michael Kammen of Cornell University for his careful reading of this essay, and to William Bruce Wheeler of the University of Tennessee for assisting me in its preparation.

1. Richard Hofstadter, *The Progressive Historians* (New York, 1968, 1970), xi–xii, xiv. Privately, Hofstadter offered a less generous estimate. He had once read and liked Becker, he disclosed in a 1960 interview, but hadn't "reread him in years" and didn't think "as much of his work now." Quoted by Arthur M. Schlesinger, Jr., "Richard Hofstadter," in Marcus Cunliffe and Robin W. Winks, eds., *Pastmasters: Some Essays on American Historians* (New York, 1969), 280.

the same impassioned approval or criticism as did Turner's boldly provocative essay on the frontier, Beard's sweeping interpretation of *The Rise of American Civilization,* or Parrington's beautifully imaginative elegy on the evolution of American democracy. Neither is it to Hofstadter's discredit that he chose to exclude Becker from his gallery of Progressives. The Cornell historian might well have proved as enigmatic and misplaced under that designation as under any other.

Not all prominent American historians have been distinguished for consistency, but Becker's methodological and philosophical idiosyncrasies have proved more than ordinarily frustrating to the many "sensitive commentators" who have tried to understand him. If Becker possesses a particularly "strange fascination" for historians, as one such commentator observes, it is perhaps his very inconstancies no less than his scholarly attainments that account for the attraction.[2] Still another critic, puzzled by Becker's greater subtlety of mind yet lesser "clarity and consistency" than other New Historians, took refuge in the somewhat whimsical conclusion that Becker's importance arose from "the rich confusion of his thought."[3]

The historiographical efforts to resolve or clarify the paradoxes in Becker's writings are misdirected; for *paradox* is their overriding universal. Its recurring employment by Becker was more than a literary device; and, as Bernard Bailyn so astutely observes, it was neither accidental nor indeliberate. The juxtaposition of opposites—phrases, ideas, men; the use of clichés turned upside down; the artfully formed examples of circular reasoning are all part of the Becker style— "disarmingly lighthearted" but deliberately designed to add "another dimension of thought" to the initiated.[4] Such Becker devices could be

2. Robert A. Skotheim, *American Intellectual Histories and Historians* (Princeton, 1966), 110n.; James L. Penick, Jr., "'Carl Becker and the Jewel of Consistency," *Antioch Review,* XXVI (1966), 235–246. For some of the many recent writings on Becker, see John C. Rule and Ralph D. Handen, "Bibliography of Works on Carl Lotus Becker and Charles Austin Beard, 1945–1963," *History and Theory,* V (1966), 302–314.

3. Milton Gold, "In Search of a Historian," *Centennial Review,* VII (1963), 282–305, especially 286.

4. Bernard Bailyn, "Becker, Andrews, and the Image of Colonial Origins," *New England Quarterly,* XXIX (1956), 522–534.

seen in Samuel Adams vs. Thomas Hutchinson in *The Eve of the Revolution;* Jeremiah Wynkoop vs. Nicholas Van Schoickendinck in "The Spirit of '76"; and John Jay vs. Peter van Schaack in the essay so titled. The *philosophes*—"having denatured God, they deified nature"; Jefferson—where he "got his ideas is hardly so much a question as where he could have got away from them"; Henry Adams—his "genius for reflection was always at war with his desire for 'power' "; Einstein—he was guilty of a slight error in saying that "God is probably a mathematician . . . he meant to say that a mathematician is probably God." "Some men are born stupid. And some achieve stupidity"; "The eyes of the law must have been poor, since they did not see things as they really were." On the colonists' attempt to distinguish between taxes for trade and taxes for revenue: "Ha! You would determine the nature of an act by the intention of the framers, and the intention of the framers by the nature of the act. Excellent!"[5] *The Heavenly City of the Eighteenth-Century Philosophers,* perhaps Becker's most widely known work, is so replete with aphorisms, paradoxes, and verbal gymnastics that Peter Gay concludes it must not have been intended as serious history at all but as a "jeu d'esprit."[6]

Becker's own advice to students on the art of writing emphasized the congruity between style, on the one hand, and writer and subject on the other.[7] The point is illustrated perfectly in Becker's own writing. If paradoxes pervade his literary efforts, it is because they mirror with such dazzling clarity the anomalies of his own life and career. His interpretation of the nature of the American Revolution not only

5. *The Heavenly City of the Eighteenth-Century Philosophers* (New Haven, 1932, 1959), 63; *The Declaration of Independence* (New York, 1922, 1942), 27; "The Education of Henry Adams," in *Everyman His Own Historian* (New York, 1935; Chicago, 1966), 168; *Progress and Power* (New York, 1949), 113; Charlotte Watkins Smith, *Carl Becker: On History and the Climate of Opinion* (Ithaca, 1956), 146; Becker, *Modern History* (New York, 1931, 1942), 146; "The Spirit of '76." in *Everyman,* 61.

6. Peter Gay, "Carl Becker's Heavenly City," in Raymond O. Rockwood, ed., *Carl Becker's Heavenly City Revisited* (Ithaca, 1958; [New York], 1968), 27–51, especially 28 and 33.

7. "The Art of Writing," in Phil L. Snyder, ed., *Detachment and the Writing of History: Essays and Letters of Carl L. Becker* (Ithaca, 1958, 1967), 121–144. The essay is discussed and analyzed by Smith, *Becker,* ch. 4.

exercised a decisive influence on the contemporary image of the colonial past but also stimulated a controversy among historians that still dominates the historiography of that conflict.[8] His scholarly writings were almost entirely in American history. Yet when the near-certain prospect of the Harmsworth Professorship in American History at Oxford was made known to him in 1935, he declined on the ground that he had never taught American history and knew very little of its essential details![9] He had a devoted following of graduate students who became important historians themselves—Louis Gottschalk, Leo Gershoy, Geoffrey Bruun, Robert R. Palmer—but while they described themselves as "Beckerites," they represented no "Becker school," simply because their field was modern European history, which Becker taught for his entire professional career but in which he produced little scholarship himself.[10]

Becker received his doctorate under Turner, for whom his admiration was near-adulatory, and his reputation was "made" by his essay on Kansas—strongly evocative of Turner; but his doctoral dissertation, while feebly undertaking to incorporate the frontier thesis, directly challenged it in emphasizing the role of the urban lower classes in the advance of American democracy.[11] The dissertation more nearly resembled the approach of Herbert L. Osgood, under whom Becker started his graduate work in the colonial period; but

8. Robert E. Brown's recent book, *Carl Becker on History and the American Revolution* (East Lansing, Mich., 1970), is an extended critique of Becker's view of colonial history and the Revolution.

9. Felix Frankfurter to Becker, Jan. 9, 1935, in Burleigh T. Wilkins, *Carl Becker: A Biographical Study in American Intellectual History* (Cambridge, Mass., 1961), 145 and note; Becker to Frankfurter, Jan. 10, 1935, in Brown, *Becker,* 184.

10. Brown, *Becker,* 188, 198; Wilkins, *Becker,* 147n.

11. Frank Klingsang, one of Becker's students at Kansas, said of this essay that it "did almost as much for Becker as Turner's essay on the Significance of the Frontier did for him." Klingberg to Phil L. Snyder, Nov. 19, 1955, Cornell University Collection of Regional History and University Archives. The Kansas essay originally appeared in *Essays in American History Dedicated to Frederick Jackson Turner* (New York, 1910), 85–111, and was republished in *Everyman,* 1–28. Of it, Claude H. Van Tyne said that the author had "cultivated Professor Turner's own field, and . . . reaped a new and varied harvest." *American Historical Review,* XVI (1911), 636.

having made his bow to his mentor's technique of assembling masses
of data and the Columbia historian's focus on the imperial connection, Becker abandoned both Osgood's "plodding methods" and his
interest in Anglo-American relations. Becker's enthusiasm for history
came from Turner, who provided the young Iowa farm boy not so
much with historical information or even ideas as with the magic of
his personality and the warmth of his companionship.[12] But Becker
was unable to emulate his teacher in this respect. If he tried, it was an
inner effort which he abandoned early. He provided none of the same
excitement to his own undergraduates, and he refrained from warm
attachments with his graduate students until after they had left his
classes. Unlike other graduate professors, he did not invite his students to his home, nor did he engage in dialogue with them "to develop divergent ideas." To one of his ablest graduate students, he
appeared in retrospect to have exhibited "a kind of intellectual loneliness."[13]

As a historiographer, Becker is famed for his warning to historians
that they could not hope to achieve objectivity by "mental detachment" from their subject, a note he sounded as early as 1910, reiterated in 1926, and climaxed in his famous "Everyman" address to the
American Historical Association in 1931. His subsequent writings
merely repeated the earlier theme: historical facts were no more than
the historian's mental images, in the creation of which some part of
his own individual experience, preoccupations, and purposes inevitably entered. The historian's account of the past was a product of the
present and an expression of the contemporary milieu of the writer, of

12. "I was interested in history, and in the companionship of men like
yourself," Turner wrote Becker in 1925, disclaiming any virtue as "a teacher,"
a view he reiterated in 1927 after reading Becker's tribute to him. Avery
Craven, "Frederick Jackson Turner," in William T. Hutchinson, ed., *The
Marcus W. Jernegan Essays in American Historiography* (Chicago, 1937),
267; Wilkins, *Becker*, 44. Becker's admiring portrait of Turner appeared in
Howard W. Odum, ed., *American Masters of Social Science* (New York,
1927), 273–318, and was republished in *Everyman*, 191–232.

13. Smith, *Becker*, 26–28; Wilkins, *Becker*, 73–74, 104–106; Klingberg to
Snyder, Nov. 10, 1955, Robert R. Palmer to George H. Sabine, Nov. 17, 1945,
in Cornell U. Archives. Becker, of course, did not lack for admirers among
students, and he submitted his later manuscripts for criticism to former students
like Robert R. Palmer and Leo Gershoy.

the "dominant ideas of his own age." The effort at complete detachment was fruitless; were it possible, it would "produce few histories, and none worth while; for the really detached mind is a dead mind. . . ."[14]

Now no one could accuse Becker of intellectual torpor or charge his writing with lack of animation, yet the literary art he practiced to perfection was the very detachment he assured the historical guild was impossible. Becker's graduate students were awed by his ability to "sit on the moon and unconcerned but interested watch the world go by," and his artful cultivation of an air of detachment—"the detachment of a keen observer who stands apart from the human comedy and watches it with quizzical interest." Their impression was not devoid of substance. One of man's—and the historian's—most successful tricks, Becker admitted, was the ability to "hold himself at arm's length in order to observe himself as an object from the outside." The vantage point should be "near enough to discern the course of human history . . . but sufficiently removed not to be startled by the form and pressure of particular events." Becker's own preference was for a spot on the Olympian Heights with the Greek gods, where he could observe the Earth Creatures whose fate he did not share![15] It is not accidental that among the reasons for Becker's appreciative sketch of Benjamin Franklin was the Philadelphian's "disposition to take life with infinite zest and yet with humorous detachment."[16]

The areas of scholarly investigation which interested Becker extend

14. The quotations are from "Detachment and the Writing of History," *Atlantic Monthly,* CVI (1910), 524–536. The other two essays in this vein are "What Are Historical Facts," originally delivered as a paper in 1926 but first printed in the *Western Political Quarterly,* VIII (1955), 327–340; and "Everyman His Own Historian," *American Historical Review,* XXXVII (1932), 221–236.

15. The observations of the graduate students are those of Louis Gottschalk and Geoffrey Bruun, cited in Brown, *Becker,* 190, and Rockwood, ed., *Heavenly City Revisited,* 73. Becker's own lighthearted expression of the theme is in *Progress and Power* (New York, 1949), 19–20. Leo Gershoy, another of Becker's students, in his introduction to the last-mentioned book (xxxi), also acknowledges the controlled quality of Becker's style and the absence of any "impressions of physical turmoil" or of "emotional agitation."

16. The sketch appeared in the *Dictionary of American Biography,* VI, 585–598. It was reprinted, with an introduction by Julian Boyd (Ithaca, 1946). The quotation above appears on p. 34 of the reprint.

the realm of paradox even more. He began his professional career
with a detailed exposition of the role of extremists in bringing on the
American Revolution, and he expressed a tolerant understanding of
the lower-class "radicals" who, in the process, advanced the course of
democracy. In later years, he more than once expressed his firm belief that civilization could advance on the foundations of democracy
and science. But his subsequent writings revealed far more interest in
the philosophers than the makers of revolutions, and he became increasingly distrustful of "a mass intelligence that functions at the level
of primitive fears and tabus" and of advanced scientific technology
which, far from liberating, merely caged mankind. If he "never left
the age of the enlightenment," as Leo Gershoy insists, he found himself in the uncomfortable position of challenging the premises on
which its "humane and engaging faith" was based. For the scientific
view of nature in which it was rooted also made man the helpless
victim of the power which science generated. With a gloom that
contradicted the optimism of the *philosophes,* Becker more than once
lamented his "devastating" discovery about modern man, that "in an
indifferent universe which alone endures, he alone aspires, endeavors
to attain, and attains only to be defeated in the end." Like Diderot,
of whose dilemma he wrote a magnificently perceptive essay, Becker
himself was torn by the knowledge that a natural world, governed by
impersonal scientific forces, could neither be held responsible for evil
nor credited with beneficence and progress.[17]

Becker wrote about the eve of two revolutions, George Sabine
observes, but never about a revolution. Seeking to understand the
meaning of a revolution by an exploration of its philosophical and
intellectual underpinnings, he lost interest in the event itself as he be-

17. *Progress and Power,* xxix, 104–105; *Freedom and Responsibility in the
American Way of Life* (New York, 1945, 1951), xxi–xxii; *Modern Democracy*
(New Haven, 1941), 19; *New Liberties for Old* (New Haven, 1941), 83–84.
"The Dilemma of Diderot" appeared in the *Philosophical Review,* XXIV
(1915), 54–71, and was reprinted in *Everyman,* 262–283. For a discussion
of the conflict between optimism and pessimism in Becker's writings, see John
C. Cairns, "Carl Becker: An American Liberal," *Journal of Politics,* XVI
(1954), 623–644; and David W. Noble, "Carl Becker: Science, Relativism, and
the Dilemma of Diderot," *Ethics,* LXVII (1957), 233–248.

came persuaded that "every revolution is betrayed, because history is a cynical, tough old nut that always betrays our ideal aspirations."[18] Convinced that only human intelligence could solve the complex problems of an industrial society, he acknowledged the paradox which made the mass of mankind suspicious of the very brainpower that could ease its distress and promote its happiness. Despite his own preachments of the pragmatic role of history and historians in the effort to save mankind, he eschewed practical involvement in the contest and evaded philosophic resolution of the intellectual conflict he perceived. A perplexed and saddened Robert Palmer conceded that his mentor must be judged guilty of retreating from the issue by "a skeptical and modest acknowledgment of dichotomies which admit of no final answer."[19]

Perhaps the penultimate paradox, but one that may help to explain Becker best (an irony he himself might have enjoyed), is the fact that despite his reputation for wide-ranging and many-sided interests —American history, European history, political history, economic history, intellectual history, philosophy of history, historiography, secondary school history—all of Becker's work "moves within a somewhat limited circle of ideas which recur again and again." The observation is that of George Sabine, a colleague of Becker's at Cornell, but it is reaffirmed by Robert Palmer, one of his students. The wide variety of Becker's subject matter, he concluded, was confined to the same "philosophical framework," and encompassed within "a rather limited sphere." The phrases themselves were reiterated so often in his books that they seem "echoes of each other" and "self-plagiarism."[20] It was not the poverty of his mind which explains this pre-

18. Sabine, *Freedom and Responsibility*, xxxi; Becker to Gottschalk, Dec. 26, 1938, in Snyder, ed., *Detachment*, 85.

19. *Progress and Power*, 108–110; Palmer to Sabine, Nov. 17, 1945, Cornell U. Archives. Two reviewers have made a virtue of this limitation in Becker's thought: "While he could not answer all the questions he raised, he did have the insight to ask them." John Braeman and John C. Rule, "Carl Becker: Twentieth Century *Philosophe*," *American Quarterly*, XIII (1961), 539.

20. Sabine, *Freedom and Responsibility*, vii–viii; Palmer to Sabine, Nov. 17, 1945, Cornell U. Archives. Charlotte Smith agrees that Becker remained preoccupied with "a few central ideas through which he approached all the

occupation with so limited a number of ideas but rather his self-critical temperament. Just as he reworked his sentences and paragraphs to give them letter-perfect grace and lucidity, so he worked over his central ideas in order to reduce them to the lowest—or sharpest— level of understanding. It is not altogether surprising, then, that they should evidence a unity and consistency belying the many apparent contradictions in Becker's life and work.

In his writings on public affairs and his lectures on the contemporary social scene, the idea that emerges most obviously and repeatedly is that democracy, based on the free use of intelligence, is, despite all its limitations, the surest guarantor of the good society. But this perception offers little help in understanding Becker, the historian of colonial America. The idea is not fundamental or even always visible in his major writings on American history. What provides thematic unity and comprehension to Becker as a colonial historian is less substantive than philosophical and methodological: first, his intellectual skepticism, which caused him to challenge with irony, however gentle, each orthodoxy in historical interpretation, including his own; and second, his fascination with the operation of men's minds under conditions of stress. While these two elements of his intellectual outlook are not universally evident in all of his writings in American history, the exceptions are few enough to make the generalization tenable.

Becker's earliest writings in American history—two articles in scholarly journals—did not particularly foreshadow his later interests. The first, an essay on the development of the unit rule in the national nominating conventions of the Democratic, Whig, and Republican parties, was an outcome of his first two years of graduate work at Wisconsin under Turner. Written without much of Becker's later grace of style, it was competent enough to be published in the *American*

---

problems of man." Smith, *Becker,* 42. Bailyn notes that "phrases, whole sentences, even pages, were lifted intact from one essay to the next, appearing in one volume after another." "Becker, Andrews, and the Image of Colonial Origins," *New England Quarterly,* XXIX (1956), 524.

Historical Review.[21] In 1898, Becker received a fellowship at Columbia University in constitutional history, and his second scholarly effort reflected the interests of his new mentor, John W. Burgess. It dealt with the constitutional basis for the acquisition and government of overseas territories. More constitutional law than history, the piece concluded that while Congress could exercise plenary powers over the residents of the new possessions, it had to operate within certain constitutional limits.[22] Appearing in late 1900, Becker's essay anticipated with remarkable precision the Supreme Court's position on the subject the next year in the Insular Cases.

Becker's studies with Herbert L. Osgood at Columbia redirected his interest to the colonial period, and he now found it possible to return to his earlier research on the nominating convention, with special emphasis on its colonial origins. The result was an article on nominations in colonial New York, published in early 1901.[23] By now, Becker had committed himself to the study of political parties in colonial New York, and during the next few years three other essays on the subject were published.[24]

All four of these articles were incorporated into Becker's dissertation, two reappearing with little change as separate chapters; but none of them proclaimed with any vigor what was to become in the dissertation itself the "Becker thesis." The elements, however, were present along with manifestations of the central concerns of his intellectual life: the interest in democracy's progress from an earlier prerevolu-

21. "The Unit Rule in National Nominating Conventions," *American Historical Review*, V (1899), 64–82. Apparently Becker intended to write a history of the nominating convention as his doctoral dissertation.

22. "Law and Practice of the United States in the Acquisition and Government of Dependent Territory," *Annals of the American Academy of Political and Social Sciences*, XVI (1900), 61–76.

23. "Nominations in Colonial New York," *American Historical Review*, VI (1901), 260–275.

24. "Growth of Revolutionary Parties and Methods in New York Province, 1765–1774," *American Historical Review*, VII (1901), 56–76; "The Nomination and Election of Delegates from New York to the First Continental Congress, 1774," *Political Science Quarterly*, XVIII (1903), 17–46; and "Election of Delegates from New York to the Second Continental Congress," *American Historical Review*, IX (1903), 66–85.

tionary aristocracy; the search for an understanding of the economic
and social forces that lay behind the formal instrumentalities of colonial government; the effort to comprehend the mainsprings of action
that determined the conduct of revolutionary Americans; and the willingness to challenge accepted interpretations of the coming of the
Revolution.

Becker's analysis of the political and social structure of colonial
New York disclosed an oligarchy of wealth, social position, and political privilege that monopolized the machinery of government and controlled it in quasi-feudal fashion. The foundations of aristocratic power
lay in the disfranchisement of large numbers of the citizenry and over-
lord domination of the enfranchised. The instrumentalities of aristocratic influence were familial rather than political. Seeds of change
were sown in the mid-eighteenth century in the form of popular political literature and open, if informal, devices for nominating candidates
for office. The imperial contest after 1763 provided impetus to these
developments, as issues and principles were employed by the oligarchy
to pursue the struggle with the mother country, and as individuals
came together in public political associations unrelated to family connections. The entrance of the masses into the political arena, particularly after 1765, converted the traditional and somewhat immature
division between "court" and "popular" factions into more meaningful and modern political groupings. The line of division became one
between "radicals" and "conservatives," the former including the
previously disfranchised masses. Their growing "consciousness of
equality" intruded new issues of political democracy into the more
conspicuous struggle with Britain for colonial rights. By 1774, the
masses had, by the force of events, secured "vital control of the business of government," thus completing the process begun earlier in the
century of pulling down authority from the top and placing it on the
ground. Conservatives, intent upon the business of combating English
restrictions, lost control of the machinery of government to the "lowest" classes of society. Alternately allying with and divorcing themselves from such radical company between 1765 and 1775, seeking to
control when they could not dominate the various committees and

extralegal bodies formed to prosecute the contest, extreme conservatives finally made the decision to withdraw. They had grown more fearful of mob violence and the loss of their own political privileges than of British rule. Thus was born the party of the Loyalists.

While these articles had both unity and continuity, they still lacked the integrating thread of the "two revolutions" for which Becker was to become famous. The link was added in the dissertation itself, but Becker made public its central thought at least five years earlier in reviewing a rather obscure book for *The Nation*. Viewing the revolutionary movement in Pennsylvania, Becker was struck by the extent to which public interest centered on the organization of the new state government: "the war seems almost to have been of secondary importance." From this, Becker concluded that "there were bound up in the Revolution, in fact, two great questions . . . the relation of the colonies to England, and the . . . extension of political privileges to the unfranchised in the colonies." Out of the second struggle arose a division between "extreme radicals" and "moderate conservatives." The latter resisted the democratic spirit, fostered by the contest against Britain, which was expressed by the entrance into the political arena of those "who had previously had no share in political action." The Revolution, Becker emphasized, could not be understood as a movement for home rule alone, since basic to that issue was "whether home rule, if allowed, was to be based on equality or restriction of political privilege."[25]

In his dissertation, published in 1909, Becker restated the proposition in more felicitous language: "The American Revolution was the result of two general movements; the contest for home-rule and independence, and the democratization of American politics and society. Of these movements, the latter was fundamental; it began before the contest for home-rule, and was not completed until after the achievement of independence."[26] Insofar as New York's political history was

25. Review of Burton A. Konkle, *Life and Times of Thomas Smith*, in *The Nation*, LXXIX (Aug. 18, 1904), 146–147. Brown, *Becker*, 21, is responsible for calling attention to this review.
26. *History of Political Parties in the Province of New York, 1760–1776* (Madison, Wis., 1909), 5.

concerned, the application of the thesis resulted in redefining the nature of the province's party divisions. Between 1765 and 1776, the old medieval-like factional politicking, led by aristocrats, gave way under pressure of the controversy with Parliament to extralegal instrumentalities, popularly controlled. The real issue for the old political leadership was not merely how to conduct the crusade for self-government but how to keep the lower classes from usurping control of the local political structure. "From 1765 to 1776, therefore, two questions, about equally prominent, determined party history. The first was whether essential colonial rights should be maintained; the second was by whom and by what methods they should be maintained. The first was the question of home rule; the second was the question, if we may so put it, of who should rule at home."[27]

Carrying his account only to 1776, Becker nevertheless suggested in his closing pages the shape of things to follow. With extreme conservatives fleeing the fray to become Loyalists, the new battleground would pit moderate against radical Patriots; and in the new republic the radicals would become the followers of George Clinton, the opnents of the Constitution, and eventually the Jeffersonians and Jacksonians.[28]

Becker's thesis corresponded well with the Progressive view of American history which was emerging at the turn of the century, and it reflected most of the attitudes and assumptions of that school of historiography: a subordination of ideas to economic and social process; a tendency to see politics in polarized terms; an emphasis on conflict as an underlying theme in the development of American democracy; and an interest in the dynamics of change rather than the evolution of institutions from their germinal origins.[29] Turner's influence had already shifted the interest of American historians to the study of diversity and conflict; and Becker drew heavily for his in-

27. *Ibid.*, 22.
28. *Ibid.*, 274–276.
29. On Progressive history and its central ideas, see John Higham, *History: The Development of Historical Studies in the United States* (Englewood Cliffs, N.J., 1965), 171–173; and Charles Crowe, "The Emergence of Progressive History," *Journal of the History of Ideas*, XXVII (1966), 109–124.

spiration on Turner's suggestion that American democracy was not transplanted from abroad but generated in the crucible of West-East conflict. With respect to the Revolution, Turner had written in 1903 that the conflict was more than a war for independence from Britain; it was also a battle against "the aristocracy that dominated the politics" of the colonies. The place of honor in the struggle, however, had been given not to Becker's urban workers and mechanics but to the small landholders and indentured servants of the frontier.[30]

Becker's own papers do not reveal the source of his idea of the dual revolution, but he had ample progenitors to draw upon. With respect to Pennsylvania, which evoked his first pronouncement of the thesis, Charles H. Lincoln had developed the theme fully in his own doctoral dissertation, published in 1901.[31] Here, too, the Revolution was portrayed as a twofold affair, "a colonial as well as a national revolution," the former emerging from the long-held hostility between the entrenched Quaker oligarchy and the "dissatisfied" masses. Here, also, there developed a contest between conservatives and radicals for leadership of the revolutionary movement, with the former recoiling from the violent tactics employed by the lower classes. The use of extralegal machinery permitted the disfranchised elements to "make their influence felt," and for them, the overthrow of the local oligarchy was more important than freedom from Parliamentary restrictions. Lincoln, indeed, went a step further than Becker. For him, the war against England was merely incidental to the major issue—the desire of the masses to "revolutionize their own colonial condition." The internal revolution would have occurred anyway. The contest with Parliament simply provided the lower classes with "a plausible excuse" to democratize local politics under cover of the larger movement for independence. Success produced "a double change of government."[32]

30. The idea appeared in Turner's "Contributions of the West to American Democracy," *Atlantic Monthly*, LXXXIX (1903), 83–96, reprinted in *The Frontier in American History* (New York, 1920, 1947), 243–268.
31. *The Revolutionary Movement in Pennsylvania, 1760–1776* (Philadelphia, 1901).
32. *Ibid.*, 3–4, 15, 37, 53–54, 78, 96, 189–190, 223.

Becker employed no such emphatic language in his own book, but he made the identical point in almost the same words as Lincoln's in a letter to Turner in the year in which his dissertation was published: "I am immensely confirmed in my idea that the Revolution was only incidentally a matter of home rule, and primarily a matter of democratization of politics and society."[33]

Although no historian prior to Becker had analyzed the revolutionary movement in New York in such detail, or from the internal perspective, neither the idea of class conflict nor the notion of two revolutions in that colony was entirely original with him. As early as 1814, John Van Ness Yates, an Albany Jeffersonian politician and an amateur historian, had hinted at an early division in the province between "court" and "popular" parties. In 1859, Henry Dawson, a prolific essayist and speaker on historical subjects and later editor of the *Historical Magazine,* in a brief work on the Sons of Liberty in New York bluntly stated that the Sons had two enemies: Britain, on the one hand, and the merchant-landlord-lawyer conservatives on the other. The latter, accustomed to managing the affairs of the province, professed constitutional principles of government which they never intended to extend to the "great body of the people." When they realized that the generality of the population took these principles too literally, the great families worked strenuously to restrain the protest movement and, at the same time, to preserve their own privileges.[34]

Later in the century, Theodore Roosevelt elaborated the notion more fully. His approach to history was more literary than analytical, but he was not unaware of the significance of great crises and cataclysms in the past. The Revolution in the northern colonies was just

33. Becker to Turner, March 19, 1909, in Brown, *Becker,* 24. Becker added: "The history of revolutionary parties must be rewritten on that line, I think."

34. William Smith, *History of New-York . . . with a Continuation . . . to the . . . Year 1814* (Albany, 1814), 400, 408, 417, 445. Yates wrote the continuation. Dawson, *The Sons of Liberty in New York* (Poughkeepsie, N.Y., 1859), 106–111. In a later work, Dawson reiterated that two parties emerged in the course of the Stamp Act resistance: the Sons of Liberty, representing the people, and the conservatives, whom Dawson dubbed the "friends of Mammon and the Government." *The Park and Its Vicinity* (Morrisania, N.Y., 1867), 19–20, 42–43, 45, 48.

such a crisis, because the struggle "had two sides; . . . it was almost as much an uprising of democracy against aristocracy as it was a contest between America and England."[35] The roots of the internal struggle he found in the "peculiarly aristocratic structure" of New York society and the aspirations of "the democracy" to end the domination of "the local oligarchy." Roosevelt escaped the trap of a class conflict interpretation, however. The real power, he stated, lay in the hands of the "moderate men" who rejected the extremes of both aristocrats and the mob, assumed leadership of the revolutionary movement, and enlisted the "intelligent working-classes" in the patriotic effort against England. Aristocrats like the Livingstons and Schuylers accepted mob support, however distasteful, because their "belief in freedom" and their "profound Americanism" were stronger than their conservatism. Thus, when independence came, the "best men" in New York were on the American side.[36]

Several historians had also antedated Becker's general interpretation of the coming of the Revolution and the nature of the struggle. Woodrow Wilson, in his popular *History of the American People*—distinguished less for original scholarship than for readability—called attention to the division between radicals and conservatives among the opponents of Parliamentary restrictions, the "plain men" being the former, led by Samuel Adams, and the latter comprising the men of large fortune and business. However, Wilson used the terms "radical" and "conservative" to denote variant positions on the pattern of resistance to be employed in the imperial conflict rather than differences over local political issues.[37] J. Allen Smith, one of the fathers of Progressive historiography, alluded to the dual nature of the Revolution in his *Spirit of American Government,* published two years before

35. *Gouverneur Morris* (Boston and New York, 1888, 1898), 26. On Roosevelt's historiography, see Herman Ausubel, *Historians and Their Craft: A Study of the Presidential Addresses of the American Historical Association, 1884–1945* (New York, 1950), 132–137, 329–331; and Harrison J. Thornton, "Theodore Roosevelt," in Hutchinson, ed., *Jernegan Essays,* 246–247.

36. *New York* (New York, 1891, 1895), 111–114, 121, 128.

37. *History of the American People,* 5 vols. (New York and London, 1902), II, 156–157, 210, 297.

Becker's dissertation. Smith viewed the War for Independence as the catalyst which permitted latent democratic tendencies in the colonies to be given political expression; but within Smith's conceptual framework the antidemocrats were the Loyalists. It was not until the framing of the Constitution that Smith resurrected the conservative opponents of democratic rule.[38]

A remarkably prescient statement of the Becker thesis appeared in a doctoral dissertation on the Declaration of Independence, published five years before Becker's own work. Herbert Friedenwald expounded the view that in the middle colonies, at least, internal political revolutions took place alongside the larger struggle with Britain. The democracy, formerly held in check by the local aristocrats who controlled the administrative machinery, was powerfully affected by the abstract theories of equality and the rights of man put forth in the course of the contest with Parliament. The battle between conservatives and radicals over the democratization of local government was often hushed, Friedenwald noted, by "the rattle of musketry and the war of artillery." As the fight for independence progressed, however, it became "not less one between the people and the aristocrats for control, than one between the United Colonies and Great Britain for the establishment of a separate government."[39]

If Becker himself drew upon any of these earlier statements of the case, his book does not disclose the fact. In any case, these studies made so little impact upon the historiography of the Revolution that they are scarcely noted by modern students. That Wilson's and Roosevelt's allusions to the internal division among the Patriots should have been lost to view among professional historians is not especially surprising. Friedenwald's presentation of the thesis had attractive possibilities but was not further explored by him, since it was peripheral to his own primary focus on the Declaration of Independence. Lincoln's obscurity is more baffling, since his exposition of the dual nature of the conflict in Pennsylvania is, in many respects, more clearly

38. *The Spirit of American Government,* ed. by Cushing Strout (Cambridge, Mass., 1965), 13–16, 18, 27.
39. *The Declaration of Independence* (New York, 1904), 79–81.

delineated and closely argued than Becker's own.[40] What is unquestioned is that Becker's book and name became associated with the dual-revolution theme, and it was soon extended beyond New York to constitute a general and major interpretation of the Revolution as a whole.

One can only guess at the reasons why Becker was so surprisingly successful in gaining recognition as the "founder" of a large school of historical interpretation. It was surely not because his book "was the first carefully documented study of the existence of class struggle in America at the time of the Revolution, the peculiar American class struggle of the 'people' against an artificial un-American aristocracy," as one historiographer flatly stated.[41] Certainly, the influence of Turner must have been a measurable factor in extending the popularity of the two-revolution thesis. The Wisconsin historian liked it "exceedingly," he told his former student. Privately, Turner expressed doubts about the book's excessive detail and unreadability. To Van Tyne he wrote that the work was "an illustration of a delicate conscience and a training under Osgood, fighting successfully against a literary instinct." The interpretation was more to Turner's taste, agreeing with his own feeling that the social reorganization emerging from the Revolution was as important as independence from Britain. A year after the dissertation's appearance, Turner had incorporated the main outline of the Becker thesis in a paper of his own: "in substantially every colony there was a double revolution, one for independence and the other for the overthrow of aristocratic control."[42]

Becker himself did no further scholarly work on the two-revolutions

40. David Hawke is one of the few historians who seem aware of Lincoln's contribution, observing that Lincoln "has never received the praise he deserves, for it was he who set the pattern for interpreting the American Revolution as a twofold movement." See Hawke, *In the Midst of a Revolution* (Philadelphia, 1961), 62–63n.

41. David W. Noble, *Historians against History* (Minneapolis, 1965), 78.

42. Turner to Becker, June 8, 1907, in Brown, *Becker*, 23; Turner to Van Tyne, Feb. 24, 1911, to Max Farrand, Mar. 21, 1909, in Wilbur R. Jacobs, ed., *The Historical World of Frederick Jackson Turner* (New Haven and London, 1968), 99, 210; "Pioneer Ideals and the State University," *Indiana University Bulletin,* VII (June 15, 1910), 6–29, reprinted in *The Frontier in American History,* 269–289. The quotation appears on 274 of the latter.

generalization, but he was as responsible for its spread as anyone. He reiterated the theme frequently, and he extended it to all the colonies rather offhandedly—a step he took with surprising ease considering his caustic commentary on persons who expounded historical propositions "without fear or research." Reviewing the third volume of Channing's *History of the United States,* Becker criticized the Harvard historian in 1912 for ignoring the dual nature of the Revolution. Besides "the desire of the colonists for home rule," which Channing understood well enough, was "another aspect of the Revolution, not so important, perhaps . . . but still very important. . . . This may be called the class conflict within the colonies themselves." In explaining it, however, Becker blurred his own earlier identification of the parties in dispute: "it was a struggle between 'East' and 'West,' between franchised and unfranchised, rich and poor, . . . common-weal and special privilege. . . ." In the most general terms, however, he defined the issue as simply one between "democratic and aristocratic interests and ideals." All the other elements in his dissertation were repeated, however: the oligarchic nature of colonial government and politics; the rise of a dissident democracy; conservative fears of the mob as the movement against Parliament progressed; and the dilemma of the conservatives as they sought to limit the aspirations of the radicals while enlisting their support. Extending his argument, Becker projected the conflict to 1828, stating that the radical victory of 1776 was partially undone by the events of 1789, partly restored in 1800, and finally victorious with Jackson—although it was "frontier democracy" that triumphed in this case.[43]

Two years later, in a well-written but rather simplified interpretive treatment of the whole period of American history from discovery to independence, Becker enlarged upon his earlier theme. Colonial governments "in every colony" were in the hands of "the eminent few." Disfranchisement of the majority was common. "Interests" rather than parties dominated the political process. The aristocrats employed Lockean principles "to justify the natural right of English-

43. *The Nation,* XCV (Nov. 21, 1912), 482–483.

men to become free while remaining unequal." The inevitable conflict between classes was foreshadowed by Bacon's Rebellion, "an
early instance of that struggle between rich and poor, between ex-
ploiter and exploited, of that stubborn insistence upon equal opportunity which have so often characterized the most decisive periods of
American history." The major issue dividing Britain and America was
the constitutional nature of the empire, but the conservatives who
argued the American case would never have allowed the contest to
reach the stage of independence had they not been pushed by the
underprivileged. "Not for home rule alone was the Revolution fought,
but for the democratization of American society as well." The Revolution was the "Heaven-sent opportunity" of the masses to end monopoly privilege in the colonies.[44]

In an even less distinguished survey of American history, written
as part of Becker's contribution to the work of the Creel Committee
on Public Information during World War I, the dual-revolution thesis
was repeated in almost the same language as the doctoral dissertation
and reiterated at least three times within twenty pages. When the language was varied, it was in one of Becker's characteristic wordplays:
The aristocracy "wanted home rule, but they wanted to rule at home."
The disfranchised became the "humble folk," and their leaders the
"young radicals, backed by the people of the back-country." The
Revolution was transformed by pressure from the democracy into "a
social as well as a political movement," aiming at equal rights for
"poor and rich alike."[45] In extending his contention that the movement inaugurated in the Revolution to democratize American society
and politics was "the central theme of American history," Becker
utilized the frontier thesis to demonstrate the point. Contemporary
critics were quick to characterize the book as a popularization of
Turner, and Becker was quite willing to accept the charge. He had
appropriated his mentor's views, he told Turner appreciatively, "with-

44. *Beginnings of the American People* (New York, 1915; Ithaca, 1960),
80, 165–166, 172, 182, 240–241.
45. *The United States: An Experiment in Democracy* (New York, 1920),
10–11, 34–36, 39, 46–50.

out scruple, without fear . . . , without reproach I hope, and certainly without research."[46]

Becker continued to propound his interpretation without benefit of any of these attributes—often in the very same words, in books, book reviews, articles, and lectures. At times, he added modifications, reservations, and qualifications that challenged the very heart of the thesis. Becker frequently admitted that the great difference between America and Europe was the wide degree of freedom and equality that abundant land and resources conferred from the beginning. He conceded that America's aristocrats were quite different from Europe's, and he even anticipated modern critics of his thesis by suggesting that "America was free before it won independence." He assured William E. Dodd that he did not see history "quite as much in terms of a conscious class struggle of conflicting economic interests," as did some of his fellow historians; and he disclaimed any censure of the propertied classes for acting in their own economic self-interest—he was referring specifically to Beard in this respect. Men of property were not any less "good patriots" for seeking to keep what they possessed than were those who "profess principles designed to get it away from them." But on the general proposition, he continued to assert, as late as four months before his death, that the Revolution "was as much an uprising of the populace against the better sort as it was an uprising of the better sort against British control."[47]

46. *Ibid.*, 35; Becker to Turner, Oct. 24, 1920, in Brown, *Becker*, 108. Farrand called its Turnerian emphasis the book's "dominating characteristic." See his review in the *Mississippi Valley Historical Review*, VII (1921), 407–409.

47. *Freedom and Responsibility*, 11; Becker to Dodd, [1923], in Snyder, ed., *Detachment*, 81; Becker to Arthur M. Schlesinger, n.d., Schlesinger Papers, Harvard University. Among the many references to the thesis are Becker's reviews of H. R. Eckenrode's *Revolution in Virginia*, *Political Science Quarterly*, XXXI (1916), 613–614, and of H. E. Egerton's *Causes and Character of the American Revolution*, *American Historical Review*, XXIX (1924), 344–345; "Liberalism—A Way Station," in *Everyman*, 91–93; and *Modern Democracy* (New Haven, 1941), 42–43. His references to the basic equalitarianism and freedom of the colonies may be found in *Political Parties*, 16; *Beginnings of the American People*, 31, 73–74, 79, 174–175, 180–181; *Experiment in Democracy*, 5–6, 144, 308; "Political Freedom: American Style," in *Safeguarding Civil Liberty Today* (Ithaca, 1945), 10; and *Freedom and Responsibility*, 6–7, 10, 16–17.

Perhaps the most charitable explanation of Becker's unyielding adherence to his doctoral thesis so late in life, in juxtaposition with interpretations essentially at variance with it, is that he was flattered by its acceptance among fellow historians. The notion that colonial governments were essentially aristocratic instrumentalities and engendered conflict between the nascent democracy and an entrenched oligarchy became widely accepted within little more than two decades after Becker first presented the case in his article on New York in the *American Historical Review.* At least such was the opinion of the reviewer of Becker's *The United States: An Experiment in Democracy* in 1921, who commented that there was little new in the book's emphasis on "the aristocratic methods and practices which largely controlled the colonial governments," since this was the viewpoint already "part of most recent works in general American history or . . . government."[48]

The dual-revolution thesis was accepted as it was given support by men like Arthur M. Schlesinger, Sr., and J. Franklin Jameson in their own books, extended into the postrevolutionary era by the writings of Charles A. Beard and Merrill Jensen, and incorporated into standard history texts.[49] Not surprisingly, economic historians like Louis M. Hacker came to regard Becker's description of the coming of the Revolution in New York as "one of the great monographs in American colonial history." Hacker claimed in 1936 that the thesis "still stands," and a few years later he incorporated it into his economically oriented history of the United States: the Revolution was the instrument by which the "lower classes" sought to "attain their *own* freedom"; and alongside the war with England raged "a struggle for power

48. The reviewer was Charles G. Haines, in the *American Political Science Review,* XV (1921), 616–617.

49. Schlesinger, *The Colonial Merchants and the American Revolution, 1763–1776* (New York, 1918); Jameson, *The American Revolution Considered as a Social Movement* (Princeton, 1926); Beard, *American Government and Politics* (New York, 1910), *An Economic Interpretation of the Constitution of the United States* (New York, 1913), and, with Mary R. Beard, *The Rise of American Civilization,* 2 vols. (New York, 1927, 1930); Jensen, *The Articles of Confederation* (Madison, Wis., 1940). Brown, *Becker,* 205–207, gives a partial listing of texts incorporating the Becker thesis, but it could be multiplied.

between the right and left wings of the revolutionary host." The statement in Samuel E. Morison's and Henry Steele Commager's *Growth
of the American Republic* is best illustrative of the orthodoxy of the
dual-revolution interpretation in textbooks at about the time of Becker's death: "Fully as important as the question of home rule in the
empire was the question of who should rule in the colonies. . . .
There were really two American revolutions at the same time: the
sectional revolt of thirteen colonies against imperial centralization;
and a democratic upheaval against vested interests and local governing cliques."[50]

The attacks on the Becker thesis began almost with its first enunciation, but they gathered strength in the 1950's as the pendulum of
historiographical interpretation swung away from the conflict history
of the Progressive school and toward the "cult of consensus." The
reasons, as Hofstadter has perceptively noted, were not merely that
the milieu in which the newer historians worked influenced their outlook and made them more conservative and nationalistic but that
"ideas have an inner dialectic of their own." Progressive historians
had simply pushed polarized conflict as a conceptual framework for
understanding the Revolution so far that it could go no further "without risking self-caricature."[51] Certainly the outer limit of the two-
revolution thesis had been reached when one historian could claim
that no movement for separation from England would have occurred
without the tensions caused by the internal conflicts within the colonies and another flatly state that victory over England was the "least
important aim of the Revolution." It was rather merely "a necessary
prerequisite" to "a social revolution of the most profound sort."[52]

Criticisms of the Becker interpretation of the colonial period and

---

50. Hacker in the *New Republic,* LXXXV (Jan. 8, 1936), 260; *The Triumph
of American Capitalism* (New York, 1940), 167, 172; *Growth of the American
Republic,* 2 vols. (New York, 1950), I, 163.
51. Hofstadter, *Progressive Historians,* 439.
52. Frank Thistlethwaite, *The Great Experiment: An Introduction to the
History of the American People* (New York, 1955, 1968), 34; Gordon S. Wood,
The Creation of the American Republic (Chapel Hill, 1969), 91, 128.

the Revolution have followed the general lines of attack on conflict history, stressing the centrist tendencies in American history, whether designated conservative or liberal, the absence of sharp class or ideological polarities, or, alternatively, the multifarious factors in American life—religious, ethnic, racial, social—which make the two-class view of our society oversimplified, exaggerated, and untrue.[53] What is surprising, however, is that it should have taken so long for the Becker interpretation of the causes and character of the Revolution to have come under attack; since, in a very real sense, Becker's own statement of the case in his doctoral dissertation was feeble, inconsistent, and unconvincing.

One of the earliest reviewers of the volume called attention to the book's numerous weaknesses in a critique that, for some unexplained reason, escaped the notice of Becker's subsequent critics. The review appeared in the most obvious of places, the *American Historical Review*. Its neglect may have been a consequence of the author's anonymity.[54] The reviewer commended Becker for carefully describing the evolution of the extralegal machinery of committees and congresses during the period 1765–1776, and for pointing up the division between conservatives and radicals arising in the course of this development. But he criticized Becker for failing to link the radical-conservative split over tactics and policy to the internal party structure of the colony. Becker's analysis of the colony's political and social structure —the aristocratic-democratic syndrome—was challenged as hasty and superficial. How could anyone understand the political dynamic of the colony, the reviewer asked, if he ignored the "continuous active political life" of the province, which dated from well before 1765 and

53. General statements of the consensus viewpoint appear in Daniel Boorstin, *The Genius of American Politics* (Chicago, 1953); Louis Hartz, *The Liberal Tradition in America* (New York, 1955); and, implicitly, in Hofstadter, *The American Political Tradition* (New York, 1948). The criticism of polarized economic history for ignoring other divisions in American society is best stated in Lee Benson, *Turner and Beard: American Historical Writing Reconsidered* (Glencoe, Ill., 1960).

54. The present editors of the *American Historical Review* were unable to identify the author from their files. Letter, John T. Appleby, Assistant Editor, *American Historical Review*, to author, July 22, 1971.

involved vital issues like the bitter strife between Anglicans and Presbyterians; the contest between governor and assembly over judicial tenure, supplies, and salaries; and the deep-seated and rancorous divisions within the aristocratic families themselves? Finally, with greater appreciation of the complexity of New York's political history than Becker, the reviewer questioned any account which minimized personalities so much that "powerful and interesting" figures like William Livingston, William Smith, James DeLancey, Cadwallader Colden, Isaac Sears, and Alexander McDougall became no more than names in a catalog.[55]

Subsequent critics of Becker's New York study have done little more than document the perceptive remarks of this earliest reviewer. They have demonstrated the caricature Becker drew of New York's static, medieval-like, family-dominated, oligarchic political structure before 1765. They have shown how badly he underestimated the extent of the suffrage and the dynamism of the colony's political process—perhaps as far back as the 1730's; ignored the interplay of British imperial interests with the colony's politics; missed the political force and implication of such provincial issues as the efforts to establish the Anglican Church within New York, Presbyterian demands for legal incorporation of their own churches, the attempt to organize King's College as an Episcopal seminary, and the quarrel between the governor and the lawyer-led Assembly over the tenure of judges and the inviolability of jury decisions; and oversimplified the unity of the great families.[56]

55. The piece appeared in *American Historical Review*, XV (1910), 395–397.
56. On the extent of the franchise and the nature of the political process, see Milton M. Klein, "Democracy and Politics in Colonial New York," *New York History*, XL (1959), 221–246, and "Politics and Personalities in Colonial New York," *ibid.*, XLVII (1966), 3–16; on the Anglo-American cast of politics, Stanley N. Katz, *Newcastle's New York: Anglo-American Politics, 1732–1753* (Cambridge, Mass., 1968); on church issues, Carl Bridenbaugh, *Mitre and Sceptre* (New York, 1962); on King's College, Klein, "Church, State, and Education: Testing the Issue in Colonial New York," *New York History*, XLV (1964), 291–303; on the judicial issue, Klein, "Prelude to Revolution in New York: Jury Trials and Judicial Tenure," *William and Mary Quarterly*, 3d. ser. XVII (1960), 439–462; on divisions within the aristocracy, Roger Champagne, "Family Politics versus Constitutional Principles: The New York As-

The strongest element in Becker's account of the revolutionary movement in New York was the gradually deepening rift between conservatives and radicals, the former representing the old-line colonial leadership—merchants, lawyers, and landlords—and the latter, the newer coalition of artisans, tradesmen, and men of smaller property. But Becker failed abjectly to demonstrate that the split between these groups was, in fact, over the nature and form of local government, i.e., the democratization of provincial society and politics. The bulk of his book disclosed largely that the disagreement within the New York revolutionary leadership centered upon the character and tactics of the colony's response to the imperial crisis and, by 1774, upon the issue of pursuing the contest within the empire or outside.

A close examination of Becker's history of the period reveals too much ambiguity, inconsistency, and contradiction to sustain the claim either of sharply marked class divisions or of an emerging popular democracy.[57] Lawyers and merchants appear variously as conservatives and radicals; and radicals like Alexander McDougall are conceded to be as much disturbed over the "licentiousness of the people" as the arch-conservative, Cadwallader Colden.[58] Radicals are shown to be content to employ the existing franchise in creating the machinery of extralegal government. When a broader suffrage was adopted for a popular canvass of opinion on the ending of nonimportation in 1770, the result of the "vote of every inhabitant" was a victory for the

---

sembly Elections of 1768 and 1769," *ibid.,* XX (1963), 57–79. For an able summary of much of this literature, see Bernard Mason, "The Heritage of Carl Becker: The Historiography of the Revolution in New York," *New York Historical Society Quarterly,* LIII (1969), 127–147.

57. Brown, *Becker,* ch. 3, is a detailed exposition of many of these internal contradictions in Becker's "dual-revolution" interpretation. For critiques of Lincoln's comparable delineation of the dual character of the Revolution in Pennsylvania, see Hawke, *In the Midst of a Revolution,* especially 67–68, 184, 197–200, and James H. Hutson, "An Investigation of the Inarticulate: Philadelphia's White Oaks," *William and Mary Quarterly,* 3d. ser. XXVIII (1971), 3–25, particularly 15–17. Patricia U. Bonomi, in her *A Factious People: Politics and Society in Colonial New York* (New York, 1971), offers a far more sophisticated and satisfactory analysis of the nature of the colony's political process than Becker's simplified division into aristocrats and lower classes.

58. Becker, *Political Parties,* 44, 59, 60, 83, 266n.

conservatives, not the radicals.[59] And Becker's "radicals" encompass men of as divergent views as Gouverneur Morris, John Morin Scott, Alexander McDougall, and Isaac Sears.

Conservatives may well have "dimly perceived" the precariousness of their domination of local politics and the difficulty of preserving their monopoly against "popular encroachments" as the revolutionary struggle progressed, but the evidence does not appear in Becker's presentation. And for one who continued to link the backcountry small holders with the urban, propertyless masses as the base of the democracy, Becker failed signally to show any support for the revolutionary movement in New York City among the upstate freeholders and tenants.[60]

The antidote Becker offered to the oversimplified, ultranationalistic interpretation of the colonists rising as one man behind the leadership of "the best men" in the colonies was genuinely wholesome and historically more accurate.[61] But both he and Schlesinger afterward were guilty of overextending their interpretation. Neither in New York nor in any of the other colonies, as Bernard Bailyn has shown, was there a "merchant class" unified by "class consciousness." There were men of trade who did not fit the Becker-Schlesinger "merchant" characterization in origin, life style, or political interests; and they were deeply

59. *Ibid.,* 93, 134, 153, 227, 252.

60. As he tried to resolve the dilemma of the hostility between New York's urban and rural lower classes, so Becker sought also to escape the problem posed by Turner's insistence that the Revolution was a regional conflict between the East and the West. The latter generalization did not apply to New York, Becker explained to Turner, simply because New York was "all coast," without regional configurations or antagonisms. (Becker to Turner, March 19, 1909, Turner Papers, Huntington Library, San Marino, Calif.) This explanation merely compounded the dilemma by merging city and country without being able to clarify the absence of unanimity between their respective "democracies."

61. In his *Causes of the War of Independence* (Boston, 1922), Van Tyne, who thought Becker's dissertation a "thorough, scholarly, patiently but heavily executed work," quoted liberally from it and Schlesinger, adopted the position that opponents of Britain split into conservative and radical factions, conceded that the "Jack Cades" began to think of the "rights of man" as they became active in the struggle against Parliament, but reiterated that the Revolution was a rising of a whole nation already "the freest of peoples" (chs. 16, 18). For the comment on Becker's book, see Van Tyne to Turner, Feb. 16, 1911, in Jacobs, ed., *World of Frederick Jackson Turner,* 209.

divided in numerous ways in their response to British measures.[62] For a Becker who soon became absorbed by the intriguing question of human motivation, his account of New York was surprisingly superficial and shallow in inquiring into the reasons for the behavior of conservatives, radicals, Patriots, and Loyalists. The questions were there, implicit in the whole exposition, but the response ignored the nuances, complexities, ironies, and subleties of men's conduct which Becker came to believe conditioned their response to their social experience. Above all, there was gross inattention to the ideas and ideals which comprised the rhetoric of the revolutionary struggle and which, for a later Becker, became the necessary prelude to any political action.

The supreme irony of the "Becker thesis" is that it should have consumed so much professional energy in the years since its enunciation and so narrowly constricted scholarly inquiry into the causes and nature of the Revolution. It is almost certain that Becker would not have wanted it so. He delighted in challenging orthodoxies of interpretation, in destroying ancient shibboleths, and in poking fun at historians for serving as no more than "bards and story tellers and minstrels, . . . soothsayers and priests, . . . keeping . . . the useful myths."[63] He would have been amused, as one of his Cornell colleagues observed upon the occasion of a reassessment of another of Becker's writings, to hear his words "discussed with great solemnity as . . . a pretentious monograph" on so large an event as the American Revolution, or to see his book regarded as a summation of, rather than an introduction to the subject.[64]

One reason for Becker's bemusement would surely have been the enshrinement of his thesis in the temple of Progressive historiography, with Becker himself raised to scholarly sainthood; for Becker was no ordinary Progressive historian. While he continued to preach, with

62. Bailyn, "The Blount Papers: Notes on the Merchant 'Class' in the Revolutionary Period," *William and Mary Quarterly,* XI (1954), 98–104, and "The Beekmans of New York: Trade, Politics, and Families," *ibid.,* XIV (1957), 598–608.

63. "Everyman His Own Historian" (1932), in *Everyman,* 247.

64. Henry Guerlac in Rockwood, ed., *Heavenly City Revisited,* 4, 25. Also Palmer and John Hall Stewart in *ibid.,* 125, 161.

other Progressives, that objective history was impossible and that the only valuable history was one that served a contemporary social purpose, he departed from his co-workers in continuing to profess the dogma without practicing it. Most Progressives who began as colonial historians moved into later periods as they became interested more in the outcome than the origin of the Revolution. They preferred to investigate the environmental factors that advanced—or retarded—American democracy, not the ideological. Many engaged actively in the Progressive Era's campaign to reform American society. They candidly confessed that their historical writings were not an end in themselves but part of the campaign to improve America. Becker was different in almost every respect. He shifted his interest to ideas, remained largely in the eighteenth century, focused on individuals rather than on broad social or economic forces, eschewed active involvement in politics, and wrote a kind of history which was committed to social purpose only in a very general way. If history was helpful at all, Becker observed early in his career, it was "in getting the world's work more effectively done," but Becker's notion of precisely what that involved was uniquely personal.[65]

In a characteristic Becker paradox, he lent his support to James Harvey Robinson's "New History," with its emphasis on the conscious exploitation of the past not only to understand the present but to advance the future, yet he rarely practiced its principles. The possibility of progress he considered too important not to enlist the aid of all intellectuals, including historians. They should properly be concerned with "what ought to happen" and not merely with what happened; they should, indeed, "care greatly what happens"; they should study the past "as something to be practically appraised in the light of ends

65. Becker's utilitarian view of history appeared in "Some Aspects of the Influence of Social Problems and Ideas upon the Study and Writing of History," *American Journal of Sociology,* XVIII (1913), 642. Louis Hacker, who accepted Becker as a Progressive historian by virtue of his monograph on New York, criticized him sharply for his seeming preoccupation with middle-class intellectuals who talked about revolutions rather than with the inarticulate lower classes who made them. He urged Becker to abandon the role of disinterested observer and ally himself with "the living forces in society." "Historian of Revolutions," *New Republic,* LXXXV (Jan. 8, 1936), 260–261.

that are thought to be desirable and attainable in the future."[66] But while other Progressives, like Beard, were assuring historians that by their "act of faith" they could make the past serve the present, Becker cautioned them not to expect the enterprise to be too successful. Hopeful of progress, he was uncertain that mortal man could master his environment sufficiently to improve it. Desirous of useful history, he was aware of the changing uses to which every generation of historians and "everyman" could put that history. Eager to have society reformed, he was not confident of his ability to participate successfully in the effort. While others were more certain of the pragmatic possibilities of the new history to change society, Becker was certain only that society must first be understood. Torn between doubt and hope, he veered toward the former, allowing his fellow scholars to move forward confidently while he continued to warn them not to expect too much in the process.

Other Progressive historians, like Beard and Harry Elmer Barnes, were inclined to attribute blame to individuals in history. Becker, because of his own sensitivities to human frailties, could not; but he also rejected the Beard-Barnes approach because he believed men to be victims of their environment and the contemporary current of opinion. He would not blame individuals without blaming the whole society as well.[67] Individual character counted, to be sure, but in the cosmic view of history, man was "after all but a speck of sentient dust, a chance deposit on the surface of the world," a product of purposeless forces he could not easily control.[68]

66. Review of Robinson's *The New History* in *The Dial*, LIII (July 1, 1912), 19; "Detachment and the Writing of History," in Snyder, ed., *Detachment*, 28; "Mr. Wells and the New History," *American Historical Review*, XXVI (1921), 650.

67. Becker to Barnes, Feb. 21, 1926, in Smith, *Becker*, 116. Of Beard's tendency to portray the propertied classes as "conscious hypocrites," Becker observed that the assumption was based on an inadequate psychology. There was no necessary contradiction between self-interest and principle in explaining human behavior. Becker to Arthur M. Schlesinger, Sr., n.d., Schlesinger Papers, Harvard.

68. "The Dilemma of Diderot" (1915), in *Everyman*, 273. This tragic view of man appears frequently in Becker's subsequent writings, usually in the very same language. See especially *Progress and Power*, 9, 59, 107–108, 114–115.

There was confusion in Becker's search for the roots of human conduct. Acknowledging that it was important for a writer to reflect "the life and feeling" of an individual, he was at times persuaded that this could be accomplished best by "analysis of character," by "sympathetic appreciation of the conscious motives and purposes that determined their action."[69] A Jefferson, a Marshall, could not be explained by environmental influences alone. The decisive thing was the "individual temperament, the personality, the innate slant of the mind, or whatever term it is that best describes those inherited characteristics which react to the pressure of the external world but are not created by it."[70] But he also came to believe that there were "unconscious influences that activate the human animal," and that among these was the influence of the "spirit of the age," which could be ascertained not by the material interests of the time but by its ideas—"the state of mind" that conditioned events, "the complex of instincts and emotions that lie behind the avowed purpose and the formulated principles of action."[71] The "facts" of history might be important, but even more so was what men thought about them—"the revolution that occurs in people's heads." Evidence could be mustered in our own day, Becker observed, to demonstrate that miracles could not have occurred in the Middle Ages; but this was less important than the disposition of people at the time to accept evidence that miracles *could* occur.[72] Shifting his focus, however, he then insisted that principles, faith, and ideals were all unknowingly at the mercy of "complex and subtle instinctive reactions and impulses." Man was too

69. "Wild Thoughts Notebook," Feb. 6, 1894, in Wilkins. *Becker,* 32; reviews, *American Historical Review,* XXIII (1918), 619; XXIV (1919), 267.
70. Review of vols. 1 and 2 of Beveridge's *John Marshall* in *The Nation,* CIV (Feb. 1, 1917), 133.
71. Becker to Geoffrey Bruun, Dec. 6, 1931, in Smith, *Becker,* 128; review of James B. Perkins, *France in the American Revolution, The Nation,* XCII (June 15, 1911), 605; *Progress and Power,* xli; review, "The Memoirs and the Letters of Madame Roland," *American Historical Review,* XXXIII (1928), 784.
72. Reviews of Bernard Fay, *L'Ésprit Revolutionnaire en France et aux États-Unis,* and of Ernest C. Mossner, *Bishop Butler and the Age of Reason, American Historical Review,* XXX (1925), 810; XLIII (1938), 117.

complex to be manipulated and controlled by ideas or events![73] Becker discovered no theory of behavior to explain his simultaneous rejection of individual will, the force of ideas, and the influence of environment to explain historical development.

As he became more interested in the working of men's minds and the force of will in history, and correspondingly cognizant of the continuing struggle between the rationalism he prized and the irrationality of mass mankind, Becker decided that before society could be managed, men must learn to manage themselves. "Don't try to reform men, it can't be done. Reform yourself." This was the advice he jotted down for himself in his undergraduate notebook.[74] The thought was expressed frequently in later life. "The value of history," he said in 1915, was "not scientific but moral: by liberating the mind, by deepening the sympathies, by fortifying the will, it enables us to control not society, but ourselves."[75] A year before his death, he reiterated that he was "one of those who are more interested in finding out so far as possible what men are like and how they think than in 'doing them good.' "[76]

Becker was uncertain of his own role because he was not sure what direction progress should take or which particular set of historical truths could help man to achieve it. His sensitive conscience made him concerned for that future; his own deep insecurities—deceptively concealed by his air of serene detachment—made it impossible for him to work very actively to achieve it. The best contribution he could make, he decided, was to get men to think intelligently about the task, to understand their traditions, to recognize realities in human existence. "The business of history is to arouse an intelligent discontent, to foster a fruitful radicalism."[77] With his own keen mind, insatiable

73. Becker to Dodd, June 14, 1920, in Phil L. Snyder, "Carl Becker and the Great War: A Crisis for a Humane Intelligence," *Western Political Quarterly,* IX (1956), 6; "Afterthoughts on Constitutions," in *New Liberties for Old,* 93.
74. "Wild Thoughts Notebook," March 5, 1894, in Smith, *Becker,* 11.
75. Review of L. C. Jane, *The Interpretation of History* in *The Dial,* LIX (Sept. 2, 1915), 148.
76. Becker to Thomas Reed Powell, Dec. 3, 1944, in Smith, *Becker,* 39.
77. Review of Robinson's *New History, The Dial,* LIII (July 1, 1912), 21.

curiosity, and perennial skepticism, he could do this perfectly. Others might rouse men to fight for democracy; he would get them to think more clearly about it before it was too late. And his work could best be performed in the "sheltered corner" of academia, which was not only a congenial retreat for his shy, nervous, troubled soul but also the very place where intellectual skepticism could be practiced and rewarded. A professor was "a man who thinks otherwise," and for one who had "no faith in the infallibility of any man . . . , or of the doctrines or dogmas of any," the role suited him perfectly.[78]

There is no evidence in Becker's letters that he expressed specific reservations about his first book, but the rigidity of interpretation to which it led and its ready acceptance by historians must have disturbed him. Certainly its dogmatic character was inconsistent with his many subsequent criticisms of all historical dogmas. As he became more interested in the "whys" of history, he must have felt dissatisfied with the gross explanations of men's conduct he had proffered in his account of New York. He had shown how conservatives had been pushed to revolution and how others had shied away from that extremity, but he had not really explored their motivations. He may have taken to heart the criticism of his most severe reviewer that he had ignored the force of personality. In any case, he soon began the long process, which occupied him for the next two decades, of probing more deeply into individual behavior and of studying the social forces which conditioned men's conduct. At the same time, he warned his co-workers not to be deluded into accepting any line of historical interpretation. His debt to Turner for both of these new lines of thought is clear. From his teacher he had learned that a historian "was not God," that all historians had a philosophy of history whether

78. "On Being a Professor" (1917), in Snyder, ed., *Detachment*, 112–113; "The Marxian Philosophy of History," in *Everyman*, 125, 131; Smith, *Becker*, 44, 60–62, 166. Becker's troubled nature was not entirely the product of his intellectual uncertainties. A persistent stomach ailment, the mental condition of his stepdaughter, and the intellectual gulf that separated him from his wife created personal and family problems that must have been profoundly disturbing. See Wilkins, *Becker*, 68, and Gershoy, *Progress and Power*, introd., xxiii–xxiv.

they were aware of it or not, and that the "whys" of history were as important as the "whats."[79] He took all of these lessons to heart.

Between 1918 and 1932, Becker produced a book and a number of biographical sketches which showed his new interest in the psychological determinants of behavior and two books on intellectual history which revealed his growing conviction that ideas determined as much as mirrored men's conduct. During this period, Becker became strongly influenced by the philosopher Alfred North Whitehead, whose study of the emergence of modern science maintained that "each age has its dominant preoccupation" and that its ideas reflect the world view held at the time by its educated leadership. Whitehead's phrase to describe this collective mentality—"climate of opinion"—became a guiding principle in Becker's search for explanations of men's behavior in history. By 1932, Becker was echoing Whitehead in insisting that human conduct was determined less by independent intelligence than by "an intelligence that is conditioned by the very forces that it seeks to understand and to control." The progress of his explorations led Becker dangerously close to disavowing the force of personality entirely and making of man "but a foundling in the cosmos."[80] The end of this new quest for historical truth was no more satisfactory to the humane Becker than the disquietude that had initiated it. But of this, Becker was unaware when he embarked on the exploration.

In *The Eve of the Revolution,* which appeared in 1918 as one of the multivolume Chronicles of America Series, Becker wrote what he admitted, and what reviewers quickly recognized, was a mood piece rather than a traditional chronicle of events from 1763 to 1776 or an

79. "Frederick Jackson Turner," in Odum, ed., *Masters of Social Science,* 287, 290, 298. Becker credited Robinson, too, for his "abiding interest in learning why people think as they do." See his review of *The Human Comedy* in *The Nation,* CXLIV (Jan. 9, 1937), 49–50.

80. Becker, *Heavenly City,* 5, 14–15. On Whitehead's use of the climate of opinion concept, see his *Science and the Modern World* (New York, 1924; Mentor ed., 1948, 1964), vii, 11. For Becker's admiration of Whitehead, see Wilkins, *Becker,* 191.

interpretation. What he sought to convey was an impression of "the quality and texture of the state of mind" of individuals at the time, of its "intellectual atmosphere." He apparently did little or no research for the book. It was the product of reflective thinking, uncluttered by reference to sources, dates, or historical interpretations. As such, it was not conventional history so much as an "illusion" of history. So much he forewarned his readers.[81] Despite its "questionable orthodoxy," most reviewers were charmed by its style, its "smartness," its delicate humor, its gentle, pervading irony. There was little about causes in the volume and no mention at all of Becker's earlier dual-revolution thesis, although the presence of "little colonial aristocracies" was noted. No alternative thesis was offered, either. The division between radicals and conservatives over the response to the Stamp Act was described, but not in terms of ideological differences. The issues separating Americans from Britons were represented as practical and constitutional—the defense of the empire, the enforcement of the Acts of Trade, the rights of the colonial legislatures, the powers of Parliament, and the interests of fair traders versus smugglers among the colonial merchants.

The novelty of the volume, and the heart of Becker's new interest, was his symbolization of Sam Adams and Thomas Hutchinson as archetypal Americans and their personalities and states of mind as evocative of the antithetical position of radicals and conservatives. Adams, the "tribune of the people" with "the soul of a Jacobin," was the man best fitted by "talent and temperament" to push the continent into rebellion. Politics was his life's commitment, for which he had willingly embraced poverty. He was "born to serve on committees" and to intrigue in secret clubs. His opposition to British measures was less a response to their effects in the colonies than the product of his "faculty of identifying reality with propositions about it." The crisis was not so much real as imagined in Adams's mind, involving dark conspiracies and evil men on the one side, and virtue on the other. In opposition stood Hutchinson, symbol of reason, status, and the

81. *The Eve of the Revolution* (New Haven, 1918), pref., vii–viii.

cultivated man. No enemy of America, he was converted into such by Adams's skillful manipulation of the public representation of his actions. "Discreet conduct" on both sides might have avoided the conflict, but what was natural for Hutchinson was for Adams "a point of principle to avoid." Hutchinson's chief limitation was not his inability to analyze the constitutional issue in dispute or to appreciate the American position but his failure to fathom the intricacies of Adams's mind. Thus a "reciprocal exasperation engendered by reasonable propinquity" produced the crisis. As for other Patriot leaders, they played the role they imagined for themselves as opponents of tyranny, protesting "as a matter of course" in rhetoric somewhat more florid and exaggerated than the occasion demanded. Using skillful dialectic, the Americans moved ahead step by step from a restricted to a broad ground of opposition, almost unwittingly arriving at independence.[82]

The book was highly praised by reviewers for its happy phrasing, its light touch, and its imaginative reconstruction of reality, but few understood Becker's purpose. Louis Hacker paid Becker a left-handed compliment, calling it a "little masterpiece" because it bespoke so well the cause of Tories and British placemen; and, in fact, Hutchinson does appear as a high-minded and much-maligned victim of Adams's propaganda and the credulity of historians thereafter.[83] But Becker was not aiming to rehabilitate Loyalists so much as to point up the helplessness of individuals caught in a web of impersonal historical circumstances. The Adams-Hutchinson confrontation, he explained to William Dodd, illustrated perfectly how good and bad men

82. *Ibid.*, 60–61, 64, 131, 254–255 and ch. 5, passim.
83. Hacker's comment on *The Eve of the Revolution* appeared in "Historian of Revolution," an essay-review of *Everyman His Own Historian* (*New Republic*, LXXXV [Jan. 8, 1936], 260). Among the favorable reviews of *The Eve of the Revolution* at the time of its appearance were those of Van Tyne, *American Historical Review*, XXIV (1919), 734–735; Walton H. Hamilton, *Dial*, LXVI (Feb. 8, 1919), 135–137; and William R. Thayer, *Yale Review*, VIII (1919), 652. Jameson thought the book "quite a gem in its way." Jameson to J. Holland Rose, Sept. 19, 1925, in Elizabeth Donnan and Leo F. Stock, *An Historian's World: Selections from the Correspondence of John Franklin Jameson* (Philadelphia, 1956), 311.

could become embroiled in a war neither wanted by forces they did not understand and could not control, "although they amuse themselves with the pleasing illusion that they do." As for the rights and principles—of democracy or otherwise—employed in the course of the argument, these were not to be taken as literal explanations of political positions. "Very few people think with their minds. . . . People commonly think with their emotions." If the word "democracy" was used by the American revolutionaries, it did not mean they knew what they were talking about, however sincere they sounded. Democracy was an instrument which men "lay hold upon as a means of obtaining what they want." History was not to be explained so simply; it required "a more subtle psychology."[84]

This Becker tried to provide in an article on John Jay and Peter Van Schaack, a year later.[85] Having in his volume on New York shown that conservatives joined with and led radicals until the very eve of the conflict, only to have some of them draw back, Becker now sought to explain what differentiated the conservative-turned-Loyalist from the conservative-Patriot. Explanations based on differences in life style, such as with Adams and Hutchinson, were not satisfactory. Jay and Van Schaack were portrayed as close friends, similar in their social standing, professions, and political and religious principles. The source of their rupture was to be sought in the "subtle and impalpable influences, for the most part unconscious and emotional, which so largely determine motive and conduct." Becker found these influences to include Van Schaack's rigidity of temperament alongside of Jay's disposition to conciliate and compromise; Jay's pragmatism in contrast to Van Schaack's doctrinaire and legalistic mind; and Jay's active involvement in the various committees and congresses which unconsciously but relentlessly compelled him to acquiesce in their measures. Van Schaack, conversely, was removed from the

---

84. Becker to Dodd, June 14, 1920, in Snyder, "Becker and the Great War," *Western Political Quarterly*, IX (1956), 6; to Dodd, ca. 1923, in Snyder, ed., *Detachment*, 79–81.

85. It was published in the New York State Historical Association *Quarterly Journal*, I (1919), 1–12, reprinted in *Everyman*, 284–298, and again in *New York History*, L (1969), 442–453.

scene, and thus able to exercise greater objectivity and reason in weighing the consequences of the revolutionary movement. Ultimately Van Schaack chose neutrality and adherence to the Crown as his form of protest against loyalty enforced by social compulsion. Jay placed the welfare of his country above his personal preference for a more ordered society and grudgingly acceded to principles of government he disliked. The larger issue, as Becker saw it, was not one of loyalty or disloyalty, patriotism or treason, but individualism versus conformity.

Becker's focus, if not his sympathies, in this piece was on the Loyalist, Van Schaack. Seven years later, he tried to explain Jay's position more understandingly, this time in the form of a fictionalized essay in which Jay—or men like him—was personified by a mythical Jeremiah Wynkoop. With his fondness for polarity, Becker also created Nicholas Van Schoickendinck, Wynkoop's father-in-law.[86]

More explicitly than in the previous essay, Becker demonstrated how much doubt, hesitation, and introspection entered into the decision for independence, at least on the part of moderate men. Wynkoop was one of that "considerable class of substantial men" who were repelled by the violence which increasingly accompanied the opposition to Britain. Like his father-in-law, he had a great affection for the British constitution but no particular love for Britishers; he feared the loss of local leadership to "a mob of mechanics and ne'er do wells," and suspected their "precious democratical phrases." But while the older man would content himself with orderly, constitutional protests against Britain's manifestly illegal measures, Wynkoop was practical enough to recognize the value of force: "a little rioting may be necessary on occasion to warn ministers that legislative lawlessness is likely to be met by popular violence." Advancing step by step, under pressure of events, always rejecting the thought of separation as "fantastic," Wynkoop ultimately found himself compromised by his steady retreat from his original stance. With his conservatism and his fear

86. "The Spirit of '76," was first given as a lecture at the Brookings Institute on Nov. 19, 1926, and published as *The Spirit of '76 and Other Essays* (Washington, 1927), 9–58.

of the mob unchanged, all that Wynkoop could do was to rationalize his final position. He had joined the radicals to restrain them; he had accepted election to extralegal congresses and committees not out of disloyalty but the better to keep the province loyal; in the Continental Congress, his was a voice of moderation which might have been lost if he had declined participation. Thus, he consoled himself at the end, "the situation that confronted him was not of his making." The fault was not his, he concluded in self-deception, but Britain's in forcing him to the wall. He could not renounce either his friends, with whom he had shared in every measure thus far, or America, his country. And, in final self-justification, he persuaded himself that the advantages of union with Britain had always been illusory. Thus, once again, good men as well as bad had been forced by the logic of events into decisions which they could themselves only vaguely perceive but which they were helpless to control.

The thematic similarity in the three writings above was obvious, as was the form. There was much imaginary conversation, preoccupation with mental attitudes, and attention to the climate of opinion. Above all, however, was the reminder that great events could not be reduced to an impersonal level, that the "social soul" of an era must be understood to comprehend the actions of its individuals, that these actions were not easily explained in simple terms, and that "civilization is not understood as action but as motive to action."[87]

During the next few years, Becker pursued further his interest in historical personalities and their motivations in biographical sketches for the *Dictionary of American Biography* and the *Encyclopaedia of the Social Sciences*. Written in more scholarly vein than the earlier essays, these brief biographies applied the technique of psychological portraiture initiated in the previous, more imaginative works. Merle Curti accorded Becker high praise for these attempts at lay psychology. Reviewing *Everyman His Own Historian,* in which the essays on Jay and Van Schaack and the "Spirit of '76" were republished, Curti observed warmly that "while bold spirits were talking about the

87. The latter remark appears in Becker's "Influence of Social Problems upon. . . . History," *American Journal of Sociology,* XVIII (1913), 674.

necessity of enlisting psychology in the service of historical writing, Carl Becker in his quiet way was actually doing so without any borrowing of strange new terms."[88] Becker responded appreciatively that such had been his very purpose, "but not many historians seem to notice it, for the reasons, I suppose, that I make no use of technical jargon."[89]

However laudable his intention, Becker's execution was marred by a multiplicity of errors, logical inconsistencies, and erroneous conclusions. Reviewers and contemporary critics pointed out many; others arise from the contents themselves. Upon reading the biography of Henry Adams that appeared in the *Encyclopaedia of the Social Sciences,* James Truslow Adams exploded that it had more errors of fact in it than he had ever found "made by any scholar in similar compass before." The article, in Adams's view, was "really rather a scandal."[90] The sketch on Franklin in the *Dictionary of American Biography* was considered so outstanding that it was reprinted as a small book in 1946, on which occasion three colonial scholars felt compelled to temper their high praise of it with a catalog of some twenty factual errors in its text.[91] Becker's portraits of Sam Adams and Thomas Hutchinson scarcely resemble those drawn by a more critical if less illusive biographer like Clifford K. Shipton.[92] While the emphasis on Adams and Hutchinson in the *Eve of the Revolution* was provocative in its focus on motivation and personality, events were placed so far in the background that the substantive issues in dispute between the

88. *American Historical Review,* XLI (1935), 116.
89. Becker to Curti, Oct. 12, 1935, in Harold Bauman, "The Historiography of Carl L. Becker" (unpubl. Ph.D. dissertation, University of Iowa, 1938), 54.
90. The Henry Adams article is in the *Encyclopaedia of the Social Sciences,* I, 431–432. James T. Adams's complaint is in his letter to Allan Nevins, Oct. 22, 1932, in Nevins, *James Truslow Adams, Historian of the American Dream* (Urbana, Ill., 1968), 224.
91. *William and Mary Quarterly,* 3d ser. IV (1947), 232–234; *Mississippi Valley Historical Review,* XXXIV (1947), 123–124.
92. In addition to his sketches of Samuel Adams and Hutchinson in the *Eve of the Revolution,* Becker wrote one of Hutchinson for the *D.A.B.,* IX, 439–443, and one of Adams for both the *D.A.B.,* I, 95–101, and the *E.S.S.,* I, 435. Shipton's sketches are in his *Sibley's Harvard Graduates,* VIII, 149–215, and X, 420–464.

colonies and Britain were almost lost to view. Becker's mechanics and artisans scarcely appeared in its pages; the principles espoused by the colonists came close to being represented as mere rhetoric; the Whig leadership seemed more cynical than patriotic; and the crisis became less a matter of interests and principles than of conflicting personalities.

The portraits of Van Schaack and Jay were deliberately overdrawn to make Becker's point. The first was represented as more principled than pragmatic, but he judged the propriety of the American stand in 1776 in terms not of rights but of "general expedience, and policy"! Jay was characterized as unperturbed by legal niceties when, as a matter of fact, he was a stickler for legality. Van Schaack, according to Becker, liked "plain yes and no" answers, which scarcely made intelligible his pained, long-delayed decision for Crown or country until well after independence had been declared. Van Schaack's ability to view the scene dispassionately was accounted for by his residence in the country, removed from the scene of action; but Robert Livingston, the manor lord, even farther removed in his rural retreat, opted for independence. Jay's ultimate decision was explained by his active involvement in the revolutionary movement. Another New Yorker, however, equally conservative and even more involved, Isaac Low, was able to resist the inexorable force of events that dictated Jay's decision and remained loyal. His brother, on the other hand, chose the path of independence. The Van Schaack who turned Loyalist because he prized personal liberty more than the power of the state scarcely resembled the Van Schoickendinck of the "Spirit of '76," whose fears were largely of the libertarian spirit of the Revolution.

The criticism would not have bothered Becker. He always preferred "right questions" to "right answers." His factual errors might have disturbed him, but he was never sure of the meaning of facts in any case. Nothing was duller to him than facts, he confessed to Turner shortly after the publication of his dissertation. Their meticulous accumulation in monographs was "a dreary waste," the kind of history that "lies inert in unread books."[93] And if the critics expected him to refine his theories of motivation and become a full-fledged psychological historian, they were wrong. Becker's thinking would not be so confined. The realm of ideas, which he had only hinted at in his *Eve of the Revolution,* now engaged his fuller attention. The product was *The Declaration of Independence,* Becker's most enduring work in American history.[94]

The field of ideas was an even more treacherous and difficult arena for historical inquiry than that of human behavior, Becker admitted, but it was nonetheless essential. Accordingly, he undertook to discover the "state of mind" which conditioned the writing and acceptance of the Declaration of Independence.[95] Unlike the *Eve of the Revolution,* which emphasized the circumstances that propelled men farther than they wished to go, the *Declaration* stressed the ideals that were determinants of those actions. His historiographical reflections had convinced him that ideas were less important as absolutes or as actual representations of historical situations than as reflections of a contemporary climate of opinion. The Declaration, he concluded, represented the beliefs or rationalizations of the American revolutionaries. Whether they were true or false by any absolute standard was irrelevant. What mattered was that Jefferson and his colleagues considered them sufficiently valid to justify an unprecedented revolt and to bring their seemingly aberrant actions "into harmony with a rightly ordered universe." By the nineteenth century, Becker concluded, the theory of natural rights on which the Declaration was based had been replaced by a more utilitarian philosophy which asked not what rights society assured men but what benefits it could confer

93. Review, *American Historical Review,* XLV (1940), 593; Becker to Turner, May 16, 1910, in Jacobs, ed., *World of Frederick Jackson Turner,* 206; "Everyman," in *Everyman,* 252.

94. New York, 1922. The book was rated sixth highest, second only to Andrews's *Colonial Period* in the colonial field, in a poll of some 125 historians of the best works in their field published between 1920 and 1935. John W. Caughey, "Historians' Choice," *Mississippi Valley Historical Review,* XXXIX (1952), 298–302.

95. Review of Fay's *L'Esprit Revolutionnaire, American Historical Review,* XXX (1925), 810.

upon them.[96] To a nineteenth-century Europe that was antirevolutionary and a slaveholding United States that was defensive about human inequality, natural rights bore few of the connotations they possessed for Jefferson's America. Becker neither condemned nor praised either generation. He wanted only to explain their reactions. So well did Becker conceal his own position that Arthur M. Schlesinger saw the author "in the role of an entomologist studying a quivering specimen impaled with a pin." Another reviewer commended the book for its freedom from dogmatism.[97]

Much of the praise accorded the book, then and since, arose from its literary craftsmanship. Its substance, in large part, was unoriginal. The history of the drafting of the Declaration and its textual evolution had been discussed in a volume by John Hazelton fifteen years earlier. The natural rights philosophy in the Declaration had been analyzed by another writer at about the same time.[98] The unfolding of the theory of pluralistic empire—expressed, in Becker's view, as a "minor premise" of the Declaration—was elaborated much more fully in a study by Randolph G. Adams which appeared the same year as Becker's book.[99] That Jefferson's ideas were less imitative of French than of English political theory, moreover, was scarcely a new discovery in 1922.

By the standards of modern historical knowledge, there are more substantial weaknesses in the book. The ideas discussed in it are largely dissociated from the events which produced them, appearing merely to have passed from Locke to Jefferson through various intermediaries without ever acting on the minds or emotions of men. One reviewer's criticism of the *Heavenly City* applies equally to the *Declaration of Independence:* "He is so concerned with giving us the climate of opinion that he forgets about the sort of opinion."[100] The

96. *Declaration of Independence* (1942 ed.), 236, 277–278.
97. *Mississippi Valley Historical Review,* IX (1923), 334; F. A. Ogg in *Yale Review,* XIII (1924), 600–601.
98. Friedenwald, *Declaration of Independence,* especially ch. 9; John H. Hazelton, *The Declaration of Independence: Its History* (New York, 1906), especially chs. 4–7.
99. *Political Ideas of the American Revolution* (Durham, N.C., 1922).
100. Quoted in Rockwood, ed., *Heavenly City Revisited,* vii.

inevitability of the acceptance by Americans of Jefferson's principles is belied by the long, heated debates in the press and in the Congress over the separation from England. Becker's own earlier essays on Jay, Van Schaack, and Wynkoop had demonstrated not the ease with which Americans accepted independence and its rationale but their painful, halting progress toward that decision. Stressing Jefferson's dependence on Lockean thought, Becker missed the irony in the British Whigs' admiration for that same ideology. If Britons, too, looked "with reverence, almost amounting to idolatry," as the British General Burgoyne put it in a classic letter to Charles Lee, upon these same "doctrines of Mr. Locke," what explained the impassable chasm between Americans and Englishmen? Becker's treatment possessed none of the sophistication of Bernard Bailyn's later analysis of the differences between English and American Whig political ideologies as each evolved in its own separate milieu.[101]

No one could have expected Becker to remain constant in his historical evaluations. It is not surprising, then, that in time, as the threat to democracy from abroad became more visible, he should have dropped some of his somewhat cynical detachment with respect to Jefferson's "glittering generalities." In 1922 he believed that the principles enunciated by Jefferson had secured their immortality not because of their intrinsic validity but because the success of the Revolution gave them the distinction of success. He saw these principles, founded upon "naïve faith" in human virtue, being crushed by the harsh realities of the modern world.[102] By 1930, he conceded that the Declaration served discontented people everywhere as "a charter of human liberty." When the *Declaration of Independence* was reissued in 1942, Becker was more confident that the "glittering generalities" of that document were "the fundamental realities" for which men fight. He praised Jefferson for the "humane and liberal spirit" which was unaffected by events, and he lauded the "rights of man-

101. Bailyn, *The Origins of American Politics* (New York, 1967, 1970), *Ideological Origins of the American Revolution* (Cambridge, Mass., 1967). The Burgoyne letter is quoted in Clinton Rossiter, *Seedtime of the Republic* (New York, 1953), 353.
102. *Declaration of Independence* (1942 ed.), 225, 278–279.

kind" explicated in the Declaration as the only principles consistent with democratic government.[103]

Within three more years, Becker was gone, his dilemmas resolved, his paradoxes silenced. His long and troubled quest for assurance of man's morality in an amoral world and of his intelligence in a cosmic universe was ended; his unceasing search for meaning in a history that played tricks upon the historian, terminated. In a characteristically final irony, his fellow historians have played their own tricks on Becker. He has been honored as a leader of Progressive historiography, though he did not share most of the philosophical convictions of that school. He has been labeled a relativist despite his insistence that the acquisition of objective historical knowledge was possible and desirable: he merely cautioned that the effort was fraught with hazards. He has been called a psychological historian, but he never probed very deeply into the subconscious of men's minds—although he perhaps thought he did. He has been acknowledged as a preeminent intellectual historian, but his dissection of ideas never went very far below the surface. He has been lauded for his warm and engaging faith in humanity and democracy, but for long periods of his life he expressed grave doubts about mankind's capacity to govern itself and frank cynicism about its own deep commitment to the democratic way.

That historians, years after his death, should seek to categorize him represents an irony which Becker would have enjoyed. He eschewed categorization himself. "To say of any historian, ancient or modern, that he is scientific, or literary, or patriotic tells me little that I care to know."[104] His own heterodoxy put him outside all of them. "I don't claim to be new or old or anything that a label can be attached to." He preferred to consider himself less a historian than a thinker about history and historians. His forte, he said, consisted "in having thought a good deal about the meaning of history rather than having achieved

103. "Declaration of Independence," in *E.S.S.*, V, 47; "What Is Still Living in the Political Philosophy of Thomas Jefferson?" *American Historical Review*, XLVIII (1943), 691–706; *Declaration of Independence* (1942 ed.), xvi. See also "Some Generalities That Still Glitter," in *New Liberties for Old*, 127, 149–151, and *Freedom and Responsibility*, 18.

104. "Labelling the Historians," in *Everyman*, 135.

erudition in it."[105] He delighted, too, in being regarded as a writer and must have appreciated Beard's compliment: "I have heard on good authority that you are no Historian; nothing except a Man of Letters. It makes me jealous."[106] He would have warmed, also, to the witty tribute of a later admirer: "Becker had the dangerous gift of being able to make utter nonsense sound completely plausible."[107]

The compliment was, at best, oblique. Becker provided American historians with more than plausible keys to an understanding of their past: a view of the American Revolution more subtle, complex, and disordered than they had theretofore imagined; an introduction to the possibilities in the study of motivation, character, and ideology; an awareness of the interaction between men and their climate of opinion; and, above all, a warning about the dangers of all orthodoxies of interpretation, if history was to serve the useful purpose of enabling men to understand the past, manage the present, and anticipate the future. That his readers were often beguiled and entrapped by his magnificently lucid and tranquilizing flow of words was their error, not his. He had urged his own students to take courses that would unsettle rather than settle them, make them ask questions, not answer them. He never ceased raising questions himself. "What is it all about?" he wrote to some troubled Cornell freshmen in 1926. "That is a pertinent question. I have been asking it for thirty-five years, and I am still as bewildered as they are." Two decades later, on the eve of his death, he knew no more than that "to expect to find any final answer to the significance of history is as futile as to expect to find any final answer to the meaning of life." Like Socrates, whom he admired, he was glad that he had not discovered any final truth. Hence, he was never "in a position to rest on his laurels and abandon the search for it."[108]

105. Becker to George Lincoln Burr, Jan. 4, 1917, in Brown, *Becker,* 97; Becker to Merle Curti, Oct. 1935, in Wilkins, *Becker,* 186.

106. Beard to Becker, Sept. 26, [?], in Cushing Strout, *The Pragmatic Revolt in American History* (New Haven, 1958), 85.

107. Ralph H. Bowen, in Rockwood, ed., *Heavenly City Revisited,* 144.

108. Becker to the *Cornell Daily Sun,* Dec. 10, 1926, in Snyder, ed., *Detachment,* 158; *Freedom and Responsibility,* 56; review of Fulmer Mood, *The Development of Frederick Jackson Turner as a Historical Thinker,* in *American Historical Review,* XLIX (1944), 265.

Becker's dilemma was as old as America's. He sought answers knowing they were evanescent, because they always raised new questions; just as the Puritans sought perfection in a world they knew was destined to be imperfect. Each found strength and refreshment in the possibilities along the way, not in the probability of traversing the road completely. In 1927, Becker wrote: "As a young man I was encouraged to look forward hopefully to the day when all fields of history having been 'definitely' done and presented in properly dull and documented monographs, the final synthesis could be made. Wondering what historians would do then, I secretly hoped that day would not come in my time. It hasn't."[109] Becker's testamentary advice to his profession, for whom that day has still not come, would be to worry less about the end and to enjoy every minute of their never-ending task of understanding American history.

109. Review of J. B. Black, *The Art of History, American Historical Review*, XXXII (1927), 295.

RICHARD B. MORRIS

The Spacious Empire of Lawrence Henry Gipson

TWO NOTEWORTHY EVENTS make the year 1880 distinctive in
the annals of American historiography. That patriarch among American historians, George Bancroft, then in his eighty-first year, was
busily engaged in preparing his two-volume *History of the Formation
of the Constitution of the United States,* which became a part of "The
Author's Last Revision" to appear within a few years. In that same
year Lawrence Henry Gipson, the present dean and patriarch of
American historians, was born in Greeley, Colorado. I suggest that this
is more than coincidence, for something of that quality of timeless
energy which Bancroft possessed in full measure seems to have been
infused into the bloodstream of our distinguished colleague. One who
at the ripe age of eighty-six can demonstrate a capacity, intellectual
and physical, to bring to completion a grandiose design might well be
compared with that earlier historian, who at the age of eighty-five
wrote to Oliver Wendell Holmes: "On one of the days in which I
wrote my little tribute to your *Life of Emerson,* I was yet strong

*This paper was originally delivered in the Centennial Lecture Series at
Lehigh University on March 26, 1966, and published the following year in the*
William and Mary Quarterly, *3d Ser., XXIV (1967), 169–189. Professor Gipson died in 1971. The nature of a* festschrift *precluded our consulting Dr. Morris about revisions he might have wished. Therefore the essay appears here as
originally published, except for minor editorial adjustments that make it consistent in format with the rest of the volume (eds.). Reprinted by permission of
the* William *and Mary Quarterly, copyright held by the Institute of Early
American History and Culture.*

enough to rise in the night, light my own fire and candles, and labor with close application fully fourteen hours consecutively, that is, from five in the morning till eight in the evening, with but one short hour's interruption for breakfast; and otherwise no repast; not so much as a sip of water." To which the Autocrat of the Breakfast Table made a characteristic response: "You must be made of iron and vulcanized india-rubber, or some such compound of resistance and elasticity."

Now, synthetic chemistry has invented many more compounds than were known in the late Doctor Holmes's day. If Lawrence H. Gipson has partaken of these new elixirs, for trade reasons he has kept it a secret. But anyone who for some score of years could survive a daily round-trip commutation stint on the Reading Railroad between Rydal and Bethlehem and still write history in the grand style deserves a very special tribute. Lawrence Gipson is something more than the most durable commuter of our time. He is a historian whose powers of concentration and physical energy are matched by erudition and ingenuity. In combination these elements have produced a masterly series unrivaled in its general area, and considering its breath-taking range, definitive in its execution.

At this point, however, I think I should make clear that I am not trying to suggest some lineal connection between the point of view of George Bancroft and that of Lawrence Gipson. Ranke needled Bancroft when he told him that his *History* was "the best book ever written from the democratic point of view," and he may have been right, for Bancroft's writing sounds a far more polemical note than is present in the Revolutionary histories of the previous generation. To Bancroft the Americans were pressing along the path of progress according to God's plan. Not only was it a democratic plan of progress, but it was a culmination of manifest destiny, and it was even an exposition of the virtues of low tariff, which one might expect of a strong Jacksonian Democrat. As an opponent of trade barriers Bancroft gave to the British mercantile program a more important dimension than most earlier writers, and he viewed the colonial mercantile systems as the "head-spring which colored all the stream" of independence. To almost all these generalizations Lawrence H. Gipson would take strong exception, as he would to Bancroft's curious scholarship. Although no man prior to Bancroft took as much pains as he did to search out and copy pertinent materials from the foreign archives, he signally and unaccountably failed to utilize much of the documentation that he had gathered, too often substituting purple prose for a reasoned evaluation of the evidence. To a prodigious researcher like Lawrence Gipson, whose footnotes are a testament to the care with which he has utilized his evidence and made the sources fully available to other investigators for their own verification, Bancroft's failure to drink from the very well which he himself had dug must stand as a lesson to all historical scholars: "Go thou and do the contrary."

It was fortunate for Lawrence Gipson and for his wide circle of admirers that his formative years of intellectual growth coincided with an extraordinary change in both the intellectual and the political climate of this country. On the intellectual side, the eighties and nineties of the last century witnessed the rise of graduate education, of scientific and specialized research, with its complementary emphasis on objective history and more dispassionate—if a lot duller—writing by historians. The changing climate which affected historical writing reflected the great diplomatic rapprochement that was in the course of being cemented between the British and the American peoples. The *fin de siècle* was notable, among other things, for the appearance on the world stage of the gauche, impulsive Kaiser Wilhelm II, whose bellicosity did more to patch up long-strained British-American relations than the efforts of a long line of American secretaries of state and their counterparts at Whitehall. With Germany, that Continental behemoth, suddenly looming large and formidable on the world horizon and posing a massive threat both to Britain's naval and maritime supremacy and to that European balance of power so delicately reassembled by the old Congress of Vienna and kept pasted together by later treaties, the British permitted their long and understandable irritation over the proprietary attitude that America had assumed toward the Western hemisphere, along with America's espousal of the cause of Ireland, to be deflected against Germany.

How much of this was felt on the campus of the University of

Idaho in the year 1900 is, of course, speculative, but there is no question that Lawrence Gipson as a Rhodes Scholar at Oxford some four years later must have been acutely sensitive to the changing horizons. Men like his tutor Owen Edwards of Lincoln College contributed to his growing awareness. Even Englishmen who had never forgiven the rebellious provincials for seceding from the Empire felt the change— or at least some Englishmen did, conspicuously among them the liberal-minded Sir Charles Dilke, whose current vogue unfortunately derives from more lurid reasons.

During the days when Lawrence Gipson was enjoying Oxford's then cloistered life, George Otto Trevelyan, joining literary artistry with political intention, was currently laboring on his multivolume account of the American Revolution, of which the first two volumes had already appeared by the time Lawrence Gipson went to England. Carrying on the Whig tradition of W. E. H. Lecky, Trevelyan did full justice to the Patriot cause and was severely critical of the King and his ministers. For the new imperial school of American historians then achieving notice Trevelyan's portraits of the Patriots must have seemed, however, too pure and undefiled, and his representation of the North ministry as a collection of rogues, scoundrels, and dunderheads to have been painted with colors a bit too deep-dyed. The later Namierites were to protest that Trevelyan's work provided an oversimplified view of a Whig opposition joining forces with Whigs across the sea to fight for a concept of a British Constitution which the King and his supporters, with some justice, considered archaic.

While in England Trevelyan was audaciously publishing a sympathetic account of the American Revolution, a subject which was understandably distasteful to the British public at any time, American scholars were beginning to take a more dispassionate view of the struggle and to reexamine with considerable objectivity the role of the traditionally maligned Loyalists and even of the parts played by Crown, Ministry, and Parliament. More balanced treatments of an ancient quarrel than one could have found in earlier works of history published in this country were being presented by Moses Coit Tyler, by Sydney George Fisher, and by Claude Halstead Van Tyne. But it was Herbert L. Osgood who, at the turn of the century, set the stage for entrance thereon of the imperial school of colonial historians. He was among the first to stress the need for mastering the details of England's commercial policy as a key to the understanding of colonial developments on this side of the water. He was also among the first to stress the importance of research into the dark ages of American history, the seventy years following 1690, and, above all, he stands as a pioneer in his caution that in studying the colonies "full justice must be done" to both the British and the colonial sides. An institutional and administrative historian, Osgood initiated that whole series of administrative studies of the operation of the British Empire, a series principally carried out by his own graduate students and surviving as the chief glory of the imperial school of historiography.

It was left to two others at this time to complete the ambitious program that Osgood had laid out in his seven-volume study of the colonies in the seventeenth and eighteenth centuries. The most notable of Osgood's students to take American colonial history out of its provincial setting and make it a part of the history of the British Empire was George Louis Beer. Following the completion of his master's essay, written in 1893 when he was but twenty years old and entitled "The Commercial Policy of England toward the American Colonies," Beer researched in England during the same period that Lawrence Gipson studied at Oxford. The results of his investigations were exhaustive analyses of British colonial policy, 1754–1765, and probings into the background of the Navigation Laws of 1660. Beer's main thesis that the colonial system was mutually advantageous to England and the colonies profoundly influenced the thinking and writing of Charles McLean Andrews. Almost by coincidence Lawrence Gipson's future mentor was in England in 1904 on sabbatical leave from Bryn Mawr, the very year that the new Rhodes Scholar was to begin his studies at Oxford. The fruit of Andrews's digging and cataloging appeared in the years 1908, 1912, and 1914, in the form of notable guides to the manuscript materials for the history of the United States to 1783 in the British Museum and in the Public Record Office. In many respects the most substantial and lasting of Andrews's scholarly contributions, these guides opened up a whole new world to American scholars who were now to stand in Whitehall and Westminster rather than in Boston, Philadelphia, or Charleston and view the empire as a whole.

This coincidence in time in the careers of student and mentor seems more than a little fortuitous; for in 1910, Charles M. Andrews took up his duties at Yale as Farnam Professor of American history, devoting himself exclusively to the colonial period, and in that same year, Lawrence Gipson began his studies at Yale as a Farnam Fellow. Even by that early date his teacher's pronounced views as an imperial historian had been well publicized through numerous addresses and papers and, above all, through his superb volume in the American Nation Series on *Colonial Self-Government,* a treatment which at that date marked something of an innovation. A historian of the new scientific school that eschewed literary effect, that concentrated on administration rather than administrators, that was concerned with causes and patterns rather than with people, Andrews as a director of graduate studies discouraged anything that smacked of pretension to style, cautioning that a monograph be prepared in accordance with the most stringent dictates of historical scholarship and with substantial impersonality. Himself a vital and positive personality, genial, charming, and sympathetic to his students' problems, Andrews insisted that his students work in institutional and administrative history, and avoid biographical subjects. One student, the retiring, modest, even diffident Lawrence Gipson, possessed an equal share of tenacity. He clung to his notion of working on the biography of Jared Ingersoll, an able Connecticut lawyer, who served as his colony's agent in England and then had the bad fortune to follow Franklin's advice and to accept an appointment as a stamp distributor in Connecticut. For the failure to predict how his countrymen would react Ingersoll suffered ill-deserved obloquy. His career, expertly and sympathetically handled by Lawrence Gipson, illumines the conflict facing those Americans who loved their country and yet could not renounce the obligations to Crown and empire.

Gipson was never to lose sight of people, either in his warm personal relationships or in his later work. It would be perhaps idle to speculate about how much his sturdy decision to write a biography as a dissertation molded his later historical views, but all one has to do is to read his magnum opus, *The British Empire before the American Revolution,* and discover a series of skillful portraits woven into the majestic tapestry. Take, for example, his account of the Abbé Le Loutre in his struggle with Thomas Pichon for the allegiance of the French settlers of Acadia. One a cleric, the other a layman, one, as Mr. Gipson puts it, "fanatically of the robe, the other wantonly of the world; one clinging to the past, a child of the Middle Ages," yet "ruthless with the present"; the other, "scorning the past, a child of the age of rationalism," and "all-absorbed in the significant present; one a Frenchman who saw the summum bonum in concepts that would subordinate all mankind to the autocratic rule and will of both church and state authorities, the other a Frenchman who saw it in concepts that would subordinate the church and state to the inherent natural rights and general will of mankind." Each had a record of treachery; yet each was convinced of the correctness of his own course. "Each contributed mightily, although working at cross-purposes, to the destruction of the old French Empire."[1]

Or consider Gipson's stouthearted defense of Governor William Shirley, whose replacement by the Earl of Loudoun he tells us was little short of disastrous. When Shirley was recalled he was, as Gipson depicts him, "the symbol of something that disappeared from British continental America never to return. For never again would a royal governor in any colony be able to harmonize to the same extent as Shirley the interests of the mother country—imperial in nature—with those of the vigorous corporate colonies—local in nature. Never again would a native Englishman enjoy in eighteenth-century America the vast prestige that came through the exercise of superior capacities directed to the enlistment of the voluntary support of the colonials for certain common and important ends." "Doubtless the secret of his power," our author suggests, "lay in the fact not only that his spacious

1. Lawrence H. Gipson, *The British Empire before the American Revolution* (New York, 1936–), VI, 240.

and disinterested views on American affairs appealed to most colonials but also that he understood Americans, he respected them, and was inclined to support them whenever possible against the claims of superiority of his fellow Englishmen."[2] If Shirley were to run on the Gipson ticket in the next British by-election, one could be sure that he would command the moral support of the horde of American scholars laying the Public Record Office under perpetual siege.

Or take Gipson's revisionist portrait of William Pitt the Elder. Gipson portrays him as ever the opportunist, whether as a cocky young man prior to joining the government in 1746, or as a mature leader outside the government after 1761, or as an aging valetudinarian after he finally gave up all thought of continuing in office in 1768. To Gipson, unmoved by the uncritical acclaim of Pitt's admirers, there are many facets of the elder Pitt that do not show him to advantage, notably his irresponsibility in opposition. While giving Pitt his due as the inspiring war leader whose direction changed the course of the Great War for the Empire, Gipson portrays him during the crucial moments of the tragic Pitt-Grafton Ministry which proposed the Townshend Acts as unstable of mind and temperamentally unsuited to dealing with domestic problems, notably to concentrating on the tedious details of finance.[3] These portraits are memorable, and they reveal a historian who, after a measured evaluation of the evidence, is willing to express moral judgments, who, like Trevelyan, although perhaps from a different point of view, believes there is right and there is wrong, and is not content to stand on neutral gray ground.

Jared Ingersoll, published in 1920, quickly received deserved recognition, including the Justin Winsor Prize of the American Historical Association.[4] For Gipson, scholar and teacher, these have been busy years indeed since Oxford—years of teaching, first in Idaho, then at Wabash College, and finally, since 1924, at Lehigh, where for some forty years he has held high the torch of Clio, whereby countless col-

2. *Ibid.,* 210–211.
3. *Ibid.,* VII, 7. For a full discussion of Pitt, see 3–26.
4. Lawrence H. Gipson, *Jared Ingersoll, A Study of American Loyalism in Relation to British Colonial Government* (New Haven, 1920).

lege generations have developed a taste for the new scientific history as well as a real feeling for the colonial past, and where his colleagues have had constantly before them a living exemplar of the dedicated scholar, not content with worn-out ideas and yellowing old notes, but insisting upon an ever fresh and seemingly inexhaustible re-examination of old evidence and new opinions.

A dozen years of careful preparation, indefatigable sleuthing, and profound reflection went into the initial volumes of *The British Empire before the American Revolution,* published in 1936, when Lawrence Gipson was fifty-six years old. He spoke then of having "intermittently haunted the leading depositories of documents and other rare sources," and his diligence and wide curiosity were abundantly disclosed in the first three volumes. Originally planned as a multivolume work, the series ultimately has burgeoned to a dozen volumes with two more projected. A thirteenth volume will cover areas outside the mainland colonies in North America, provide a "Summary of the Series," and discuss historiography. There will be a final bibliographical volume. In his timing as well as in his systematic planning for this magnum opus, Mr. Gipson was perhaps more felicitous than his old master Charles McLean Andrews. The latter had only given us fragments of his vast storehouse of knowledge before the publication in 1934 of Volume I of *The Colonial Period of American History.* Andrews was then seventy-one years old, and as he remarked amusingly to me, he considered his completion of the project "a race with death." That he was able to produce three more volumes within four years was a tribute to his extraordinary vitality, but it was indeed a tragedy that his series left us in mid-air, that he did not live to do his volume on social life, for which he had gathered innumerable notes, nor give us a concluding volume on the coming of the American Revolution.

Lawrence Gipson was more provident in the allocation of his time and energy. Between 1936 and 1965 at regular intervals we have had one dozen volumes of the great series come off the presses, at the rate of about one every two and a half years, and now the latest volume, published at the age of eighty-five, inspires comparison with George

Bancroft's work on his last revision and gives us assurance that the grand design will be brought to completion. I might add that the first three volumes were initially brought out by The Caxton Printers, a distinguished Gipson family enterprise located in Caldwell, Idaho, but that subsequently the firm of Alfred A. Knopf has undertaken the responsibility for publishing the series, including the recent reissue of the first three volumes in a revised form.

The Gipson series has constituted a massive assault upon the old-line nationalist interpretation of the period, a critical questioning of patriotic assumptions about our Revolutionary past, combining the most recent researches of the imperial school of historians and the followers of Sir Lewis Namier. The panorama is as broad as the whole world, the treatment is crowded with detail, and the subject has enormous complexities, but I should like to confine my analysis to some of the areas where Gipson's contribution is especially distinctive and original.

It is clear from the start that Gipson is sympathetic to the British Empire and its imperial administrators in the year 1750, and that he does not regard mercantilism as a system of tribute, but rather as an effort to provide imperial protection "for all those great interests that were sources of material wealth and power." Conceding its inconveniences and occasional gross injustices, he regards these flaws as inherent even in the most modern legislative scheme imposing national or imperial restrictions. There were restraints, to be sure, but for each of them he sees reciprocal benefits either direct or indirect to the colonies.[5]

Some of Gipson's most powerful and original ideas are spelled out in his massive treatment of what Parkman handled almost as a private war between Montcalm and Wolfe. The old name for it, "The French and Indian War," Gipson would discard on the ground that it stems from the Patriot's hostility to Great Britain, a hostility originating at the time of the American Revolution. That tradition was bound up with the following propositions: (1) that the connection of the colo-

_____

5. Gipson, *British Empire before the Revolution,* III, 287.

nies with Great Britain was a malevolent one, dragging the colonists into wars with England's enemies, especially France, in which they had no interest; (2) that North America was predestined to be Anglo-Saxon in culture regardless of what Britain did, and that the French and Indian War was "nothing more than one of a series of so-called French and Indian wars . . . a mere interlude in the resistless westward march of the American pioneers"—the Fourth Intercolonial War Osgood unimaginatively labeled it; and (3) that the colonists were quite able to fend for themselves and owed nothing to Great Britain, whose role in the war was motivated by self-interest and whose troops in America were a hindrance rather than a help because of their devotion to "European methods of fighting unsuited to the American scene." All these views Professor Gipson dismisses as devoid of historical foundation, distortions resulting from patriotic American hindsight.[6]

To Gipson the war was primarily an *American* war, triggered by the *Americans* themselves, and one that determined whether English or French civilization was to prevail in North America and whether the Appalachians were to constitute a permanent barrier to the westward spread of American settlements. In the light of massive contemporary evidence Gipson disabuses us of the notion that the colonists were able to defend themselves without British assistance. "All well-informed Americans," Gipson reminds us, "felt that all-out British aid to them was imperative if they were to be saved from irretrievable disaster."[7] Even Braddock's defeat, he insists, did not destroy the faith of colonial assemblies and popular opinion in the performance of regular troops as compared with irregulars fighting in Indian fashion.[8]

Away with the "French and Indian War," Gipson admonishes. It was "the Great War for the Empire," Benjamin Franklin to the contrary notwithstanding.[9] Some of the most luminous pages in this mul-

6. *Ibid.*, VI, 4–9, 10–11, 12.
7. *Ibid.*, 13.
8. *Ibid.*
9. *Ibid.*, VI, viii.

tivolume treatment deal with the operations and consequences of this "Seven Years' War," which started two years earlier on this side of the Atlantic than it did in Europe. Why did France lose the war? Not because of Continental setbacks, argues Gipson, but rather because she lacked sea power. She did not have the economic and logistical strength to get the timber, naval stores, and trained seamen necessary to maintain sea power. France was in fact stretching her resources too thin. She was fighting a major European war as well as a major overseas war, and fighting it not by economic aid to allies, as was Britain for the most part, but by her own blood and industry.[10] Like Louis XIV and Napoleon, she took on too many foes, foes that she had accumulated because on balance more Europeans felt France rather than Great Britain to be the aggressor.

True, the war started in America and may have been fought for America, but it is presented to us on a global scale. We see the French project for invading the British Isles in 1759,[11] a project to be revived with even less satisfactory results twenty years later, as is set forth in *The Peacemakers*. We see the privateers and the neutrals island-hopping in the Caribbean,[12] the mopping up of French posts in Africa,[13] and the crushing defeat of the French in India.[14]

One of Gipson's most moving pieces of research was prompted by the fate of the Acadians. Humane and kindly disposed though the author must always be, he shows very clearly that the Acadians were a fifth column, that they continued as uprooted and hapless exiles in a state of sullen defiance, seeking to get back to Acadia one way or the other, or to French-speaking areas. The extraordinary itineraries of the Acadians in the Thirteen Colonies are painstakingly traced. Isolated and even forgotten remnants of the Acadian exile are turned up in this major piece of sleuthing. More sympathetic to the British side of the controversy than Bancroft or Henry Wadsworth Longfellow, Gipson makes patent to his readers the threat the Acadians posed to

10. *Ibid.*, VIII, 290–291.
11. *Ibid.*, 3–27.
12. *Ibid.*, 65–82.
13. *Ibid.*, 173–177.
14. *Ibid.*, 106–171.

the military security of the British possessions in wartime, and reveals the disillusionment of that substantial group of Acadian exiles who finally reached the soil of France.[15]

As compared with Parkman, Gipson has given us a deglamorized version of the Great War for the Empire, one that lays stress on the virtues of the established canons of military science and tactics, one that points out that Wolfe's decision regarding the landing place for his troops was ill-judged,[16] and one that sees Wolfe's bravery in leading in person the famous bayonet charge of his grenadiers, in which he met his heroic death, as a reckless and irresponsible disregard of sound military practice and precept.[17] Perhaps the grenadiers would not have made the charge if Wolfe himself had not led them, the small quiet voice of the reader might ask? In his handling of military operations Gipson is amazingly sure-footed. Thus, his defense of young Washington's criticism of the projected wilderness road from Raystown to the Forks of the Ohio—known as the Forbes Road—is justified on the ground of military judgment. Gipson has no sympathy for the view that as a Virginian, Washington preferred Braddock's Road which began on the Potomac rather than one which lay entirely within the province of Pennsylvania. Washington was not unaware of business opportunities, but both Douglas Freeman and Gipson quite independently exonerate him of interested motives in this case.[18]

From the beginning to the end of the Great War for the Empire Gipson provides us with illuminating analyses. He has done probably the most exhaustive study of the various schemes of intercolonial union which the Albany Congress debated in 1754 in the face of the growing French military threat, including the plan he attributes to Thomas Hutchinson. He details the rejection of the final plan by the provincial governments and the refusal of the British ministry to impose it in the form of a parliamentary enactment.[19] All in all, Gipson is happy about the Albany Plan of Union, which would have provided the kind of

15. *Ibid.,* VI, 243–344.
16. *Ibid.,* VII, 194–195.
17. *Ibid.,* 420–421.
18. *Ibid.,* 262–265.
19. *Ibid.,* V, 113–166; for Hutchinson's plan, see 128–130.

viable and possibly permanent relationship between colonies and mother country within the empire that he would have liked to have seen. Despite its shortcomings he characterizes it as a "glowing tribute to the capacity of the commissioners who assembled at Albany to rise, at least temporarily, above local and selfish interests, to think in terms of the general welfare of the English colonies."[20] Later in the series he is to remind us that Franklin, who in 1754 was to advocate Parliamentary enactment of the plan of union, was after 1766 to deny all Parliamentary authority over the colonies whatsoever.[21]

Since Lawrence Gipson has spent the greater portion of his life on the East Coast, most of us seem to have forgotten that he is a westerner by birth and early rearing, and that the Idaho country of his childhood must have had many of the elements of Turner's last frontier. What we should remember is that he is at home in the trans-Appalachian West as much as in London or Philadelphia, and that he can lay down the details of the treaties of Hard Labor, Fort Stanwix, and Lochaber with as much gusto as he can describe French plans for expansion on the Carnatic or moves in the Senegal or the West Indies. His treatment of the Proclamation of 1763 is revisionist and in many ways definitive.[22] He shows that it was no permanent line, but rather that it created a temporary[23] but vast Indian reserve by laying down as a barrier the crest of the mountains beyond which there should be no white settlement except by specific permission of the Crown. He refutes the charges that the Proclamation was a blunder, that it resulted from carelessness or ignorance on the part of those responsible for drafting it, or that it was a cynical attempt by the British ministry to embody mercantilistic principles in an American land policy that in itself ran counter to the charter limits of many of the colonies and the broader interests of all the colonials. The Indians had been assured during the previous war, he reminds us, that they would be

20. *Ibid.*, 138.
21. *Ibid.*, X, 411.
22. *Ibid.*, IX, 41–54.
23. For a new look at the alleged temporary character of the Proclamation Line, see Francis S. Philbrick's revisionist treatment, *The Rise of the West, 1754–1830* (New York, 1965), 6–7.

secure in their trans-Appalachian lands as a reward for deserting their allies, the French. Unfortunately, this step, which was both politic, humane, and, according to present-day standards, conservationist, ran counter to the interests of various groups of land speculators as well as those of the irrepressible frontiersmen who spilled across the mountains in defiance of the Proclamation Line.

True, the Proclamation might have become a formidable issue, he concedes, but the British were flexible enough to acquiesce in various Indian treaties by which speculators and western settlers secured areas they coveted, and in fact bent and stretched the Proclamation Line. Should the British government thereafter have withdrawn their troops and dropped onto the lap of the old continental colonies the entire responsibility for maintaining the garrisons in Canada, about the Great Lakes, in the Ohio and Mississippi valleys, and in east and west Florida? An utterly chimerical notion, Gipson declares. Considering the extent of intercolonial rivalry over the West and the exceptionally bitter feeling between Pennsylvania and Virginia over the control of the upper Ohio Valley, the author insists that control of the West would have required not only a vast expenditure of funds but highly complicated intercolonial arrangements, neither of which seemed practical possibilities. Imagine the American with his aversion to the dull routine of garrison duty isolated on a frontier post for months or years at a time! Gipson reminds us of the dispatches of Colonel George Washington in 1756 and 1757 denouncing the militiamen for their shameful desertions when they were ordered to hold the chain of posts on Virginia's western frontier.[24] No, postwar garrison duty was clearly a task for regulars held to their duty under firm discipline and capable of being shifted from one strategic point to another as circumstances might require.[25]

If we accept Gipson's argument that only the regulars could do this job, then we are confronted with the bill for doing it—a sum ranging from three to four hundred thousand pounds for the maintenance of ten thousand troops. Was it not reasonable for the home government

24. Gipson, *British Empire before the Revolution,* IX, 43.
25. *Ibid.,* X, 5.

to assume that the colonies would underwrite some share of the costs of protecting and guarding their own frontiers?[26]

The answer to this question constitutes the nub of Gipson's closely reasoned argument developed in his later volumes. Gipson argues, first, that the colonies were in a financial position to shoulder a share of that fiscal burden,[27] and second, that the colonies were *undertaxed* on the eve of the Revolution while the British at home were *overtaxed*.[28] As regards the first contention, Gipson gives us a full-scale exposition of the pattern of Parliamentary reimbursement of the colonies for expenses incurred in the course of the intercolonial wars. While the British government never contemplated total reimbursement, the program that was carried out reflected, in Gipson's judgment, a degree of generosity unparalleled in the previous relations of a mother country to her colonies. In addition to the sums received as reimbursement, the colonies, as Gipson shows us, had moved rapidly on their own to the liquidation of the remaining war debts that they had incurred.[29]

Years ago, in the early 1920's, Gipson dug extensively into the tax structure of pre-Revolutionary Connecticut,[30] and his later researches draw heavily upon this early investigation. Earlier, Edward Channing had insisted that colonial appropriations were underestimated by the Treasury officials, and stressed the vast indirect taxation imposed under the Navigation Laws. In disputing Channing, Gipson would also seem to controvert his own hero Jared Ingersoll, Connecticut's Stamp Act collector. His views should also be related to the recent researcher William Marcuse, who has laid stress on the role of the town rather than the colony in colonial Connecticut as the predominant taxing and spending unit and offered evidence to show that the normal peacetime colony rates were at best a third as large as local tax

26. *Ibid.*
27. *Ibid.*, 12–19.
28. *Ibid.*, 109–110.
29. *Ibid.*, 38–110. The question will also be discussed in pt. II of vol. XIII, which is forthcoming.
30. Lawrence H. Gipson, *Connecticut Taxation, 1750–1775* (New Haven, 1933).

rates. Thus, Marcuse contends that, local taxes included, the Connecticut colonist, particularly as a result of the French and Indian War, paid heavier taxes than are usually realized.[31] These issues of financial solvency and comparative tax burdens probably can never be settled, as there would seem to be too many intangibles not susceptible to proper audit, but it is clear that the colonists disliked visible taxes even more than we do, and that John Adams with some justice said in 1780: "America is not used to great taxes, and the people there are not yet disciplined to such enormous taxation as in England."[32]

Central to the Gipson thesis is the view that, under the functioning of the imperial system from 1650 to 1750, great mutual advantages were enjoyed by mother country and colonies, with a fair division, taking everything into consideration, of the financial burdens necessary to support the system.[33] However, with the outbreak of the Great War for the Empire, the old equilibrium was destroyed, and the colonists were in a highly favored position in comparison with the taxpayers of Great Britain. Unprepared and unwilling to consider representation in Parliament, the colonists suggested no viable alternative to taxation by Parliament. When the Ministry decided to tax, it precipitated a constitutional crisis out of which came the Revolutionary War. Ironically, to Gipson, that was Britain's return for entering upon a war with France in 1754, begun, as many members of Parliament affirmed, for the "security of our colonies upon the continent."[34]

In recent years much has been made by Edmund S. and Helen M. Morgan of the fact that the colonists really did not accept the distinction between external and internal taxes and therefore cannot be charged with flagrant opportunism in shifting their constitutional stand

31. William Marcuse, "Local Public Finance in Colonial Connecticut" (unpubl. Ph.D. dissertation, Columbia University, 1956), 202–229.
32. John Adams to Mr. Calkoen, Oct. 17, 1780, in C. F. Adams, ed., *The Works of John Adams*, VII (Boston, 1852), 294.
33. Lawrence H. Gipson, *The Coming of the Revolution, 1763–1775* (New York, 1954), 26–27.
34. Gipson, *British Empire before the Revolution*, VIII, 308, citing *The Parliamentary History of England* . . . (London, 1806–   ), XV, 1271–1272.

from tax to tax.[35] Gipson, and I must say that the evidence would seem to bear him out, reiterates the classic view that there was a clear distinction drawn between internal and external duties in the minds of most colonists from the date of the passage of the Molasses Act of 1733 down to 1766. He has on his side such learned contemporaries as Benjamin Franklin, Thomas Hutchinson, the Connecticut Assembly, the Massachusetts House of Representatives, and Daniel Dulany.[36]

Both in *The Coming of the Revolution,* a book written for the New American Nation Series, and in Volume XII of his *British Empire before the American Revolution,* Gipson lays great stress on the role of planters' debts in fomenting discontent against the empire in Virginia.[37] In reading his pages one is reminded of the sneers the Irish poet Tom Moore aimed at:

> Those vaunted demagogues who nobly rose
> From England's debtors to be England's foes,
> Who could their monarch in their purse forget
> And break allegiance but to cancel debt.[38]

In this area Gipson also stands on firm ground, for the issue of the debts due British and Scottish creditors is fundamental to an understanding of the politics of Virginia not only in the pre-Revolutionary period, but also for more than a decade following the ending of the war.

Like David Ramsay and James Schouler before, Gipson recognizes the role of maturing American nationalism as a catalyst touching off Revolutionary ferment. He attributes the rupture between colonies and mother country neither to wicked men in England nor to

35. Edmund S. and Helen M. Morgan, *The Stamp Act Crisis* (Chapel Hill, 1953), especially 114–115. See also Edmund S. Morgan, "Colonial Ideas of Parliamentary Power, 1764–1766," *William and Mary Quarterly,* 3d. ser., V (1948), 311–341.

36. *Ibid.,* X, 285.

37. *Ibid.,* XII, 199, 203–207. For further discussion of planters' debts see Gipson, *The Coming of the Revolution,* ch. 4, and Gipson, "Virginia Planter Debts before the American Revolution," *Virginia Magazine of History and Biography,* LXIX (1961), 259–277.

38. "To the Lord Viscount Forbes," in *The Poetical Works of Thomas Moore,* ed. by A. D. Godley (London, 1910), 115.

radicals in America, but to the growing maturity of the English-speaking community on this side of the Atlantic "with a mind of its own and a future that it considered peculiarly its own." He does not exculpate British statesmen of all blame. He concedes their failure to realize that the old system of imperial control was no longer applicable to so advanced, so populous and highly cultivated a society. Nor does he exculpate American radicals of responsibility for violent words and acts which he feels were provocative of coercion rather than conciliation. In a closing chapter to Volume XII he points out the extraordinary significance of the new concept of loyalty, not to a person, but to a country, "to America, to its people and its land."[39] Paying tribute to the nobility of concept and expression of much of the Declaration of Independence, he recognizes that it voiced what was in the minds and hearts of the people.[40] Not of all the people, though, Gipson is careful to remind us. Expressing doubts as to whether before the outbreak of the Revolution there was ever a majority of one mind, he credits the Revolutionary movement to "a hard core of dedicated men." Gipson stresses the strength and diversity of the Loyalists, people of all ranks, people of quiet or conservative temper, people numbering the highly educated and the illiterate, who seemed to be present in greatest strength in the West and along the coastal areas of the middle Colonies.[41]

The cause of the Loyalists did not prevail, and although a mighty empire was severed, what survived enjoyed a new and great rebirth. Gipson contrasts the readiness of the British in the twentieth century to repudiate their earlier position that sovereignty was indivisible within the Empire and to concede to different units and nationalities complete freedom with the increasing tendency of the United States since the Civil War to emphasize the supremacy of the Union and the subordination of the states.[42] With gentle irony, too, he contrasts the earlier position of Americans on the issue of taxation without repre-

39. Gipson, *The Coming of the Revolution,* 232; *British Empire before the Revolution,* XII, 354.
40. *Ibid.,* 367–368.
41. *Ibid.,* XIII, pt. ii, 368–370.
42. Gipson, *The Coming of the Revolution,* 233.

sentation to the more recent one, when representation has been denied to the District of Columbia, to territories, and to overseas possessions at the same time that power over such areas has been affirmed by the Supreme Court in the Insular Cases, thereby asserting a right of taxation over people who are not and may never be represented in Congress.[43]

Having plunged into the seas of controversy, Gipson cannot escape some stormy sailing en route. Having directed some of his best aimed shafts at supercharged patriotic legends, he must expect that a few slings and arrows will be hurtling his way. With patience, understanding, and high tolerance he has painted the portraits of the British rulers as well-meaning and beneficent gentlemen. Yet Sir Lewis Namier and his disciples have spent a whole generation proving that political factions were moved less by principle than by a desire for the spoils of office. If we are persuaded by the Namierite contention that parochial issues prevailed in English politics in the pre-Revolutionary period, then it is difficult to understand how men dominated by local, familial, and other narrow ties possessed that breadth of vision needed to encompass the administration of a great empire or sufficient awareness of the maturing and dynamic political situation in America to come to terms with the Americans.

That British administrators did not stumble by accident on the plan of reshaping imperial relations is suggested by a number of pieces of evidence. Most recently, in their fragmented biography of Charles Townshend, Sir Lewis Namier and John Brooke disclose that it was "Champagne Charlie" who, as a junior minister back in 1753, drafted instructions for Sir Danvers Osborn, governor of New York, that Horace Walpole caustically described as "better calculated for the latitude of Mexico and for a Spanish tribunal, than for a free, rich British settlement." These instructions charged the New York Assembly with trampling upon the royal authority and prerogative by assuming "to themselves the disposal of public money," and directed it to make permanent provision for the salaries of the governor, judges, and other officials, and for the security of the province and any fore-

43. *Ibid.*, 233–234.

seeable charges. The money was to be applied by warrants from the governor advised by the Council, the Assembly being merely permitted "from time to time to view and examine . . . accounts." If carried out, Townshend's instructions would have rendered the royal executive financially independent of the colonial assembly. As Namier and Brooke point out, Townshend aimed at a reshaping of colonial government, to which the raising of a revenue by act of the British Parliament became a necessary corollary.[44]

Or consider the views of that much-maligned colonial secretary, Lord George Germain. During the debates on the Coercive Acts, he supported his arguments for changing the government of Massachusetts and putting an end to the town meetings with views such as these: "I would not have men of a mercantile cast every day collecting themselves together, and debating about political matters; I would have them follow their occupations as merchants, and not consider themselves as ministers of that country." The "tumultuous and riotous rabble," he again insisted, "ought, if they had the least prudence, to follow their mercantile employment and not trouble themselves with politics and government, which they do not understand."[45] In 1774 there was, it now seems obvious, a chasm separating American Patriots and British leaders in power, a chasm too wide to be bridged. In Volume XIII Gipson concedes "the failure of British statesmanship at this most crucial period in the life of the eighteenth century British Empire," and holds George III to be a party to that failure, along with Opposition leaders like Burke and Chatham.

It is understandable that Gipson, in his deep concern for the old empire, should share some of the views of his old mentor, Charles M. Andrews, who spoke with scorn of the "muscular radicals." And one might say that some of the portraits of the Patriot leadership are rather one-dimensional. Otis is dismissed as an astute agitator, vacillating from one extreme to another.[46] That "petty county lawyer," Patrick Henry, is portrayed as a "sharp-featured young man, with deep-set,

44. Quoted in Sir Lewis Namier and John Brooke, *Charles Townshend* (London, 1964), 37.
45. *Parliamentary History,* XVII, 1195–1196.
46. *Ibid.,* X, 126n.

piercing eyes, aquiline nose, heavy eyebrows, hollow cheeks, and a mouth that never really wreathed a smile."[47] Granted that the extreme left had its full share of angularity and demagoguery, I am sure that Mr. Gipson would be generous enough to concede that hidden depths, complexity, a talent for rationalizing public interest and private motive, along with strength of purpose and a sense of dedication, constitute some of the keys to the characters of the men who took this nation to the brink of Revolution, then successfully guided the craft over the cataract to a safe haven. As Gipson himself points out in his illuminating discussion of the Declaration of Independence, there was more to the American Revolution than the relatively narrow issue of self-determination. There was the larger dimension of human freedom.

Mr. Gipson is too subtle a scholar not to recognize that the implications of his lawyerlike brief on behalf of the imperial authorities place him squarely in the camp of the economic determinists. After all, if demagogues could stir up discontent among Virginia debtors and disappointed western land speculators, and if disaffection took root and flourished among big-time smugglers smarting from humiliations suffered at the hands of royal officials as well as among penny-pinching taxpayers who put their pocketbooks ahead of the welfare of the empire, then it would seem that the Patriots seceded, not from any different conception of the British Constitution from that prevailing in England, but rather because of narrow notions of economic self-interest. I feel sure that Mr. Gipson would not want others to press this thesis too rigorously, and that he would concede the important role played by cultural nationalism in separating the destinies of the two great families of English-speaking peoples. The American Revolution may have been triggered by disputes over taxes, but the final break came because of a difference over ideas. It was not just a bourgeois revolt from the confines of a tight mercantilist system, as the Marxist historians would view it, but a broad movement of liberation that has not yet run its course.

47. Gipson, *The Coming of the Revolution,* 53.

So much has been said about Lawrence Gipson as a scholar that there is a danger of neglecting a warm-hearted, generous human being, whose dedication to the cause of early American history and whose selfless gift of time to seekers of knowledge are proverbial in our profession. Despite his vast achievements and his commanding stature among his contemporaries, Lawrence Gipson has a becoming modesty, a readiness to accept suggestions as well as to give them, that might well serve as an example and a constant reminder to the younger and less patient group of American historians. Dig, dig deeply before you generalize! In the course of the years that I have been coediting the New American Nation Series I have had to deal with a good many authors. Now, as an author myself, I know that the breed can be prickly and supersensitive, highly intolerant of suggestions for revisions, and indignant at intimations that theirs is not necessarily the noblest prose since Edmund Burke. Not so with Lawrence Gipson, who is as ready to take suggestions as he is to offer his counsel. As regards the latter commodity, I have as an editor had occasion to call rather frequently upon Lawrence Gipson for such counsel regarding other manuscripts in his field. Despite his pressing burdens, he has always responded promptly. His thoughtful and penetrating observations reveal enormous funds of bibliographical learning and an extraordinary knowledge of close detail—of royal ordinances, and forts, and trails, and old maps. Only such scholarly vigilance can safeguard a series against blunders both egregious and minute.

If by some miracle Lawrence Gipson could be placed in a time capsule and transplanted to Rittenhouse or Berkeley Squares in his beloved eighteenth century, I feel somehow that there are two personages with whom he might feel most at home. One of them, it goes without saying, would be his old friend William Shirley, who had a lofty vision of an empire as a whole with proper participation by each of the parts. The other would be my old friend John Jay, who, like Mr. Gipson, could sniff French or Spanish intrigue from afar, and who looked forward, once the Revolution's bitterness had ebbed, to the establishment of amicable relations between America and Britain under a liberal trade system. I am confident that Lawrence Gipson would have approved Jay's stand as Chief Justice when he told the Virginia debtors that they would have to pay to their British and Scottish creditors the debts honorably contracted before the war. I am sure that he would not have joined the chorus of criticism but instead have applauded the stubborn but high-minded New Yorker when, on his mission to William Wyndham, Lord Grenville, in 1794, he refused to press the claims of the southern planters to slaves removed or liberated by the British armies during the war, declining to carry out this instruction on the ground that to press the issue would be to put America morally in the wrong before the world.

The spacious empire of Lawrence Henry Gipson has in truth been more enduring than the first British Empire, which crumbled on the rock of revolution, or even the second, which, recognizing the inevitability of decolonization, has shrunk to a shadow of its former magnitude. That spacious empire has embraced an abiding community of interest among the English-speaking people on both sides of the Atlantic, a community of interest that passed the test of two world wars and has withstood sniping and sabotage within the Atlantic alliance. If George III might have been astonished to see the present *entente cordiale* between mother country and former insurgent plantations, the Earl of Shelburne might well regard this present fact of diplomatic life as a vindication of his creative statesmanship. To Lawrence Henry Gipson it is, fittingly, the re-creation, if not the fulfillment, of his spacious empire.

CHANGING PERSPECTIVES

EMIL OBERHOLZER

Puritanism Revisited

IN HIS PRESIDENTIAL ADDRESS to the American Society of Church History twenty years ago, James Hastings Nichols observed that the study of Puritanism was "probably the most important single current in recent American church history."[1] Since then, the literature on American Puritanism has grown beyond anything one might have expected in 1950.[2] At that time, one could count on the fingers of one hand the great writers on American Puritanism. Perry Miller easily topped the list with his *Orthodoxy in Massachusetts*[3] and *The New England Mind*.[4] Then there were his three colleagues at Harvard: Samuel Eliot Morison, author of *The Puritan Pronaos*,[5] Kenneth Mur-

1. "The Art of Church History," *Church History*, XX (Mar. 1951), 7.
2. What follows cannot pretend to be an exhaustive survey of the recent writings on the subject, but at best will attempt to trace some developments, indicate some impressions, draw some conclusions, and offer a few suggestions. For recent historiographical studies, see Edmund S. Morgan, "Perry Miller and the Historians," American Antiquarian Society *Proceedings*, LXXIV, pt. I (1964), 11–18, and "Historians of Early New England," in Ray Allen Billington, ed., *The Reinterpretation of American History* (New York, 1969); David D. Hall, "Understanding the Puritans," in Herbert J. Bass, ed., *The State of American History* (Chicago, 1970), 330–349, and Michael McGiffert, "American Puritan Studies in the 1960's," *William and Mary Quarterly*, 3d ser., XXVII (1970), 36–67. McGiffert's study is noteworthy for its use of questionnaires. Good bibliographical essays appear in many of the books cited below.
3. Cambridge, Mass., 1933.
4. New York, 1939.
5. New York, 1936.

dock, known for his *Literature and Theology in Colonial New England,*[6] and Ralph Barton Perry, whose *Puritanism and Democracy*[7] was packed with pungent phrases which stuck in the mind. Protestantism (which for Perry was almost synonymous with Puritanism) "sought to be more Christian than the Christians,"[8] and the Calvinists were "the shock troops of protestantism."[9] (For some unknown reason, Perry always capitalized "Catholic," but never "protestant.") And who could forget his picture of "The Moral Athlete"?[10] The remaining finger was allotted to a professor at Columbia University, Herbert Wallace Schneider, for his book *The Puritan Mind.*[11] Had there been a sixth finger, it would have been divided between the two writers on the English background: Marshall M. Knappen, for his *Tudor Puritanism,*[12] and Barnard College's William Haller, whose interest in John Milton's *Areopagitica* had led him to delve into the writings of the theologians as well as the poets and to write *The Rise of Puritanism.*[13] But the one name which invariably came up when Puritanism in New England was mentioned was that of Perry Miller.

Of all the contributions Perry Miller made, none has occasioned more investigation and aroused greater controversy than his thesis that the Puritans were covenant theologians. The teachings of John Cocceius, with at least some reference to his English followers, had been examined long before,[14] and as Miller himself observed, his thesis had been anticipated by others.[15] But it remained for Professor Miller, in a paper read in 1935 and published two years later, to show how great had been the influence of the covenant theology on the teachings of the New England ministers.[16] That the New England

6. Cambridge, Mass., 1949.
7. New York, 1944.
8. Perry, *Puritanism and Democracy*, 87.
9. *Ibid.*, 91.
10. *Ibid.*, ch. 10.
11. New York, 1930.
12. Chicago, 1939.
13. New York, 1938.
14. Gottlieb Schrenk, *Gottesreich und Bund in älteren Protestantismus* (Gütersloh, Germany, 1923).
15. *Errand into the Wilderness* (Cambridge, Mass., 1956), 49.
16. "The Marrow of Puritan Divinity," Colonial Society of Massachusetts

Puritans were covenant theologians has not been denied. But had Miller understood the covenant aright? And did the covenant theology place the Puritans beyond the range of Calvinism? Ralph Barton Perry considered the covenant theology "a form of Calvinism,"[17] but a year later Peter Y. De Jong concluded that federal theology and Calvinism did not mix.[18] Studying early American Presbyterianism, Leonard J. Trinterud noticed the influence of covenant theology, via New England and Northern Ireland, and concluded that "the Federal Theology took form so gradually within Puritanism that its incompatibility with [John] Calvin's thought was seldom noticed."[19] Trinterud then turned to examine the origins of English Puritan teaching and, in one of the most important articles on Puritanism in the last twenty years, demonstrated that the influence of Calvin had been negligible. The covenant theme as interpreted by Ulrich Zwingli and Heinrich Bullinger at Zürich, by Johannes Oecolampadius at Basel, and by Wolfgang Capito and Martin Bucer at Strasbourg, to mention only the most important, was known in England when Calvin was just emerging as a Protestant. In the reign of Edward VI, Bucer and his Italian colleague, Peter Martyr Vermigli, visited England; during the Marian reaction, the majority of the exiles went to northern Switzerland or the Rhineland and only a small group to Geneva, and in the early years of the reign of Elizabeth I, the Geneva party lost its bid for power.[20] This conclusion was supported by Jerald C. Brauer, who observed "an almost wholesale adoption of Covenant Theology" in England;[21] and John T. McNeill, who also called attention to

---

Proceedings, XXXII (1937), 247–300, and reprinted in *Errand,* 50–98. An earlier presentation of the thesis is found in "The Puritan Theory of the Sacraments in Seventeenth-Century New England," *Catholic Historical Review,* XXII (1936), 409–425.

17. *Puritanism and Democracy,* 93.

18. *The Covenant Idea in New England Theology* (Grand Rapids, Mich., 1945).

19. *The Forming of an American Tradition* (Philadelphia, 1949), 171–172.

20. "The Origins of Puritanism," *Church History,* XX (March, 1951), 37–61.

21. "Reflections on the Nature of English Puritanism," *Church History,* XXIII (1954), 99–108. Cf. Knappen, *Tudor Puritanism,* 4–5, and Ernest F. Kevan, *The Grace of Law* (Grand Rapids, Mich., 1964), 40.

Lutheran and Zwinglian elements in Puritanism, referred to Bullinger as "the greatest Continental ally of Tudor Puritanism."[22]

The alleged incompatibility of covenant theology and Calvinism has given rise to considerable discussion. Trinterud's assertion elicited a rebuke from a reviewer,[23] and a year later Everett Emerson suggested that the federal theology sought to mitigate the rigors not of Calvin's own teaching but of Reformed scholasticism. But because the Puritans were out to convert people, and because Calvin preached to presumably converted Christians, the covenant was less obvious in the work of the Genevan theologian.[24] Other writers supported Emerson's argument by showing that Cocceius's purpose had been to recover biblical thinking in the face of the new scholasticism[25] and by reassessing the covenant idea in the light of predestinarian doctrine.[26] In a study of John Bunyan's teachings, Richard L. Greaves distinguished three principal types of covenant theology, two of which had plainly Calvinistic roots,[27] and in a brilliant study, *The Elizabethan Puritan Movement,* Patrick Collinson considered the federal theology as not necessarily a distortion of Calvinism.[28] John Dykstra Eusden, who may be the most important contemporary scholar of the covenant theology, in 1968 brought out a new edition of Ames's *Medulla.*[29] Ten years earlier, Eusden had observed the similarities between Puritanism and Calvinism, but also had recognized the contributions from

22. *Modern Christian Movements* (Philadelphia, 1954), 26. See John T. McNeill, *The History and Character of Calvinism* (New York, 1954), 309. McNeill notes that the word "Calvinist" (and the earlier "Calvinian") was broadly construed to comprehend "Helvetic" and "Zwinglian" as well as what was distinctively Genevan.

23. G. D. Henderson, *Journal of Ecclesiastical History,* II (1951), 240–242.

24. "Calvin and Covenant Theology," *Church History,* XXV (1956), 136–144. Also see David D. Hall, "Understanding the Puritans," in Bass, ed., *State of American History,* 335.

25. Charles S. McCoy, "Johannes Cocceius: Federal Theologian," *Scottish Journal of Theology,* XVI (1963), 352–370.. Cf. J. A. Ross Mackenzie, "The Covenant Theology," *Journal of Presbyterian History,* XLIV (1966), 198–204.

26. John von Rohr, "Covenant and Assurance in Early New England Puritanism," *Church History,* XXXIV (1965), 195–203.

27. "John Bunyan and Covenant Thought in the Seventeenth Century," *Church History,* XXXVI (1967), 151–203.

28. (Berkeley and Los Angeles, 1967), 435.

29. William Ames, *Marrow of Theology* (Boston, 1968).

Zürich, Basel, and Strasbourg.[30] In his introduction to Ames's work, Eusden noted the novelties in Ames's thought and observed that, covenant theologian though he was, Ames had not repudiated predestination.[31] That the controversy raised by Perry Miller is by no means concluded is suggested by a recent article which once more accuses Miller of misrepresenting both Calvinism and the covenant theology.[32]

Perry Miller's work also came under attack from critics who complained that, in his concern with the Puritans' intellect, he had neglected their feelings.[33] In *Puritanism in Old and New England,*[34] Alan Simpson, who acknowledged a "special debt" to both Miller and A. S. P. Woodhouse,[35] implicitly—and ever so gently—rebuked Miller for his omission and noted that the Puritans "suffered and yearned and strived with an unbelievable intensity; and no superstructure of logic ought to be allowed to mask that turmoil of feeling."[36] Five years earlier, Jerald C. Brauer had called attention to Puritan mysticism.[37] As if to remedy the omission of the theme in Miller's works, Geoffrey Nuttall devoted an entire volume to *The Holy Spirit in Puritan Faith and Experience,*[38] and Fulton J. MacLear demonstrated the importance of the Holy Spirit in early New England thought.[39] A study of Cotton Mather's correspondence with August Hermann Francke has

30. *Puritans, Lawyers, and Politics in Early Seventeenth-Century England* (New Haven, Conn., 1958), 19–27.

31. Ames, *Marrow,* especially 26–27, 47–48.

32. George M. Marsden, "Perry Miller's Rehabilitation of the Puritans: A Critique," *Church History,* XXXIX (1970), 91–105.

33. In fairness to Perry Miller, one should note that the titles of his two greatest works plainly state that they are concerned with the Puritans' intellect: *The New England Mind: The Seventeenth Century,* and *The New England Mind: From Colony to Province.*

34. Chicago, 1955.

35. *Ibid.,* vii.

36. *Ibid.,* 21.

37. "Puritan Mysticism and the Development of Liberalism," *Church History,* XIX (1950), 151–170.

38. Oxford, Eng., 1946.

39. " 'The Heart of New England Rent': The Mystical Element in Early Puritan Piety," *Mississippi Valley Historical Review,* XLIII (1955–56), 621–652.

shown that Mather was both an ecumenist and a Christian with a
profound sense of the Holy Spirit,[40] and researches into religious
autobiography have disclosed that a strong pneumatic element per-
vaded both Puritan and Quaker writings.[41] Robert Middlekauff has
questioned the assumption that emotions necessarily are the cause of
ideas and suggests that the interaction of piety and intellect found in
the diaries of Cotton Mather and Samuel Sewall be considered a
determinant of Puritan character.[42]

By the time Simpson called for a closer look at the Puritans' hearts,
Perry Miller's juridical interpretation of the covenant[43] had already
been questioned by Leonard Trinterud. Miller, who had little interest
in the Bible or in creeds, and who certainly had no genius for abstract
theology, regarded the covenant as a useful device to bring the people
into the churches by assuring them of their salvation. Trinterud perceived that the covenant theology answered the needs of the heart
because "it could so readily and simply give intellectual expression to
the Augustinian theology, the lush, warm flow of mystical piety and
devotion, the bride-mysticism, the rich, highly allegorical interpretation of the Bible, especially the Song of Songs, the preaching of peni-
tence, the love of pilgrimages and the pilgrim motif, all of which had
since medieval times played so great a role in English religious life,
and all of which was quite specifically English."[44] Two years later,
H. Richard Niebuhr discussed the covenant theme in a much wider
context and almost casually remarked that its principal sources were
biblical.[45]

40. Ernst Benz, "The Pietist and Puritan Sources of Early Protestant World
Missions (Cotton Mather and A. H. Francke)," *Church History,* XX (June
1951), 28–55.
41. Daniel B. Shea, Jr., *Spiritual Autobiography in Early America* (Princeton, N.J., 1968). Also see J. William Frost, "The Dry Bones of Quaker
Theology," *Church History,* XXXIX (1970), 503–523, and Charles E. Park,
"Puritans and Quakers," *New England Quarterly,* XXVII (1954), 53–74.
42. "Piety and Intellect in Puritanism," *William and Mary Quarterly,* 3d ser.,
XXII (1965), 457–470.
43. Miller, "Marrow," in *Errand,* passim, but especially 71–74.
44. Trinterud, "Origins of Puritanism," *Church History,* XX (March
1951), 50.
45. "The Idea of Covenant and American Democracy," *Church History,*
XXIII (1954), 130.

In *The Heart Prepared*,[46] Norman Pettit considered the scriptural basis of the covenant theology and demonstrated that one school of early Puritan thought considered conversion as a gradually unfolding experience for which one could prepare. From his study of the English and American "preparationist," Pettit concluded that this theory was widely accepted in New England until John Norton drastically altered the meaning of preparation in 1657 and Giles Firmin, an English Nonconformist who had been ejected from his living in 1662, introduced moralism into the religion of New England. While none of Pettit's conclusions vitiate the thesis that the Puritans were covenant theologians, they radically change the "bargain" theory and raise the question whether the covenant theology was the door to religious experience or its intellectual expression.[47] The year after Pettit's book appeared, David Kobrin published an article which also showed that the clergy of early Massachussetts regarded conversion as "a process with definite steps continuing over a period of time."[48] By 1650, Kobrin observed, the churches had adopted membership policies in accordance with this theory and considered the Eucharist as an efficacious instrument of salvation. These studies partly complemented and partly conflicted with Edmund S. Morgan's earlier study of the actual admissions procedures of the churches. In *Visible Saints,* Morgan came to the startling, but amply documented, conclusion that what was to become the standard Congregational practice had begun in Massachusetts, whence it had spread to Plymouth and England, rather than the invention of the Separatists on the Cape. In Plymouth, the churches had required that prospective communicants assent to the covenant and demonstrate some understanding of the

46. *The Heart Prepared: Grace and Conversion in Puritan Spiritual Life* (New Haven, Conn., and London, Eng., 1966). Also see Norman Pettit, "Lydia's Conversion: An Issue in Hooker's Departure," in Cambridge Historical Society *Publications,* XL (1967), 59–83.

47. Pettit, *Heart Prepared,* especially 9–11, 217–222. That Calvin, in a passing reference, alluded to preparation is shown in Emerson, "Calvin and Covenant Theology," *Church History,* XXV (1956), 140.

48. "The Expansion of the Visible Church in New England, 1629–1650," *Church History,* XXXVI (1967), 189–209.

church's teaching; the Bay Puritans went further and demanded evidence of saving grace.[49]

The Halfway Covenant, together with the closely related question of a possible decline in religious fervor, also received attention from Morgan, who in 1961 queried whether the change inaugurated in 1662 necessarily indicated a decline. Was it not possible, Morgan asked, that many members of the second generation showed "an extraordinary religious scrupulosity" by refraining from the Lord's Supper lest they enter too lightly upon the covenant obligations?[50] That this possibility was not in the least far-fetched is indicated by a Scotsman's observation that in the Highlands "the high standard of holiness demanded by public opinion deters many people from joining the Church, who attend it regularly."[51] Darrett Rutman, who may have read too much into Morgan's article, took issue with his colleague and insisted that the Halfway Covenant could not be understood apart from a decline.[52] In accordance with a promise made to his critic,[53] Morgan affirmed and elaborated his argument in *Visible Saints*.[54] In the most thorough recent study of the Halfway Covenant, Robert G. Pope supported Miller and Morgan in their judgment that the synod of 1662 had acted wisely. Pope believes the Halfway Covenant had a salutary effect on the churches, and that the repeal of the charter in 1684 did much more harm than the admission of the children of noncommunicants to baptism. Nevertheless, Pope observed, it had a divisive influence and opened the door to a proliferation of polities.[55]

49. *Visible Saints: The History of a Puritan Idea* (New York, 1963).

50. Edmund S. Morgan, "New England Puritanism: Another Approach," *William and Mary Quarterly*, 3d ser., XVIII (1961), 236–242.

51. Andrew Landale Drummond, *Story of American Protestantism* (Boston, 1951), 57n.

52. "God's Bridge Falling Down: 'Another Approach' to New England Puritanism Assayed," *William and Mary Quarterly*, 3d ser., XIX (1962), 408–421.

53. Letter to the Editor, *ibid.*, 642–644.

54. Ch. 4.

55. *The Half-Way Covenant* (Princeton, N.J., 1969). That many Congregationalists regarded the measure as a betrayal of their principles and believed the Baptists to be closer to the ideal of pure churches is shown by E. Brooks Holifield in "On Toleration in Massachusetts," *Church History*, XXXVIII (1969), 188–200.

Roger Williams has been a new man since the early 1950's, when Mauro Calamandrei and Perry Miller produced the prototype of the new Williams portrait.[56] Miller had "long been persuaded" that recent biographers inspired by political liberalism had hopelessly romanticized Williams, but it remained for the obscure Italian scholar to serve as a catalyst for the expression of Miller's ideas.[57] In an article published in 1952, Calamandrei showed that Williams was not the liberal Baptist, or the freethinker, or the political theorist he had been portrayed to be. He was a democrat in politics, but only because of his religious presuppositions, which were anything but democratic.[58] His political ideas were the incidental by-product of his religious convictions, and these were the result of his reliance on typology in biblical interpretation.[59] Although the work of Calamandrei and Miller has not gone entirely unscathed, it may fairly be said that these scholars have wrought one of the most thoroughly accepted changes in our understanding of the colonial period.[60] Alan Simpson has emphasized that we cannot understand Williams unless we see him as "a religious enthusiast";[61] Ola Winslow, in a biography devoid of theological depth, implicitly warned against present-mindedness in the interpretation of Williams,[62] and Edmund S. Morgan, in a study of Williams's theory of church and state, followed the lead of Calamandrei and

56. Mauro Calamandrei, "Some Neglected Aspects of Roger Williams's Thought," *Church History*, XXI (1952), 235–258; Perry Miller, *Roger Williams: His Contribution to the American Tradition* (New York and Indianapolis, 1953). See Le Roy Moore, Jr., "Roger Williams and the Historians," *Church History*, XXXII (1963), 432–451, which shows that the realistic approach of Calamandrei and Miller was anticipated in the eighteenth century by John Callender and Isaac Backus.

57. Miller, *Williams*, xiii.

58. Calamandrei, "Some Neglected Aspects," *Church History*, XXI (1952), 256.

59. Also see Perry Miller, "Essay in Introduction," in *The Complete Works of Roger Williams*, VII (New York, 1963), 5–25.

60. A few recent publications show no signs of being influenced by the new interpretations: Robert C. Whittemore, *Makers of the American Mind* (New York, 1964), and Shirley Barker, *Builders of New England* (New York, 1965).

61. "How Democratic Was Roger Williams?" *William and Mary Quarterly*, 3d ser., XIII (1956), 52–67.

62. *Master Roger Williams: A Biography* (New York, 1957).

Miller.[63] Nevertheless, some flaws in the thesis have turned up. The assertion that Williams regarded the New Testament as repudiating, rather than fulfilling, the Old has been refuted by Le Roy Moore,[64] and Sacvan Berkovitch has shown that the typology on which Williams relied was in common use at the time.[65] Jesper Rosenmeier has called attention to the importance of the Incarnation in the Puritan view of *Heilsgeschichte;* John Cotton and Roger Williams were of one mind about the importance of the God-made-man, but they differed in interpreting his significance for the coming kingdom of God.[66] None of these revisions vitiates the most important elements in the new portrait of Williams, and it is safe to assume that it will be a long time before he will again be depicted as a romantic freethinker,[67] a political theorist who anticipated Thomas Jefferson,[68] or an "irrepressible democrat."[69]

Thomas Hooker's position may be approaching a reevaluation similar to that accorded to Williams. In 1931, Perry Miller questioned the extravagant claims earlier historians had made for Hooker as a democrat and observed that Connecticut was patterned on the same principles as Massachusetts.[70] Some time elapsed before this challenge found a response, and in 1952 Clinton Rossiter (who created a little confusion by using the words "judicious Hooker" with reference to Thomas, instead of reserving them for his more famous namesake Richard) also concluded that colonial Connecticut was no democ-

63. *Roger Williams: The Church and the State* (New York, 1967).

64. "Religious Liberty: Roger Williams and the Revolution," *Church History,* XXIV (1956), 57–76.

65. "Typology in Puritan New England: The Williams-Cotton Controversy Reassessed," *American Quarterly,* XIX (1967), 166–191.

66. "The Teacher and the Witness: John Cotton and Roger Williams," *William and Mary Quarterly,* 3d ser., XXV (1968), 408–431.

67. Vernon Louis Parrington, *Main Currents in American Thought* (New York, 1930), I, 62–75.

68. James Ernst, *Roger Williams: New England Firebrand* (New York, 1932).

69. Samuel Hugh Brockunier, *The Irrepressible Democrat* (New York, 1940). The most recent biography, Henry Chupack's *Roger Williams* (New York, 1969), was not available to the writer when this essay went to the editor.

70. "Thomas Hooker and the Democracy of Connecticut," *New England Quarterly,* IV (1931), 663–712, and reprinted in Miller, *Errand,* 18–47.

racy.[71] Roland Bainton disposed of the older view in Churchillian language when he bluntly declared: "Never have claims so great been supported by evidence so quantitatively slender."[72] In 1963, however, Sidney Ahlstrom, one of Bainton's colleagues at Yale, called attention to Hooker's real significance, which was not as a politician, but as a theologian. Ahlstrom implicitly agreed with Thomas Prince's description of Hooker as the John Chrysostom of New England.[73]

Of all the American Puritan leaders, none has received as much attention as Jonathan Edwards, who appears to be enjoying a significant renaissance. Several theological schools and religion departments are now offering semester-long seminars on Edwards, and the Yale University Press is republishing his works. Under Perry Miller's direction, Paul Ramsey edited Edwards's most difficult work, *Freedom of the Will*,[74] and John E. Smith did the same for his *Religious Affections*.[75] After an interruption caused by Miller's death, the work has been resumed under the general editorship of John E. Smith. To date, Clyde Holbrook's edition of *Original Sin*[76] and Clarence C. Goen's edition of *The Great Awakening*[77] have appeared. The editors' introductions are in themselves worth study; Holbrook, for instance, examines Edwards's sources and concludes that he used Calvin less frequently than is generally supposed, and Goen provides a good map showing the location of the revivals.

The merits of Edwards as philosopher and theologian remain open to question. Two years after Parrington had portrayed Edwards as a tragic figure whose fame—or notoriety—rested chiefly on his hellfire

71. "Thomas Hooker," *The New England Quarterly*, XXI (1952), 459–488.
72. "Thomas Hooker and the Puritan Contribution to Democracy" (first published in 1958), in *Christian Unity and Religion in New England* (Boston, 1967), 239–251.
73. "Thomas Hooker—Puritanism and Democratic Citizenship: A Preliminary Inquiry into Some Relationships of Religion and American Civic Responsibility," *Church History*, XXXII (1963), 415–431.
74. New Haven, 1957. The new editions, it will be noticed, mercifully use shorter titles.
75. New Haven, 1959.
76. New Haven and London, 1970.
77. New Haven and London, 1972.

and damnation sermons,[78] Arthur Cushman McGiffert, Jr., sought to
redeem Edwards in a biography which emphasized his role in the
Great Awakening and concluded that the noted divine was "a well-
balanced character."[79] Next came a volume by Ola Winslow, which
remains the best introduction to Edwards's life,[80] and this was followed
by Perry Miller's great intellectual biography.[81] The new Edwards
was radically different from the one Parrington had depicted. Gone
was the "anachronism" that had sacrificed a good mind for the "ig-
noble ends" of reconciling philosophy with theology. The new Edwards was a man well ahead of his time, open to Newtonian and
Lockean ideas. But soon after the publication of Miller's book, a
critic reverted to the older tradition and argued that Edwards was a
medievalist because he made philosophy subservient to theology.[82]
Then, in 1960, appeared a book which made Edwards look almost
contemporary: Douglas J. Elwood's *The Philosophical Theology of
Jonathan Edwards*.[83] (The language of this book immediately reminds
one of the late Paul J. Tillich; at the very beginning the author refers
to "the principle of correlation.") Elwood sees Edwards as drawing
on Scripture and Newtonian physics, on Christian experience and
Lockean empiricism, on faith and on reason in his effort to understand man's relationship to his Creator. The question whether man is
a being of reason or emotion becomes irrelevant; important is that
he is a religious being. Elwood's Edwards, living in an age still governed by religious ideas that were aloof from the newer currents of
thought, is distinctly avant-garde. Six years later, however, two
scholars questioned Edwards's "modernity" anew. In a cleverly dia-

78. Parrington, *Main Currents,* I, 148–163.
79. *Jonathan Edwards* (New York, 1932), 111.
80. *Jonathan Edwards, 1703–1758* (New York, 1941).
81. *Jonathan Edwards* (New York, 1949). Also see Perry Miller, "The
Rhetoric of Sensation" (first published in Harry Levin, ed., *Perspectives of
Criticism* [Cambridge, Mass., 1950]), in *Errand,* 168–183.
82. Vincent Tomas, "The Modernity of Jonathan Edwards," *New England
Quarterly,* XXV (1952), 60–84. Also see H. G. Townsend, "The Will and the
Understanding in the Philosophy of Jonathan Edwards," *Church History,*
XVI (1947), 210–220, and Claude M. Newlin, *Philosophy and Religion in
Colonial America* (New York, 1962), 25.
83. New York, 1960.

grammed article inspired by what he considered to be Elwood's misrepresentation of Edwards's Neoplatonism, Robert C. Whittemore found that by adhering to an ontology of being instead of becoming, Edwards was a medievalist after all.[84] About the same time Peter Gay, a champion of the enlightenment, implicitly concluded that Parrington had been right after all. Gay regards Edwards as a tragedy and as "the last medieval American—at least among the intellectuals."[85]

Studies of a less controversial nature, or on more limited aspects of Edwards's life and work, also have added to our knowledge of the great divine. In a slim volume which eschews all criticism and evaluation, Alfred Owen Aldridge has provided a succinct summary of Edwards's ideas.[86] That Edwards was both a Calvinist and a federal theologian is the argument of an article by C. Conrad Cherry, which also provides a much needed warning that both Calvinism and the covenant theology are easily misrepresented if certain features are considered out of context. Moreover, Cherry draws attention to the importance of the Incarnation in the covenant theology,[87] and another writer has shown that Edwards preached the "visibility of God" in Christ.[88] Others have written on Edwards's work as an evangelist,[89] on his profound sense of the invisible Church and his doctrine of justi-

84. "Jonathan Edwards and the Theology of the Sixth Way," *Church History*, XXXV (1966), 60–75. Edwards's Neoplatonism is also discussed in Gerhard T. Alexis, "Jonathan Edwards and the Theocratic Ideal," *ibid.*, XXXV (1966), 328–343. Also see Whittemore, *Makers of the American Mind*.

85. Peter Gay, *A Loss of Mastery: Puritan Historians in Colonial America* (Berkeley and Los Angeles, 1966).

86. *Jonathan Edwards* (New York, 1964). A biography by James Wood Playsted, *Mr. Jonathan Edwards* (New York, 1968), makes no contribution to scholarship, but William Boyd Duff, *Jonathan Edwards Then and Now: A Satirical Study in Predestination* (Pittsburgh, Pa., 1959), wherein the author invents a dialogue between Edwards and a contemporary interviewer, at least reflects some imagination.

87. *The Theology of Jonathan Edwards: A Reappraisal* (Garden City, N.Y., 1966). Also see C. Conrad Cherry, "The Puritan Notion of the Covenant in Jonathan Edwards's Doctrine of Faith," *Church History*, XXXIV (1965), 328–334.

88. James Carse, *Jonathan Edwards and the Visibility of God* (New York, 1967).

89. John H. Gerstner, *Steps to Salvation: The Evangelistic Message of Jonathan Edwards* (Philadelphia, 1960). Also see Gerald J. Goodwin, "The Myth of 'Arminian-Calvinism' in Eighteenth-Century New England," *New England Quarterly*, XLI (1968), 213–237.

fication,[90] on his mysticism,[91] and on "Jonathan Edwards and Melancholy,"[92] and C. G. Goen has shown that Edwards was "America's first post-millennial thinker," whose eschatology blended orthodox Calvinism with a chiliasm not found in the teachings of the Geneva reformer.[93] In a study based on a careful reading of his sermons, Ralph G. Turnbull finds that the real justification for Edwards's greatness lies in his work as preacher and pastor: Edwards was the model parish minister.[94]

Among the other biographical works worth noting are Raymond Stearns's life of Hugh Peter,[95] and books on John Winthrop, Ezra Stiles, the Mathers, John Cotton, and Anne Hutchinson. Cotton, long neglected, has been the subject of a biography by Larzer Ziff, whose work also throws light on the Congregational churches of the time.[96] Cotton's writings have been briefly described by Everett Emerson,[97] and his most important works edited by Larzer Ziff.[98] The life of Cotton's erstwhile friend, Anne Hutchinson, has been thoroughly reexamined by Emery Battis, whose combination of historical research, sociological inquiry, psychiatric (and gynecological!) investigation, and generous use of the imagination (the latter limited to nonessentials) has resulted in a unique biography.[99] The "Antinomian" label

90. Thomas A. Schafer, "Jonathan Edwards's Conception of the Church," *Church History*, XXIV (1955), 51–66, and "Jonathan Edwards and Justification by Faith," *Church History*, XX (Dec. 1951), 55–67.

91. David C. Pierce, "Jonathan Edwards and the New Sense of Glory," *New England Quarterly*, XLI (1968), 82–95. Also see Elwood, *Jonathan Edwards*, 135.

92. Gail Thain Parker, "Jonathan Edwards and Melancholy," *New England Quarterly*, XLI (1968), 193–212.

93. "Jonathan Edwards: A New Departure in Eschatology," *Church History*, XXVIII (1959), 25–40. Also see Alexis, "Jonathan Edwards," *Church History*, XXXV (1966), 328–343.

94. *Jonathan Edwards the Preacher* (Grand Rapids, Mich., 1958).

95. *The Strenuous Puritan: Hugh Peter, 1598–1660* (Urbana, Ill., 1954).

96. *The Career of John Cotton: Puritanism and the American Experience* (Princeton, N.J., 1962).

97. *John Cotton* (New York, 1965).

98. *John Cotton and the Churches of New England* (Cambridge, Mass., 1968).

99. *Saints and Sectaries: Anne Hutchinson and the Antinomian Controversy in the Massachusetts Bay Colony* (Chapel Hill, 1962). See the equally unusual review by Bernard Bailyn in *William and Mary Quarterly*, 3d ser., XXI (1964), 123–127.

seems to be firmly stuck to Mrs. Hutchinson, although earlier scholars had perceived that it was a misnomer.[100] The word appears again in the title of a collection of documents, whose editor has concluded that Mrs. Hutchinson was the scapegoat in a quarrel between John Cotton and his colleagues.[101] How one Puritan leader dealt with the problem of the Christian politician in a less-than-perfect world is depicted in a biography of John Winthrop,[102] whose author has also given us a life of the distinguished divine and educator Ezra Stiles.[103] The intellectual contribution of the Mather dynasty is the subject of a recently published book by Robert Middlekauff,[104] which shows the influence of Pettit's work on preparation. Interesting in relation to Miller's treatment of the covenant is the observation that Increase Mather regarded the church covenant not as a bargain, but as "total capitulation" by the church member.[105]

The significance of Perry Miller as the single most important cause of researches into American Puritanism notwithstanding, not all that has been wirtten on the subject touches on the theses he propounded and the controversies he engendered. Nor can Miller's work explain the growing interest in American Puritanism among students, to which the recent output of source books bears witness.[106] Michael McGiffert

100. Charles Francis Adams, *Three Episodes in Massachusetts History*, 2d ed. (Boston and New York, 1892), I, 435; Williston Walker, *Ten New England Leaders* (New York, 1901), 81; Charles M. Andrews, *The Colonial Period of American History*, I (New Haven, Conn., 1934), 475.

101. David D. Hall, ed., *The Antinomian Controversy, 1636–1638: A Documentary History* (Middletown, Conn., 1968).

102. Edmund S. Morgan, *The Puritan Dilemma: The Story of John Winthrop* (Boston, 1958).

103. Edmund S. Morgan, *The Gentle Puritan: A Life of Ezra Stiles, 1727–1795* (New Haven, Conn., 1962). Also see Richard D. Birdsall, "Ezra Stiles versus the New Divinity Men," *American Quarterly*, XVII (1965), 248–258, and Edmund S. Morgan, "Ezra Stiles and Timothy Dwight," Massachusetts Historical Society *Proceedings*, LXXII (1960), 101–117.

104. *The Mathers: Three Generations of Puritan Intellectuals, 1596–1728* (New York, 1971).

105. *Ibid.*, 164.

106. The reprinting of many older works also suggests a growing interest in the topic. Even the lapse of nearly seventy years has not relegated Frank Hugh Foster's *A Genetic History of the New England Theology* (Chicago, 1903) to oblivion; this recently reprinted work remains the only comprehen-

has produced an interesting collection which combines selections from
the Puritans' writings with excerpts from the works of modern
scholars,[107] and David D. Hall[108] and Sydney V. James[109] have edited
extracts from twentieth-century writers on Puritanism. Selections from
Puritan political writings have been compiled by Edmund S. Morgan,
whose definition of Puritanism is broad enough to encompass Bullinger.[110] A fifth collection, on the relationship of religion to the
American Revolution, is marred by an introduction which fails to
grasp the complexity of the situation and shows little understanding
of theology.[111]

Among the monographs, George L. Mosse's study of the adoption
of Machiavellian ideas by Puritan leaders, and the attempt to relate
them to Christian ethics, is perhaps the most distinguished work.[112]
Although Mosse emphasizes the English Puritans, notably William
Perkins and William Ames, there is a good chapter on John Winthrop.
In a book intriguingly entitled *The Grace of Law,* Ernest F. Kevan
suggests that for the Puritan there was no conflict between the two,
for he saw the law as the Jew saw the Torah; therefore, Samuel
Rutherford could speak of "making friends" with the law.[113] In the
first thorough history of the Puritan lectureships, Paul S. Seaver notes
the great influence these lectures had and shows that the lectureships
indicated "a power drive among the laity to control the Church."[114]

---

sive history of the school of thought that began with Edwards and by the
third quarter of the nineteenth century dominated American theological
education.

107. *Puritanism and the American Experience* (Reading, Pa., 1969).

108. *Puritanism in Seventeenth Century Massachusetts* (New York, 1968).

109. *The New England Puritans* (New York, 1968).

110. *Puritan Political Ideas, 1558–1794* (Indianapolis, 1965).

111. Peter H. Carroll, ed., *Religion and the Coming of the American Revolution* (Waltham, Mass., 1970).

112. *The Holy Pretence: A Study in Christianity and Reason of State from William Perkins to John Winthrop* (Oxford, Eng., 1957). Also see George L. Mosse, "Puritanism and Reason of State in Old and New England," *William and Mary Quarterly,* 3d ser., IX (1952), 67–80, and Perry Miller, "Jonathan Edwards," in *Errand,* 164–165.

113. See 1951 edition of work cited in fn. 21.

114. *The Puritan Lectureships: The Politics of Religion and Dissent, 1560–1662* (Stanford, 1970).

Two recent books consider aspects of Puritanism in relation to Anglicanism. As its subtitle implies, John F. H. New's *Anglican and Puritan: The Basis of Their Opposition, 1558–1660,* is a study in contrasts. What makes New's book refreshing is that the author stresses differences in the doctrines of man, the church, the sacraments, eschatology, and ethics, rather than in polity and ceremonial.[115] Ironically, this is also the weakness of New's method. As the present writer has observed in a review,[116] the author not only ignored some important Anglican evidence (the Prayer Book!) but also blithely assumed that issues of church government are necessarily "subsidiary to theology."[117] One man's adiaphora may be another man's essentials, and the Puritans are noted for having had little of the former. In the other book, C. F. Allison shows that the moralism of the Puritans is not lacking in the teaching of some of the Caroline divines, notably Jeremy Taylor. John Donne had regarded sin as a condition; as a logical consequence, his soteriology stressed the new life in Christ. Taylor, like the Puritans, was more interested in sins than in sin, and like the Puritans denied that an unsanctified person was capable of salvation.[118]

Turning to the purely American scene, we must first mention Marion Starkey's general history of Congregationalism through the time of Horace Bushnell.[119] Good as this book is, it differs from her admirable study of the Salem witchcraft trials[120] in that it makes no contribution to learning (and does not claim to make one); the book may best be described as religious education material of an exceptionally high quality. Still good reading is Ola Winslow's *Meetinghouse*

115. Stanford, 1964.
116. *Archiv für Reformationsgeschichte,* LVIII (1967), 142–143.
117. New, *Anglican and Puritan,* 107.
118. *The Rise of Moralism: The Proclamation of the Gospel from Hooker to Baxter* (London, Eng., 1966). Another study, Timothy Hall Breen, "The Non-Existent Controversy: Puritan and Anglican Attitudes on Work and Wealth, 1600–1640," *Church History,* XXXV (1966), 273–287, shows that both sides thought alike on this question.
119. *The Congregational Way: The Role of the Pilgrims and Their Heirs in Shaping America* (New York, 1966).
120. *The Devil in Massachusetts: A Modern Inquiry into the Salem Witchcraft Trials* (New York, 1949).

Hill, which reflects no great interest in theology but is the better social history for that.[121] An inveterate collector of gossip has exploited the church records to recount the Puritans' misdeeds in early Massachusetts.[122] In his book on the relations between Puritans and Indians, Alden T. Vaughan has devoted three of his twelve chapters to an excellent study of missions,[123] and John Eliot (who, as Vaughan carefully points out, was not the only apostle to the Indians) was the subject of a recent biography by Miss Winslow.[124] In "The Rule of the Saints in American Politics," Jerald C. Brauer has shown that the Puritan ideal of a theocracy survived the Puritan age and the disestablishment of the Congregational churches. "Theocracy," the writer reminds us, does not mean government by the clergy. It means the rule of God, whom the Puritans expected to govern society through his saints, who, though there were ministers among them, were mainly of the laity. As Brauer notes, do not the voters expect the President to go to church and demand that he be a "godly" man?[125]

The recent revival of interest in the Great Awakenings amply justifies Edwin Gaustad's remark that the recent books on the topic "constitute some sort of 'Awakening' of their own."[126] The last five years have witnessed the publication of no fewer than five source books, three of which appeared in 1970 alone! The books vary widely in content and arrangement, and range from a massive volume of more than 700 pages[127] to slim paperbacks obviously meant for mass consumption on college campuses. One focuses on enthusiasm,[128] an-

121. New York, 1952.
122. Emil Oberholzer, *Delinquent Saints: Disciplinary Action in the Early Congregational Churches in Massachusetts* (New York, 1956).
123. *The New England Frontier: Puritans and Indians, 1620–1679* (Boston, 1965).
124. *John Eliot, Apostle to the Indians* (Boston, 1968).
125. *Church History,* XXVII (1958), 240–255. Also see H. Richard Niebuhr, "The Idea of Covenant," *Church History,* XXIII (1954), 133.
126. Book review in *William and Mary Quarterly,* 3d ser., XXVIII (1971), 315.
127. Alan Heimert and Perry Miller, eds., *The Great Awakening: Documents Illustrating the Crisis and Its Consequences* (Indianapolis, 1967).
128. David S. Lovejoy, ed., *Religious Enthusiasm and the Great Awakening* (Englewood Cliffs, N.J., 1969).

other on piety,[129] and still another likens the eighteenth-century revivals to civil rights demonstrations and student unrest of the present
day.[130] The compilation by Darrett B. Rutman[131] is distinctive for
two reasons. It includes selections not only from eighteenth-century
writers but also from modern interpretations, and it is peculiarly designed to meet the modern student's demand for that elusive thing
called "relevance."[132] A curious feature of all five volumes is that their
titles imply that the evangelical movements of the time constituted a
unified whole; references to the Great Awakenings, in the plural,
though probably more correct, are rare in recent writing.[133] Two of
the editors have also written interpretative studies. In *From Puritan
to Yankee,* Richard L. Bushman suggests that somewhere between
1690 and 1769 the Puritans became Yankees and shows that in
Connecticut the Great Awakening and economic ambition combined
to break down the older institutions.[134] Alan Heimert's massive work
*Religion and the American Mind: From the Great Awakening to the
Revolution*[135] is in scope comparable to Perry's *Puritanism and
Democracy.* Heimert's book reflects an enormous amount of reading
and a quite unusual method of interpretation. Convinced that words
do not mean what we think they mean, Heimert examines every
minister's utterance in relation to what he believes was its author's
intention. What were the preacher's presuppositions? How did he

129. J. M. Bumsted, ed., *The Great Awakening: The Beginnings of Evangelical Pietism in America* (Waltham, Mass., 1970).
130. Richard L. Bushman, ed., *The Great Awakening: Documents on the
Revival of Religion, 1740–1745* (New York, 1970).
131. *The Great Awakening: Event and Exegesis* (New York, 1970).
132. The editor solemnly assures the readers that the subject is "relevant"
(p. 2) because it influenced the American sense of "mission and morality,"
and "the black man has been a victim of the mission" (p. 7). In a prefatory
note, he refers to "the overall result." Here, in a few pages, we have all the
contemporary student demands: the unnecessary adjective, the reference to the
black man, and the assurance of "relevance." This makes one wonder whether
the spate of source books reflects a revival of student interest in the eighteenth
century or an artificial effort by the compilers to create a demand for their
wares.
133. See Edwin S. Gaustad, *The Great Awakening in New England* (New
York, 1957), 102.
134. Cambridge, Mass., 1966.
135. Cambridge, Mass., 1967.

assess his congregation? What did he hope to accomplish? Every minister of the period is seen either as a liberal, which is to say a rationalist, an opponent of the Great Awakening, and a conservative in politics, or as a Calvinist, which means an evangelical and what most people would consider a liberal in politics. Heimert concludes that the evangelical spirit of the Calvinists broke down local allegiances, united the people, stimulated intercolonial and interdenominational unity, and ultimately provided the inspiration for the Revolution. The validity of this author's conclusions necessarily depends on the validity of his hermeneutics. When one learns that the spirit of Calvinism provided the foundation for Jeffersonianism, one may be forgiven for imagining the rationalist of Monticello turning over in his grave and may wonder what Heimert has wrought. Edmund S. Morgan is not unjustified in concluding his review of this book with the remark that what Heimert "finds beyond the lines [of his sources] . . . partakes more of fantasy than of history."[136] In an earlier work, Edwin S. Gaustad demonstrated, among other things, that while the New England Awakening was not devoid of social and economic aspects, it transcended all class lines.[137] The religious divisiveness which the Great Awakening engendered and the emergence of the Calvinistic Baptists have been examined by C. G. Goen.[138] Isaac Backus has been included in the Library of American Biography,[139] and the role of the Anglican evangelist George Whitefield has been treated in an article.[140]

136. Review in *William and Mary Quarterly*, 3d ser., XXIV (1967), 454–459.
137. Gaustad, *The Great Awakening*. The thesis of this work is also found in Edwin S. Gaustad, "Society and the Great Awakening in New England," *William and Mary Quarterly*, 3d ser., XI (1954), 566–577.
138. *Revivalism and Separatism in New England, 1740–1800: Strict Congregationalists and Separate Baptists in the Great Awakening* (New Haven, Conn., and London, Eng., 1962).
139. William G. McLoughlin, *Isaac Backus and the American Pietistic Tradition* (Boston, 1967). Also see McLoughlin, "The First Calvinistic Baptist Association in New England, 1754?–1767," *Church History*, XXXVI (1967), 410–418.
140. William Howland Kenney, 3d, "George Whitefield, Dissenter Priest of the Great Awakening, 1739–1741," *William and Mary Quarterly*, 3d ser., XXVI (1969), 75–93.

Some writers have used long-neglected sources; others have struck out in new directions. Theological treatises, manuals of polity, devotional writings, polemical literature, and particularly sermons—these were the principal sources used by Perry Miller and by most of his followers and critics. But the pleasure experienced in working with church records, which had been rarely used except by genealogists, induced one writer to encourage further use of these documents, preferably in conjunction with civil records.[141] Some years later Darrett B. Rutman again urged further study of these papers[142] and used them himself in his excellent history of Boston in its first two decades.[143] In an unusual reversal of a common practice, a sociologist has relied on the history of Puritanism to explain a sociological phenomenon,[144] and a writer who seems to be as well-versed in the theories of Sigmund Freud and Karl Menninger as in the writings of Perry Miller and Norman Pettit has compared and contrasted the Puritan conversion experience with the practice of psychoanalysis.[145] No less *sui generis*, but probably devoid of anything save bulk and the pretense of scholarship, is a pompous volume which advances some complex theory concerning the decay of Puritanism and the rise of American culture.[146] To end this section on a happier note, we may call attention to some contributions from the pen of Roland H. Bainton. Anything by Bainton is bound to be good in content and delightful in form, and his history of

---

141. Emil Oberholzer, "The Church in New England Society," in James Morton Smith, ed., *The Seventeenth Century: Essays in Colonial History* (Chapel Hill, 1959), 164–165.

142. "The Mirror of Puritan Authority," in George Athan Billias, ed., *Law and Authority,* 149–167.

143. *Winthrop's Boston: Portrait of a Puritan Town, 1630–1649* (Chapel Hill, 1965).

144. Kai T. Erikson, *Wayward Puritans: A Study in the Sociology of Deviance* (New York, 1968).

145. Howard M. Feinstein, "The Prepared Heart: A Comparative Study of Puritan Theology and Psychoanalysis," *American Quarterly,* XXII (1970), 166–176.

146. Chard Powers Smith, *Yankees and God* (New York, 1954). Just what is this book: a hopelessly presented attempt at interpretation? Or an exercise in finding footnotes to document preconceived notions? Or the work of a genius not understood? See the review by Stow Persons, *William and Mary Quarterly,* 3d ser., XII (1955), 494–497.

the Yale Divinity School[147] and paper on "The Office of the Minister's Wife in New England"[148] are no exceptions.

"The chief difficulty in writing about the Puritans," A. L. Rowse complained, "is one of definitions. Who were the Puritans? Whom are we to regard as Puritans?"[149] In the quest for definition there have been some interesting developments, but no agreement seems in sight. We know that Lutheranism is that form of Christianity which Martin Luther taught, or its derivatives, and that Anglicanism is that form which is manifested in the Church of England and her sister churches of the Anglican communion. But no single person can be named as the fount of Puritan doctrine, nor can Puritanism be identified with any one ecclesiastical body. Perry Miller's now famous definition of Puritanism as "that point of view, that philosophy of life, that code of values, which was carried to New England by the first settlers in the early seventeenth century"[150] has been found untenable. Its regional bias is obvious. A more subtle, and therefore more serious, flaw is that it assumes that all aspects of New England life were the effects of Puritanism and thus ignores the common English heritage of all the colonists.[151] William Haller's definition, "a spiritual attitude, moral temper, and way of life preached in England after the accession of Elizabeth,"[152] which reverses the geographical bias, thoughtfully begins with an indefinite article, but fails to specify which attitude of Elizabethan England is Puritan. John Eusden's simple definition, "evangelical Calvinism,"[153] presupposes that Puritanism was in fact

147. *Yale and the Ministry: A History of Education for the Christian Ministry at Yale from the Founding in 1701* (New Haven, Conn., 1967). The book is charmingly illustrated by Bainton's drawings.

148. In Bainton, *Christian Unity and Religion in New England*, 265–282.

149. A. L. Rowse, *The England of Elizabeth* (New York, 1951), 464.

150. Perry Miller et al., eds., *The Puritans* (New York, 1938), 1. Cf. Hall, ed., *Puritanism*, 1.

151. Oberholzer, "Church in New England Society," in Smith, ed., *The Seventeenth Century*, 165; Rutman, *American Puritanism*, 7.

152. "The Puritan Background of the First Amendment," in Conyers Read, ed., *The Constitution Reconsidered* (New York, 1938), 136. Cf. Haller, *Rise of Puritanism*, 9: "That spiritual outlook, way of life, and mode of expression which eventually flowered so variously and magnificently in Milton, Bunyan, and Defoe."

153. Introduction to Ames, *Marrow*, 19.

a form of Calvinism, and Norman Pettit's "a form of piety within the English Church"[154] can easily be construed to include the Caroline divines and Nicholas Farrar, but to exclude the Separatists, Independents, and Quakers. Perhaps Horton Davies's definition, "the outlook that characterised the radical Protestant party in Queen Elizabeth's day,"[155] comes nearest the truth, but "radical" is a vague word. Presumably it includes the Brownists, but does John Hooper still qualify as a Puritan?

Not surprisingly, some writers have given up trying to define Puritanism. Kenneth Murdock found himself so baffled that he sought refuge in a good description.[156] In 1956, I found it "almost impossible to define Puritanism accurately";[157] three years later I suggested that others do what I could not.[158] Of course, one can attempt a definition by listing the individuals or species one includes in the genus,[159] be it *Piers Plowman*[160] or the Quakers,[161] or, following Geoffrey F. Nuttall, anybody who manifested "that spirit in religion which has driven men at all times to seek a purer way of life, one that was simple and good as opposed to the insincere conventionalities and corruptions in the world around them."[162] Given this definition, one cannot object to its author's inclusion among the Puritans of persons as diverse as Bernard of Clairvaux and the Cistercians, Dante Alighieri and Desiderius Erasmus, the Quakers, the Anglican archbishop William Temple, and

154. *Heart Prepared*, 6. Cf. Everett Emerson, *English Puritanism from John Hooper to John Milton* (Durham, N.C., 1968), 3.
155. *The Worship of the English Puritans* (Westminster, 1948), 1.
156. *Increase Mather: The Foremost American Puritan* (Cambridge, Mass., 1925), 8–9.
157. Oberholzer, *Delinquent Saints*, 6. In retrospect I would omit both adverbs.
158. Oberholzer, "Church in New England Society," in Smith, ed., *The Seventeenth Century*, 165.
159. A peculiarly awkward example of this method is found in John Dillenberger et al., *Protestant Christianity Interpreted Through Its Development* (New York, 1954), 99–118.
160. G. M. Trevelyan, *English Social History: A Survey of Six Centuries, Chaucer to Victoria*, 2d ed. (London, Eng., 1946), 2.
161. Simpson, *Puritanism*, 1–2.
162. *The Puritan Spirit, Essays and Addresses* (London, Eng., 1967), 11. Also see his *Visible Saints: The Congregational Way, 1640–1660* (Oxford, Eng., 1957), 3.

even Virginia Woolf.[163] The definition is not without charm, but it is hardly helpful to the historian. It encompasses Amos and Hosea, Isaiah and Micah, Jeremiah and Ezekiel, not to mention Jesus and Paul, and perhaps includes the contemporary WASP mendicants who, though their Hinduism be only paint deep, chant Vedic hymns on urban streetcorners. Were Nuttall's definition to find general acceptance, we would have to find a new term to designate the still-undefined movement we call Puritanism.

Two writers recently have addressed themselves to the problem of definition. Darrett B. Rutman, who rightly insists that "New England has a history apart from Puritanism,"[164] seeks to isolate the Puritan element in colonial society. After explaining his conception of Puritanism as "a gift from the preachers to the hearers,"[165] he examines the theologically determined message of the clergymen and the laity's psychologically conditioned response. Admittedly an experimental work, the book presents an ingenious but not wholly convincing approach to a difficult problem. The author's presupposition that laymen regarded the ministers as having a sort of monopoly on grace and truth, and themselves as the recipients of mere handouts, is questionable, as is his reliance on the notion of a fellowship of ministers. The Congregationalists of New England were more interested in the fellowship of churches, and the churches were overwhelmingly constituted of lay persons. No doubt Rutman's book will stimulate any number of studies, either along the lines he suggests or in opposition to his method, but probably more scholars will follow David D. Hall. In a recent essay, Hall discusses definitions, the function of Puritanism in society, and the relationship of Puritanism to the Reformed tradition and Pietism.[166] Unlike Rutman, Hall offers no startlingly new method, but he reflects a sounder understanding of Puritan theology. Conceding that the Puritan ideal could be more readily realized in America than in England, Hall urges less emphasis on

163. Nuttall, *The Puritan Spirit*, passim.
164. *American Puritanism, Faith and Practice* (Philadelphia, 1970), 125.
165. *Ibid.*, 17.
166. "Understanding the Puritans," in Bass, ed., *State of American History*, 330–349.

American Puritanism and more research into the Puritans' place in the Reformed tradition, which, he warns, must not be judged by the teachings of Calvin alone. It may be helpful at this point to recall a suggestion made in 1954 by John T. McNeill, who observed that "a recklessly extensive application of the word 'Puritan' has become habitual and virtually unavoidable."[167] As a remedy, McNeill recommends the study of distinct groups, such as Presbyterians or Separatists or "spiritual sectarians and miscellaneous fanatics." Each class will be found to have its peculiar features, but from such studies a view of Puritanism showing the traits common to all groups will emerge.

The observation which James Hastings Nichols made in 1950 might as well have been made at the last meeting of the American Society of Church History. Indeed, a similar remark was made in 1970, when Ahlstrom noted that "Puritanism has become the area of American historical work where the greatest sophistication has been achieved; hence it continues to attract keen historians who are doing impressive work."[168] Even this fragmentary survey of the recent literature conveys some suggestion of the vast amount of work that has been done. The production of books and articles witnesses to a still growing interest in Puritan studies, and *The William and Mary Quarterly,* indubitably the most important journal for students of early American history, reflects this trend in the approximately double number of articles on the subject.[169]

Nichols also noted that of the six leading scholars in American

167. *Modern Christian Movements,* 19.

168. In a letter to Michael McGiffert, quoted in McGiffert, "Puritan Studies," *William and Mary Quarterly,* 3d ser., XXVII (1970), 37.

169. A count of the articles on Purita*nism,* as distinguished from the non-religious aspects in the lives of the Puritans and of New England history generally, shows that in the 1950's 5 of the 234 articles were on that topic; in the 1960's, there were 12 out of 242. The figures will vary depending on whether one counts notes and essay-reviews, as well as on the criteria applied, but by adhering to any uniform standard one will find a marked increase. In *Church History,* the absolute number of articles on Puritanism has increased, but the magazine has grown in size, and the proportion of such articles over any period of two or three years has remained fairly constant.

Puritanism in 1950, "not one is a church historian by profession."[170] The work continues to be done by persons of varied backgrounds. Before the time of Miller and Haller, the general historians wrote on Puritanism. Then Perry Miller, sitting on the edge of a Congolese jungle, found his vocation. "It was given to me," he recounted, "to have thrust upon me the mission of expounding what I took to be the innermost propulsion of the United States."[171] Less dramatically, Haller found that in order to understand Milton, he must first understand Puritanism. Thus the literary scholars became the principal explorers of the Puritan tradition. Today's Puritanists are drawn from several disciplines, with the historians and literary scholars in the foreground. With the gradual disappearance of the giants of 1950 (only Haller and Schneider are still at work in retirement; Morison has become absorbed in nautical matters), it is impossible to say whether Nichols's second observation is still precisely true, but only a relatively small number of the present Puritanists have any formal training in church history. Nevertheless, most of these scholars display a far deeper understanding of the theological problems inherent in their subject than did their predecessors twenty years ago.

Now that students of Puritanism in America have recognized that the subject cannot be studied in isolation from its English (and European?) counterparts and are prepared to deal with theological niceties, perhaps the next logical step is to bring the study of Puritanism into closer relationship with the whole of church history. Such an approach may not only uncover some common factors or suggest previously ignored nexuses but may also help avert some pitfalls. Consider, for instance, the incredulity or amazement implied in this statement: "Orthodoxy in Massachusetts was to be a curious thing. It involved no great statement of creed or belief. Truth in such matters was defined in negative terms by virtue of the condemnation of Anne [Hutchinson]'s multitude of errors."[172] If one remembers that nearly three centuries elapsed before the early church came to some agreement on

---

170. Nichols, "The Art of Church History," *Church History*, XX (March 1951), 7.
171. Miller, *Errand*, vii–viii.
172. Rutman, *Winthrop's Boston*, 124.

the nature of the Trinity, that more than another century was needed to define orthodox Christology, if only for the West, that this was done largely under the aegis of emperors motivated by political considerations, that in the process numerous errors and the devout persons who held them were condemned, and that Christians everywhere usually have found it easier to decry heresy than to define orthodoxy, is it really "a curious thing" that the New Englanders needed a few years in which to arrive at some agreement, that politics influenced the process, that they did this as doctrines arose which threatened the unity of the society, and that orthodoxy was defined by rejecting heresies and heretics?

After fifteen years' absence from any serious work on Puritanism, it may be presumptuous for me to offer much in the way of suggestion or criticism, but perhaps a few comments may be permitted. Could it be that contemporary scholarship, diverse as its directions are, has almost wholly neglected certain lines of investigation? Calvin wrote a great deal about the Eucharist, but the historians have told us very little about what the Puritans believed. Hall dismisses the subject with the observation that they were Zwinglian memorialists.[173] Assuming that there are sufficient references in the sermons and books of the Puritan theologians, one might investigate the subject more thoroughly, not only with reference to Calvin and Zwingli, but also to such mediating and irenic statements as the First Helvetic Confession and the Consensus Tigurinus, both of which considerably modified Zwingli's own teaching.[174] Moreover, Kobrin's observation that the Lord's Supper was considered as an efficacious means toward conversion[175] calls for a reevaluation of Stoddardeanism. Did Solomon Stoddard consider himself as an innovator or as reviving an older practice?

Another possibly fruitful but almost wholly neglected area of study

173. David D. Hall, "Understanding the Puritans," in Bass, ed., *State of American History,* 334.
174. I have no knowledge of the Puritans' use of these statements, but the date of the Zürich consensus, 1549, is suggestive. This was the last major declaration on the subject by the Reformed theologians before the Marian exiles arrived in Europe.
175. Kobrin, "The Visible Church," *Church History,* XXXVI (1967), 189–202.

is Puritanism in the colonies outside of New England. It has been suggested that a study of the sermons, books, and practices of the clergy in colonial Virginia might uncover evidence of Puritan influence in colonial Anglicanism.[176] If this be true of Virginia, there is no reason to assume that similar influences could not be found elsewhere, perhaps in Pennsylvania after the Keithian schism, when many former Quakers joined the Church of England. Indeed, it is a peculiar trait of American Puritanists to ignore those manifestations of Puritanism that appear within the framework of the Church of England.

The colonists who sought to plant the holy commonwealth in New England were Puritans, but their world was not shaped by Puritanism alone. We must distinguish between Puritanism, which was a particular form of Christianity, and its adherents, who were not Puritans only, but, in the case of New England, Englishmen as well. The first step toward avoiding, or at least alleviating, some of the recurrent confusion which confronts students of New England history might be to use the words "Puritan" and "Puritanism" only with reference to the particular Christian movement they designate. This is not intended to deprecate other investigations into New England history, but unless it is clearly demonstrable that the topic under consideration is related to Puritanism, and not only to those who happened to be Puritans, it might be helpful to speak of *Massachusetts* law, or *Boston* trade, or *Connecticut* society.[177] Such an approach would help to bring the study of Puritanism into a more intimate relationship with church history, which Cyril C. Richardson so gracefully described as "the

176. This was an "off-the-cuff" remark by a distinguished historian who asked to remain unidentified.

177. Perhaps a piece of paper which I recently found may illustrate this point. It contains the answers to a quiz given in a seventh-grade history course. Presumably the teacher asked her pupils to list three characteristics of the Puritans. My answers were: "1. They read the English Bible a lot. 2. They thought the Church of England should have been reformed more. 3. They ate venissen [sic]." Although the teacher accepted the answers, only two were really related to Puritanism, and only one was distinctive of it. Being Puritans, they read the Bible a lot, but they read it in English because they were Englishmen; the Anglicans also read it in English. They ate venison because it was readily available. Only the fact that they were dissatisfied with the extent of the English Reformation was a distinctively Puritan trait.

tale of redemption; and while in a sense it embraces world history, its central thread is the story of the Holy Community (known under various guises and found in manifold and surprising places), which is the bearer of revelation and through which God acts in human history."[178]

Perry Miller was not a professional church historian, but perhaps he broke out "in a cold sweat in the loneliness of the night at the realization that he was, in fact, writing church history!"[179] And he performed an enormous task, for which all Puritanists should be grateful. Unfortunately, some of the recent writers seem to take more delight in rebuking him than in discovering truth. Miller was not infallible. He overlooked the emotional life of the Puritans, sometimes drew unwarranted conclusions, and occasionally displayed a shocking lack of theological understanding. But it is only fair to give equal weight to the vast bulk of his work which still stands, even if modified in some details. His labors inspired many researches which resulted in corrections Miller would have welcomed. "The career of Perry Miller rebukes us all."[180] This was the tribute to a Harvard man by a Yale man, and one who was far from an uncritical disciple but who dedicated a volume to the scholar whose conclusions he modified.

178. "Church History Past and Present," *Union Seminary Quarterly Review,* V (1949), 13.

179. Nichols, "The Art of Church History," *Church History,* XX (March 1951), 7.

180. Morgan, "Perry Miller," American Antiquarian Society *Proceedings,* LXXIV, pt. I (1964), 11.

JOHN J. WATERS

From Democracy to Demography: Recent
Historiography on the New England Town

THOMAS JEFFERSON, in declaring that the New England towns "have proved themselves the wisest inventions ever devised by the wit of man for the perfect exercise of self government," merely clothed in republican rhetoric an already old Yankee belief.[1] Tocqueville continued this tradition when he envisioned these towns as democratic-egalitarian nations "independent in all that concerns themselves."[2] In the last decades of the nineteenth century the newly emerging historical craft enriched this tradition by grafting onto it Anglo-Saxon and Teutonic ancestors and institutions.[3]

This continuing belief in the existence of free local government, best seen in small farming towns settled by northern Europeans who are assumed to have shared an egalitarian ethos, is the heart of what I call the "populist-traditional" interpretation; it is the first in three

1. Thomas Jefferson to Samuel Kercheval, Monticello, July 12, 1816, as quoted in Ruth R. Wheeler, *Concord, Climate for Freedom* (Concord, 1967), 92; Ralph Waldo Emerson's version of this idea reads: "In a town meeting the great secret of political science was uncovered, and the problem solved, how to give every individual his fair weight in the government"; see Townsend Scudder, *Concord: American Town* (Boston, 1947), 16.
2. Alexis de Tocqueville, *Democracy in America* (New York, 1961), I, 56–64.
3. See Herbert B. Adams, *The Germanic Origin of the New England Towns* (Baltimore, 1882), 8–9; Charles Francis Adams, "Genesis of the Massachusetts Town," Massachusetts Historical Society *Proceedings,* 2d ser., VII (1892), 172–211.

current approaches in the writings dealing with these preindustrial communities. If the "populist-traditional" school recruits its authors mostly from the localities being studied, the second school, the "middle-class-democratic" interpretation (which contributed to the consensus mentality of Cold-War American historiography), comes overwhelmingly from professional academic institutions. Implicitly, this "democratic" approach agrees with the basic premises of the "populist-traditional" school. As such it supports an essentially conservative political view of colonial society; and in fact, Robert E. Brown, one of the founding fathers of this school, consciously rejected the class-conflict interpretation of what he called the eastern establishment's "Old Left" and its thesis that "colonial political and economic life was dominated by the upper economic classes."[4] The third school, the "sociodemographic model builders," while also of academic background, has been heavily influenced by the behavioristic theories of the social sciences; as such its foci and methodology depart from the overwhelmingly political and economic interests of its "democratic" predecessors.

The unity of these three schools comes from a concurrence with Samuel Flagg Bemis's view that by the study of local communities "scholars are replowing the base and marking out the contours of our Republic" and that future historians "must stand on this revised base and follow these smaller contours" if they wish "to feel and portray the real American heritage."[5] The schools' revisionistic intent is obvious, as is the rejection of the centralistic focus of most colonial historiography, which they charge with an overconcern with the "high culture"—Puritan theology, Harvard, the General Court, and an imperial elite—while remaining ignorant of popular life and local institutions.

As might be expected, the "populist-traditional" interpreters, amateurs and professionals alike, have a profound emotional involvement

4. Robert E. Brown, *Middle-Class Democracy and the Revolution in Massachusetts, 1691–1780* (New York, 1969), preface, vii–viii, xi.

5. Jasper Jacob Stahl, *History of Old Broad Bay and Waldoboro* (Portland, Maine, 1956), I, xxvii.

in *their* towns. The authors of three of the very best studies—Amos and Emily Jewett of Rowley, Massachusetts; George Abbot Morison of Peterborough, New Hampshire; and Jasper Jacob Stahl of Old Broad Bay and Waldoboro, Maine—descend from their town's early settlers. This is also the case with Rehoboth's outstanding genealogist, Richard LeBaron Bowen. In short, they are from those "old families" in which Allan Nevins believed "experience and wisdom descend from generation to generation; they have a strong local pride, rooted in history; they let their life be shaped, in part, by the scenery, geology, and natural productions of the area."[6] These innately conservative local historians, like Nevins, use the past to support their contemporary social and political beliefs.

The Jewetts in their study of the settlement patterns of the new Rowley posited the movement of an already formed Yorkshire group —and their evidence for this affinity group came from a careful analysis of the interlinkage of will witnesses. This Puritan community shared the religious values of its charismatic minister, Master Ezekiel Rogers; not surprisingly, three-fourths of its fifty-four founding males are *"known* to have been members" of his reformed church.[7] For the professional historian this is an intriguing example of popular participation in the church. If from one point of view these early men of Rowley epitomized reformed religious radicalism, they were at the same time social conservatives. In placing house lots these Yorkshiremen retained the spread-out village pattern, even though this deviated from the Bay Colony's mandate that "noe dwelling howse shalbe built above halfe a myle from the meeting howse." The size of the house lot, as well as the rights in the commons, followed one's contribution to the £ 800 cost of the "Rowley Company," thus continuing the existing wealth concentrations. The Jewetts see these middle-class planters, once in the new land, passionately desiring to own soil and

6. Allan Nevins, "Foreword," in Silvio A. Bedini, *Ridgefield in Review* (Ridgefield, Conn., 1958), xi.

7. Amos and Emily Jewett, *Rowley, Massachusetts, "Mr Ezechi Rogers Plantation," 1639–1850* (Rowley, Mass., 1946), I, v, 23, 28–29; and for wills see A. D. J. MacFarlane, *Witchcraft in Tudor and Stuart England* (New York, 1970), 170–171.

establish families: they relate that one family declared: "We will risk our scalps for the land," when warned of a possible Indian attack. The Jewetts assert, without demonstration, that Rowley became a stable town in which the eighteenth century would find "the sons and grandsons of the first settlers at the head of affairs."[8] Finally, this meticulously documented book has as its collective hero the English race; an ethnocentric leitmotif marks almost all of the "populist-traditional" narratives.

George Abbot Morison shared most of the historical bias of the Jewetts. However, his founding fathers (and hence his heroes) were "Scotch-Irish." A more crucial difference in Morison's work was his dynamic overview of economic developments which changed Peterborough from a colonial preindustrial New Hampshire hilltop town to a water-powered industrial center in the nineteenth century. And Morison realized that his study could represent "the changes in a typical New England town brought about by changing economic developments."[9]

Peterborough really came into being with the arrival of the Scotch-Irish in 1749–1750. By then the "New England Way" had an established format: church and minister, school, town meeting, and commons constituted the community ideal.[10] Morison's Presbyterian immigrants, coming mostly from the Bann Valley in Ireland, above all desired to "have an opportunity of worshipping God according to the dictates of conscience and the rules of His inspired word" as opposed to the dictates of the Anglican Church. The families of Peterborough had not come to New Hampshire either to compromise or to assimilate. Morison declares that his ancestors had "kept their racial integrity and their religious integrity during the one to three genera-

8. *Ibid.,* 17–18, 62; Louis E. Roy in his *Quaboag Plantation alias Brookefield: A Seventeenth Century Massachusetts Town* (Worcester, Mass., 1965), 62, also realized that the size of land grants suggests "the probably relative social stature of the individuals concerned. . . ."

9. George Abbot Morison, *History of Peterborough, New Hampshire* (Rindge, N.H., 1954), I, 3.

10. Petition of the Inhabitants of Peterborough, Nov. 14, 1785, *ibid.,* 72–73; Conrad Arensberg, "American Communities," *American Anthropologist,* LVII (1955), 1148–1151.

tions they lived in Ulster," and for more than a century after settling in Peterborough these Scotch-Irish "did not intermarry to any extent with the other settlers who came from the English settlements of eastern Massachusetts."[11] One of the fascinations in reading about early Peterborough derives from an awareness of its retention of Old Country ethnic-cultural and religious values; while today we see major similarities between the Scotch-Irish Presbyterians and the colonial New Englanders, the sectaries of colonial America lived in a world fixated by the differences. These immigrants were traditional folk. When they assembled with blackened faces, the "tinkling of cowbells, blowing of horns and much shouting," and rode on a rail a wife beater, it was to enforce collectively by this "rough music" the mores of their community.[12]

Politically the Scotch-Irish chafed under the rule of Peterborough's absentee Yankee proprietors. That within a decade's time these settlers had organized themselves as a political pressure group, challenged the proprietors, successfully petitioned the legislature, and gained legal autonomy as a township bears witness to a shared complex of assumptions between the immigrant and the host culture. These Scotch-Irish quickly took to the town meeting. It became a prime instrument for reaffirming what Michael Zuckerman called the group's "broadly diffused desire for consensual communalism as the operative premise of group life in America." One townsman seemed to sense this function. When asked what happened at meetings, he replied: "Oh, there was George Duncan, he got up and spakit awhile, and Matthew Wallace, he got up and talkit awhile, and Matthew Gray, he got up and blathered awhile; and then they dismissed the meeting." To modern ears this sounds like a communal-ritual activity. Morison, however, remained true to the "populist-traditional" myth, and insisted that participation in the meeting meant adherence to the democratic creed. In fact, Morison, in his opinion that the "New England towns are the outstanding example of the successful practice of true democracy" in the

---

11. Morison, *Peterborough*, 57–62.
12. *Ibid.*, 159; the Scotch-Irish settlers of Oakham were also Presbyterian "zealots"; see Henry Burt Wright et al., *The Settlement and Story of Oakham, Massachusetts* (New Haven, 1947), I, 4, 116.

world, is one with Jefferson.[13] While I find such a view ahistorical, it does not obviate Morison's accomplishment in his intelligent study of early Peterborough.

Jasper Jacob Stahl, the author of the final work in this settlement trio, had the task of making meaningful the experiences of his Palatinate-German ancestors who had immigrated in the 1730's to Old Broad Bay and Waldoboro, Maine. These peasants, with their feudal loyalties, pietistic Christianity, and earthy customs, contrast sharply with both Rowley's English and Peterborough's Scotch-Irish. As long as their leaders spoke German, the Palatinate immigrants endured incredible exploitation, chicanery, and fraud. They asked no more than the right to preserve their customs, till the soil, and leave a wife as security with the lord until a cow could be paid for; the Moravian missionary Georg Soelle corroborated this mentality when he wrote: "I can see that this folk here is more concerned about its cattle than about the souls of its children." The civil and religious institutions of the "New England Way" had no appeal in this transplanted German village. It easily spent its first thirty years under the autocratic rule of the hereditary lord of Broad Bay, Samuel Waldo. As Stahl saw it, these folk supported a system in which "their class was fixed; their economic status predetermined; their obedience to the word of the ruler complete; their attitude to authority one of obsequious respect."[14] The advent of Yankee settlers after 1765, their successful move for incorporation as a town in 1773, and the Revolution all united to shatter the fabric of that system. While the majority of Germans passively supported George III, they were no match for the organized Yankee minority which now controlled institutional life.[15] The future meant assimilation. The unusual variation of this German town from the New England mold sharply points out the existence of cultural differences in the colonial past. At the same time it delineates by contrast the cultural and institutional unity of Yankeedom.

The town histories by the Jewetts, Morison, and Stahl deserve a

13. Morison, *Peterborough*, 92–94. See also George C. Homans, *English Villagers of the Thirteenth Century* (Cambridge, 1941), 265.
14. Stahl, *Old Broad Bay*, 306, 317.
15. *Ibid.*, 399, 433, 474–479.

larger reading on the part of professional historians than they have received. Their trio contains valuable insights into migration, ethnicity, and social stratification. Moreover, each of these monographs contains a precise map locating the homesteads of the first settlers. The authors' careful references to documents susceptible to quantification should be of value to current research in demography and social structure—interests which were also the concerns of the economic historian Ernest Bogart and the genealogist Richard LeBaron Bowen.

Ernest Bogart firmly stated the connection between the local scene and the national marketplace. Moreover, he was conscious of the importance of transportation factors, population growth, economic activity, and their mutual interdependence in the hundred-and-fifty-year history of the Vermont hilltop town of Peacham. Yet this sophisticated study adhered to the myth that the development of Peacham is a history "in microcosm, of the forces which have created American democracy at its best." He could be right. Yet there is a certain irony in his tale of the harsh lives of the barely literate settlers, of rampant speculation, and of an out migration rate of 40 to 20 percent per decade for the period 1780 to 1800. And while in the 1790's 80 percent of this primitive frontier village's seventy-three heads of families owned farms averaging 137 acres—of which only five acres were under tillage—eleven families, or 15 percent of the population, owned no land. Peacham's warning out notices show that it gave no legal status to the unfortunates who could not meet its communal standard of competition.[16] Their 1813 "Confession of Faith" declared "all mankind are naturally destitute of all moral goodness, are dead in trespasses and sin, and are, by nature, children of wrath, being children of disobedience."[17] I think this creed mirrored the fierce, fundamentalistic, uncompromising world of its Yankee inhabitants.

Finally, Bowen's "Population Estimates" in his *Early Rehoboth* are in my opinion the single most original contribution of any of these local studies. Baldly stated, through a lifetime of counting heads and

16. Ernest L. Bogart, *Peacham: The Story of a Vermont Hill Town* (Montpelier, 1948), preface, recto, 24, 57, 73, 100.
17. *Ibid.*, 172. See also John W. Reps, *Town Planning in Frontier America* (Princeton, 1969), 145–183.

an uncanny luck in discovering tax and census records, Bowen established the first scientific population estimates on seventeenth-century New England: the concluding figures for 1690 are Plymouth Colony, 10,105; Connecticut, 20,210; and Massachusetts, 33,700. Bowen's is a technical, nonnarrative opus in which the calculations dealing with tax and militia lists, as well as data on the decline over time in the size of the colonial family, are of import to today's demographers. Equally novel is Bowen's all-too-short essay on the town of Swansea, in which he departs from the belief in pure democracy characteristic of this genre. There he unearthed an explicit class system of land division consisting of three orders, in which a first-rank man would hold half the land, a second-rank man a third, and a third-rank man a sixth. Bowen believed that this "system of land division, under the direction of a committee composed of *first rank* officials, who had the arbitrary power of assigning ranks, established a landed aristocracy that lasted for nearly a quarter of a century."[18] Some historian ought to tell us how this system functioned.

The works of the Jewetts, Morison, Stahl, Bogart, and Bowen separate themselves from the vast majority of local histories by their insights and high craftsmanship. Yet it is obvious that they share a core of central thematic concerns. And since these books are usually written *in vacuo*—with no reference to any other study save the records and local histories of the particular town—such unity flows from popular tradition.

The first common vision of the "populist-traditional" school affirms an egalitarian democratic past, where "everybody knew everybody else" and where town leaders had "worked their way up from small beginnings."[19] Allied to this view is the concept, expressed by the town of Westminster in 1778, that all power belonged to the people: "Where can the power be lodged so well as they, or who has the bold-

18. Richard LeBaron Bowen, *Early Rehoboth: Documented Historical Studies of Families and Events in This Plymouth Colony Township*, 4 vols. (Rehoboth, Mass., 1945–50), I, ix, 1–24, 74–76; IV, 87–112, 117; cf. John Demos, "Families in Colonial Bristol, Rhode Island: An Exercise in Historical Demography," *William and Mary Quarterly*, 3d ser., XXV (1968), 41, n. 3.

19. Aubigne L. Packard, *A Town That Went to Sea* [Thomaston] (Portland, Me., 1950), 1–18; Claude M. Fuess, *Andover, Symbol of New England: The Evolution of a Town* (Andover, 1959), 6.

ness without blushing to say that the people are not suitable to putt in their own officers—if so why do we wast our blood and treasure to obtaine that which when obtained we are not fitt to enjoy, or if but a selected few only are fitt to appoint our rulers, why were we so uneasie under George?"[20] It would be foolish to dismiss the truth of this congregational view, however inadequately expressed by local historians, just as it would be unwise to negate the inherent idealism in Westminster's belief that each man ought to have a say in the decisions affecting his own life.

What meaning do these local historians give to their past? I see three approaches. First is a nostalgic identity with its memories of "arching elms over shady streets flanked by well clipped lawns, of painted cottages with cool green shutters, or meticulously stocked wood piles, and white church spires rising aloft to catch the last brightness of the sunset glow." Such a view recognizes New England as *patria;* at the same time it realizes that the sun has set on that lost agrarian world. As Catherine Fennelly succinctly put it, the "New England known to John Adams . . . to Charles Chauncey and William Ellery Channing and Lyman Beecher is gone, beyond even the memory of any man now living."[21] Such is not the case with the germinal view.

This second approach, supported by social conservatives such as Allan Nevins, who believed that "experience and wisdom descend from generation to generation" in a handful of select families, implicitly denies the necessity for institutional change. Horace A. Hildreth, a former governor of Maine, gave a classic rendition of this ideology in his declaration that in the "human and physical characteristics of our early New England communities" repose the "essence of

20. Catherine Fennelly, *Life in an Old New England Country Village* (Sturbridge, 1969), 41.

21. *Ibid.,* 191; Harold R. Phalen, *History of the Town of Acton* (Cambridge, Mass., 1954), 1; and Charles D. Hubbard, "And now all sleeps—beautifully—as a New England village can sleep, with a hush almost as complete as the silence which enfolds the dust of the early settlers resting there so quietly before the old meeting-house," *An Old New England Village* (Portland, Me., 1947), 18. This is also the tone of Edward M. Chapman, *New England Village Life* (Cambridge, 1937).

American purpose and the seed of our destiny." Even in a modified (and less Anglo-Saxon) version such a belief in prototypical American communities, which are conceived of as repositories of freedom, by definition limits the options and the freedom of men living today.[22] The third, or exemplary, view, while sharing the institutional prejudices of the germinal view, has come to terms with such new ethnics as the Irish, the Poles, and the Swedes. What matters is to recognize that the values and ideals of the past constitute the models for the present. Indeed, one can display "many of the characteristics of the first settlers" by working "for the same objectives as did the forefathers—good roads, good schools, and a peaceful, well-ordered community." This is the legacy of the founding fathers, and it would be folly to tamper with success; after all, "these dedicated and farsighted people had built a new town and made laws and established patterns still found just and good."[23] As I see it, this view must fade, undermined by the new complex of life experiences, moral conduct, black and female awareness of past exploitation, and above all by a technology which makes tomorrow already out of date.

It is not surprising that the "populist-traditional" histories in their asides and editorial comments support a static, Calvinistic concept of human nature, criticize the policies of the Roosevelt administration, and sing praise to a colonial past "in which men of brains and vision rose rapidly from wage-earners to capitalists."[24] After all, a usable,

22. Hubbard, *An Old New England Village*, preface; Bedini, *Ridgefield*, xi, xiii.
23. The quotations are from Lura Woodside Watkins, *Middleton, Massachusetts, A Cultural History* (Salem, 1970), 328, and Louise K. Brown, *Wilderness Town: The Story of Bedford, Massachusetts* (n.p., 1968), 5; Edward Pierce Hamilton, *A History of Milton* (Milton, Mass., 1957), 4, holds that the newcomers have maintained the "old Yankee spirit of service to the community and the desire for integrity in local government. . . ." Charles A. Morse hits the patriotic note with his prayer: "We must never cease to honor those founders of our country and impress future generations with the tremendous debt we owe those who fought for us . . . ," *Warwick, Massachusetts: Biography of a Town, 1763–1963* (Cambridge, Mass., 1963), 97.
24. Roy, *Quaboag Plantation*, 136, holds that the Puritan idealism must fail because "human nature being what it is, desire for self-enhancement, greed, avarice and the other vices of man" would dominate. Hamilton, *Milton*, 113, states that he is convinced "that, despite the passage of many years, human na-

adaptable, and rather polemic past has always been part of the "populist-traditional" school. More recently, in the Cold War Era of the 1950's, Samuel Chamberlain and Henry Flynt continued this tradition when they turned to the frontier town of Deerfield for the calm strength America needed to face the Communist menace. More than two centuries ago the white inhabitants of that village, animated by "fiery patriotism and love of life," met and overcame the challenge of a savage horde just "as we are meeting it in Korea today, with the lives of brave men and women."[25] These Cold War currents also influenced the ideological considerations of the "democratic" historians writing at the same time.

The unity of a culture is a wondrous thing: there exists a wholeness between its political life and its social modes of behavior. In the town of Boston the Puritan leaders governed the commonwealth, took first place in the distribution of land, and shaped sermon and society to mirror ideological values. The seating patterns in churches reflected the shared sensibilities of this new order, just as the central dominance of the pulpit symbolized the triumph of the Word over the Anglican liturgy.[26] Likewise, in looking at the works of B. Katherine and Robert E. Brown, who studied the franchise in Puritan and colonial Massachusetts, and Clinton Rossiter, whose *Seedtime of the Republic* returned to the germinal approach of the last century, we discern a conservative focus which marks their prize-winning writings as distinct products of the Cold War Era of the 1950's. At no point in recent times had the definition of what was "American" been so important, nor had the demand for historians been so great. Society needed and found praiseworthy the works of Brown and Rossiter.

---

ture has not really changed," a position also supported by Phalen, *Acton*, 18. For politics see Morison, *Peterborough*, I, 91–92, and James Duncan Phillips, *Salem and the Indies* (Boston, 1947), 3–9.

25 Samuel Chamberlain and Henry Flynt, *Frontier of Freedom* (New York, 1952), 1–7.

26. Darrett B. Rutman, *Winthrop's Boston: Portrait of a Puritan Town, 1630–1649* (Chapel Hill, 1965), 73; John Coolidge, "Hingham Builds a Meetinghouse," *New England Quarterly*, XXXIV (1961), 457–459; Watkins, *Middleton*, 254; Robert J. Dinkin, "Seating the Meeting House in Early Massachusetts," *New England Quarterly*, XLIII (1970), 450–464.

Their books reflected the dominant ideological concerns of a culture in crisis which considered itself under attack; when it heard the "tom-tom" of communism it turned to its past for strength and solace.[27]

The past desired was the past found. Rossiter's colonial garden brought forth the fruit of "ethical, ordered liberty." He shared the "devotion Americans continue to pay to the political values of the colonial and Revolutionary periods" and declared his opposition to any "rude rejection of the past. . . ." He believed that the values of the New England town meeting and covenant theology could still serve an urban, secular, and industrial society. To this picture Robert E. Brown added pragmatic details on economics and voting which he saw as proving the absence of both class conflict (that Marxist engine for social change) and elites. The Massachusetts towns had a "relatively equalitarian, middle-class society in which there was a great deal of economic opportunity." Both Rossiter and Brown agree that the Revolution was essentially legal, peaceful, and conservative—"a revolution to preserve a social order rather than to change it."[28] In myriad forms the American public of the fifties shared this vision: President Dwight Eisenhower accepted the Presbyterian covenant; our universities committed resources to publishing virtually the entire works of the founding fathers; our builders constructed more colonial-type houses than had been built in the period before 1789; and Early American furniture gracefully cabineted the televisions and computers in our homes and offices.

In the rehabilitation of our colonial past the Browns assured nerv-

27. John Higham, in his "The Cult of the 'American Consensus': Homogenizing Our History," *Commentary*, XXVII (Feb. 1959), 93–100, called attention to this phenomenon, as has John B. Kirby in his recent "Early American Politics—The Search for Ideology," *Journal of Politics*, XXXII (1970), 808–838. Strangely enough, neither author focused on the Brown-Rossiter contribution to consensus history.

For the demand for historians see W. David Maxwell, "A Methodological Hypothesis for the Plight of the Humanities," and Paul L. Ward's "Graph," American Association of University Professors *Bulletin*, LIV (1968), 80, 397.

28. Clinton Rossiter, *Seedtime of the Republic: The Origin of the American Tradition of Political Liberty* (New York, 1953), 2, 446, 448–449; Robert E. Brown, *Middle-Class Democracy*), 19, 401. However, Rossiter in his *Seedtime*, 19–20, favored the interpretation supporting a limited franchise in colonial America, since that would be closer to the English model, which is typical of his Anglophilia.

ous Americans that their ancestors and institutions always had been democratic. Moreover, the evidence for this thesis came from the New England towns with their local tax records, voting lists, petitions, probate files, and town meeting minutes. B. Katherine Brown argued that the Bay Colony's law requiring church membership as the first condition for freemanship voting was probably inclusive of the population's male majority. Why not? After all, the Puritans controlled both the immigration to their confessional state and the right to settle in any community. The end result, obviously, was a "great degree of uniformity in religious beliefs in most of the towns." Although on a theoretical level the Puritans conceived of the government as an "aristocracy," they also held for the consent of the governed; B. Katherine Brown read this to mean that in "form, then, Puritan aristocracy bears a strong resemblance to our modern democracy." She continued that then, "as in our modern democracy, wealth and heredity carried no weight in government."[29] Her husband, Robert E. Brown, made an even stronger case for the existence of primitive democracy in the Massachusetts Charter government of 1691. There, full exercise of the franchise depended upon a man's owning property worth £40 sterling: Brown's analysis of tax and voting lists for Stockbridge and seventeen other towns indicated that in the eighteenth century 53 to 97 percent of the adult males could vote. Brown concurred in Crèvecoeur's vision of agrarian innocence, picturing the "Sunday congregation of respectable farmers and their wives" in which "there was not an esquire except the unlettered magistrate, and even the minister himself was a simple farmer who did not live in luxury on the labor of others." Brown found no ruling elites, no seaboard aristocracy, no oligarchy. "Obviously the common man had come into his own in Massachusetts long before the time of Andrew Jackson."[30]

29. B. Katherine Brown, "Freemanship in Puritan Massachusetts," *American Historical Review*, LIX (1953–54), 868–880; and, "A Note on the Puritan Concept of Aristocracy," *Mississippi Valley Historical Review*, XLI (1954–55), 112.

30. Robert E. Brown, "Democracy in Colonial Massachusetts," *New England Quarterly*, XXV (1952), 295–298, 300–301, 313; *Middle-Class Democracy*, 3–4.

The key point in the Browns' argument dealt with the inclusiveness of the various Massachusetts franchises, which they found to embrace a majority of the adult males. This position generally has been confirmed. And their "middle-class democratic" view of society agreed with that of the Jewetts, who held that a majority of Rowley's early settlers had been church members and voters, just as it reechoed Morison's loud cheers for Peterborough's town meeting democracy. In this respect it represented a union with the "populist-traditional" town history school (and a return to the republican nationalism of George Bancroft circa 1840). Both the Browns and the "populist-traditional" authors rejected the "progressive" historians who saw "early Massachusetts as a class-ridden oligarchy."

But does the existence of a wide franchise equal democracy? Does the sharing of a world view by the governed and the governors mean liberty? Can anyone really believe that "wealth and heredity" carry no weight in "our modern democracy"or that these factors were unimportant in the Bay Colony?[31] Even so sympathetic a scholar as Robert J. Taylor, whose account of the extensive franchise in Hampshire County helped confirm the Browns' research, found class conflict. In the period of stress following the Revolution—and stress tests the true parameters of any system—Taylor realized that "what troubled [the Massachusetts] westerners was that their votes were not doing them any good." When their views differed from their leaders they faced a "continued unresponsiveness of elected representatives" which the democratic Shaysites resolved by armed rebellion.[32] As Richard B. Morris perceptively remarked, Brown had failed to "take into account the leadership of the élite, which was one of the marked phenomena of New England town life."[33] Yet both B. Katherine and Robert E. Brown had set the terms for future case studies. And they had placed

31. For a competent survey of the problem, see James A. Thorpe, "Colonial Suffrage in Massachusetts: An Essay Review," Essex Institute *Historical Collections,* CVI (1970), 169–181, as well as Michael G. Kammen, ed., *Politics and Society in Colonial America* (New York, 1967), which is a careful anthology of central articles in this controversy.

32. Robert J. Taylor, *Western Massachusetts in the Revolution* (Providence, 1954), 3, 36, 143, 176, 207.

33. *American Historical Review,* LXII (1956–57), 636–637.

town history in the mainstream of American historiography. Micro-studies on Kent (1955), Newburyport (1959), and Plymouth (1963) testified to this new direction.

In 1738 Kent, Connecticut, started with forty settling families, extensive economic opportunity, and basic agreement on the value of acquisitiveness. The resident proprietors comprised a dominant group. High mobility matched the endemic "speculation by local men in local lands." At this point the franchise included 71 percent of the adult resident males. The local power structure broadly represented its frontier farmers, who themselves had come from middle-class families and were related to the ruling "eastern families." And democratic Kent supported the aristocratic governing clique in the Assembly because "this hierarchy appeared to govern in the best interests of the Kent citizen." Moreover, Kent gave witness to its belief in traditional status, piety, and wealth in its church seating formula: "We shall seat each person according to age, dignity, and [property on the tax] list."[34] This shows that while we have focused most of our attention on the franchise, which is obviously important in a secular-political culture, the Kent townfolk gave primary attention to the religio-symbolic ordering of themselves on Sunday morning. Charles S. Grant so far had confirmed a substantial part of the Brown thesis on "middle-class democracy." However, Grant realized that just as available farm land supported the political and economic opportunities of the first generation, so the lack of land constrained the second and third generations. "Less land meant less opportunity to qualify as freemen." By the 1790's hard times had come to overcrowded Kent. The franchise, which in 1777 embraced 79 percent of the adult males, now covered but 63 percent, and a permanent proletariat had made itself visible on

34. Charles S. Grant, *Democracy in the Connecticut Frontier Town of Kent* (New York, 1961), 32, 106, 111, 162. In trying to comprehend the values of these colonial people it should be remembered that they were more likely to fight over the church seating than over town politics. See Hamilton, *Milton,* 128, Phalen, *Action,* 45–53, Frank P. Rand, *The Village of Amherst: A Landmark of Light* (Amherst, 1958), 17, for seating arrangements. B. Katherine Brown in "Puritan Democracy: A Case Study [Cambridge]," *Mississippi Valley Historical Review,* L (1963–64), 384–385, shows a higher popular participation in church affairs than in "freemen" politics.

the bottom. Why? Grant's answer is as simple as his research was complex: "pressure of an increasing population on the available supply of local land."[35]

Benjamin W. Labaree in writing about colonial Newburyport and its dominance by a "merchant aristocracy" maintained "that wherever social and economic democracy does not exist, political democracy is impossible." Nothing could be more antithetical to the Brown thesis than Labaree's portrait of government by a mercantile elite. An "irreconcilable breach" with its backland farmers brought about the town's birth in 1764. Into its 647 acres—the size of five Kent farms—crowded 2,882 inhabitants who looked "out to the sea for their fortune." Sea captain, artisan, sailor, found common cause in that orientation. They knew their "basic interdependence" upon one another and the sea. The inhabitants allowed a "minority group of less than 200 men" to control this truly urban, stratified, and economically dynamic town because of a "habit of deference" learned before the mast and confirmed in school and church. The unequal distribution of the franchise reflected the town's hierarchy: of Newburyport's 699 adult males in 1773, 24.8 percent were merchants and professional men of whom 79.1 percent were qualified to vote; 3.9 percent shopkeepers and innholders with 77.8 percent qualified; 25.3 percent domestic artisans with 63.8 percent qualified; 19.4 percent maritime artisans with 51.5 percent qualified; 15.3 percent unknowns with 44.8 percent qualified; and finally 11.3 percent laborers and others with 36.7 percent owning enough property to share in the franchise. In this class society 40.2 percent (281/699) of the adult males failed to qualify as voters. Theirs was a "life balanced on the line of subsistence, finding employment as it came along, on the docks as wharfingers or at sea as fo'c's'le hands." Although it was statistically possible for the lower orders to gain political control, since "the merchants and shipmasters, with their professional allies, the lawyers, doctors, and other gentlemen, constituted only about one third of the electorate," the fact is that these voters overwhelmingly gave office to their betters from the "uppermost

35. Grant, *Democracy*, 102, 111, 172.

class."[36] In Labaree's hands the franchise becomes a prime indicator of economic activity: that 73.8 percent of adult males could vote in the state election of 1793 and 92 percent in 1807 meant prosperity, while the decline to 70 percent in 1820 reflected depression.[37] But whether the franchise was high or low, a vote in either circumstance was cast for one's betters in this era of deferential politics.

By the time George Langdon came out with his study of Plymouth Colony in 1966 most of the necessary clues had been assembled to resolve the "middle-class" democratic riddle. Langdon built upon the results and insights of his predecessors. He knew that the Plymouth government in general represented the aims of its denizens; and in the early years of the Old Colony a majority of adult males would become freemen as the Browns predicted. And just as Grant found population pressure in Kent reducing opportunity for the third generation, so Langdon realized that by 1675 Plymouth faced a land shortage. Moreover, the "same deputies seemed to return year after year" to the Plymouth Court as they had in Labaree's deferential Newburyport. In the 1670's orthodoxy favored a contracted franchise, and one-third of the Plymouth townsmen were purged from the voting list: "Seventeenth-century Plymouth, then, produced a society in which the opportunity to share in the political life of the colony was initially great but became more exclusive."[38] Langdon believed that the original wide participation "in the colony's political life" was a means of obtaining and holding a "consensus of support for an established civil authority."[39] Michael Zuckerman imaginatively grasped the larger implica-

36. See Benjamin W. Labaree, "Newburyport," American Association for State and Local History Bulletin, II, 9 (1959), 225–234, and Patriots and Partisans: The Merchants of Newburyport, 1764–1815 (Cambridge, 1962), 1–5, 13–15.

37. Labaree, Merchants of Newburyport, 104, 133, 203. See also Donald W. Koch, "Income Distribution and Political Structure in Seventeenth-Century Salem, Massachusetts," Essex Institute Historical Collections, CV (1969), 50–69.

38. George D. Langdon, Jr., "The Franchise and Political Democracy in Plymouth Colony," William and Mary Quarterly, 3d ser., XX (1963), 525–526.

39. Langdon, Pilgrim Colony: A History of New Plymouth, 1620–1691 (New Haven, 1966), 98.

tion of this idea. He realized that in the Massachusetts towns effective "action necessitated a public opinion approaching if not attaining unanimity, and public policy was accordingly bent toward securing such unanimity." In the context of the colonial world, men "were allowed to vote not out of any overweening attachment to democratic principles *per se* but simply because a wide canvass was convenient, if not indeed critical, in consolidating a consensus in the community."[40] One went to the town meeting to affirm communal unity, not to be a democrat.

Fortunately for the historian, Jackson Turner Main in 1965 offered a typology for viewing town settlement, growth, and development. New England towns fell into four regional types, the first of which was the frontier community with its high mobility and the concentration of a third of its land in the hands of the top 10 percent of its farmers. Kent of the first generation fits in there, as does early Peacham. Next was a subsistence farm town such as Old Broad Bay with its great diffusion of land of little market value. The third type was the commercial farm communities with fertile soil and access to market, in which the top 10 percent of the farmers owned half the land. Both Kent and Plymouth of the third generation probably approached this model. Finally, there were the urban societies such as Newburyport in which the top group controlled 60 percent of the wealth.[41] Hence, what is crucial in understanding a town's history is the ability to place it in its proper setting. Accidentally, the democratic focus of the fifties had cast light on this factor and the sociocultural realities of the colonial towns, although its primary concern, in the words of Robert J. Taylor, had been "political and economic developments." The decade of the sixties would now turn explicitly to sociodemographic analysis.

40. Michael Zuckerman, "The Social Context of Democracy in Massachusetts," *William and Mary Quarterly*, 3d ser., XXV (1968), 526–528, and reprinted in Stanley N. Katz, ed., *Colonial America: Essays in Politics and Social Development* (Boston, 1971), 230–231.

41. Jackson Turner Main, *The Social Structure of Revolutionary America* (Princeton, 1965), 39–41. See also Edward M. Cook, Jr., "Local Leadership and the Typology of New England Towns, 1700–1785," *Political Science Quarterly*, LXXXVI (1971), 586–608.

The emergence of a new generation of colonial historians, sharing basic theoretical premises, occurred in the early sixties. Theirs was a host of common concerns dealing with the settlers' British backgrounds, family structures, land and kinship networks, and population, all united to bring cumulative light upon the multifaceted life of the early New England towns. And just as one cannot separate Robert E. Brown's attempt to provide us with a democratic past from the Cold War defensiveness of American culture, so the "sociodemographic model builders" reflected both in the mode of analysis and in the questions asked certain current trends; this is most obvious in concerns with quantification, population problems, sexual mores, and social protest movements. The day of explicit conceptualization had come and with it a conscious colonial "sixth section," which like its French prototype believes that social history must be rewritten from the bottom up. And like the *sixième section* these studies borrow from the insights of cultural anthropology, historical demography, and social psychology. Moreover, they share a common ethos, which Philip Greven sums up as the conviction that "historians must seek to explore the basic structure and character of society through close, detailed examinations of the experiences of individuals, families, and groups in particular communities and localities."[42]

John Demos, Philip Greven, Kenneth Lockridge, and Darrett Rutman—authors of works dealing with Plymouth, Andover, Dedham, and Boston—ask not only what happened in the view of modern behavioristic theories, but also what did people think was happening, and what did they want to happen; and their answers to this quest for the perceptions and ideals of the colonial folk come by and large from such nonnarrative data as family reconstitution forms, land division records, tax rolls, deeds, estate inventories, court cases, and settlement patterns. These authors have been influenced by Louis Henry's *Anciennes familles Genevoises* (Paris, 1956), Pierre Goubert's *Beauvais et le Beauvaises de 1600 à 1730* (Paris, 1960), the English edition

42. Philip J. Greven, Jr., *Four Generations: Population, Land, and Family in Colonial Andover, Massachusetts* (Ithaca, 1970), viii; John Demos, *A Little Commonwealth: Family Life in Plymouth Colony* (New York, 1970), vii.

of Philippe Ariès's *Centuries of Childhood* (New York, 1962), the various population studies of the Cambridge Group for the History of Population and Social Structure, and of course such microstudies as Charles Grant's work on the Connecticut town of Kent. These historians realize that if we are to speak of something being "American" in this early transplant period we must have valid comparative data about equivalent English and French societies; a colonial historian must be a specialist in the "Atlantic Community" world of the seventeenth and eighteenth centuries.

In looking at the European backgrounds of the first settlers Crèvecoeur saw nothing but "involuntary idleness, servile dependence, penury, and useless labour" in contrast to the freedom, innovation, and "ample subsistence" of the American experience.[43] Until very recently historians allowed their views of the settlement process to be imprisoned in Crèvecoeur's mythic dichotomy which saw America as the virgin land and Europe as the villainous, corrupt, crowded, Old World. Yet the fact is that we know very little about the *real* pasts of the first planters and of their experiences in both the "old" and the "new" Englands.

Sumner Chilton Powell, by focusing his attention on the English backgrounds of Sudbury's founders, saw a diversity of farming and leadership patterns tempered by the American experience. The town's dominant reality continued to be the traditional open field village system of farming which had characterized the past experiences of a majority of Sudbury's transplanted Englishmen. Just as they had done in Weyhill, so these settlers shared their oxen, farm equipment, and labor, and lived back to back in a nucleated village. Yet one of the reasons they had left England was to form "godly, orderly communities"; they showed what they meant by this when they ranked all settlers in an "economic hierarchy" headed by the minister, Edmund Brown. Moreover, their own selectmen rather than a manor lord now governed them. Powell rightly draws attention to the granting of house lots to each and every inhabitant, "free and clear," thus making every adult

43. J. Hector St. John de Crèvecoeur, *Letters from an American Farmer* (New York, 1957), 40.

male a landowner. The full implications of individual landholding in Sudbury were not realized until the second and third generations reached maturity; by any past norms their willingness to leave the village and live on distant farms was radical; at the same time they insisted upon using the "pagan" calendar and the conservative common law which their parents had rejected as corrupt norms.[44]

In the account by Philip J. Greven, Andover, Massachusetts, also started as a "replica of an English village . . . in which all of the inhabitants dwelt side by side and tilled their lands in small plots adjacent to those of their neighbors in the general fields." Within a generation, this community-centered ideal likewise had been transformed by the sheer abundance of available land into an individually oriented farming area.[45] John J. Waters, in his study of Hingham, also realized that prior local and regional identifications, crystallized in divergent farm customs, religious rituals, dialects, even in the styles of door hinges, meant that the first settlers came with fixed loyalties. He found ethnic conflict between the town's "West Country" men and the more numerous East Anglian immigrants dominating the first generation's life. The men from old Hingham were patriarchs, determined to keep their familiar religious and political leadership patterns intact. They did form a community more traditional than the compromising Sudbury or the youth-oriented Andover.[46] These three studies make apparent an amazing cultural diversity.

To speak in any meaningful way of generations the historian must come to terms with the vital statistics of actual colonial families. After all, Ecclesiastes tells us there is a time to be born and a time to die. Yet most historians remained ignorant of this truth when writing about western preindustrial families. Scholars were content with the myth of early marriages, large families, high infant mortality, and early death.

44. Sumner Chilton Powell, *Puritan Village: The Formation of a New England Town* (Middletown, 1963), xvii, 81–84, 138–140, 144–145.

45. Philip J. Greven, Jr., "Old Patterns in the New World: The Distribution of Land in 17th Century Andover," Essex Institute *Historical Collections,* CI (1965), 147–148.

46. John J. Waters, "Hingham, Massachusetts, 1631–1661: An East Anglian Oligarchy in the New World," *Journal of Social History,* I (1967–68), 351–353, and reprinted in Katz, *Colonial America,* 52–53.

John Demos's research on Plymouth, published in 1965, established a new set of boundaries: the colonial family averaged from seven to ten children and could expect an infant mortality rate of one out of ten; moreover, every fifth woman died from causes associated with child-birth. Now while these families were large they had not reached maximum possibilities. The spacing of births at "roughly two-year intervals" indicates family planning. Demos thinks that "Plymouth couples simply eschewed sexual contact over long periods of time," although as Louis Henry has shown in his study of Geneva, other methods of contraception ought not to be ruled out as possibilities for this period.[47] The low rate of infant mortality, approximately half of what is considered as normal in the Third World, speaks for a high standard of life, as do the longevity figures of 69.2 for adult males and 62.4 for women. Another sign that these people had some control over the life process may be seen in the relatively late age for marriage: the age for men went from a high of 27 to a low of 25 years; for women the movement went from a low of 20 years in the early colony to 22 years at the end of the seventeenth century. These people lived in a fluid, dynamic, highly mobile, almost rootless society which is in marked contrast to "hermetically sealed" Dedham.[48]

The people in Kenneth Lockridge's Dedham lived and died where they had been born. If Dedham never saw a stranger, neither did it see famine or war. Its "births recorded for each marriage" in a century's time were 4.64. At first its conceptions occurred cyclically, peaking in May and with a secondary ascendancy in December, just as happened in rural France and England. What is remarkable is that by the end of its first century its people had departed from the "cyclic yearly pattern of conception" and now spaced conceptions throughout the year.[49] By implication, Dedham's people in the eighteenth century had

47. John Demos, "Notes on Life in Plymouth Colony," *William and Mary Quarterly*, 3d ser., XXII (1965), 270–271 and n. 3; Louis Henry, *Anciennes familles Genevoises* (Paris, 1956), 93–99; Robert V. Wells, "Family Size and Fertility Control in Eighteenth-Century America: A Study of Quaker Families," *Population Studies*, XXV (1971), 73–82.
48. Demos, 275 (see n. 47), and reprinted in Katz, *Colonial America*, 81.
49. Kenneth A. Lockridge, "The Population of Dedham, Massachusetts, 1636–1736," *Economic History Review*, 2d ser., XIX (1966), 318–344.

partially mastered the procreative drive. Lockridge in his extremely
sophisticated analysis produced a people-centered history rather than
a narrative of politics and great events. And what impressed Lockridge
was the remarkable similarities which unite the experiences of the inhabitants of Dedham, Massachusetts, Clayworth, England, and Crulai,
France.

Philip J. Greven's *Four Generations* details the land and kinship
networks of Andover's first twenty-eight families and their descendants unto the fourth generation. Andover, open to colonization in
1646, had by 1662 formed a core community which dominated the
town for the next hundred years. Within twenty years of the town's
founding, the first settlers had garnered almost 8,000 acres, most of
which would not be cultivated in their lifetimes. The ownership of this
land meant control; it enabled the fathers to place their sons in surrounding plots near the parental homesteads without the elders sur-
rendering title until death separated them from their beloved acres.
This dependency created and maintained the extended "patriarchal
families characteristic of the first and second generations in Andover."[50] The promise of parental land meant that nearly four-fifths
of the second generation men abided all their lives in Andover. Such
overwhelming stability is in marked contrast to the geographical mobility Demos described in Plymouth, but it is very close to Lockridge's
figures on Dedham and Waters's data for Barnstable.[51] Andover's first
two generations shared a golden age of much land, high fertility and
large families, low mortality, and lives which equaled the biblical
three score and ten. The third generation, as in Kent, inherited a land
shortage. It also witnessed a willingness on the part of the fathers and
a desire on the part of the sons for "economic autonomy and personal
independence"; they knew that the boom days had passed; two-fifths
of the third-generation sons left Andover for greener pastures. The
fourth generation lived in an overcrowded, stagnating town, had a

50. Greven, *Four Generations,* 99.
51. *Ibid.,* 39; Kenneth A. Lockridge, *A New England Town: The First
Hundred Years* (New York, 1970), 139–140; John J. Waters, *The Otis Family
in Provincial and Revolutionary Massachusetts* (Chapel Hill, 1968), 49–50.

lower life expectancy than their fathers, and a notable decline in fertility: in the peak days of the 1690's births per marriage were 7.6, whereas for 1720 to 1789 the figure drops from a high of 4.8 to a low of 3.0.[52] These conclusions rest upon a data pool of 2,000 individuals. The careful outline of their activities through a century and a half shows the great relevancy of a controlled generational study for the social historian. In Andover we see a cycle of growth, stability, flux, decline, and the intimate connection of population to land in that pre-industrial peasant farming community.

By now it should be obvious that human beings are not everywhere the same, that human personality may be shaped differently, and that behavior varies considerably over time. Yet the obviousness of this remark cannot disguise the many difficulties involved in trying to comprehend past psychological phenomena. Fortunately, John Demos and Richard Bushman have addressed themselves to this complex problem in complementary studies dealing with character formation and change.

From the outset Demos has been influenced by Erik Erikson's concept of "life cycles" as a way of understanding individual development. This model, applied to the early period of child rearing and character formation, holds that in the first year of life the Puritan baby could expect a "relatively comfortable and tranquil time"—it was wanted, breast-fed, kept warm, and free from swaddling or binding restraints. The second year, with its weaning, the confronting of another new child, and the culture's insistence that any assertion of the will on the part of the child must be broken, must have been a traumatic experience. And all of this happened in a small crowded house where privacy as we understand the term did not exist. This crowding combined with the culture's attack against a child's will indicates that the Puritan's hangup was not sex but rather a "tight cluster of anxieties about aggression."[53] As a result, fear of aggression, of conflict situations, and loss are the dominant motifs of childhood, adulthood (for adolescence

52. *Ibid.*, 123, 172, 181–183.
53. Demos, *A Little Commonwealth*, 134–137.

did not yet exist), and old age in seventeenth-century Plymouth. Such training produced feelings of inadequacy in Connecticut townsmen as they faced a "series of stern fathers who stood over them in the homes of their childhood, in the church, in society, and in the state." Under this repressive system, Bushman believes, these men lived in tension, made sharper when material improvement brought society away from its Puritan ideals of restraint. The Great Awakening, when the "ALL" touched the sinner, liberated man from past guilt, for the Lord took man as he was: "In making peace with themselves, converts inwardly revolted against the old law and authority, and, as time was to show, they would eventually refuse to submit to a social order alien to their new identity." The Puritan had become a Yankee; what was inward guilt became outward conflict; the avid pursuit of gain was by 1765 considered acceptable rather than sinful.[54]

The cumulative insights of this third school have converged with peculiar intensity to illuminate colonial Boston. In 1962 Emery Battis led the way with a sociological analysis of Boston's Antinomians before 1638. First of all, he showed the import of past family relationships and regional origins in bringing together the critical "core group" of supporters for Anne Hutchinson. They came overwhelmingly from Lincolnshire and were trade-and-craft oriented as distinct from the dominant "agricultural yeomen and gentry" sectors. In short, "Mrs. Hutchinson's doctrines were most attractive to those persons whose economic interests were frustrated by the organic morality of the orthodox clergy and gentry."[55] But as Darrett Rutman showed, John Winthrop's victory over the merchants was temporary. His ideal of a corporate, medieval state perished before his death. Winthrop's gentry followers who "had received almost one-half of the land granted by the town" helped bring about commercial change. Boston had taken a distinctly modern, secular air, condemned in the countryside as a "can-

54. Richard L. Bushman, *From Puritan to Yankee: Character and the Social Order in Connecticut, 1690–1765* (Cambridge, 1967), 18, 187–191, 286–288.
55. Emery Battis, *Saints and Sectaries: Anne Hutchinson and the Antinomian Controversy in the Massachusetts Bay Colony* (Chapel Hill, 1962), 257–259, 264.

cerous sore" where "trade and commerce ruled."[56] James A. Henretta continued the documentation of this drift when his analysis of the tax lists of 1687 and 1771 showed the emergence of a modern, urban, stratified society.[57] Finally, Allan Kulikoff in a technical *pièce de résistance* demonstrated that for the revolutionary era, 1771 to 1790, not a "less stratified, but an even more unequal society developed in Boston." In fact changes in the distribution of wealth were greater in these two decades than they had been in the preceding nine; by 1790 the top 1 percent of the population held 27.14 percent of the wealth, while that of the "lower middle group" had been cut in half. Ministers might preach to the rich on their duty to the poor, and elite literature might still give the impression of noblesse oblige, but such sentiments were fantasies. The hard quantifiable evidence leads to the conclusion that the "groups of near poor who manned preindustrial crowds in Europe—apprentices, journeymen, and artisans—lived in greater profusion in Boston than in contemporary European towns."[58] Kulikoff has made us conscious of the socioeconomic realities of a capitalistic, urban structure. He has given us a real image to replace the ideal of a communal past which never existed for colonial Boston.

The modern historiography on the New England town can tell us a great deal about how the historian serves as the selective memory for his culture. His concerns clearly reflect the times in which he lives. The "populist-traditional" views of Amos and Emily Jewett mirrored a belief, common for their generation, in Anglo-Saxon superiority, republicanism, and institutional stability. The town of Rowley exemplified the normative virtues of WASP America. Likewise, B. Katherine and Robert E. Brown in their Cold War quest for "middle-class" colonial democratic voters reflected the defensiveness of our culture as it sought comfort in a conflict-free, status quo past. In turn, the "sociodemographic model builders" such as Philip Greven and Kenneth

56. Rutman, *Winthrop's Boston*, 22, 87, 256, 272.
57. James A. Henretta, "Economic Development and Social Structure in Colonial Boston," *William and Mary Quarterly*, 3d. ser., XXII (1965), 75–92, and reprinted in Katz, *Colonial America*, 450–465.
58. Allan Kulikoff, "The Progress of Inequality in Revolutionary Boston," *William and Mary Quarterly*, 3d ser., XXVIII (1971), 376, 381, 388, 409–410.

Lockridge speak for today's concerns. However, the difference from the two earlier schools is the explicit consciousness of both historical relativity and creativity. We recognize that historians serve society as its perceptual screen through which the past is filtered. Of necessity, the end results ignore or downplay some aspects of the past and exaggerate others. Yet to be aware of this truth makes one more conscious of the strengths and weaknesses of research models. It should lead to a more logical, systematic program of regional town research. We need studies of towns which failed and of those which deviated from the norm by not having churches and schools.

The collective picture emerging from recent town studies shows a more conservative, primitive, and fundamentalist society than historians had suspected. The first settlers came as peasants; they shared plows and common fields; they lived in nucleated villages just as they had in the old country. On the local level they supported a hard-line damnation theology; it contrasts sharply with the academic religion of Harvard dons. If the settlers rejected certain aspects of Tudor-Stuart hierarchy they created a new hierarchy, new space, and new farms. We see this in local government, church seating, and individual farming. The element of gain, violating certain traditional communal norms, is central in understanding this new order and with it the formation of a colonial bourgeoisie in the second and third settlement generations. The emergence of a capitalistic order in Newburyport and Boston rested upon this shared ethos. We now realize that at any stage in a community's life there exists an equation between land and people; this realization helps us to explain the generational changes in Kent, Andover, and Dedham. We now understand that our colonial ancestors had some control over family size as well as the will to adjust to changing socioeconomic norms.

Finally, we historians realize that the settlement and development of these pre-industrial towns constitutes a priceless record in social experimentation. Indeed, as John Murrin observed, the "colonies provide the best social laboratory we can find for early modern England."[59] More than a decade ago, Peter Laslett saw that the settlements

59. John M. Murrin, *History and Theory*, XI (1970), 275.

tell us "what was transferred intact" from the Old World "undisturbed, subjected neither to criticism and rejection nor to circumstances which forbade their continuance."[60] And as a result of current research we can write with some meaningfulness about innovation, selectivity, and creativity in New England. The host of comparative and interdisciplinary insights derived from such studies has placed the New England towns in the very center of contemporary research.

60. Peter Laslett, *New England Quarterly*, XXXVI (1963), 547.

HERBERT ALAN JOHNSON

American Colonial Legal History:
A Historiographical Interpretation

NEARLY THIRTY YEARS AGO Professor Julius Goebel commented that "American legal history is in its infancy, and if it is to be reared in accord with the high standards which have prevailed in the writing of English legal history, the matter of tutelage is critical."[1] Although the past three decades have witnessed considerable maturity in the field, there is still a persistent need to give careful attention to the education of a new and larger group of young legal historians. Historiography, one of the most effective pedagogical tools, has been and remains "the foster child of legal history,"[2] in spite of a revived interest in the history of law and the establishment of graduate-level programs at the University of Virginia and Harvard University. To condemn neophytes to wander aimlessly through the maze of American colonial legal history without the aid of historiography is to frustrate them and to elicit from them harsh words of criticism for their elders. One can easily imagine them rephrasing the lament of Peter Van Schaack, one of the many pre-Revolutionary law clerks trained in New York before the advent of the blessed Blackstone, "How many hours have I hunted, how many books turned up, for what three

1. Julius Goebel, Jr., and T. Raymond Naughton, *Law Enforcement in Colonial New York: A Study in Criminal Procedure* (*1664–1776*) (New York, 1944), xxxiv.
2. The phrase is that of John P. Reid, in *1962 Annual Survey of American Law* (New York, 1963), 742.

minutes of explanation from any tolerable lawyer would have made evident to me."[3] In training legal historians, as in educating colonial law clerks, there is a time for complication through the contemplation of variables, and there is also a time for simplification through the consideration of general principles. Generalization is fostered and facilitated by historiographic analysis and criticism. Thus, if American colonial legal history is to remain a viable academic discipline in the present and to flourish in the future, we must make the initial effort necessary to understand the subject as it has been studied and presented in the past. Based upon the insights gained from considering past writings in the field, we might determine what approaches might prove fruitful for future explorations.

The history of colonial American law came to scholarly attention around the turn of the century when the "frontier thesis" of Frederick Jackson Turner occupied the focal point of historical debate.[4] Not surprisingly, the work of certain legal historians reflected Turnerian influences. The work of Paul S. Reinsch, in particular, was notable for its emphasis on the unique qualities of seventeenth-century American colonial law, and the relationship which the relatively civilized frontier communities in the New World had with the development of legal rules and procedures that differed from Old World models.[5] Although

3. Henry C. Van Schaack, *Life of Peter Van Schaack* (New York, 1842), 9.
4. Turner's exposition of his "frontier thesis," originally delivered as a paper before the American Historical Association annual meeting in 1893, is printed in Frederick J. Turner, *The Frontier in American History* (New York, 1920), 1–38; an excellent critical and historiographic study of the Turner thesis is Ray A. Billington, *The American Frontier* (Washington, 1959), particularly 14–17. John Higham indicated that Turner's was a "divided heritage" encouraging both the use of the frontier and section theses, as well as stressing the importance of western history, *Writing American History* (Bloomington, 1970), 121. In the legal history field it is, of course, the frontier thesis which has the broadest applicability. Richard Hofstadter pointed to a basic contradiction in Turner's work; while Turner was a theorist of historical causation, he was nevertheless opposed to "one idea systems" in the interpretation of historical events and development, *The Progressive Historians* (New York, 1968), 120.
5. Reinsch's doctoral dissertation at the University of Wisconsin was first published in 1899, and is his principal work in American colonial legal history. Its republication in "The English Common Law in the Early American Colonies," in *Select Essays in Anglo-American Legal History,* 3 vols. (Boston, 1907–9), I, 367–415, has made it a classic exposition of Turnerian interpreta-

Reinsch's emphasis on the influence of primitive conditions upon legal development for the most part has been discredited; there were, nevertheless, a number of valid interpretive insights gained from the Turnerian analysis. First and foremost, it was recognized that geographical factors were vitally important considerations to the student of early American law.

This influence of geography on the development of colonial law was profound, indeed. As a rule, colonial court jurisdictions were territorially larger than those in the mother country. Moreover, the cruder systems of transportation made actual distances in the colonies vastly greater than they were in England. Within any given American colony the court systems served both isolated frontier communities in which no trained lawyers practiced, as well as large provincial capitals and trading centers where the bar flourished. Here colonial practitioners equaled in knowledge and skill all but outstanding among their English contemporaries.[6]

---

tion. In a later work, *Colonial Government* (New York, 1902), 244, Reinsch rather inconsistently found that British institutions were successfully adopted by nineteenth-century British colonial possessions; however, Reinsch also discovered these same colonists to be making "decidedly novel experiments" with British forms of government. *Ibid.*, 244–246.

6. The Massachusetts General Court exercised relatively limited jurisdiction over the western counties of the province, and the local courts were initially endowed with powers far in excess of those authorized by the charter. Those same local courts were content with a six-man rather than a twelve-man jury. Joseph H. Smith, ed., *Colonial Justice in Western Massachusetts (1639–1702): The Pynchon Court Record* (Cambridge, Mass., 1961), 66, 90–91. Smith's conclusion is that the court structure and practice was not responding to "frontier" influence, but rather "in shaping the jurisdiction of the lower courts of the judicial hierarchy the General Court [i.e., legislature] followed an eclectic policy grounded upon expediency and pragmatism." *Ibid.*, 198. Clearly one of the practical considerations was the physical impossibility of close supervision over the distant courts of the western counties.

A somewhat similar situation existed in remote Albemarle County, North Carolina, where the local county courts followed their own mode of procedure in spite of proprietary orders to the contrary. Mattie E. W. Parker, ed., *North Carolina Higher-Court Records: 1670–1696*, 3 vols. to date (Raleigh, N.C., 1961–   ), II, lxxiii–lxxiv. Among the manuscript records of the Tryon County (New York) Court of Common Pleas, I have found unusual motions in arrest of judgment and for a new trial; the routine method of correcting error in counties nearer to the provincial capital at New York City was to take an appeal by writ of error to the Supreme Court of Judicature.

Density of population and landholding patterns, as well as familial relationships, likewise created the need for new principles of law and altered procedures in the courts. We have only begun to appreciate the impact that population density can have on legal development. Clearly, as the number of individuals in a given jurisdiction increases, the number of their legally cognizable controversies also begins to rise. Necessarily the law must exercise an increasing amount of social control as men and communities change from independent, relatively isolated agrarians, into interdependent urbanites.[7]

An emerging school of historical demographers, although primarily concerned with the political and social aspects of statistical studies, has begun to provide the basis for a reevaluation of the connection between population density, family structure, and the law. Philip Greven, for example, has noted the gradual abandonment of a community-wide preference for equal portions being given to all sons under wills and inter vivos deeds of gift in early Andover. This rejection of what is inaccurately termed "partible inheritance" coincided with a growing scarcity of land that persisted in the later years of settlement. By way of contrast, the town of Dedham held fast to the customary rule of equal division of agricultural lands among all the sons of the testator or grantor, according to Kenneth Lockridge, leading to severe economic hardship by the time the fourth generation reached maturity.[8] In a sense the legal rule in Massachusetts Bay remained static—partible inheritance applied to intestate succession in both Andover and Dedham—but in actual practice, those who took positive steps to arrange their estates in those two communities were

7. The legal consequences of population density can best be seen through the experiences of colonial city administrations. As settlement became more dense, the need for greater protection against fire became apparent and water supply became a matter of public concern, as did the increase of crime, violence, and vice. Carl Bridenbaugh, *Cities in the Wilderness* (New York, 1955), 55–93, 206–248. "Townspeople tended to greater violence in their behavior toward one another." *Ibid.*, 222.

8. Philip J. Greven, Jr., *Four Generations: Population, Land and Family in Colonial Andover, Massachusetts* (Ithaca, 1970), 37, 4–78, 83. Kenneth A. Lockridge, *A New England Town: The First Hundred Years* (New York, 1970), 157–159.

guided by sharply different attitudes toward the proper distribution
of land.

The Greven and Lockridge studies also demonstrate the conservatism followed by the town proprietors of Andover and Dedham in
their initial distribution of land among the original settlers. Lockridge
suggests that the preference for small land grants, revolving around
the future town common, was for the purpose of achieving social and
economic cohesion, and to advance the religious and utopian purposes
which formed the basis for the township enterprise. Greven stresses
the originally strong preference for an open-field system of agriculture,
which made it necessary to maintain land in small tracts reasonably
proximate to the town commons and house lots. As an alternative,
Greven suggests that the lack of grown children in the new settlement
may have limited the supply of labor which each family could devote
to its lands; consequently, smaller grants were necessary to avoid waste
or inefficient cultivation.[9]

Scarcity of labor is, of course, just another aspect of population
density; the sparse population of colonial America had an impact on
all phases of community activity, including the formation of the law.
As an example of this phenomenon, Sung Bok Kim's study of New
York tenants and their jural relationship to their landlords shows that
the economic reality of labor scarcity forced the magnates to waive
whatever may have remained of their ancient legal privileges and im-
munities. They provided their prospective tenants instead with substantial advantages in their leases, before adequate settlement of
manorial lands could be obtained.[10]

It may be argued that these influences did not alter the law as it
existed in the statute books, or as practiced in the courts, but such an
interpretation is undoubtedly too narrow a conception of what the
law is. Customary usages have always played an important role in the
development and modification of the law, and colonial America was

9. Greven, *Four Generations,* 49; Lockridge, *New England Town,* 12, 13.
10. "A New Look at the Great Landlords of Eighteenth-Century New York,"
William and Mary Quarterly, 3d ser., XXVII (1970), 599–610; attempts to
regulate labor in colonial America are discussed in Richard B. Morris, *Government and Labor in Early America* (New York, 1946).

forced to utilize custom when New World conditions dictated alterations from the English pattern. As settlements aged, their economic and social circumstances began to approximate those of the mother country, and early variations from English practice undoubtedly began to fall into disuse as a consequence. However, variations built into the American situation—large tracts of land on the western frontier and an undersupply of labor in the older sections of the colonies—continued to make their inroads into the monolithic adoption of English common law throughout the colonial period.

Few students of American colonial history have failed to marvel at the appetite for litigation displayed by the early Americans. Historical demographer John Demos has examined the architecture of Plymouth Colony homes in the seventeenth century. When the limited space, and hence small opportunity for privacy, is compared with the large size of the individual family units, it becomes obvious that the living arrangements of Plymouth residents were fraught with possibilities for intrafamilial conflict. Some of these arguments actually reached the courts of law, where Demos discovered them along with a strikingly large number of law cases between neighboring families. Demos advances a "germ of a hypothesis" which should cause legal historians to pause and contemplate: that these colonists redirected their feelings of anger and aggression, aroused by overcrowding, by arguing with and suing their neighbors.[11] Certainly this is as plausible an explanation as has ever been given for the multitude of small and inconsequential matters which came before many of the seventeenth-century colonial courts.

While these historical demographers are not Turnerians in the narrow sense of the term, they, and indeed most modern historical writers, share in the rich heritage that Turner left to the profession. Turner was the first to break with the old institutional school which attempted to trace the gradual and unilateral historical development of sharply segregated portions of human and community life. In legal

11. John Demos, *A Little Commonwealth: Family Life in Plymouth Colony* (Oxford, 1970), 46–51. This volume is filled with insights that will be helpful to all colonial legal historians.

history, as Roscoe Pound has argued persuasively, this approach resulted in a severe categorization and a compartmentalization of historical study which eliminated the need to consider the overall impact of formative influences upon the law derived from all sorts of human experience and thought.[12] By way of contrast, the "Turnerverein" returned to the historian's task of assessing *all* causative factors and of isolating those which appeared to be most determinative in shaping the new American nation.[13] In that sense their history was more catholic than that of the old institutional school they intended to replace. While Turnerianism has come into disrepute because of the emergence of internationalism and intellectual history,[14] the revisionism has been directed primarily at the western provincialism of the school and its tendency toward overemphasis of environmental determinism. American history in general partook of this revisionism, as did American colonial history, but both have preserved the most valuable of Turner's lessons concerning the influence of environment on human life and thought, and particularly on the development of legal institutions and principles. The Turnerians anticipated the use of social science methods in historical analysis and writing, and it is in this context that the school has the most to offer to the study of American legal history.[15]

12. Pound rejected the historical jurisprudence of the nineteenth century, and found its interpretations of legal history too narrow and compartmentalized. As far as he was concerned, the dynamic nature of the law was not taken into account in institutional studies which stressed gradual legal development along experiential lines. Roscoe Pound, *Interpretations of Legal History* (Cambridge, 1923), 12, 52, 74, 85–88, 92–93, 103, 188. He counseled, "Physical environment may not be ignored by jurist or legal historian." *Ibid.,* 117.

13. Higham, *Writing American History,* 118; Hofstadter, *Progressive Historians,* 66–67.

14. Higham, *Writing American History,* 122.

15. *Ibid.,* 125. Higham attributes the revival of Turnerian emphasis in the years 1941 to 1946 to the contributions of the social scientists. It is this period which I have, for convenience, termed "neo-Turnerianism." There is undoubtedly a great deal of Turnerian influence in the work of James Willard Hurst and his disciples, who stress the interaction between law and society in nineteenth-century America, but I have not discussed this school because its techniques are not generally applicable to the materials for colonial legal history.

Turnerianism undoubtedly has meant a variety of things to different historians, and it was only within the narrow circle of his disciples that Turner was followed with any semblance of orthodoxy. Among the true Turnerian colonial legal historians, Reinsch stands alone. But Richard B. Morris in his *Studies in the History of American Law,* first published in 1930, can be said to be one of the earliest legal historians in the "neo-Turnerian" school which stressed the social sciences and multiple causation. There is a paradox in all this. For Morris by virtue of his place of birth and training, as well as by intellectual inclination, was a more fit candidate for inclusion in the "asphalt flowers" school of historical writing, which because of its international sentiments and urban inclinations attacked the midwestern provincialism of Turner. Morris's dissertation, written under the direction of Evarts B. Greene—an institutionalist of the Osgood school—exhibited striking parallels to Turnerian thought and method in legal history. For example, Morris noted that it was the topography and barren soil of New England that forced the abandonment of the English inheritance system of primogeniture, and the concentration of landholdings into freehold tenements arranged in compact settlements.[16] Following Reinsch's example, Morris examined all of the colonies, rather than the experience of only one jurisdiction, and found among them certain common characteristics which seemed to justify the use of the term "American law" in pre-Revolutionary America.[17] His hypothesis, that "profound changes in social outlook can be traced to conditions on the frontier and to a changed intellectual and theological equipment," was to be tested by a comparative study of three topics of substantive law that would show "social engineering evolving out of the frontier."[18] Morris's inclusion of intellectual and theological factors undoubtedly represents an alteration of, or even a departure from, the Turnerian pattern, and it is in this sense that his disclaimer of membership in the "indigenous law"

16. Richard B. Morris, *Studies in the History of American Law,* 2d ed. (Philadelphia, 1959), 75–77.
17. *Ibid.,* 11.
18. *Ibid.,* 10–11, 20–21.

camp of the Turnerians must be understood.[19] In the larger sense that we have viewed the writings of the "Turnerverein," there was much in *Studies* that entitled it to be included within the Turnerian or, perhaps more accurately, the "neo-Turnerian" school.

The controversial and pioneering approach of *Studies* was evident in two aspects of the work. First, it was a pilot work which attempted to study, in a comparative way, certain principles of law as they evolved in the American colonies. Second, it treated three topics of substantive law—the distribution of land, the rules of tort liability, and the legal rights of women—which were most susceptible to social, intellectual, and environmental influences. In retrospect it might be said that there were two inherent limitations to Morris's approach. His selection of topics was not at all representative of a valid cross section of colonial law; moreover, his attempt to employ the comparative method across jurisdictional lines utilized a scholarly format which encouraged disregard for the subtle differences between the colonies with respect to their institutions, environment, social structure, and their constitutional position within the British Empire.

But we must realize that Morris considered his monograph only a pilot study to point the way toward a new approach in American colonial legal history. The important thing was not that he chose topics which were most likely to reflect alterations because of American conditions, but rather that he was willing to come to grips with the substantive law. Limitations in source materials made it extremely difficult to study such subjects, and vast preliminary searching was required to develop the necessary documentation for analysis. The value of a multijurisdictional approach to substantive law materials might be justified on these grounds alone. Morris's aim was not to trace the detailed evolution of legal principles and institutions, but rather to identify those factors of environment, society, and intellectual activity which influenced the development of law in colonial

19. Significantly, Morris did not expressly repudiate the "frontier thesis," of an indigenous form of law developing in America, in his 1959 introduction, but rather asserted that its impact should be closely evaluated, region by region. *Ibid.*, vi, viii.

America. While writing in the framework of a traditional institutional historian, heavily influenced by Turnerian analysis, he transcended the methodology of both fields, and throughout *Studies* there were thoughtful commentaries that can still lead scholars down new and unexplored investigatory paths.

Morris noted, for example, the seventeenth-century New England policy for the wide distribution of the ownership of real property and the consequent evolution of rules of descent and distribution of intestate estates to encourage that policy. The work of Greven and Lockridge, discussed above, continues this exploration through a more detailed analysis of the history of given New England localities. Morris commented on the Kentish origins of New England settlers, and surmised a connection between partible inheritance and Kentish gavelkind. While the connection has been disproved in a later article by George L. Haskins, the examination of English customary law and its impact on American colonial legal institutions has become an important part of the analytical tools of all historians, including those working in legal history.[20]

The section in *Studies* dealing with tort law in colonial America remains unique in the subtlety of its analysis and the scope of its coverage. Since the various forms of modern liability had not evolved by the end of the eighteenth century, it was extremely difficult to determine precisely what English common law was at any given point during the American colonial period.[21] Naturally the lack of any colonial law reports before the end of the eighteenth century prevented other than the most general surmises concerning the principles

20. *Ibid.*, 69–125; the material on gavelkind is in *ibid.*, 103–111. Haskins, "The Beginnings of Partible Inheritance in the American Colonies," *Yale Law Journal*, LI (1941–42), 1280–1315, as reprinted in David H. Flaherty, *Essays in the History of Early American Law* (Chapel Hill, 1969), 204–244. For studies stressing the influence of English customary law on colonial legal institutions see Julius Goebel, Jr., "King's Law and Local Custom in Seventeenth Century New England," *Columbia Law Review*, XXXI (1931), 416–448, as reprinted in Flaherty, ed., *Essays*, 83–120; and Sumner Chilton Powell, *Puritan Village: The Formation of a New England Town* (Middletown, 1963).

21. For a general discussion covering developments from Anglo-Saxon times to 1850, see John H. Wigmore, "Responsibility for Tortious Acts: Its History," in *Select Essays in Anglo-American Legal History*, III, 474–537.

of tort liability which the colonists considered applicable to their peculiar circumstances. In regard to trespasses of animals, Morris noted that the English colonies universally imposed a duty on land-owners to fence their fields against wandering livestock, while English law required that cattle and other animals be "fenced in."[22] American colonists in the seventeenth century did not resort to the futility of the deodand—a procedure for inflicting punishment upon animals, or even inanimate objects, which caused tortious injuries. However, Morris pointed out that as English common law rules gained greater acceptance during the eighteenth century, American courts began to utilize the deodand with increasing frequency.[23] By way of contrast, American colonials preceded their English contemporaries in passing laws for the prevention of cruelty to animals.[24] These and other diver-gences from English common law rules of tort liability demonstrate invaluable insights into the social conscience and value systems of colonial America. They reveal, moreover, the extent to which legal history studies in this area can advance our general understanding of colonial civilization.

Significant though these discoveries were, it was Morris's com-parative method which made *Studies* a classic in the field, and one worthy of careful attention by the present generation of legal his-torians. Although the colonies differed markedly from one another, each was more like its sister provinces than it was like the mother country. Colonials were as troubled by the variations between pro-vincial legal systems as they were by the uncertain adoption of Eng-lish case law and statutes by the courts of colonial America. The New York Moot, meeting during the last decade of the colonial period to debate points of law, found that most of its sessions dealt with con-

22. *Studies,* 208–217; see also "Statutory Modifications of the Common Law Trespassing Cattle Rule," in Young B. Smith and William L. Prosser, eds., *Cases and Materials on Torts* (Brooklyn, 1951), 662–665; and William L. Prosser, *Handbook of the Law of Torts* (St. Paul, 1941), 434.
23. *Studies,* 225–230; a more detailed consideration of colonial deodands is in Cyrus H. Karraker, "Deodands in Colonial Virginia and Maryland," *American Historical Review,* XXXVII (1932), 712–717.
24. *Studies,* 231, 232.

flict of laws between the province of New York and the precedents and statutes of her sister colonies.[25] Morris suggested the connection between the New England codes, the Duke's Law of New York, and the Pennsylvania "Great Law" of 1682. This phenomenon of intercolonial statutory borrowing was later more fully explored by George L. Haskins and Samuel E. Ewing.[26]

In retrospect it becomes apparent that Morris was far in advance of his time when *Studies in the History of American Law* was published. The work of succeeding generations of legal historians has benefited immensely from these early scholarly explorations. Although more recent and detailed monographs have modified certain of Morris's conclusions, his overall approach in his *Studies* has successfully met the test of time. It has been unfortunate that more of the topics he explored were not reconsidered and expanded as new materials became available. Perhaps even more significant in a historiographic sense is the fact that Morris's grand design for the study of colonial legal history has not been given its proper due; as a result much remains to be accomplished before the fullest potentialities of his creative pioneering work can be fulfilled.

While Turner's influence predominated in the early twentieth-century writing of colonial legal history and, as we have seen, was carried to new levels of utility by the work of Morris, the older institutional school of history had by no means surrendered its place to the exponents of the frontier thesis. Nor, for that matter, had all legal historians embraced the "indigenous law" principle. Throughout these early years, the flow of institutional monographs continued. The work of German-trained institutional historians, particularly that

25. For a discussion of the Moot, see Herbert A. Johnson, "John Jay: Colonial Lawyer" (unpubl. doctoral dissertation, Columbia University, 1965), 177–181.

26. "The Spread of Massachusetts Law in the Seventeenth Century," *University of Pennsylvania Law Review*, CVI (1957–58), 413–418, as reprinted in Flaherty, ed., *Essays*, 186–191. An interesting general article on statutory borrowing is Stefan A. Riesenfeld, "Law-making and Legislative Precedent in American Legal History," *Minnesota Law Review*, XXXIII (1948), 103–144.

of Herbert B. Adams, stressed the remote European heritage of colonial American law, thereby promoting an exaggerated sense of continuity across the ages.[27] It was monographic studies such as these which drew the sharpest criticism from Turner and his students. However, we should note that Adams's studies of colonial legal institutions *predated* Turner's "frontier" speech by more than ten years. The leading institutional historian of American colonial history, Herbert L. Osgood, wrote *after* Turner had come to public attention and redirected the historiographical thought of the profession. Osgood was emphatic about showing the use of English institutions in the New World. But he was also careful to point out that these applications of English antecedents were not mere slavish imitations, but a conscious selection of Old World forms and rules in which the colonists resorted to "natural selection" to choose those that seemed suitable to meet the needs of their frontier conditions.[28]

Osgood was the first professional historian to treat the American colonies and the colonial period in totality, and his monumental works remain essential basic reading for students in the field.[29] Unquestion-

27. Adams's principal works in legal history are "The Germanic Origin of New England Towns," in *Johns Hopkins Studies in History and Political Science,* ser. 1, no. 2 (1882), 5–38; "Saxon Tithing-men in America," *ibid.,* ser. 1, no. 4; and "Norman Constables in America," *ibid.,* ser. 1, no. 8 (1883). His contemporaries John W. Burgess and Albert B. Hart were more active in political history and political science.

28. *The American Colonies in the Seventeenth Century,* 3 vols. (New York, 1904–7), I, 426; II, 437; III, 14–15. In an earlier address Osgood had also stressed the need for a study of the colonies as a group, from the viewpoint of a general American colonial history, as well as forming a part of the British Empire. "The Study of American Colonial History," in *Annual Report of the American Historical Association for the Year 1898* (Washington, 1899), 65–66, 70. In the same article he stressed the need to study colonial political and constitutional institutions, for "it is only through law and political institutions that social forces become in a large sense operative." *Ibid.,* 68.

29. Totality in the sense that quantitatively Osgood covered the chronology of colonial America with a thoroughness not previously achieved, and at the same time qualitatively "total" in the sense that while his focus was on political developments, he was quite sensitive to economic influences on history, as well as certain religious and intellectual considerations. In a sense my use of the term "totality" for Osgood's work seems similar to the "unity" which Avery Craven discovered in the work of Turner. Compare Avery Craven, "Frederick Jackson Turner," and E. C. O. Beatty, "Herbert Levi Osgood,"

ably his close analysis of institutional development and his expertise in the presentation of a highly objective and factual narrative place him in the front rank of those historians in the institutional school. Yet his work also exhibits familiarity with the methodology of the Turnerians as well as a certain sensitivity to the use of social science methods. Indeed, as we have indicated, there are passages which contain so much environmental determinism that they could, if taken out of context, be assumed to have been written by Turner himself.

While tracing colonial legal historiography it is essential that one recognize the pervasive impact of Frederick Jackson Turner upon even the institutionalists, and particularly upon Osgood. It is only by tracing the institutional school backward in time to the essays written by Herbert B. Adams on colonial legal institutions that we can uncover a pure institutional approach. Adams's work by modern standards is somewhat cumbersome in its reasoning, and unpersuasive in its treatment of the problems of causation. The abundance of doctoral dissertations and narrow monographs in the institutional school which follow Turner in time, but reject his influence, have not made any perceptible impact on the history of American colonial law.[30] Osgood's great work on colonial America, however, outshines the efforts of his contemporaries, simply because he was willing to

---

both in William T. Hutchinson, ed., *The Marcus W. Jernegan Essays in American Historiography* (Chicago, 1937), 259, 279–283. Beatty comments, "With all his attention to minutiae, Osgood possessed the power of clear and forceful generalization." *Ibid.,* p. 289.

Osgood's volumes on the eighteenth century were published posthumously as *The American Colonies in the Eighteenth Century,* 3 vols. (New York, 1924). His studies of the land system of the seventeenth-century colonies and the court system of the later proprietary colonies are particularly valuable for legal historians. Osgood, *Seventeenth Century,* I, 424–467; II, 16–57, 277–308.

30. Many of these monographs provide valuable descriptions of legal systems and institutions; however, their failure to deal with the problems which are fundamental to colonial legal history is unfortunate. See Arthur P. Scott, *Criminal Law in Colonial Virginia* (Chicago, 1930); Elmer B. Russell, *The Review of American Colonial Legislation by the King in Council* (New York, 1915); Edwin L. Page, *Judicial Beginnings in New Hampshire, 1640–1700* (Concord, N.H., 1959); Charles J. Hilkey, *Legal Development in Early Massachusetts* (New York, 1910); and Oliver P. Chitwood, *Justice in Colonial Virginia* (Baltimore, 1905).

adapt what was best in the institutional methods and to accommodate that substantial residue to what he deemed valid in the Turnerian historiography.

While Osgood's work bears the mark of Turner's pervasive influence, it remains nevertheless one of the outstanding contributions of the institutional school to American colonial history. In countless graduate schools throughout the nation, students turned their attention to the study of the evolution of institutions. Those interested in legal history examined with increasing care the legislative acts and court records of colonial America. Supposedly following Leopold von Ranke's dictum "to tell history as it really was," they aimed for objective truth by remaining free from any preconceived ideas. For American colonial legal history this meant placing major emphasis on institutional developments rather than on the evolution of legal thought. Indeed the inheritance of the institutional school is at once the greatest glory, and the most stultifying influence, on the writing of legal history at the present time.

An institutionalist attempts to avoid any amount of speculation or interpretation of the meaning of his primary sources. This approach requires that his subjects be those which can be explained through the examination of substantial amounts of primary source material—not only for information and explanation, but also for verification of one's findings. Before writing institutional history in the classical manner, one must first be certain that the sources are adequate, lest research lead the scholar down paths where his evidence will become too sparse to provide the definite information and gratifying verification which is essential to the objective institutionalist. In other words, the accidents and vagaries of documentary preservation become inherent limitations upon the scope of the work which any institutional historian may undertake.

One result of this archival determinism has been that little has been written about the substantive law of colonial America. Practically no serious institutional work has been done on the legal history of the southern colonies other than Maryland. Procedural matters, on the other hand, are well documented in the many surviving court records of the seventeenth century, and the less informative, but nevertheless useful, court minute books of the eighteenth century. While southern court records, and indeed all court archives other than those of New England, were in serious disarray during the nineteenth century, and for most of the present century, Massachusetts documentation has been preserved in great bulk, and has served to feed the note cards of countless graduate students working in American colonial legal history. One can safely venture the assumption that the legal history written about seventeenth-century Massachusetts Bay and Plymouth exceeds in sheer volume the history of all of the other colonies put together.[31]

Despite the narrowness and conservatism of institutional legal history, it should be abundantly clear that an understanding of legal procedure is absolutely essential to telling the overall story of legal development. The law now is, and has always been, predicated upon certain preordained systems of adjective law which dominate not only the substance of the law but also the very manner in which lawyers and laymen customarily think about their courts and the law administered therein. Because procedural law is the best-documented area of early American law, it offers to the legal historian his best hope to understand the fundamental assumptions upon which all of colonial jurisprudence was founded. Yet those who write upon procedural matters tend to consider them the alpha and the omega of colonial legal history, which only leads to interpretive difficulties.

Matters of procedure are generally isolated from public interest and concern; as professional topics they fall entirely within the expertise of lawyers and judges. For centuries adjective law was virtually immune to legislative alteration, and evolved through court

---

31. For the lack of southern studies see Flaherty, ed., *Essays,* 12–13. Pennsylvania has suffered neglect despite the presence of a strong history department at the University of Pennsylvania throughout this century. Massachusetts' preeminence may be attributable to the location of Harvard University, but a substantial number of the Massachusetts articles and monographs are by non-Harvard-related scholars. Columbia University, by way of contrast, seems to have sent its students and faculty members to concentrate their efforts on the relatively meager and inaccessible source material for New York colonial history.

rulings and customs of the profession. Thus procedural law is something very special in the spectrum of legal knowledge, and it is unwise to inflate it beyond the limits of its importance. To consider procedural law a bellwether of legal development is highly misleading, for by doing so scholars—like the blind man grasping the tail of the elephant—may wind up accounting the characteristics of but one part of the beast. It is true that Maitland admonished his hearers, "The forms of action we have buried, but they still rule us from our graves," but earlier in the same speech, he had noted that his preference for procedural matters was not shared by all, and many felt that "substantive law should come first—adjective law, procedural law, afterwards." In the shadow of Maitland, we have perhaps fallen victim to an overemphasis on the very topics which were most neglected in his day. It is time that the pendulum of historical study swung back in the direction of substantive law topics, for as Maitland also pointed out, it is through greater knowledge of procedure that we are enabled to better understand the substantive law.[32]

Among the institutional historians of early American law, none has equaled the stature of Julius Goebel, Jr. Trained at Columbia's Faculty of Political Science under John Bassett Moore, Goebel completed his doctoral dissertation in diplomatic history in 1915,[33] and then moved on to study and teach at Columbia Law School until his retirement in 1968. After several years studying medieval English criminal procedure, Goebel turned his scholarly talents toward the study of criminal procedure in colonial New York. In collaboration with T. Raymond Naughton he published the definitive monograph on this subject in 1944.[34] The work shows all of the insights to be

32. The oft-quoted expression is from a lecture Maitland delivered in London which was published posthumously in 1909. Frederic W. Maitland, *The Forms of Action at Common Law,* ed. by A. H. Chaytor and W. J. Whittaker (Cambridge, Eng., 1968), 1.

33. Julius Goebel, Jr., *The Recognition Policy of the United States* (New York, 1915), 8.

34. *Law Enforcement in Colonial New York: A Study of Criminal Procedure (1664–1776).* Goebel's earlier study was *Felony and Misdemeanor: A Study in the History of English Criminal Procedure* (New York, 1937); earlier he wrote an exploratory article on the New York manorial system, which re-

gained from an encyclopedic knowledge of English criminal procedure and its application to colonial adaptations. Crisp and precise in its discussion of details, *Law Enforcement* is an outstanding example of institutional history at its best.

Goebel, following the more expansive tradition of Osgood, clearly recognized the limitations of the earlier and more orthodox institutional legal history. His introductory remarks to *Law Enforcement* leave little doubt that he was interested in the influences and social forces which shape the law. "The legislation of another age has meaning only if examined in connection with the social, economic and political factors which conditioned its enactment," he counseled.[35] There were certain differences between American colonial law and its English precedents, but Goebel stressed the cultural background of the settlers, which he believed was most responsible for determining the nature of the legal rules they wished to apply in their American settlements.

Aware of the separateness of the American colonies from the mother country, as well as from one another, he commented on the variations in intellectual "pull" which English tradition exerted on each colony. Goebel denied, in general, both Turner's "frontier theory" in the development of American law and Roscoe Pound's rejection of colonial legal history as irrelevant to the subsequent development of American law and legal institutions.[36] According to Goebel, the study of American colonial legal history was concerned with "the problem . . . of accounting for historical reality and it is

---

mains one of the best legal history studies of these remnants of feudalism. "Some Legal and Political Aspects of Manors in New York," *Order of Lords of Colonial Manors in America, Publications,* no. 19 (1928).

35. *Law Enforcement,* xxix. The close analysis of statutory materials per se is of course important to the legal historian's craft. See the works of Mark DeWolfe Howe, "The Sources and Nature of Law in Colonial Massachusetts," in George A. Billias, ed., *Law and Authority in Colonial America* (Barre, Mass., 1965), 1–16; "The Recording of Deeds in the Colony of Massachusetts Bay," *Boston University Law Review,* XXVIII (1948), 1–6; and "The Process of Outlawry in New York: A Study of the Selective Reception of English Law," *Cornell Law Quarterly,* XXIII (1937–38), 559–573, as reprinted in Flaherty, *Essays,* 433–450.

36. *Law Enforcement,* xix, xx, xxi.

more profitably approached as one in the mutations of a transplanted culture. Like every bit of Old World civilization brought overseas, the law underwent a process of indenization, of acquiring a New World identity."[37] In other words, the legal historian had to understand all of the forms of English law, both common and local, in order to be able to accurately trace their growth and adaptations in the alien soil of the American colonies. Goebel concluded that there were only slight variations between colonial New York's criminal procedure and that utilized in the mother country. The degree to which English procedural standards had been transplanted was what governed the proficiency of New York lawyers, and not any influence of the "frontier."[38]

Goebel restored the importance of institutional studies as much by the excellence of his work as by his allowance for the influence of nonlegal factors. Although he cannot in any way be said to have advocated a "social science" approach to legal history, he was very much concerned with the impact of the total human experience upon the development of American law. When viewed within this context, the law was not a subject isolated from general historical development in the American colonies as a whole.

Legal historians view Goebel and Morris as representatives of two different "schools" of colonial legal history, yet the foregoing discussion blurs many of the most facile distinctions which have been made between them. Clearly Morris searched for general rules in the development of colonial law, and was intent upon those changes from English practice which might demonstrate the existence of an indigenous law in seventeenth-century America. Equally obvious is the fact that Goebel worked in a more restricted jurisdictional framework, with a primary interest in examining the growing professional expertise of colonial lawyers and their relationship to the gradual acceptance of English rules. As we have indicated, substantive law subjects lend themselves to broad and general treatment, and the absence of adequate sources for each colony might frustrate or discourage institutional historians. Conversely, criminal procedure is so well docu-

37. *Ibid.*, xx.
38. *Ibid.*, xxi, xxviii–xxix, 760.

mented in each of the provincial systems that a comparative approach to all the colonies would lead to mountains of detail that would engulf the reader, if not the would-be author.

Part of the distinction between the two men is thus inherent in their subject matter, but in terms of thematic interpretation of their materials they differ even more markedly. Simply stated, the two legal historians differed in their allocation of importance to the law itself. Morris used legal history to provide a body of evidence for an extended commentary on colonial Americans and their society. Goebel treated legal history as the central focus of his study, subordinating all other considerations, and considering only those other historical forces and events which were directly relevant to legal development. Goebel's work was "legal-centered" while that of Morris was "society-centered."[39] These differences in scholarly viewpoint are what account for the variety in their legal history, but essentially both men were products of the institutional school as altered by Turner. Being younger, Morris was more profoundly influenced by the social sciences and their impact on historical analysis. However, the distinctions do not seem sufficiently large to justify the differentiation of a "Goebel" school and a "Morris" school of American colonial legal history.

A variety of viewpoints, rather than true historiographic distinctions, has typified the writing of American colonial legal history since the publication of *Studies* and *Law Enforcement*. Joseph H. Smith, a former student of Julius Goebel who assisted in the preparation of *Law Enforcement*, turned to the paths developed by the imperial school of colonial history and wrote a superb monograph covering the legal and constitutional aspects of Privy Council appeals from the colonies.[40] Conforming to the "imperialist" format, Smith included

39. See Richard B. Morris, "The Sources of Early American Law: Colonial Period," *West Virginia Law Quarterly*, XL (1933–34), 215–216, for the clearest statement of this viewpoint which underlies much of Morris's work in legal history. A similar statement stressing the social history possibilities for legal history sources is George L. Haskins, "Court Records and History," *William and Mary Quarterly*, 3d ser., V (1948), 550, 551.

40. Joseph H. Smith, *Appeals to the Privy Council from the American Plantations* (New York, 1950); see also his article "Administrative Control of the Courts of the American Plantations," *Columbia Law Review*, LXI

Jamaica and the British West Indies within his area of study; he thereby became the first American legal historian to consider imperial law as it had been understood and administered at Whitehall during the seventeenth and eighteenth centuries.

There was a wealth of local detail in Smith's *Appeals* volume, but his focus never shifted far from the Privy Council chamber. The reader was given an excellent overview of the legal development of each colony as it appeared to the bureaucrats in London. At the same time he was instructed in the intricacies of Privy Council procedural and substantive law. What was especially noteworthy in Smith's study was the care with which he delineated the impact of political pressures and the influence of the royal prerogative upon the Council's legal decisions. Smith found that the members of the Council were extremely ignorant of colonial conditions, and quite condescending in their evaluation of the legal accomplishments of colonial lawyers and judges. This official attitude, he concluded, prevented the Council from ever becoming an effective supreme court for the plantations; it tended, on the contrary, to encourage a spirit of independence on the part of the colonists.[41]

With an eye toward the advent of the American Revolution, however, Smith cautioned against placing an undue emphasis on the Council's actions in constitutional appeals from the North American plantations. Similar legal matters arising in the Channel Islands were treated as routine judicial business, he noted. The Privy Council did not manage its appellate business as if it were the supreme court of the empire, but rather as if it were the highest appellate court in each colonial jurisdiction. Moreover, colonial conditions and the internal

---

(1961), 1210–1253, as reprinted in Flaherty, ed., *Essays,* 281–335. For discussions of the imperial school see Michael Kraus, *The Writing of American History* (Norman, 1953), 242–270; Lawrence H. Gipson, "The Imperial Approach to Early American History," in Ray A. Billington, ed., *The Reinterpretation of Early American History* (San Marino, Calif., 1960), 185–199. Charles M. Andrews drew attention to the imperial approach in an early paper, published as "American Colonial History, 1690–1750," *Annual Report of the American Historical Association for the Year 1898* (Washington, 1899), 49–60.

41. Smith, *Appeals,* 654–664.

appellate systems within each colony resulted in large variations in the number and types of appeals which the Privy Council heard from each of the overseas possessions. The Council thus emerged in *Appeals* to be a tribunal charged with the overall review of legal business within each colony, rather than an instrument of the royal prerogative utilized to consolidate and unify the legal development of Britain's far-flung colonial empire.[42]

Smith's *Appeals* is as significant in constitutional history as it is in legal history. It helped to fill a substantial void in the general history of the American colonies, for little work of such careful detail had been done on the constitutional relationship of the colonial governments with the mother country and with one another. Just as a study of the present-day Supreme Court of the United States places one at the nexus of law and politics, so the study of the Privy Council placed one at a similar advantage in understanding the British Empire before 1783.

While Professor Smith's excursion into the broad world of imperial judicial activity was under way, another legal historian, George L. Haskins, emerged from his earlier studies of English parliamentary institutions to commence a reinterpretation of the legal and constitutional history of the Bay Colony. After establishing his credentials by writing a number of provocative articles on property law and decedent estates in Massachusetts and Plymouth,[43] Haskins undertook the task of rewriting the legal and constitutional history of Massachusetts for the first two decades of its existence. Like Goebel he sought, and usually found, in the background of the settlers adequate basis for the

---

42. *Ibid.,* 655.

43. Haskins's earlier books on English legal history were *The Statute of York and the Interest of the Commons* (Cambridge, Mass., 1935) and *The Growth of English Representative Government* (Philadelphia, 1948). Among Haskins's early articles are "The Beginnings of Partible Inheritance in the American Colonies," *Yale Law Journal,* LI (1941–42), 1280–1315, as reprinted in Flaherty, ed., *Essays,* 204–244; and "A Problem in the Reception of the Common Law in the Colonial Period," *University of Pennsylvania Law Review,* XCVII (1949), 842–853, which was revised and published as "Reception of the Common Law in Seventeenth-Century Massachusetts: A Case Study," in Billias, ed., *Law and Authority in Colonial America,* 17–31.

legal principles which developed in the colonies in North America. However, in writing his major work, *Law and Authority in Early Massachusetts,*[44] he focused not only on the legal institutions which the Bay Colonists had known, but also on the religious and philosophical ideals upon which they based their New World experiment in self-government. In this way Haskins brought intellectual history to bear on the problems of colonial legal history.

The years from 1630 to 1650 were crucial to the future development of law and authority in Massachusetts, for these were "the formative years during which, under the pervasive influence of Puritan doctrine, and with virtually no outside interference, the structure of civil government took shape and was completed."[45] Dealing with the evolution of both public and private law, Haskins emphasized the impact of tradition—social, political, legal, religious, and intellectual—as well as the dynamic pressures requiring a restructuring of the law, both public and private, to make it more suitable to the overall goals for which the colony was founded. Such conscious efforts toward change he denominated "design," hence the subtitle of the word, "a study in tradition and design."[46]

Rather than dealing with the detailed development of private law in the second section of his book, Professor Haskins chose to examine certain of those subjects to demonstrate the process of the reception and adaptation of English legal traditions into the law of Massachusetts. His discussion emphasized the diverse sources upon which the colonists drew to construct their early legal system. *Law and Authority* thus provides a blueprint of the manner in which a new government was erected in Massachusetts. Yet in explaining these developments even to 1650, Haskins was required to touch on nearly every aspect of the totality of life within the colony. The central theme dealt with causation—those cultural forces which made Massachusetts law different from the law of England and, at the same time, a recognizable subsystem of English law.

44. George L. Haskins, *Law and Authority in Early Massachusetts: A Study in Tradition and Design* (New York, 1960).
45. *Ibid.,* ix.
46. *Ibid.,* 228–231.

What emerged from *Law and Authority* was a particularly complex story of the convolutions of these various cultural forms and their ultimate amalgamation into a coherent system of public and private regulations for the governance of life by the Puritans within the "City upon a Hill." Yet it is not because of its institutional findings that the book is entitled to careful study by legal historians, but rather because of its inclusion of intellectual factors among those forces which shape and condition the development of law. Following the paths blazed in intellectual history by Samuel Eliot Morison and Perry Miller, Haskins made their methods an integral part of his study of Massachusetts legal development in the seventeenth century.[47] Except for a few article-length treatments,[48] no legal historian has so far been inspired to follow Haskins's example in utilizing intellectual history as a key to causation in American colonial law. Nevertheless, it is unquestionable that law responds as much to ideas which are current in society as it does to factors such as land availability, population density, and economic development. American colonial legal history can learn from Michael Kraus's perceptive teachings that the Atlantic Ocean, far from being a barrier to interchange of ideas and customs, actually served as an efficient bridge of communications and transportation, linking together the portions of Britain's colonial empire washed by its waters.[49]

We know that English lawbooks were used extensively in the colo-

47. "Religious doctrine," asserts Haskins, was one of the "principal strands which held together the web of government." *Ibid.*, 43. His fourth chapter, "A Due Form of Government," examines Massachusetts civil government in the light of Puritan political thought. *Ibid.*, 43–65. The sixth chapter, "Communities of Visible Saints," deals with public and private law ramifications of Puritan religious practices and ethical standards. *Ibid.*, 85–93. On the connection between religion and law, see Simeon L. Guterman, "The Interaction of Religion, Law and Politics in Western Society: Its Historical Character and Influence," *University of Miami Law Review*, XVII (1963), 439–468.

48. Haskins's student Ralph H. Clover published an excellent study along these lines entitled "The Rule of Law in Colonial Massachusetts," *University of Pennsylvania Law Review*, CVIII (1960), 1001–1036. Another useful study is David Fellman, "Property in Colonial Political Theory," *Temple Law Quarterly*, XVI (1942), 388–406.

49. Michael Kraus, *Intercolonial Aspects of American Culture on the Eve of the Revolution* (New York, 1928), particularly 210; *The Atlantic Civilization: Eighteenth Century Origins* (Ithaca, 1949).

nies, but we have not begun to study the extent to which they became "American" lawbooks through their influence in colonial courts and in training American lawyers.[50] There is no comprehensive list of English lawbook holdings in colonial libraries, something which would provide an invaluable guide to the number of copies of each title and its geographic distribution in North America. This would be a handy method for determining the most widely-circulated English legal literature, and make possible a much more sophisticated answer to the difficult question of how much of American law followed English precedent in the eighteenth century.

Another continuing intellectual influence on colonial legal development can be found in those members of the colonial bar who received their legal training at either the Inns of Court or some English country law office. Sending young men to England for their professional training was not a popular practice in every colony, by any means, but even those provinces which sent a token number of students were rarely without at least one English-trained attorney or barrister in their midst.[51]

Recently Joseph Smith has published a thoughtful article considering the theory of judicial precedent as it was followed in the American colonies.[52] Carefully examining the printed records of the American colonies, as well as many manuscript sources, Smith found a strong

50. Eldon R. James, "A List of Legal Treatises Printed in the British Colonies and the American States Before 1801," in *Harvard Legal Essays Written in Honor of and Presented to Joseph Henry Beale and Samuel Williston* (Cambridge, Mass., 1934), 159–211, particularly 159–179. Although James's list is an impressive one, anyone familiar with colonial law practice can readily see that a substantial number of English lawbooks were imported, since they were not locally printed. Some bibliographic work on colonial law libraries has been done. Paul M. Hamlin, *Legal Education in Colonial New York* (New York, 1939), 73–94, 171–196; Johnson, "John Jay," 168–175, 265–272; Edwin Wolf 2d, "Historical Development of the American Lawyer's Library," *Law Library Journal*, LXI (1968), 440–450.

51. Hamlin, *Legal Education*, 12–23; Johnson, "John Jay," 10–12, 17–20; Edward A. Jones, *American Members of the Inns of Court* (London, 1924).

52. "New Light on the Doctrine of Judicial Precedent in Early America: 1607–1776," in John N. Hazard and Wenceslas J. Wagner, eds., *Legal Thought in the United States of America under Contemporary Pressures* (Brussels, 1970), 9–39.

tendency in eighteenth-century American courts to follow English precedent unless their own legislature or some prior decision by their provincial courts indicated that English law did not apply. He concluded that the doctrine of judicial precedent, just beginning to develop in England, took strong root in the American provinces. In directing scholarly attention to the possibilities inherent in a multijurisdictional study of a doctrine of law, Smith reaffirmed the underlying validity of Richard Morris's multijurisdictional approach in *Studies.* At the same time, by stressing a jurisprudential aspect of colonial law, he brought into play the analysis of legal philosophy as it was practiced, if not fully articulated, in the American colonies. The materials are scarce, as Smith's article shows, but similar studies might be undertaken concerning the colonial attitude toward the statute of frauds, the principle of res judicata, or such aspects of the law of evidence as the hearsay rule, the best evidence rule, or exclusion of privileged communications.[53]

Every so often, each legal historian should take a busman's holiday into comparative studies. In a certain sense every legal historian resorts to the comparative method, for as Maitland noted in his inaugural lecture, true legal history cannot exist without comparisons between variations in the law and between one legal system and another. George Haskins's comparative study of codification—drawing parallels between the experiences, both social and legal, in early New England and similar phenomena in the Greek colonies at isolated points on the shores of the ancient Mediterranean sea—stands as a model of imaginative comparative history.[54] We have studied revolutions in a comparative way, and we are beginning to analyze imperial expansion and administration in a comparative framework.[55] Is it not

53. Morris, *Studies,* treats the privileged communication between spouses in a cursory way, 199, 200.
54. George L. Haskins, "Codification of the Law in Colonial Massachusetts: A Study of Comparative Law," *Indiana Law Journal,* XXX (1954–55), 1–17.
55. For a discussion of comparative revolutions, including a useful bibliography, see Robert R. Palmer, "The Revolution," in C. Vann Woodward, ed., *The Comparative Approach to American History* (New York, 1968), 46–61; on imperialism in the nineteenth century see Robin W. Winks, "Imperialism," in *ibid.,* 253–270; comparative colonial empires in the seventeenth and

time that men who know the law utilize one of legal education's greatest gifts to the social sciences? The more widely dispersed in time the comparisons may be, the less utility the conclusions may have for "hard-core" legal history; yet the insights into causation are enhanced by similar responses made throughout the ages to nearly identical circumstances. And increasingly what legal historians must seek is not merely factual knowledge of the past, but also a more sophisticated understanding of the nature of law and its part in the broad spectrum of human experience in society.

Within the scope of American legal history it is important to consider the effects of periodization and categorization upon the writing of legal history. Many years ago Professor Daniel Boorstin drew attention to the fact that legal historians tend to categorize and classify their topics according to subjects recognized in modern American law.[56] He criticized this tendency in terms of its propensity toward anachronism as well as its hobbling effect on historical analysis. Boorstin wished to have legal history broadened in scope, and at the same time have it recognized that the law itself was an integral part of historical development. He concluded that legal historians should concern themselves more actively with the relationship between the history of law and the growth of society and its institutions. More recently, Stanley N. Katz has suggested that another problem is one of periodization: that by adopting overly shortened time periods, legal historians do not permit themselves proper freedom to examine long-range developments in the history of law.[57] If, for example, the study of eighteenth-century colonial law were continued through the Jacksonian period, certain patterns might emerge that would not be discernible if the analysis had been terminated in 1776 or even 1800. There are, of course, vast differences between the research methods of colonial legal history and the history of later decades when the

---

eighteenth centuries are treated in John J. Tepaske, ed., *Three American Empires* (New York, 1967).

56. Daniel J. Boorstin, "Tradition and Method in Legal History," *Harvard Law Review*, LIV (1941), 424–436.

57. "Looking Backward: The Early History of American Law," *University of Chicago Law Review*, XXXIII (1966), 867–884.

number of printed reports of cases facilitates the work of the scholar in his search for rules of law. Yet the variation in research technique should not prove overly inconvenient, for most colonial legal historians have a basic acquaintance with the system of legal research necessary to gain access to the printed law reports.

In a general way, we must realize that what Professors Boorstin and Katz have suggested is that legal historians must be willing to abandon some of the conventions which they have established in the past. What they need is to strike out for a broadly conceived legal history that seeks to explain colonial law, not in contemporary legal context, but as it was conceived in the seventeenth and eighteenth centuries. The constructive criticism of these two scholars is entitled to great weight, and will no doubt receive the compliment of scholarly adoption within the next few years. As a group, colonial legal historians have adapted slowly to changing trends in historiography. But as we have seen, there is a close correlation between the writing of American colonial history in general and the interpretive and historiographic methods which have altered the writing of colonial legal history.

A major development which has made American colonial legal history a more promising field in recent years has been the slow but steady increase in the number of court records which have appeared in print.[58] This assures future generations of legal historians a readily available source of materials for conducting comparative studies among colonial jurisdictions. Coupled with the new methodological approaches, this multiplication of printed sources makes the subject at once less narrow in its research techniques, and promises to liberate the legal historian from the drudgery of scanning countless volumes and file boxes of manuscript court records, seeking one or two bits of evidence among the dirty and crumbling documents. The time conserved could well be used for more extensive evaluation of causation than has been customary in the past.

Complementing the publication of American colonial court records

58. For a survey see Michael G. Kammen, "Colonial Court Records and the Study of Early American History: A Bibliographical Review," *American Historical Review,* LXX (1964–65), 732–739.

has been the appearance of the legal papers of colonial practitioners. The most significant of these, of course, were the *Legal Papers of John Adams*,[59] which hopefully will set a standard for future publications of this nature. Law practice in the colonies was not specialized, but general in nature, and thus the legal papers of an active attorney provide a superb "lawyer's eye" view of the law as integrated in his practice. Practitioners are not permitted the academic legal scholar's leisure to view law as a large topic, divided into several distinct categories, such as contracts, torts, equity, property law, constitutional law, or domestic relations. Any given case might well involve several of these subjects, as well as the usual problems of the law of evidence and rules of practice, which can shape the issues presented to the judge or jury. The distortions of legal history caused by categorization, particularly those mentioned by Boorstin, can be neutralized by looking at the legal system through the extant law office files of a colonial lawyer. While the appearance of lawyers' papers has not as yet been sufficiently large to make a cumulative impact in this direction, we can anticipate some historiographic trend as new legal papers appear in print.

American colonial legal history has grown considerably in the past forty years, and its indebtedness to the interpreters of the general history of colonial America is readily apparent. At this time it seems abundantly clear that there is room for greater expansion of the study as well as a need for new and altered viewpoints toward the proper subjects for legal history study. Legal historians owe it to themselves as well as to the historical profession in general to undertake work in topics for which the documentation is slender and conclusions can be only tentative in nature. Problems of causation must be analyzed with care, bringing to bear upon legal development and its history all of the current discoveries in the social sciences. There is a need for

59. L. Kinvin Wroth and Hiller B. Zobel, eds., *Legal Papers of John Adams*, 3 vols. (Cambridge, Mass., 1965). For a comment on the legal aspects of the major historical publication projects, see Richard B. Morris, "The Current Statesmen's Papers Publication Program: An Appraisal from the Point of View of the Legal Historian," *American Journal of Legal History*, XI (1967), 95–106.

comparative studies, as well as expansion into the field of legal philosophy and its history in colonial America. There have been, and will continue to be, finite limits to the information which legal historians can obtain from colonial materials. Much documentary evidence has already been destroyed, and that which remains does not always contain the information which the researcher would like to have. Faced with discouragement over this state of affairs, legal historians need not despair, for the example of students of Roman law, struggling with their fragmentary and scattered collections of rescripts and monumental inscriptions, should serve to breed a sense of documentary abundance. The lack, we must admit, lies not as much within the documentary record as within ourselves—we are unimaginative and poorly-motivated.

Much has been written about the relationship between legal studies, historical scholarship, and the profession of legal history.[60] The perennial interest in this topic is, no doubt, directly proportional to the number of legal historians seeking placement in their field, either in history faculties or in the law schools. For clearly there is little need for legal history unless it be considered pertinent to one or the other of the disciplines—at least as far as job placement of legal historians is concerned. Yet the subject is a valid professional subdivision which draws upon both law and history for its techniques of study and for the training of its professionals. It can do much for both law schools and graduate schools in advancing their pedagogical purposes. To historians legal history brings a specialized knowledge of the law and the development of legal institutions. The degree to which historians of the law can broaden their perspectives to include in their works a proper consideration for the interrelationship between law and so-

60. Among the more helpful articles are Charles F. Mullett, "The Value of Law to Historians," *Missouri Law Review,* IX (1944), 144–164; Ben W. Palmer, "The Historian and the Lawyer," *American Bar Association Journal,* XXXII (1946), 530–536; Charles E. Wyzanski, Jr., "History and Law," *University of Chicago Law Review,* XXVI (1959), 237–244; Frederick B. Wiener, *Uses and Abuses of Legal History: A Practitioner's View* (London, 1962); and Calvin Woodard, "History, Legal History and Legal Education," *Virginia Law Review,* LIII (1967), 89–121.

ciety will help to determine how far legal history can lead the way toward a better understanding of the nature of man and his social activities. To legal educators and law students, legal history explains the law as it was in the past, thereby throwing light on the state of the law at the present. It has been said that the current development of legal studies places undue emphasis on "presentism," leaving students and professors without a sense of the past and consequently with an unreal view of the law and its place in the social framework.[61] Legal history can provide a useful antidote to such a tendency. It can provide lawyers and law students with a sensitivity toward the evolutionary characteristics of legal development—a kind of guide to the achievements and failures of the past in the attempts made to use legal methods to improve the state of man, his institutions, and his way of life.

In the final analysis, the history of law in colonial America, or any other field of legal history, is basically historical in its approach and methods. History as the study of human life and experience within recorded time includes within its broad commission the study of men's laws and the institutions they have erected to enforce their laws. To deny the primary historical foundation of legal history, and to make it relevant to today's problems, is to confuse the purpose of legal history and to debase its practice. Simply put, legal history is the memory bank of the legal profession; it serves lawyers best when it remains independent of their preoccupation with the present, as well as their desire to shape the progress of the future through the guiding hand of reforming legislation and court decisions. At the same time, however, legal history must communicate its findings in such a way as to make its lessons clear and meaningful to men of the law. Legal history should be expected to explain the importance of purely technical studies to the general history of the law as well as the overall history of the American people.

The challenge to legal history in the years ahead—particularly to American colonial legal history—is one of redefining its own identity.

61. *Ibid.*, 109, 112.

It must move forward to examine the history of law within a broader context than ever before, and to exhibit in its writings and its teaching the vitally important role that law has always played in our society. As we have seen, the leading scholars in the field of American colonial history have already pointed the way that must be traveled; it is for the legal historians of the present, and those who are being trained to write and teach in the future, to fulfill the great expectations and dreams of those who have so rapidly advanced the study in the past seventy years.

GEORGE ATHAN BILLIAS

The First Un-Americans: The Loyalists in American Historiography

THE NEGLECT which Loyalists have suffered at the hands of American historians reveals much about the way such scholars have interpreted our nation's past.[1] The relative disregard of the Loyalists

For help in preparing this article, I am indebted to my former student, Jeffrey Nelson, presently a doctoral candidate at Harvard University.

1. The term "Loyalist" rather than "Tory" is used throughout this essay. "Tory" was a term of opprobrium, representing an effort by American Whigs to denigrate their opponents. The word "Tory" in English political thought often carried certain connotations; e.g., within the Filmerian tradition the term implied passive submission to the king because he ruled by virtue of divine right, for ultimate authority within an organic Christian society was seen as descending from God to king. After the Glorious Revolution, however, the Tory tradition was transformed into a significant component of the eighteenth-century court ideology in which divine right was considered to inhere not in the person of the king but rested rather in the authority of the established government ruling at the time. Such an acceptance of de facto sovereignty characterized the party of the King's Friends in eighteenth-century England. Despite their being described as the "King's Friends" in America, however, most Loyalists fell within the liberal Whig tradition. Like their opponents—the American Whigs—most Loyalists generally held that the colonists possessed inalienable rights and privileges to self-government, that there were individual liberties which the British government could not transgress, and that Parliament held certain prerogatives at the expense of the Crown. Thus, many American Loyalists admitted the colonists could, within certain limits, protest and even resist British encroachments on their rights as Englishmen. In short, the Loyalists in terms of their thought patterns were often well outside the Tory tradition as defined in the Anglo-American world of the eighteenth century.

Contemporary historians, Loyalists and Whig alike, showed a keen aware-

indicates the degree to which American scholars have been prisoners of the "whig philosophy of history." That interpretation of history viewed all developments in America within the context of a single continuum. Events were judged in the light of their contribution to the forward progress of those democratic principles which characterized the so-called American way of life. Movements and men that presumably advanced the cause of democracy—the Founding Fathers, Jeffersonianism, Jacksonianism, the Populist-Progressive movements, and the New Deal—were considered representative of the mainstream of American history. Developments which ostensibly retarded progress toward the goal of ever greater democracy—the Loyalists, Hamiltonianism, the Southern Confederacy, and the conservative forces usually identified with the business community—were assumed to be peripheral to the main thrust of the nation's destiny.[2] Within the context of this Manichaean interpretation of American history, the position of the Loyalists has been misinterpreted and misstated: scholars placed them in the role of traitors during the first century after the Revolution; treated them somewhat more sympathetically around the turn of the twentieth century; rediscovered them again in order to satisfy the demands of a historical dialectic when the progressive tradition among historians became dominant; and then blurred the distinction between Loyalists and Whigs when the consensus historians began

---

ness of this semantical problem. Jonathan Boucher remarked: "Were it not that mankind in forming themselves into sects, parties, and factions very generally renounced the exercise of their reason, why should their leaders so often found it necessary to distinguish men so associated . . . by some low and ridiculous names . . . ? Hence (not to go out of our own country) such strange names as Puritans, Roundheads, Whigs, Tories, White Boys, Dippers, Ranters, Quakers, &c. . . ." Jonathan Boucher, *A View of the Causes and Consequences of the American Revolution* (London, 1897), li. David Ramsay likewise made the distinction in his history: ". . . the epithets Whig and Tory are used in the following sheets in a sense different from what has been usual. By the latter he means those of the inhabitants who were friends of the royal government; by the former, and also by the more general appellation American, he intends those who favoured the revolution." David Ramsay, *History of the Revolution of South Carolina*, 2 vols. (Trenton, 1785), I, x–xi.

2. J. R. Pole, "The American Past: Is It Still Usable?" *Journal of American Studies*, I (1967), 63–78.

writing after World War II. Despite all that has been written about them, the Loyalists have yet to be integrated into American history.[3]

The Loyalists remain, in effect, "un-Americans." As Robert R. Palmer pointed out, they have been all but eliminated from the nation's collective historical consciousness. "The sense in which there was no conflict in the American Revolution is the sense in which the loyalists are forgotten," he wrote. "The 'American consensus' rests in some degree on the elimination from the national consciousness, as well as from the country, of a once important and relatively numerous element of dissent."[4]

The Loyalists, moreover, suffer from bias as well as neglect. Many American historians have been reluctant to face the implications of the Revolution as a civil war. Brought up on certain national myths—the notion of America's "uniqueness," the concept of a "chosen people," and the idea of a national sense of mission—many American scholars have been too culture-bound to view the Loyalist position impartially. To do so would mean challenging the legitimacy of the Revolution, raising doubts about the entire American experiment, and robbing the New World of much of its historical meaning.

Bias against the Loyalists originated in the writings of contemporary Whig historians. Mercy Otis Warren—sister of James Otis, wife of James Warren, and one of the nation's first women of letters—heaped

3. For a survey of writings on the Loyalists, see Wallace Brown, "The View at Two Hundred Years: The Loyalists of the American Revolution," American Antiquarian Society *Proceedings*, LXXX (1970), 25–47. Brown claims that the "chorus of complaints about neglect and bias towards the Loyalists is exaggerated." The present essay is based on a different assumption: that the Loyalists have *yet* to enter the American historical consciousness.

Brown's article includes English and Canadian authors, and is not culture-bound as are most works. The present essay, however, is based almost exclusively on American scholars, includes only those writings which the author feels had an important impact on American historiography, and makes no pretense of an exhaustive bibliography on the subject. For a survey of British historians who sometimes touched upon the subject, see Richard Middleton, "British Historians and the American Revolution," *Journal of American Studies*, V (1971), 43–58.

4. Robert R. Palmer, *Age of Democratic Revolution: The Challenge* (Princeton, 1959), I, 190.

scorn upon the Loyalists in her three-volume history of the Revolution published in 1805. Her portrait of Thomas Hutchinson epitomized the hostile characterization which most Loyalists suffered at the hands of contemporary Whig historians. Hutchinson was "dark, intriguing, insinuating, haughty, and ambitious, while the extreme of avarice marked every feature of his character." Machiavelli was his mentor, and Hutchinson "never failed to recommend the Italian master as a model to his adherents."[5] The fact that the Hutchinsons and Otises fought a bitter family feud for control of patronage in colonial Massachusetts, that her husband and sons hungered for office after the Revolution, and that, ironically enough, she wrote part of her history in the Hutchinson home which her husband had purchased as a confiscated Loyalist estate did not make Mrs. Warren's judgment an impartial one.

Two other contemporary Whig historians—David Ramsay and William Gordon—were also critical of the Loyalists, though not to the same degree. Ramsay, a doctor, state politician, and delegate to the Continental Congress, published two histories of the event, one local and the other national: *The History of the Revolution in South Carolina* in 1785, and *The History of the American Revolution* in 1789. In discussing the Loyalists, Ramsay resorted to a sophisticated social analysis which included a generation-gap thesis:

The age and temperament of individuals had, often, an influence in fixing their political character. Old men were seldom warm Whigs. They could not relish the great changes, which were daily taking place. Attached to ancient forms and habits, they could not readily accommodate themselves to new systems. Few of the very rich were active, in forwarding the revolution. . . . The active and spirited part of the community, who felt themselves possessed of talents, that would raise them to eminence in a free government, longed for the establishment of independent constitutions: but those who were in possession or expectation of royal favour, or of promotion from Great Britain, wished that the connexion, between the parent state and the colonies, might be preserved. The young, the ardent, the ambitious, and the enterprising were mostly Whigs: but the phlegmatic, the timid, the interested, and those who wanted decision,

5. Mercy Otis Warren, *History of the Rise, Progress, and Termination of the American Revolution;* 3 vols. (Boston, 1805), I, 79.

were, in general, favourers of Great Britain, or, at most, only the luke-warm inactive friends of independence.[6]

William Gordon, the English-born clergyman, came to Massachu-setts in 1770, plunged into the politics of his adopted country, preached to the Patriots, ransacked manuscript sources throughout America, and then returned to England in the 1780's to plan for the publication of his history of the Revolution. Although he did not deal with the Loyalists at great length, Gordon betrayed his prejudice in an acrid portrayal of Governor Hutchinson. When discussing the Hutchinson-Oliver letter affair in which the governor declared that he thought American liberties should be curtailed, Gordon wrote point-edly: "a discovery has been made, which will deliver down to poster-ity the name of Gov. Hutchinson loaded with infamy."[7]

Contemporary Loyalist historians, by contrast, were too few in number and too localist in outlook to counteract the entrenched nationalistic Whig version of the Revolution. Joseph Galloway, Phila-delphia lawyer and leading Loyalist spokesman, fled to England in 1778, where he published his history of the rebellion two years later. Like many Loyalists, Galloway did not hold Britain blameless for the rupture of the imperial relationship. He took exception to the favorite metaphor of the period—that of a mother country faced by colonial offspring who had matured, grown discontent with parental control, and were demanding their own independence. Britain had made a mistake, he wrote, by granting greater civil liberties to the Americans than British citizens enjoyed in England.[8] Galloway, like many men of political moderation, was caught in a cruel dilemma. He was concerned, on the one hand, with the excess of freedom within the colonies. Thus, he regarded the tie with Britain as crucial because it helped to maintain stability in the American social order in much

6. David Ramsay, *History of the American Revolution*, 2 vols. (London, 1793) II, 314.
7. William Gordon, *History of the Rise, Progress, and Establishment of the Independence of the United States of America* . . . , 4 vols. (London, 1785), II, 28.
8. Joseph Galloway, *Historical and Political Reflections on the Rise and Progress of the American Rebellion* (London, 1780), 113–114.

the same way that the monarchy, church, and class structure did in the mother country. On the other hand, he was himself quite critical of British rule and believed that the mother country had acted in an unconstitutional manner in certain matters. Fearful of change, however, Galloway argued that republicanism was an inherent trait in the rebellious American character because of the Puritan tradition, and that the colonies would have a brighter future under the stabilizing influence of the Crown than they would as an independent nation.

Peter Oliver's history of the rebellion in Massachusetts was more typical of the kind of writings that the Loyalists produced—parochial in nature, partisan in outlook, and defensive in tone. Oliver, the last chief justice of the Bay Colony's supreme court, depicted the Revolution as a political power struggle within Massachusetts. The Whig leaders were unprincipled demagogues who deliberately aroused the passions of men, causing the populace to abandon reason and to rise up against the colony's legitimate rulers. Written in a passionate and emotional tone, Oliver's history portrayed the Massachusetts political scene in terms of heroes and villains. His heroes were the upholders of law and order—Thomas Hutchinson (his friend and relative by marriage), Governor Francis Bernard, and, of course, Oliver himself. His villains were James Otis, Jr., Samuel Adams, and Joseph Hawley—opposition politicians who plotted the downfall of royal government to satisfy their lust for power.[9]

Thomas Hutchinson, like Oliver, cast his discussion of the Revolution within the narrow confines of Massachusetts partisan politics. A shrewd observer of political affairs, Hutchinson never lost sight of those characteristics of human nature which govern the conduct of men. "Interest," he wrote, "was the governing principle of mankind."[10] "At all times there have been parties, *Ins* and *Outs,* in the

9. Douglass Adair and John A. Schutz, eds., *Peter Oliver's Origin and Progress of the Rebellion* (Stanford, 1967), passim. Evidence that the Loyalists have been neglected by American historians may be seen in the fact that Oliver's history, one of the most important statements by a leading Loyalist, was not published until the 1960's.

10. Thomas Hutchinson, *The History of the Colony and Province of Massachusetts-Bay,* ed. by Lawrence Shaw Mayo, 3 vols. (Cambridge, Mass., 1936), III, 252.

colonies as well as the parent state."[11] Massachusetts was no exception. Indeed, for Hutchinson the province in the prewar period was a case in point that proved his generalization. The Massachusetts colonists had been "influenced by groundless fears, artfully raised by men, whose views were their own advancement by the ruin of the present easy, happy model of government, and the establishment of another form, but under their own real, if not nominal authority in place of it."[12] Since Hutchinson was the leader of the "Ins," he viewed the victory of the "Outs" as a setback to his own "Interest" and a blow against the "happy model of government" in prewar Massachusetts.

Hutchinson's history of the pre-Revolutionary period was almost as emotional as Oliver's—contrary to the impression of most scholars. The original draft of his third volume betrayed a bitterness that was absent from the first two volumes—though the revised edition resulted in a published work that was much more judicious and temperate. In his unrevised version, however, Hutchinson portrayed the Whig leaders in a series of brilliant character sketches. James Otis, Jr., was "subject to strong fits of passion, and intemperate wrath"; Dr. Joseph Warren "bid as fair as any man to advance himself to the summit of political as well as military affairs and to become the Cromwell of North America"; and James Bowdoin "discovered singular talents for managing a controversy with the governor."[13]

Motivated by a drive for power, these Massachusetts politicians conspired to aim at a single goal—independence. "The design of a general independency would have been more apparent . . . [but] the leaders in America strove to keep it out of sight."[14] Hutchinson, did not believe, however, that these men reflected the general views of the populace: "If the opinion of the people of the Province could have been taken at this time, a great majority would have given it

11. *Ibid.*, 184.
12. *Ibid.*, 253.
13. Catherine Barton Mayo, ed., "Additions to Hutchinson's History of Massachusetts Bay," American Antiquarian Society *Proceedings,* LIX (1949), 24, 25, 45.
14. *Ibid.*, 29.

against measures which must bring on independency."[15] Thus, Hutchinson presented the same thesis as other Loyalist writers: the Revolution was wrought by a small, active minority of Whig leaders who foisted the rebellion upon the masses who were politically apathetic.

Of all the Loyalist historians, Jonathan Boucher produced one of the most penetrating analyses of the causes of the Revolution. A clergyman, classical scholar, and philologist, Boucher clung to many traditional ideas while living in the midst of one of the most dynamic societies of the late eighteenth century. His criticisms of America were not only trenchant but among the most complex of all the Loyalists. Accepting as his norm a hierarchically ordered, organic society, based on the Christian religion, and a patriarchal understanding of authority and deference, Boucher was horrified by the Whig historian Gordon, who appeared "to think that the Vox Populi is truly Vox Dei."[16]

Whereas certain Whig historians made a distinction between the French and American revolutions—claiming that America's was justified and France's was not—Boucher argued that both revolutions, at bottom, were products of the same ideology. The French Revolution only appeared worse because strong opposition had developed among the conservatives. On this point, Boucher could say in his history in 1797: "It is [now] beyond even Mr. [Edmund] Burke's abilities to shew, that, in point of principle, there is a shade of difference between the American Revolution and the French rebellion."[17]

What, then, was the cause of the American Revolution? Boucher was too perceptive to attribute it to a single cause. The pluralistic nature of the American society had fostered the development of social mobility, economic opportunity, and religious heterogeneity. "Everything in America," Boucher observed, "had a republican aspect."[18] The colonists, he implied, were a breed apart, and the

15. *Ibid.*, 28.
16. Boucher, *A View of the Causes and Consequences of the American Revolution*, iv.
17. *Ibid.*, xv.
18. *Ibid.*, xliii.

country latent with volatile elements. Moreover, "it was the nature of all colonies to aspire after independence," as a boy aspires to become a man.[19]

Despite these complexities, revolution required a conscious choice among men, and Boucher concluded that in the final analysis "the American war was not a war of conquest, or to repel insult or aggression, but merely a party contest." "[W]ho does not know that misrepresentation and abuse are the usual weapons of the partisans of parties?" Boucher asked. "In speaking of party in this case, I speak indiscriminately of all those persons who in any manner abetted the cause of the insurgents, or took part with the friends of Government —with but little consideration of the side of the Atlantic on which they dwelt." In other words, the components for a Revolution had always been present—all that had been required was the conscious action of men to detonate the existing explosive elements. Boucher, therefore, arrived at much the same conclusion as Oliver and Hutchinson: the ultimate cause of the Revolution was the demagogic Whig leadership which had stirred the people to rise up in rebellion.[20]

The first generation of Revolutionary historians—the participants —may not have agreed about the causes of the Revolution, but they all concurred that the Whig version of the event was the one almost universally accepted. For the most part, the Loyalist side of the story remained buried in obscurity. The results were not too surprising— few Loyalists could bring themselves to write a general history of the Revolution; to do so would have meant explaining the formation of a new nation whose very existence was anathema to their sensibilities. Loyalist writers, nevertheless, had made a major contribution to

19. *Ibid.*, xxvii. Boucher was quoting Dean Josiah Tucker (1712–1799), the Engilsh economist, theologian, and political pamphleteer. The metaphor of the colonies as children growing to mature adulthood was one offered by Whig writers as well to explain the Revolution. See Thomas Paine's "The American Crisis," III (April 19, 1777): "To know whether it be the interest of the continent to be independent, we need only ask this easy simple question, 'Is it the interest of a man to be a boy all his life?'"

20. *Ibid.*, vi. For views of other Loyalist historians such as George Chalmers, Alexander Hewat, Robert Proud, among others, see Lawrence A. Leder, ed., *The Colonial Legacy: Loyalist Historians*, 2 vols. (New York, 1971), I.

American historiography by suggesting that the Revolution had been brought on by an activist Whig minority which had motivated the apathetic masses to rebel. This theme was destined to become an important and enduring one for future historians.

The second generation of American historians writing about the Revolution was characterized by the same fierce nationalism that had marked the first insofar as the treatment of the Loyalists was concerned. Most writers of the mid-nineteenth century viewed the Revolution in black-and-white terms as a triumph of liberty-loving Americans over tyrannical Britain. They focused for the most part upon America's Patriots and either ignored the Loyalists completely or treated them as traitors to the cause of liberty.

George Bancroft, the outstanding historian of the post-Revolutionary generation, typified this ultrapatriotic approach. Son of Aaron Bancroft, the clergyman historian who produced a eulogistic biography of George Washington, Bancroft pictured the Loyalists in a few fleeting passages as men standing in the path of progress at a time when America was moving in the direction of independence. Writing multivolume works that covered American history from the colonial period through the Federal Constitutional Convention, Bancroft's view of the Loyalists—as men of "conservative influence" who were out of step with the times—remained unchanged from the 1830's when he first began publishing until his death in 1891.[21]

One major exception to this general trend among mid-nineteenth-century American historians was Lorenzo Sabine, a Maine newspaper editor. Sabine's was the first full-scale effort to present a more sympathetic view of the American Loyalists. Writing a collective biography of certain leading Loyalists in 1847, and expanding his work in 1864, Sabine sought to rescue them from oblivion and to gain a fairer hearing for their cause. He attempted to humanize the Loyalists

21. George Bancroft, *History of the United States of America from the Discovery of the Continent,* 10 vols. (Boston, 1834–74); and George Bancroft, *History of the Formation of the Constitution of the United States,* 2 vols. (New York, 1882). See especially ch. 2, vol. VIII, of the 11th rev. ed. (Boston, 1873) of the first work cited above.

by showing that they were understandable and even likable men. But Sabine was careful to protect himself against the prevailing chauvinistic attitude by pointing out that both his grandfathers had fought in the Revolution on the Patriot side. From a historiographical point of view, however, Sabine's work must be judged a failure: his writings exercised relatively little influence upon the important historians of the period.[22]

The first major revisionist interpretation of the Loyalists came, in fact, from England, not the United States. In 1882 William E. H. Lecky, a Protestant, Anglo-Irish historian, published the third and fourth volumes of his magnum opus, *History of England in the Eighteenth Century,* containing a balanced account of the American Revolution as it affected both sides of the Atlantic. Although his work focused mainly on political affairs, Lecky's analysis included a reinterpretation of the Loyalists free from the usual narrow, nationalistic outlook of most American historians. "That the position of an American loyalist was in itself a perfectly upright one will hardly indeed be questioned in England," he declared, "and I hope, be now admitted by all reasonable men beyond the Atlantic."

Lecky's history revised the approach to the Revolution in two important respects. Firstly, he undermined the developing American myth that the Revolution had been solely a rebellion by a united people who fought to wrest their independence from a tyrannical king; he highlighted instead the deep cleavages existing within American society that turned the conflict into a violent civil war. "The civil war between Whigs and Tories," he wrote, ". . . had been more savage than the war between the English and Americans; and the revolutionary party attributed with some reason the long con-

22. Lorenzo Sabine, *A Historical Essay on the Loyalists of the American Revolution* (Boston, 1847), and *Biographical Sketches of Loyalists of the American Revolution . . .,* 2 vols. (Boston, 1864). For Sabine's remark about his grandfathers, see *ibid.,* I, 139. The justificatory memoirs published by descendants of Loyalists in the post-Revolutionary generation likewise had little effect on major American historians. The same was true of the independent-minded scholar of the mid-nineteenth century, Richard Hildreth, who showed some sympathy to the Loyalists. See his *The History of the United States . . . 1788–1821,* 6 vols., rev. ed. (New York, 1877–80), III, 137–138.

tinuance of the struggle to the existence and representation of the great loyalist party in America." Secondly, he accepted in essence the Loyalist interpretation of the Revolution set forth by Hutchinson and his contemporaries. "The American Revolution . . . was the work of an energetic minority, who succeeded in committing an undecided and fluctuating majority to courses for which they had little love, and leading them step by step to a position from which it was impossible to recede."[23]

Lecky's work had its most immediate effect upon two amateur antiquarian historians in Massachusetts—George Ellis and Mellen Chamberlain—who published articles in the late 1880's which cited the Englishman as one of the main authorities on the Revolution. The chief vehicle for their interpretation was the widely heralded multivolume cooperative work, *Narrative and Critical History of America,* edited by Justin Winsor, Harvard librarian. Ellis, a Loyalist descendant and president of the Massachusetts Historical Society, contributed a sympathetic essay on the Loyalists which emphasized that these much-maligned Americans were in need of rehabilitation. A staunch conservative in the rapidly changing America of the late nineteenth century, Ellis reflected the new-found appreciation of the Loyalists and their qualities among certain members of his social class. Chamberlain, a judge and later librarian of the Boston Public Library, likewise reflected Lecky's viewpoint in his piece which dealt with the coming of the Revolution.[24] Both Ellis and Chamberlain accepted the internal-conflict thesis and viewed the Revolution as a violent civil war.

23. William E. H. Lecky, *American Revolution 1763–1783,* ed. by James A. Woodbine (New York, 1905), 224, 412, and 484. Although this essay is restricted to American historians, an exception has been made in Lecky's case because of his important influence on American scholarship. An excellent analysis of the impact British scholars have had on the historiography of the Loyalists was made by Bernard Bailyn in his yet unpublished Trevelyan Lectures delivered at Cambridge University in January, 1971. The account above of Lecky's influence in America owes much to Bailyn's work.

24. George Ellis, "The Loyalists and Their Fortunes," in Justin Winsor, ed., *Narrative and Critical History of America,* 8 vols. (Boston, 1884–89), VII, 185–214; and Mellen Chamberlain, "The Revolution Impending," *ibid.,* VI, 1–112.

But Lecky exercised a much more profound influence upon professional historians through the person of Moses Coit Tyler.[25] A minister-turned-historian, Tyler strove conscientiously to achieve the impartiality that Lecky had set up as an ideal for an American studying the Revolution. Tyler was fond of assigning Lecky to his Cornell University students as a corrective to their inbred chauvinism. Like a number of other scholars at the turn of the century, he hoped to discover general laws regarding the nation's development by examining American literature. His method was to let the participants on both sides of the Revolution "tell their own story freely . . . and without . . . being liable, at our hands, to posthumous outrage in the shape of partisan imputations. . . ."[26] In 1897 Tyler produced what must still be regarded as the pinnacle of Loyalist historiography —his monumental *Literary History of the American Revolution.*

Tyler was the first to approach the Loyalists from the point of view of intellectual history. His methodology was new and represented a distinct break from the rather narrow political and institutional framework that had characterized much of the writing of American history to this time. Tyler hoped to write, as he put it, the "inward history" of the Revolution—"the history of its ideas, its spiritual moods, its motives, its passions . . . as these uttered themselves at the time, whether consciously or not, in the various writings of the two parties of Americans who promoted or resisted that great movement."[27] By viewing the Loyalists primarily in terms of their ideas, Tyler arrived at three main insights.

The Loyalists, he concluded, were men of "positive political ideas." Although they took exception to Whig thought and behavior, the Loyalists were not a party of "mere negation and obstruction" as

25. For the full impact of Lecky on American historians, see Charles F. Mullett, "W. E. H. Lecky," in Herman Ausabel, John B. Brebner, and Erling M. Hunt, eds., *Some Modern Historians of Britain: Essays in Honor of R. L. Schuyler* (New York, 1951), 128–149.

26. Moses Coit Tyler, *Literary History of the American Revolution,* 2 vols. (New York, 1957 ed.), I, v. All quotations in this essay are from this edition. Tyler's views appeared first in his article "The Party of the Loyalists in the American Revolution," *American Historical Review,* I (1895), 24–26.

27. *Literary History,* I, v.

they were usually identified. Tyler characterized their ideas as "creative statesmanship," and argued that the Loyalist conception of parliamentary sovereignty and virtual representation could be justified on the basis of past constitutional practices. Secondly, the Loyalists were not reactionaries—persons opposed to any changes in the imperial relationship or reforms that might have extended human rights and liberties in America and elsewhere. They agreed with the Whigs that the constitutional relations between the colonies and mother country should be changed. Their disagreement with their opponents concerned the nature of the reforms to be undertaken. Thirdly, Tyler defended the patriotism of the Loyalists. They championed measures which might have given America major reforms without the disruption of a civil war or a breakup of the British Empire.[28]

Tyler's greatest insight, however, was his analysis of why the Loyalists had failed. Their major flaw was their overconfidence and inability to grasp the threat of imperial dissolution facing them. Having seen earlier Anglo-American crises from which the empire had emerged unscathed, most Loyalists from the Stamp Act to the calling of the Continental Congress clung to the belief that this particular dispute would likewise run its natural course without any permanent rupture. Hence, many of the "ablest conservative writers in America refrained . . . from engaging very actively in the discussion." Unlike many recent historians, Tyler concluded that the tragedy of the Loyalists lay not in their being dragged into the conflict on the Whigs' own terms but rather in their complacency and disdain for those tactics necessary for political survival. His views along these lines remain one of the most suggestive hypotheses for explaining the weakness of the Loyalist response.[29]

Besides his insights, Tyler was significant for perpetuating the Loyalist interpretation of the Revolution. In terms of primary sources, no other historian had documented the Loyalist case so thoroughly. From such secondary sources as Lecky and Ellis, whom he cited,

28. *Ibid.,* 313–315.
29. *Ibid.,* 294.

Tyler repeated the Loyalist theme that the Revolution had been brought about by a demagogic Whig minority.[30]

His study, however, had several serious limitations. For one thing, Tyler failed to provide a coherent overview of the Loyalist system of thought. Aside from one synoptic chapter entitled "The Party of the Loyalists and Their Literature," his work suffered from fragmentation and an atomistic approach; he analyzed each Loyalist writer individually and according to his literary function, e.g., pamphleteer, satirist, or historian. His approach reflected Tyler's belief in the importance of the individual in conveying and acting upon ideas, but his methodology prevented him from arriving at much of a synthesis. For another, Tyler's aim was literary as well as historical.[31] He often dealt with primary sources as examples of stylistic expression rather than plumbing them for their political ideas, attitudes, and beliefs. Although Tyler did not write the kind of intellectual history conceptualized by more recent historians, his work marked the greatest single advance made in Loyalist historiography.

Tyler was a product of his age, and his work reflected many of the major influences affecting the writing of American history around the turn of the century. He personified the professionalization of the discipline that took place during the last quarter of the nineteenth century when he became one of the founders of the American Historical Association. Tyler reflected also the results of the growing Anglo-American rapprochement around the turn of the century—a development which made it somewhat easier for him to write on such a touchy subject as the Loyalists. The superiority of the Anglo-Saxon "race" was a major theme stressed by scholars at the time, and Tyler, like others, deplored the "race feud" that had separated the English-speaking peoples in 1776.[32] Finally, scholars were prone to overemphasize the influence of New England in the nation's development, and Tyler's work was guilty of an imbalance in this regard. Despite these deficiencies, Tyler's study is a classic, and it remains unsurpassed to this day.

30. *Ibid.*, 299–300, 303.
31. John Higham, *Writing American History* (Bloomington, 1970), 50–51.
32. Tyler, *Literary History*, I, ix.

Claude H. Van Tyne, who also wrote on the Loyalists around the turn of the century, reflected other influences prevalent in the profession. His study *The Loyalists in the American Revolution* represented the methodology of the so-called scientific school of historians. Such scholars set as their goal the writing of objective history; they sought to apply the same methodology to the facts of history as did the scientific investigator to the elements in a laboratory. Their definition of "scientific history" consisted of a search for the facts alone; they distrusted ideas, theories, and generalizations. Trained in America as well as in Germany, where this approach to history had its origins, Van Tyne attempted in his work to bring more emphasis on factual data and a greater objectivity to his research.[33]

Van Tyne's study was distinguished more by its longevity than by its quality. It remained the standard general work on the subject for years as scholars writing on the Loyalists turned from general works to highly specialized studies. Ambitiously conceived, Van Tyne's work ranged over a vast variety of Loyalist problems—their persecution by Whig inquisitorial committees, their military activities, and their treatment at the hands of both British and Americans as the result of certain legal and administrative problems. But the study was marred by serious shortcomings: it failed to examine deeply Loyalist motivation, to explain adequately Loyalist conservatism, and to provide a satisfactory synthesis of the subject.

The pioneering work of Tyler and Van Tyne should have provided the basis for a burst of general studies on the Loyalists. The two men had succeeded in reversing a century of historical writing in America that had neglected or deprecated the Loyalists. They had restored the Loyalists to some measure of intellectual respectability— by viewing them as individuals with viable political ideas, by demonstrating that the touchy subject of loyalism could be dealt with in the more congenial climate of opinion in the country around the turn of the century, and by indicating certain fruitful approaches for

33. Claude H. Van Tyne, *The Loyalists in the American Revolution* (New York, 1902).

further research. Subsequent scholars, however, failed to follow up on this promising start.

Professionalization, for one thing, led to increasing fragmentation and specialization among scholars who dealt with the Loyalists. Historians writing from the turn of the century to World War II devoted themselves to local or limited studies rather than to large-scale works of a broad and general nature. Beginning with Alexander Flick's doctoral dissertation, *Loyalism in New York during the Revolution,* published in 1901, a rash of works were written about the Loyalists within individual states. Such state studies prevented scholars from examining loyalism as a whole or from seeking to discover what Loyalists may have held in common.[34]

There was also an increasing tendency to fragmentation as historians approached the subject by writing about individual Loyalists. Biographical studies of leading Loyalists appeared, monographs were published on the confiscation of specific Loyalist estates, and articles were written tracing the dispersal of the émigrés to England, Canada, the West Indies, and other parts of the British Empire.[35]

The advent shortly after 1900 of two groups of scholars who proposed conflicting interpretations of the Revolution—the imperial school and the Progressive historians—also failed to result in a significant advance as far as any fruitful analysis of the Loyalists was

34. Among the state studies dealing with Loyalists, the following, written from the turn of the century to World War II, are worthy of mention: James Stark, *Loyalists of Massachusetts* (Boston, 1910); Edward A. Jones, *Loyalists of Massachusetts* (London, 1930); Otis G. Hammond, *Tories of New Hampshire in the Revolution* (Concord, 1917); Oscar Zeichner, "The Rehabilitation of the Loyalists in Connecticut," *New England Quarterly,* XI (1938), 308–330; Epaphidiotus Peck, *Loyalists of Connecticut* (New Haven, 1934); Oscar Zeichner, "The Loyalist Problem in New York After the Revolution," *New York History,* XXI (1940), 284–302; Edward A. Jones, *Loyalists of New Jersey* . . . (Newark, 1927); Harold Hancock, *Delaware Loyalists* (Wilmington, 1940); Wilbur H. Siebert, *Loyalists of Pennsylvania* (Columbus, 1920); Isaac S. Harrell, *Loyalism in Virginia* . . . (Durham, 1926); and Robert O. DeMond, *Loyalists in North Carolina During the Revolution* (Durham, 1940).

35. The pioneering work of Wilbur H. Siebert in tracing the dispersion of the Loyalist émigrés was particularly instructive in this regard. For many of his articles which appeared in obscure journals, see Oscar Handlin et al. *Harvard Guide to American History* (Cambridge, 1955), 302.

concerned. Certain ingrained philosophical biases prevented such writers from coming to grips with the problem in a meaningful way.

The imperial school of historians, for example, focused on the relationship between the mother country and the colonies: they viewed the Revolution more as an international struggle than as an internal conflict within American society, and therefore they usually neglected the Loyalists and their cause. These scholars, generally speaking, pictured the British Empire as beneficent and rational, the imperial agencies of control as operating justly and efficiently in most instances, and the British ministers as motivated mainly by the ideal of a self-sufficient empire. Whenever they turned their attention to the Loyalists, these historians simply argued that the "King's Friends" had every reason to try to continue the connection with the mother country.

Once their accounts of the Revolution reached the beginning of the hostilities, however, imperial historians showed little interest in the Loyalists. The reason was that the main focus of their studies—the first British Empire—had come to an end. One indication of this lack of attention could be seen in the fact that only a single important imperial historian—Lawrence H. Gipson—was motivated to write a biographical study of a leading Loyalist.[36] Despite their tendency to overlook the Loyalists, the imperial school of historians generally viewed the "King's Friends" sympathetically whenever they did write about them.

The Progressive historians, on the other hand, made the Loyalists a major element in their interpretation of the Revolution. When Carl Becker proposed his dual-revolution thesis, he assumed that in the fight over "who should rule at home" in New York, the colonial aristocracy based on wealth and privilege served as a native complement to George III. After analyzing the clash of economic and social forces within prewar New York, Becker concluded that the Revolution in that province—to a large degree—was the result of an internal conflict between social classes. Class antagonisms frequently pitted

36. Lawrence H. Gipson, *Jared Ingersoll* (New Haven, 1920).

the common man in New York—the small farmers and urban working men—against conservative aristocrats, and compelled most men
of property to take sides during the imperial crisis: some in the upper
classes became reluctant Patriots, while others were committed to the
Loyalist cause.[37] Many Progressive historians, however, disregarded
the qualifications in Becker's class-conflict thesis. They identified the
Loyalists as being drawn almost entirely from the upper classes, and
proceeded to apply a simplified class-conflict thesis that pictured
them as a kind of monolithic aristocratic class that ruled not only in
New York but throughout the thirteen colonies.

The Progressive scholars, imbued with the whig philosophy of history and preoccupied with the idea of American history as a reflection
of a democratic ethos, saw the Loyalists as anathema. They viewed all
of American history within a dialectic that pitted the forces of liberalism against the forces of conservatism in a constant internal struggle
as the country inevitably moved on a gradual upward gradient toward
a more democratic social order. Within this dialectic, the Patriots—
the more radical and insurgent social groups in colonial society—
represented the "thesis" or main stream of American history. The
Loyalists—the aristocratic and reactionary elements—constituted the
"antithesis." The dialectic of the Progressive historians was not only
socioeconomic but also moralistic in nature—a struggle of good
versus evil. To these scholars, what emerged out of the Revolution
was a new synthesis—the triumph of a resurgent democracy that was
good for America's democratic future. If the Loyalists had never
existed, the Progressive scholars would have had to invent them to
fulfill the needs of their historical dialectic: within the context of the
democratic ethos, the Loyalists represented the forces of evil and
reaction that were destined to be overcome.

The Progressive historians, in terms of their methodology, emphasized the materialistic basis of men's motives, stressing economic
drives for the most part. They minimized the influence of ideas in
history, and tended to view ideology only as a resort to rationalization. Ideas served merely as masks to conceal self-interest and the real

37. Carl L. Becker, *History of Political Parties in the Province of New
York, 1760–1776* (Madison, Wis., 1909).

mainsprings of human behavior. Thus, the Progressive historians remained highly skeptical of the Patriots' arguments regarding natural rights and viewed the expression of such ideas largely as rhetoric. Ironically enough, in taking such a position the Progressive scholars returned to precisely the same conclusion as the Loyalist historians who had participated in the Revolution: that the Patriots were insincere in their support of natural rights and turned to such arguments only as a device to gain the support of the masses.[38]

Indicative of this Progressive interpretation was Vernon L. Parrington's three-volume work, published in the late 1920's. To the populist-minded Parrington the major theme in American thought was the enduring dichotomy throughout the nation's history between two rival political philosophies—the liberal tradition exemplified by Thomas Jefferson and the conservative one personified by Alexander Hamilton. Reading this dichotomy back into the Revolution, Parrington portrayed the Patriots as genuine liberals and the Loyalists as arch reactionaries.

> Absolutism under whatever form was doomed in America, however slowly it might linger out its life. Jonathan Boucher might seek to . . . preach to Americans the dogma of divine right through royal primogeniture from Adam, and other colonial Tories might applaud; but they were fast becoming anachronisms. The Revolution was to overthrow for Americans the principle of the absolutist state, and substitute a modified sovereignty, circumscribed by the utilitarian test of its relation to the common well-being of its citizens. . . . Monarchy, with its social appanage of aristocracy, was a caste system wholly unsuited to an unregimented America. The war brought this revolutionary fact home to the consciousness of thousands of colonials; and the liberalism that before had been vaguely instinctive quickly became eager and militant. The old order was passing; the day of the Tory in America was over for the present; the republican was henceforth to be master of the new world.[39]

The Progressive methodology of regarding ideas as rhetoric reached its most explicit exposition in the work of Philip Davidson published in 1941. In his work entitled *Propaganda and the Amer-*

38. Bernard Bailyn, *Ideological Origins of the American Revolution* (Cambridge, 1967), 158.

39. Vernon L. Parrington, *Main Currents in American Thought,* 3 vols. (New York, 1927–30), I, 194–195.

ican Revolution, 1763–1783, Davidson treated certain Loyalist writings as mere propaganda efforts. Davidson's discussion was based
on the premise that neither the Loyalists nor the Patriots believed
what they said and that both sides were interested primarily in stirring the passions of the people.[40]

The Progressive interpretation of the Loyalists—led by Parrington, Beard, Schlesinger, and Jameson among others—proved the
dominant one in American history from the publication of Becker's
book in 1909 down to the end of World War II. To a considerable
degree this interpretation was responsible for discouraging meaningful
research on the Loyalist problem for several reasons. Its methodology
precluded any analysis in depth of Loyalist political thought. Its
crude economic determinism led to a mistaken picture of the Loyalists as being drawn almost wholly from the upper classes. And its
class-conflict thesis portrayed the Loyalists as a monolithic ruling
group whose sole motivation was to preserve its economic and political power. The Progressive interpretation made few allowances for
the role of religious beliefs, failed to account for conflicting emotional and rational differences within various Loyalist groups, and
generally disregarded the "quietist Loyalists"—men who took no active part in the Revolution and either remained neutral or followed
grudgingly the dictates of Patriot leaders.[41]

40. Philip Davidson, *Propaganda and the American Revolution 1763–1783*
(Chapel Hill, 1941).

41. For the major works presenting the approach of the Progressives see
Becker's *History of Political Parties in the Province of New York, 1760–1776;*
Charles A. Beard, *An Economic Interpretation of the Constitution of the United
States* (New York, 1913); Charles A. Beard and Mary R. Beard, *Rise of
American Civilization,* I (New York, 1927); Arthur M. Schlesinger, *The
Colonial Merchants and the American Revolution, 1763–1776* (New York,
1918); and J. Franklin Jameson, *The American Revolution Considered as a
Social Movement* (Princeton, 1926).

The Progressive tradition was carried on by a later generation of historians
including Merrill Jensen and his students. See Merrill Jensen, *The Articles of
Confederation* . . . (Madison, Wis., 1940) and *The New Nation* (New York,
1950), with an important modification, that the "Revolution was a democratic
movement, not in origin, but in result," in Jensen's article "Democracy and
the American Revolution," *Huntington Library Quarterly,* XX (1957), 321–
341. See also the works of Jensen's students, E. James Ferguson, *The*

Becker, who had been primarily instrumental in formulating the Progressive interpretation, was likewise responsible for introducing one of the more fruitful cross-disciplinary approaches to the study of the Loyalists—the application of psychology to history. In his earlier study he showed that the New York conservatives split before the Revolution, and that many of them had provided leadership to the Patriot forces down to the eve of the conflict in hopes of controlling the movement from within. In 1775, however, some of these men committed themselves to the Patriot cause, while others withdrew to become Loyalists. What differentiated those conservatives who turned Loyalists from those who became Patriots was what Becker wanted to know.

In a brief essay published a decade after his New York study appeared in print, Becker examined two men—Peter Van Schaack and John Jay—with this question in mind. The solution was not to be found in the traditional approach employed by most Progressive historians, he decided, since the two men were quite similar in social status, economic standing, and political principles. The answer lay instead in those "subtle and impalpable influences, for the most part unconscious and emotional, which so largely determine motive and conduct." Employing the technique of individual psychology, Becker concluded that the differences between the men lay in their inner feelings and beliefs as well as in their intellectual perspective. He contrasted Van Schaack's doctrinaire mind, rigid temperament, and tendency to detach himself from decisionmaking bodies in order to achieve greater objectivity with Jay's pragmatic outlook. Jay's conciliatory temperament, and "associating mind" led him to plunge into committee work and generally to acquiesce in majority decisions. Becker, in the final analysis, saw the issue in terms of individualism versus conformity—as one aspect of the age-old struggle between "the One and the Many." "Their case was a concrete example," he

---

Power of the Purse . . . (Chapel Hill, 1961), and Jackson T. Main, "Government by the People: The American Revolution and the Democratization of the Legislatures," *William and Mary Quarterly*, 3d. ser., XXIII (1966), 391–407.

wrote, "of the State versus the individual, of personal liberty versus social compulsion, of might versus right."[42]

Leonard W. Labaree, writing during World War II, extended the psychological approach to Loyalist groups rather than individuals in a brief but perceptive essay. After identifying five special groups from which the Loyalists mainly sprang—royal officeholders, Anglican clergymen and parishioners, Quakers and other pacifists, large landholders, and members of the merchant class—Labaree went on to point out certain general characteristics common to them all. Reconstructing what he called the "common Tory mind," Labaree noted certain underlying conservative attitudes: a greater appreciation of "the values inherent in their colonial past," and the "tradition of government by law . . . under the British connection." The Loyalists were also differentiated from their opponents in many ways: they saw "dangers ahead" rather than "noble possibilities"; lacked the daring to risk a "present good" for a "better future"; and were wanting in sufficient faith in mankind in general and Americans in particular "to believe that out of disorder and violence, out of an inexperienced leadership and an undisciplined following could come a stable and intelligent body politic." Labaree's essay, which traced the roots of Loyalism back to conservative tendencies existing among certain groups in colonial society well before the 1770's, remained a promising yet unexplored approach to the problem.[43]

The rise of the so-called neo-Whig historians in the post-World War II period brought a sharp reaction against the socioeconomic interpretation of the Revolution postulated by the Progressive scholars. Generally speaking, the Progressive historians viewed the Revolution as a radical movement—one based on class conflict which constituted a marked break or discontinuity from the colonial era that had gone before and the counter-revolutionary Constitutional

42. Carl L. Becker, "John Jay and Peter Van Schaack," in *Everyman His Own Historian* (Chicago, 1966 ed.), 287, 289, 297.

43. Leonard W. Labaree, "The Nature of American Loyalism," American Antiquarian Society *Proceedings,* LIV (1944), 57–58.

period that came after. The neo-Whigs, on the other hand, pictured the Revolution as a conservative movement—one grounded in constitutional and political principles and undertaken primarily to defend traditional American liberties. They minimized the magnitude of conflict within colonial society. Instead they emphasized the consensus among Americans upon certain fundamental principles of self-government that made it possible for the populace to rise as a near-united people against Great Britain. To the neo-Whig historians the Revolutionary era was less of a break with the colonial past than its culmination; they traced a line of continuity in political and constitutional principles from the prewar period through to the writing of the state constitutions and the Federal Constitution in 1787.

Given the premise of a conservative Revolution, the neo-Whig scholars could not fit the Loyalists comfortably into their interpretation. How could conservatives, like the Loyalists, oppose a conservative Revolution? The neo-Whig historians, for this reason, either failed to mention the Loyalists in their discussion of the Revolution— incredible as this may seem—or made only superficial references to them and their arguments. In the pages of Daniel J. Boorstin, Louis Hartz, and Clinton Rossiter, who wrote about the Revolution in the 1950's, little mention is made of the Loyalists.[44]

The decade of the 1960's—by way of contrast—witnessed a revival of interest in Loyalist studies. This phenomenon was attributable, perhaps, to four trends: a reaction against the neglect that the Loyalists had suffered at the hands of the neo-Whig scholars; a renewed emphasis on intellectual and social history; an increasing tendency to apply a cross-disciplinary approach to the subject; and a

44. Daniel J. Boorstin in his *The Americans: The Colonial Experience* (New York, 1958), *The Americans: The National Experience* (New York, 1965), and "The American Revolution: Revolution Without Dogma," in *The Genius of American Politics* (Chicago, 1953), 66–98, does not discuss the Loyalists. Louis Hartz, *The Liberal Tradition in America* (New York, 1955), 58; and Clinton Rossiter, *Seedtime of the Republic* (New York, 1953), 3, 155, 319, 322, 340, 349, say very little. Edmund S. Morgan, in *The Birth of the Republic, 1763–1789* (Chicago, 1956), makes some mention, 74, 99, and 120–121, but Benjamin F. Wright, *Consensus and Continuity* (Boston, 1958), hardly accounts for the Loyalists at all.

general interest among many scholars in all minorities and neglected groups in American history.

The most important work to appear during the decade, William H. Nelson's *The American Tory,* reflected all of these trends. "The Loyalists . . . ," he wrote in his preface, "suffered a most abject kind of failure, losing not only their argument, their war, and their place in American society, but even their proper place in history." His book, consisting of a series of essays, constituted the best general analysis on the subject since Tyler's study.[45]

One aspect of Nelson's study involved intellectual history—a synthetic study of the Loyalist mentality. Many ideas held by the Loyalists, he showed, fell well within the Whig tradition. Joseph Galloway, for example, believed in the colonists' right to be taxed only by their own representatives, in the protection of American liberties, and in the need for a major reorganization of the British Empire in 1774. In fact, Galloway found British policies prior to 1776 just as unacceptable as did the Patriots. Nelson thus made it clear that the intellectual differences between Loyalists and Patriots were subtle, contradictory, and ambiguous, and they could not be treated in terms of simplistic polarities.[46]

Nelson's work, which concentrated more on social than on intellectual history, reflected also the tendency to resort to techniques from other academic disciplines. When discussing the Loyalists, Nelson offered the hypothesis that they constituted a conglomeration of cultural minorities—minority groups who were consciously aware that they had not been assimilated into the larger society around them and who looked therefore to Britain for support against the surrounding dominant majority. Such identifiable social groups included the following: ethnic minorities—the Scots, recent British immigrants, and Germans in the South; religious minorities—Anglicans in the North, Presbyterians in the South, and Quakers and German pietists in the middle colonies; and racial minorities—certain Indian tribes and some Negroes. By defining these minorities in terms of their

45. William H. Nelson, *The American Tory* (New York, 1961), v.
46. *Ibid.;* see ch. 3.

sense of group consciousness and their feelings of alienation from what they perceived the prevailing Whig majority to be, Nelson sought to apply to history the negative reference group theory often employed by sociologists, psychologists, and anthropologists. Nelson's hypothesis presented exciting possibilities for future research in explaining the motivation of numerous Loyalist groups.[47]

Bernard Bailyn's book *The Ideological Origins of the American Revolution,* a brilliant piece of intellectual history, was likewise of utmost importance in illuminating Loyalist ideas. Although his study was concerned primarily with the larger story of Whig rather than Loyalist ideology, Bailyn's analysis of political thought in prewar America included both sides. Briefly stated, Bailyn's thesis was that the Revolution was a radical movement but that the true revolution took place in men's minds rather than in the political or social sphere. This intellectual revolution constituted a transformation in the perception that many colonists had of themselves. Before the Revolution, these Americans saw their divergences from European norms—the lack of an established church, titled aristocracy, stratified society, and cosmopolitan culture—as shortcomings, and they experienced a sense of inferiority. As the Patriots underwent this mental revolution, they came to look upon these deviations as good, not bad, and became convinced that they had to separate themselves from the corrupt mother country to realize their destiny as a virtuous people. Within the writings of certain Loyalists—primarily pamphleteers— Bailyn saw reflected an awareness of the shift in ideas and attitudes that was taking place in America regarding a hierarchical social order, the relationship of rulers to the ruled, and the traditional role of authority in governmental affairs. "What Boucher, Leonard, Chandler, and other articulate defenders of the *status quo* saw as the final threat," wrote Bailyn, "was not so much the replacement of one set of rulers by another as the triumph of ideas and attitudes incompatible with the stability of any standing order, any establishment—incompatible with society itself, as it had been traditionally known."[48]

47. *Ibid.,* 87–93.
48. Bailyn, *Ideological Origins of the American Revolution,* 318.

Bailyn's book was as significant for its methodology as for its thesis. Contrary to the Progressive scholars who exhibited a profound mistrust of men's ideas, Bailyn stressed the primacy of ideas and regarded them as determinants and causative agents in history. Bailyn tended to accept the expressions of Patriot principles and the conscious espousal of ideals at face value, and to show how these ideas themselves helped to bring about changes in colonial beliefs, attitudes, and behavior. By the same token, Bailyn dealt with the ideology of the Loyalist leaders in a similar fashion.

The 1960's also witnessed attempts by scholars to analyze religious ideas and institutions as a means of probing into the motivation of certain Loyalists. Religious ideas, some historians held, helped to shape the world view of many American colonists and determined to a large degree the position that they took in the Revolution. Both Bailyn and Nelson took up this theme in passing, but the most ambitiously conceived study along these lines was Alan Heimert's *Religion and the American Mind from the Great Awakening to the Revolution.*

Heimert's work was primarily concerned with the intellectual split that took place between two religious groupings that grew out of the Great Awakening, but he was interested also in the Loyalist view of the Revolution. One important component in the thinking of many Loyalists, Heimert concluded, was their identification of the Patriots with that group of evangelical, revivalist-oriented religious enthusiasts in America whose roots supposedly could be traced to the tradition of English Puritanism which had culminated in regicide and civil war. "Joseph Galloway, Samuel Peters, Peter Oliver, Jonathan Boucher and every other Loyalist traced the imperial crisis to the principles of the Puritan Revolution and Commonwealth," Heimert wrote.[49]

49. Alan Heimert, *The American Mind from the Great Awakening to the Revolution* (Cambridge, Mass., 1966), 357–358. Bernard Bailyn rejected the idea of any single intellectual paradigm of religious causation such as that suggested by Heimert in his work, i.e., that the so-called Liberals composed of religious rationalists—Arminians and Old Lights—were less radical in the Revolutionary movement than religious enthusiasts—the evangelical Calvinist followers of Jonathan Edwards. Bailyn wrote biographical sketches of three

Religious institutions also played an important part in the issue of loyalism. Carl Bridenbaugh, in his *Mitre and Sceptre,* showed that the fear of an Anglican episcopate in America antagonized many colonists in Congregationalist New England and the middle colonies, and was a factor in committing them to the Patriot cause. The aggressive tactics of the Anglican clergy in those colonies alienated American dissenters, and resulted in harsher treatment of Anglican Loyalists in certain sectors when the war came.[50]

Efforts to analyze the social as well as religious origins of loyalism continued during the decade. Wallace Brown, in *The King's Friends,* inquired into the socioeconomic and geographic backgrounds of the Loyalists in each of the thirteen colonies and arrived at certain conclusions. Contrary to the findings of earlier historians, Loyalists were not primarily members of the upper class; in most colonies they came from the middle or lower classes. Loyalism, moreover, was "a distinctly urban and seaboard phenomenon"—except for New York and North Carolina, where there existed "major rural, inland pockets." And despite John Adams's misquoted estimate that the Loyalists constituted one-third of the population, Brown's statistics indicated that they constituted no more than 7.6 to 18 percent of the whites. But Brown's methodology could be faulted because his findings were based mainly upon only those Loyalists who submitted postwar claims to Britain, and he proceeded on the unsupported assumption that "conclusions made about them can frequently be cautiously extended to Loyalists in general."[51]

clergymen—Jonathan Mayhew, Stephen Johnson, and Andrew Eliot—to show that Heimert's hypothesis of a Liberal versus Calvinist dichotomy was not a sufficient explanation as to why some men became Loyalists and others Patriots. See Bernard Bailyn, "Religion and Revolution: Three Biographical Studies," *Perspectives in American History,* IV (1970), 85–169.

50. Carl Bridenbaugh, *Mitre and Sceptre* (New York, 1962). Arthur L. Cross stressed the same theme in his *Anglican Episcopate and the American Colonies* (Cambridge, 1902).

51. Wallace Brown, *The King's Friends* (Providence, 1965), v. 250, 257–258, 261–267. See also Brown's *The Good Americans* (New York, 1969), which relies essentially on the same methodology.

For trenchant critiques of the use of the Loyalist claims as evidence, see Eugene Fingerhut, "Uses and Abuses of the American Loyalist Claims: A Critique of Quantitative Analyses," *William and Mary Quarterly,* 3d ser., XXV

Finally, the 1960's resulted in a revision of certain assumptions of the Progressive historians. One major controversy regarding the social consequences of the Revolution centered on the confiscation of Loyalist estates and whether the redistribution of such lands affected a democratization of American society. J. Franklin Jameson's book *The American Revolution Considered as a Social Movement,* published in 1926, suggested that the seizure, breakup, and subsequent disposition of Loyalist estates into small lots brought about a democratization of landownership. Two studies written in the 1930's took exception to Jameson's generalization as far as the democratizing effects of confiscations in certain areas of New York were concerned. During the 1960's, however, there was a rash of local studies on the disposition of Loyalist estates. Some of them supported the Jameson thesis, but others contended that the sale of estates profited land speculators and well-to-do Patriots far more than poor farmers or landless tenants. Richard B. Morris, who had students testing the Jameson thesis over the years, was forced to conclude, "The subject is indeed complex and deserves a precise county-by-county investigation before any valid generalization can be drawn about what seemed on paper to be the most social revolutionary step taken by the American patriots."[52]

(1968), 245–258. Paul H. Smith in "The American Loyalists: Notes on Their Organization and Numerical Strength," *Ibid.,* 259–277, comes close to agreeing with Brown's estimate and claims the Loyalists comprised about 19.8 percent of the white Americans.

Brown's point that there was a predominance of lower- and middle-class people among the Loyalists had been made previously in local and general studies. See Esther Clark Wright's important study, *The Loyalists of New Brunswick* (Fredericton, N.B., 1955); Richard B. Morris's "Class Struggle and the American Revolution," *William and Mary Quarterly,* 3d ser., XIX (1962), 27; and Nelson's *The American Tory.*

52. Morris, "Class Struggle and the American Revolution," *William and Mary Quarterly,* 3d ser., XIX (1962), 23.

Jameson was by no means the first to suggest that the sale of Loyalist estates had a democratizing effect, but his work had the greatest influence on his fellow historians. For other scholars who took the same position, see Van Tyne, *Loyalists in the American Revolution,* 280; Allan Nevins, *American States During and After the Revolution* (New York, 1924), 443.

In the 1930's, two studies appeared that dealt with the confiscation of Loyalist estates in New York: Harry B. Yoshpe's *The Disposition of Loyalist*

Another major assumption of many Progressive historians was that the Loyalists comprised a more or less monolithic ruling class made up of officeholders, rich merchants, large landowners, and slaveholders. Paul H. Smith in his monograph *Loyalists and Redcoats*, showed that as a military force the Loyalists failed to organize themselves and waited for British guidance and leadership. Smith's study, therefore, cast serious doubts on any ideas that the Loyalists constituted a powerful ruling class, or that they represented a socially cohesive group with a strong sense of identity.[53]

Much of the writing about the Loyalists during the 1960's, therefore, was heavily revisionist in nature. Most works revised the older Progressive interpretation of the Loyalists, primarily because the more recent neo-Whig scholars had written so little about them. Thus, no new interpretation emerged on the subject. The Loyalists had yet to enter into the nation's historical consciousness, and the American view of the Revolutionary era continued to be one-sided. But as Gordon Wood pointed out, "Any intellectually satisfying explanation of the Revolution must encompass the . . . [Loyalist] perspective as well as the Whig."[54]

Estates in the Southern District of New York (New York, 1939), and E. W. Spaulding's *New York in the Critical Period, 1783–1789* (New York, 1932).

Among the studies published in the 1960's on the disposition of Loyalist estates were: Staughton Lynd, *Anti-Federalism in Dutchess County, New York* . . . (Chicago, 1962); Robert S. Lambert, "The Confiscation of Loyalist Property in Georgia, 1782–1786," *William and Mary Quarterly*, 3d ser., XX (1963), 80–94; Richard D. Brown, "The Confiscation and Disposition of Loyalists' Estates in Suffolk County, Massachusetts," *ibid.*, XXI (1964), 534–550; Beatrice M. Reubens, "Pre-Emptive Rights in the Disposition of a Confiscated Estate: Philipsburg Manor, New York," *ibid.*, XXII (1965), 435–456.

The following students of Richard B. Morris worked on the Jameson thesis: John M. Hemphill II, "The Confiscation and Redistribution of Loyalist Property in Anne Arundel and Frederick Counties, Maryland" (unpubl. M.A. thesis, Columbia University, 1949); Nathan Adams, "The Confiscation of Loyalist Estates in New Jersey, Somerset County" (unpubl. M.A. thesis, Princeton University, 1948); Catherine Snell Crary, "Forfeited Loyalist Lands in the Western District of New York—Albany and Tryon Counties," *New York History*, XXXV (1954), 239–258; and Staughton Lynd, *Anti-Federalism in Dutchess County*.

53. Paul H. Smith, *Loyalists and Redcoats* (Chapel Hill, 1964).

54. Gordon S. Wood, "Rhetoric and Reality in the American Revolution," *William and Mary Quarterly*, 3d ser., XXIII (1966), 15–16.

What kind of research might be conducted to bring about the "Americanization" of the Loyalists? What lines of inquiry might prove fruitful for future research? What new approaches might be applied to this two-century-old subject? With the polemical approach of the Progressives on the wane and their fixed social and political categories exercising less influence upon scholars, the stage seems set for a new era of Loyalist historiography.

In the first place, historians might pay more attention to the problems of definitions. The term "Loyalist" has been applied too loosely in the past; it has often lacked clarity and exactitude. In identifying who the Loyalists were, most scholars have relied on *active* behavior as the key criteria. That is, they have generally defined Loyalists as those persons who actually bore arms, left the country to go into exile, placed a claim with the British government for property losses, or had their estates confiscated by state governments. Such a definition fails to account for those whom Wallace Brown has termed "quietist Loyalists"—*passive* persons who remained loyal to the king in mind and heart but indulged in no deeds.[55] The distinction between "active" and "passive" Loyalists is crucial for any statistical study, of course, because it would affect the count in computing estimates of their total numbers.[56]

The "neutrals" pose another problem of definition. Many Patriots tended to class moderate men who refused to join either side as being Loyalists at heart. Were there not persons, however, who remained completely neutral and longed for the status quo ante bellum? Were there not individuals who took the position of "a plague on both your houses" during the Revolution? If so, it seems unwise to lump them with the Loyalists. The study of the "neutrals," in fact, raises a major topic for further investigation. In this connection, Keith B. Berwick's pioneering study[57]—which charts "the ambiguous middle way between

55. Brown, *The King's Friends,* 250.
56. The distinction might prove useful in other ways. Some "active" Loyalists appear to have changed sides easily and gone over to the Patriots. Certain "passive" Loyalists, on the other hand, seem to have been persistent and stayed steadfast with their cause.
57. Keith B. Berwick, "Moderates in Crisis: The Trials of Leadership in Revolutionary Virginia" (unpubl. dissertation, University of Chicago, 1959).

the extremes of loyalism and patriotism" in Virginia—is both stimulating and suggestive.

Those who joined both sides in the course of the war present the historian with yet another dilemma. Should they be classed as "neutrals" on the grounds that their conflicting loyalties canceled one another out? Or should the side-changers be placed in a separate category? These questions, among others, will require greater precision on the part of future scholars who grapple with the problem of defining who the Loyalists were.[58]

Of all the major subcategories of the discipline, social history appears to offer the greatest promise for future research. One method of social history that has proved useful in studying the Loyalists since the days of Sabine has been that of collective biography. The classic model for a collective biography in terms of a series of impressionistic case studies is the work of Clifford K. Shipton, whose sketches of Harvard College graduates include analyses of numerous Massachusetts Loyalists. By taking up the life experiences of each individual, Shipton has entered into their innermost feelings and thoughts. His approach enables him to account for their emotional as well as intellectual frame of mind, to take a more objective view of the Revolution free from Whig bias, and to discuss "quietist Loyalists" as well as active claimants. By seeing the Revolution through the eyes of Harvard College contemporaries—both Loyalists and Whigs—Shipton comes closer to a two-sided interpretation of the event than any other colonial scholar.[59]

Collective biography by its very nature depends upon the literary remains of the elite in colonial society, but if the majority of Loyalists

58. The South in particular appears to have had a sizable number of sidechangers.

59. Clifford K. Shipton, Sibley's *Harvard Graduates* . . . vols. VII–XV (Cambridge, 1933–). For a discussion of Shipton's methodology, see the introductions to vols. VII and IX. Although sympathetic to the Loyalists, Shipton was by no means an apologist. Those reviewers who claimed he was pro-Loyalist were merely betraying their own Whig biases. As Shipton noted, "for nearly two centuries that witness stand has been monopolized by Whig leaders who have used it as a pulpit to establish as the truth a version of history just as biased and just as prejudiced as that presented by the Chief Justice [Peter Oliver]." Letters to the Editor, *William and Mary Quarterly*, 3d ser., X (1953), 348.

came from the middle and lower classes then different methods would have to be employed. To determine why these humbler, less articulate people committed themselves to the British cause, the Revolution might be viewed "from the bottom up" and from the perspective of "the powerless, the inarticulate, [and] the poor."[60] Among the more promising approaches in this regard were two methods used by demographers—family reconstitution and aggregative analysis.[61] Family connections appeared to play an important role in forming loyalties during the Revolution; the Whig-Loyalist split often mirrored already existing tensions between two distinct kinship groupings. By gathering data on families stretching over several generations, it was sometimes possible to discern divisions between elite kinship groups prior to the Revolution—such as the Hutchinson-Otis families—and to demonstrate that the event itself provided an opportunity to act out prevailing animosities.[62] Using the methodology of family reconstitution, scholars might inquire if lower-class families formed similar kinship groupings and whether they reacted in the same way as the upper classes during the Revolution.

Aggregative analysis, which deals with the "reconstitution of the demographic history of the community as a whole," presents another possibility for research into the attitudes of the inarticulate masses.[63] A concentrated study of the vital statistics of a single community—the births, deaths, and marriages—over a period of time often yields important demographic data. When changes in the rates of birth, fertility, and mortality are related to the landholding within

60. One of the scholars of the so-called New Left who suggested that the Revolution be viewed "from the bottom up" and that the Loyalists be seen from the perspective of class, among other things, was Jesse Lemisch; see his article from which the quotes above are drawn, "The Revolution Seen from the Bottom Up," in Barton J. Bernstein, *Towards a New Past* (New York, 1968), 4–29.

61. For a more complete discussion of these methodologies, see the introduction to Philip G. Greven's *Four Generations* (Ithaca, 1970).

62. John J. Waters and John A. Schutz, "Patterns of Massachusetts Colonial Politics: The Writs of Assistance and the Rivalry between the Otis and Hutchinson Families," *William and Mary Quarterly*, 3d ser., XXIV (1967), 543–567. Although this article did not employ the methodology of family reconstitution as such, its conclusions showed the possibilities of such an approach.

63. Greven, *Four Generations*, 5.

that community, new insights into the Revolution might be gleaned. Land was the most common form of capital at the time, and the land/man ratio within a community often played a determining role in the lives of individuals as well as for the locality as a whole. Questions regarding land—who owned it, the manner in which it was acquired and distributed, the way it was held, the uses to which it was put, and the methods employed for passing it from one generation to another—were of crucial importance.[64] By comparing the patterns of population growth and decline within a community with changes in the practices of landholding and land disposal, it might be possible to discern the relationship, if any, between the Loyalists and social mobility. In other words, the behavior of Loyalists as individuals or groups within a community might be reflected in their patterns of social mobility—upward, downward, or geographical in nature.

Local history might provide other possibilities for research, for localism was often the dominant force in determining the stance a particular community took toward the Revolution. Given the isolation of many colonial communities and the provincial outlook of their inhabitants, one way of approaching the problem might be to determine if the populace took into account the views of an adjoining community or a distant, cosmopolitan metropolis when adopting a political position toward the Revolution. To put it another way, by using the negative reference group theory it might be possible to demonstrate that the inhabitants of a given community achieved their sense of identity as Loyalists by taking a position contrary to that of an adjacent community with which they traditionally differed. Certain communities in the interior, on the other hand, might have taken a Loyalist position precisely because their local-mindedness put them in fundamental opposition to the cosmopolitan attitude taken by the major metropolis along the seaboard within their colony.

Local history and the study of Loyalists might be approached from an interior as well as an exterior point of view. Loyalist elements within a community might be examined from the same vantage point as Nelson's cultural minorities—as individuals or groups who,

64. *Ibid.*, 9.

for various reasons, felt that their position within the town's society was threatened or declining, and who cast their lot with the British as a means of regaining their previous power and influence. A case study of Deerfield, Massachusetts, for example, suggests that the issues that split the citizenry into Whigs and Loyalists were essentially local in nature. Divisions within the community were not over Britain's mercantile policy and "home rule," but rather between competing social, economic, and political groups—"between established families and newcomers, commercialists and farmers, and [old] political elites and new aspiring ones." Long before the Revolutionary crisis, such divisions smoldered beneath the surface in the form of local rivalries and jealousies, but they burst into flame with the coming of the conflict.[65]

The Deerfield study suggests another alternative for Loyalist studies on the local level. How many groups or individuals under the guise of patriotism used the Revolution to resort to violence in order to settle an old score, or to precipitate the resolution of some conflict of long standing? How many innocent people were killed, jailed, or persecuted unjustly as "Loyalists" by Whigs who gained positions of political power? A civil war raged with great ferocity throughout the country, especially in the South, and brought with it a level of violence that has yet to be examined fully. Violence as a phenomenon in the Revolutionary era has been studied, but the debate has revolved mainly around the issue of whether urban mobs were uncontrolled and pursuing their own aims or if they were being manipulated by Whig leaders instead.[66] Once the Revolution is

65. Bruce G. Merritt, "Loyalism and Social Conflict in Revolutionary Deerfield, Massachusetts," *Journal of American History* (1970), 277–289. Along these same lines, it might be of great value to examine local and county court records and to follow the process of litigation to discover whether there were any discernible patterns of conflict before 1776 between eventual Loyalists and Patriots.

66. The literature on the role of mobs in riots in early modern history is voluminous. Much of the recent research was inspired by George Rudé, who wrote about such phenomena in England and France in his *The Crowd in History* (New York, 1964). See also Edmund S. and Helen Morgan, *The Stamp Act Crisis* (Chapel Hill, 1953), 231–257; Bernard Bailyn, *Pamphlets of the American Revolution, 1750–1776* (Cambridge, 1965), I, 581–584; Gordon

recognized for the violent war that it was, the persecution of Loyalists—especially in the rural areas—should offer numerous opportunities for local research.[67]

Regional history likewise might offer research possibilities because loyalism manifested itself in different forms within various areas and among certain groups (such as religious sects whose following cut across colony boundaries). The data gathered by the Loyalist Papers project at the American Antiquarian Society might prove helpful in this regard—especially if such statistical information were subjected to intensive quantitative analysis by computers. A comparison of regional varieties of loyalism might reveal interesting differences that are not reflected in local and state studies.

Another regional approach might be to study those areas that were subjected to heavy occupation by British military forces. One hypothesis has already been advanced that "loyalism was strongest where the British army was there to support it."[68] This hypothesis suggests that the Loyalists were much more prudent and pragmatic in their behavior than is generally realized.

S. Wood, "A Note on Mobs in the American Revolution," *William and Mary Quarterly*, 3d ser., XXIII (1966), 635–642; Jesse Lemisch, "Jack Tar in the Streets: Merchant Seamen in the Politics of Revolutionary America," *ibid.*, XXVII (1968), 371–407; Pauline Maier, "Popular Uprisings and Civil Authority in Eighteenth-Century America," *ibid.*, XXVII (1970), 3–35; and Pauline Maier, "The Charleston Mob and the Evolution of Popular Politics in Revolutionary South Carolina, 1765–1784," *Perspectives in American History*, IV (1970), 173–196. Richard M. Brown has taken up violence in rural areas before and during the Revolution in his *The South Carolina Regulators* (Cambridge, 1963), his article "American Vigilante Tradition," in Hugh D. Graham and Ted R. Gurr, eds., *Violence in America*, 2 vols. (Washington, 1969), I, 154–226, and especially in his unpublished paper delivered at the Symposium on the American Revolution held at the Institute for Early American History and Culture in Williamsburg, Va., March 1971. Nelson likewise treated physical coercion of Loyalists by local committees in his *The American Tory*, 93–96.

67. The papers of the Continental Congress in this regard contain information on the ill-treatment of Loyalists who complained to authorities.

68. J. R. Pole's review of Wallace Brown's *The King's Friends* in *The Historical Journal*, X, 2 (1967), 309. The implications of this hypothesis have been explored in John Shy's creative paper "The American Revolution: The Military Conflict Considered as a Revolutionary War," delivered at the Symposium on the American Revolution held at the Institute of Early American History and Culture in Williamsburg, Va., March 1971.

Turning to another tack, historians might resort to traditional political history to learn new lessons about the Loyalists. Using the idea of interest-group politics, scholars might ask—as one did— "Was there a *developing* royal interest, and if so did its increase threaten to weaken the claims that the American home rulers might hope to make on nascent American patriotism?"[69] Was there, in short, a rise of royal power in colonial America in the eighteenth century concurrent with the rise of the assemblies, and did such interest groups within each colony fight to maintain the power and influence they had attained?[70] This interpretation, after all, was the version of the Revolution of many Whig leaders at the time, and for that reason alone deserves more serious consideration.

To pursue this theme, scholars must examine more closely the group political behavior of the "King's Friends." The nature of "court" politics in each province should be analyzed to reveal the political strategies employed by Loyalist factions. Those in power scarcely foresaw their impending defeat and exile, and the secret to their failure might be found in their perception of the political world in which they saw themselves operating.[71] Within Massachusetts— to give but one example—families away from the metropolis such as the Williamses in Northampton, the Chandlers in Worcester, and Leonards in Taunton, it would appear, were all part of an informal and fragile political faction connected with Governor Hutchinson. The causes of collapse of that faction, not merely in Boston but throughout the rest of the province, must be told before the Loyalist story is complete.

The Loyalists' political thought, as well as their political behavior, is deserving of greater analysis. Although scholars had fruitfully explored certain Loyalist concepts, they were not always successful in relating the assumptions, beliefs, and ideas of the Loyalists to their actions and political behavior. The political thought of the Loyalists, like that of their opponents, was often instrumentalist in purpose

69. Pole, review of Wallace Brown's *The King's Friends.*
70. John M. Murrin, "The Myths of Colonial Democracy and Royal Decline in Eighteenth-Century America," *Cithara,* V (1965), 53–69, but especially 66.
71. *Ibid.*

and reflected the political context out of which it sprang. Only by following the flow of manifest events and relating them to the writings of Loyalist leaders at the time would it be possible to perceive certain nuances, ambivalences, and contradictions in their thought: the shift in tone from a defensive to an offensive intellectual stance in the debate; and the growing skepticism about Britain's governmental practices in America along with the praise of her theory of government. Moreover, it should be noted that the Loyalists often placed a completely different emphasis on certain seminal political thinkers whom they quoted as did the Whigs—Locke, Montesquieu, and Blackstone—to say nothing of antiauthoritarian pamphleteers like Trenchard and Gordon.[72] In this last regard, what

72. Seminal political thinkers invariably face the problem of being interpreted in different ways. For Loyalists who resorted to Montesquieu see: Martin Howard, *A Letter from a Gentleman at Halifax* . . . (Newport, 1765), 18, 20; [James Chalmers], *Plain Truth* . . . (Philadelphia, 1776), 17, 71; Isaac Hurst, *The Political Family* . . . (Philadelphia, 1775), 6; and Henry Van Schaack, *The Life of Peter Van Schaack* (New York, 1842), 72. Montesquieu was used by both Loyalists and Whigs in their political thought because he could be read two ways. On Montesquieu's ambiguity, see Franz Neumann's introduction to *The Spirit of the Laws* (New York, 1949); John Plamenatz, *Man and Society* (New York, 1963), I, 253–298; Mark Waddicor, *Montesquieu and the Natural Law* (The Hague, 1970); and especially David Lowenthal, "Montesquieu and the Classics: Republican Government and *The Spirit of the Laws*," in Joseph Cropsey, ed., *Ancients and Moderns: Essays on the Tradition of Political Philosophy in Honor of Leo Strauss* (New York, 1964).

Blackstone likewise was of great value to both sides. This situation resulted, in part, from Blackstone's ambiguous use of natural law phraseology, which caused him to be interpreted as upholding Austinian sovereignty (if one may resort to an anachronism to express the intellectual reality) on the one hand, and defending a resort to revolution on the other. For the point of view that Blackstone was strictly Austinian, see Paul Lucas, "*Ex Parte:* Sir William Blackstone, 'Plagiarist': A Note on Blackstone and the Natural Law," *American Journal of Legal History,* VII (1963), 142–158. For the Whig use of Blackstone and a different point of view, see Gerald Stourzh, "William Blackstone: Teacher of Revolution," *Jahrbuch für Amerikastudien,* XV (1970), 184–200. An example of the Loyalists' use of Blackstone would be Thomas Bradbury Chandler, *A Friendly Address* . . . (Philadelphia, 1774), 17, and his *What Think Ye of the Congress Now?* (New York, 1775), 26. Chandler's use of Blackstone in the second pamphlet is of interest because precisely the same passage is used by the Whig writer John McKenzie in the *South Carolina Gazette,* Oct. 18, 1769. This ambiguity in Blackstone's political thought was noted by Ernest Barker: "Even Blackstone himself, in the preliminary introduction to his *Commentaries* (the argument of the *Commentaries* themselves is very different), allowed himself to be led by his reading

is needed is a more careful analysis of what the received tradition of such seminal thinkers was in the various colonies—what aspects of Blackstone's thought, for example, were accepted in a colony like South Carolina, what parts were rejected, and what did that process of selection reveal about the value system of that southern colony?

The diversities within Loyalist political thought have yet to be examined in depth. In the heat of the crisis, the Loyalists drew upon various traditions of Western political thought to find arguments that might be employed against their Whig enemies. Tracing the various strands of Loyalist thought back to their sources might prove useful in two ways: to shed more light on those traditions upon which they relied; and to learn how Loyalists from contrasting regions of the country, various social classes, and diverse religious persuasions employed the same sources in different ways to argue with their opponents.

Given Moses Coit Tyler's conclusion that the Loyalists waited too long in taking a stand during the pre-Revolutionary crisis, should not the apolitical nature of the Loyalist leaders be explored? Had Galloway been a more skillful politician and mended his fences with John Dickinson, with whose views he had much in common, could he have been more successful in the Continental Congress in 1774 and the Pennsylvania Assembly in 1775? Had William Smith been less disdainful of the hurly-burly of New York politics, might he have had greater influence in trying to keep that colony loyal? Why was Daniel Leonard so late in taking up his pen to write his Massachusetts letters? What was there about the Loyalist elite that made many of them so apolitical?[73]

---

of Pufendorf and Burlamaqui—and specially of the latter—into the enunciation of a political philosophy which quarrelled sadly with his own later exposition of the actual law of the British Constitution," "Natural Law and the American Revolution," *Traditions of Civility* (Cambridge, 1948), 278; and ch. 5 of the book by the same author, *Essays on Government* (Oxford, 1946).

For examples of citations of Locke and Trenchard and Gordon by both Loyalist and Whig pamphleteers, see the footnotes in Bailyn's *Ideological Origins*, 29–30, 37.

73. For Smith and Leonard, see Leslie F. S. Upton, *The Loyal Whig: William Smith of New York and Quebec* (Toronto, 1971), and Bernard

Other lines of inquiry have been suggested by more modern scholars. Edmund S. Morgan proposed that a study of local American institutions—religious and social as well as political and economic—might provide more clues as to why certain colonists became Patriots.[74] Might not the same approach be adopted to study both local and imperial institutions to discover why other men remained Loyalists? John M. Head, in his monograph, advanced the provocative but unproved assertion that sentiment for independence was strongest in those areas where there was social homogeneity but economic distress. Could the reverse tell us something about loyalism—that it was strongest where there was economic prosperity but social heterogeneity?[75] Jack P. Greene posed an important question for further research when he suggested that certain Loyalists seemed to feel that America needed the cultural stimulus of the mother country, for without it the colonies might remain mere cultural provinces.[76]

Breaking from such traditional approaches as political, intellectual, and institutional history, scholars in the future might apply certain cross-disciplinary techniques in studying the Loyalists. Social psychology was a method employed by Bernard Bailyn to explain, in part, the conspiracy theory held by British officials and American Loyalists. Both believed that a plot was afoot by seditious factions within the colonies to overthrow the rule of the mother country, and they tended to link the Patriot movement with certain opposition groups in England in this regard. Such fears helped to precipitate and exacerbate the constitutional crisis, Bailyn argued, because the Pa-

---

Mason, ed., *The American Colonial Crisis* (New York, 1972). For a view of Smith and Leonard, among others, who were early members of the Whig oligarchy and then became leading Loyalists, see William A. Benton, *Whig-Loyalism: An Aspect of Political Ideology in the American Revolution* (Rutherford, N.J., 1969).

74. Edmund S. Morgan, "The American Revolution: Revisions in Need of Revising," *William and Mary Quarterly*, 3d. ser., XIV (1957), 13–15.

75. John M. Head, *A Time to Rend: An Essay on the Decision for American Independence* (Madison, Wis., 1968).

76. Jack P. Greene, review of Leslie F. S. Upton's *The Loyal Whig* in *Canadian Historical Review*, LI (1970), 78–80.

triots had their own counterconspiracy theory which held that the British ministers were plotting to rob the Americans of their rights and liberties. Such nonrational fears created an atmosphere of tension and paranoia that made a peaceful settlement of the imperial crisis impossible. Scholars might examine in psychological terms other patterns of political behavior on the part of the Loyalists.[77]

Sociology, as well as psychology, might offer certain insights into the Loyalists. Questions regarding Loyalist group behavior—kinship groupings, religious sects, and the like—and their intergroup behavior have yet to be fully explored on the provincial and intercolonial level. Nor has there been much research on the relationships within Loyalist groups—partly on the dubious assumption that they shared ideas, attitudes, and values in common. Given the dynamism of American society and the way in which groups formed, dissolved, and re-formed during the Revolutionary era, it might be safely assumed that Loyalist groupings underwent similar changes.

Anthropology might also provide some conceptual tools for researching the Loyalists. After their dispersion to different parts of the British Empire, what kind of communities did the Loyalists build within the different cultures to which they had migrated? Would not a study of the new communities they created, if compared with the communities from which they came in America, tell us something of the value system of the émigrés? Canada, in this regard, presents a fertile field for such research because one needs to find communities dominated by Loyalists, if not composed entirely of them.[78]

Comparative history of entire societies, rather than communities, might also be attempted along similar lines. The pioneering work of Robert R. Palmer has already produced interesting contrasts regarding the émigrés from the American and French revolutions. Palmer showed that the percentage of émigrés to the total population was almost five times greater in the American Revolution than it was in the French. Equally important, Palmer noted that French émigrés

77. Bailyn, *Ideological Origins of the American Revolution,* 141, 152.
78. For this insight as a possibility of future research, I am indebted to my Clark colleague, Professor Paul Lucas.

returned to their native land following the Bourbon restoration, whereas most Loyalists did not. This situation, he concluded, resulted in great differences as far as the future of the two countries was concerned. The presence of royalists within French society meant that this social element continued to be an active force in France's political life, serving as a constant reminder of the French Revolution as a divisive event. On the other hand, the removal of the Loyalists presumably resulted in the elimination of a major dissident element in American society and, when they were soon forgotten, gave rise to the myth of a consensus among the American people in their rebellion against Britain. Research similar to that of Palmer might be done by comparing American Loyalists with groups in other countries that remained faithful to the status quo during those revolutions that took place in the "Age of Democratic Revolution."[79]

Comparative studies of America and Britain during the pre-Revolutionary period might likewise shed some light on the most important question of all: *To what were the Loyalists loyal?* Was there a sense of British nationalism among the Loyalists, or did they represent a different version of what American allegiance to the Crown should be? Did some Americans have a different image of kingship than Englishmen, giving rise to a semantical problem when Loyalists called themselves the "King's Friends"? Was there a sense of allegiance to Parliament on the part of certain American Loyalists, creating for them a whole host of complex constitutional questions?

Finally, the Loyalist exiles to England might be subjected to comparative studies. Why did so many of them identify with Britain before the war, and then feel so bitterly disappointed once they went to the mother country? Had some of them used their idealization of Britain as a countermodel by which to measure America before 1776, only to discover in their subsequent experiences in England that their earlier views had been unrealistic? Do their reactions to British society tell us more about what they wanted for America before their exile? Would a comparison of American émigrés to England *after*

79. Palmer, *Age of Democratic Revolution*, I, 185–206.

the Revolution with exiles during the war provide some important insights? Did the second wave of émigrés, for example, leave because they were disappointed with America or with the results of the Revolution?

The "Americanization" of the Loyalists, then, might be brought about by resorting to new research strategies, or by raising certain key questions. Did the confiscation of Loyalist estates result in the democratization of landholding and of American society? Did the departure of the Loyalists deprive the United States of a conservative tradition, and make possible an American consensus throughout most of our history at the expense of a forcible elimination of a major element of dissent? Did the reentry of many Loyalists into American society during and after the Revolutionary War affect the future course of American history in any meaningful way?

It must be concluded that a true explanation of the Revolution has eluded American historians precisely because they have failed to account adequately for the Loyalist version of that event. Most contemporaries after the Revolution looked upon the elimination of the Loyalists as the expulsion of an "un-American" element in their midst. Hobbled by the whig philosophy of history, subsequent American scholars, in the main, have upheld the same point of view. Until Patriot and Loyalist explanations are incorporated in our nation's history and placed in proper perspective with one another, an unbiased interpretation will continue to evade American scholars.

H. JAMES HENDERSON

The First Party System

THE FIRST PARTY SYSTEM was a political novelty that took shape in the midst of a succession of highly significant changes in both America and Europe. Hardly a decade after the War for Independence had been won, the Articles of Confederation were replaced by the Constitution, Hamilton launched a bold program of financial consolidation that seemed to many to strain national powers beyond legitimate bounds, three new states were admitted to the Union, and the nation was drawn ideologically and diplomatically into the vortex of the French Revolution and its attendant European wars. These rapid changes produced clashes between economic classes and regions, between state rightists and nationalists, and between men of different ideological persuasions. The numerous discords which helped produce the first party system provided materials for many different theses regarding the formation of that system. It is not surprising, therefore, that scholars have disagreed about the relative importance of key issues involved in the process. Such disagreements gave rise to a number of controversies—the credit to be accorded either to Jefferson or to Madison in the creation of the Republican opposition; the significance of such key issues as assumption, the bank, and Jay's Treaty in the formation of party organization; and the relationship between the Federalists and Antifederalists, who clashed over the Constitution, and the Federalist and Republican parties, which later emerged on the scene. Another major dispute arose from the question of whether parties emerged from the bottom up or the top down—that is, as a consequence of popular protest and grass-roots organizations or as the result of congressional parties that sought broader, more unified constituent support by stimulating state organizations or by linking themselves with partisan organizations that had already formed in the states.

Analysis of party formation has not been easy. The fact that the United States was a federal system capable of producing parties on both state and national levels has complicated the problem. There were also contemporary prejudices against factions and parties; their very existence was clouded by disclaimers and denunciations by the same individuals who contributed to their formation. Thus the need for conceptual handles to analyze the formative period of the American party system is compelling. But for a number of reasons—most notably the lengthy tradition of a two-party system in the United States, the enduring imprint of Hamilton and Jefferson, the development of the Federalist and Republican party labels, and the desire for intellectual symmetry—few historians have been able to break free from a dichotomous approach that has obscured as well as illuminated the problem. Only recently have analysts of the first party system attempted to incorporate the fact that formation of political parties was a concomitant development to the effective establishment of a nation state in the aftermath of a colonial war for independence. The use of the developing nation as a conceptual model can expand the focus of inquiry and help to account for other forces at work at the time, such as regionalism and problems of social communication, which do not necessarily culminate in a neatly organized and coherent two-party system.

The intent of this essay is to examine not all but some of the more penetrating studies of the origins of the first party system from the beginning of the nineteenth century to the present day. Particular emphasis has been placed on the earlier studies by Marshall and Hildreth, because they were less familiar than more recent studies that incorporate innovations in either concept or method. Although a full appreciation of the first party system should include its denouement during the Jeffersonian era, space prohibited such extended treatment. Moreover, although biographical and state and regional studies often provided important insights, they have not been comprehensively examined. Thus the chronological focus of the essay is on the early Federalist period, and on works that relate more or less directly to the national organization of the first party system.

Shortly after Washington's death, John Marshall began a five-volume study of the life of the first President. It was partly a labor of love and partly a moneymaking venture.[1] Unlike the ponderous and dull first four tomes, the final volume, which dealt with the Constitution and the Federalist decade, had genuine merit. It was less a biographical treatment than a study of the Washington and Adams administrations. Well organized and possessing unusual insights, it became the standard work on the Federalist decade for more than a generation. Indeed, Marshall's choice of topics and emphases on subject matter were not radically different from the analysis of many of the more recent historians.

He argued, for example, that "the first regular and systematic opposition to the principles on which the affairs of the union were administered"[2] began within Congress in response to Hamilton's fiscal program. Hamilton's system provided a natural catalyst for legislative opposition because it was that system which had pointed most directly to the establishment of national sovereignty and the "respectability of the nation." Hamilton had proposed a program that embodied most completely the "exalted and arduous duties" imposed upon the Federalists "to organize a government, to retrieve the national character, to establish a system of revenue, and to create

1. Marshall first demanded $100,000 for the copyright in the United States in the expectation of 30,000 subscribers to the projected five-volume set from the publisher, C. P. Wayne of Philadelphia. Bushrod Washington to C. P. Wayne, Dec. 11, 1801, quoted in Albert J. Beveridge, *The Life of John Marshall* (Boston, 1919), III, 225–226. Marshall and his brother at this time owed more than $30,000 to Denny Fairfax for land purchases, *ibid.*, 224.

2. John Marshall, *Life of Washington* (New York, 1969; AMS reprint of the London edition, 1807), V, 205.

public credit. . . ." Marshall did not conceal his pro-Federalist sympathies: "With persevering labour, guided by no inconsiderable portion of virtue and intelligence, were these objects in a great degree accomplished."[3]

Marshall was well acquainted with the politics of the 1790's, and he was aware that Hamilton's program had created widespread opposition. He was objective enough as an historian to admit that the fears of those who dreaded the central authority that Hamilton's system promoted were genuine. He was scrupulous enough also to note that the opponents of assumption in Congress pointed out that Hamilton was proposing a measure that had not been demanded by the public—that indeed there was no petition in Congress in favor of assumption.[4] He was prepared to recognize the inevitability of partisan disputes in a representative government, but he was intolerant of popular pressures upon the Federalist magistracy, and was unwilling to admit the legitimacy of persistent, organized opposition to established authority, whatever the source of that opposition might be. Thus he refused to view an organized two-party system as being either inevitable or desirable. Committed as a biographer of Washington and to the idea of legitimizing the national government by associating it with a charismatic symbol, he tended to minimize the seriousness and authenticity of party opposition to the first presidential administration. The stages of party development in his *History*, therefore, are often better discerned by viewing the emotional level of Marshall's rhetoric than by looking at his explicit findings.

From this angle of vision, it was perfectly clear that party opposition was maturing both in intensity and in extension to the grass roots in response to the French Revolution and Federalist foreign policy. Whereas Marshall's choice of terminology in the discussion of the congressional debate over Hamilton's program was low-keyed and reasonably balanced, his rhetoric reached hyperbolic levels when he described the meddling of Edmond Genêt, the rise of the Demo-

3. *Ibid.*, 267.
4. *Ibid.*, 210.

cratic Societies, and the infectious pressures of the populace upon
the formulation of foreign policy. Genêt's intrusion upon the sovereignty of the United States was characterized as "usurping,"
"haughty," "extravagant," "insufferable." The Frenchman's actions
placed Washington in the position of either demanding the minister's
removal or becoming the "mere servile instrument" of France—a
nation engaged in a revolution that was successively "the admiration,
the wonder and the terror of the civilized world."[5] Marshall noted
that the Cabinet unanimously opposed Genêt's outfitting of French
privateers in American ports, it being "impossible that any difference of opinion could exist among intelligent men, not under the
domination of a blind infatuation." But he chastised Genêt's American supporters—"this active and powerful party" which "openly
and decidedly embraced the principles for which that minister contended."[6]

It was never quite clear from Marshall's narrative whether the
"party" was the same opposition which had formed as "republicans"
against Hamilton's program. But it was apparent that Genêt was
strongly encouraged to pursue his course by the "labours and intrigues" of the Democratic Societies which "had constituted themselves the guardians of American liberty." The Democratic Societies
were "organized assemblages of factious individuals who, under the
imposing garb of watchfulness over liberty, concealed designs sub-
versive of all those principles which preserve the order, the peace,
and the happiness of society. . . ." Marshall criticized the tendency
of the "vast proportion of the American people" to accept the French
Revolution as "the genuine offspring of new-born liberty," and with
unmistakable condescension he ascribed this misconception to "that
hasty credulity which, obedient to the wishes, cannot await the sober
and deliberate decisions of the judgement. . . ."[7]

Marshall's dedication to the idea of national legitimacy under the
stewardship of the Federalists clouded his perception of the meaning

5. *Ibid.,* 363, 315–317, and ch. 6, passim.
6. *Ibid.,* 340, 349.
7. *Ibid.,* 350, 507, 379.

of the Jeffersonian opposition. Recognizing the existence of "two great parties in America" which "brought forward their chiefs" in the election of 1796, Marshall discussed the election largely in terms of foreign policy rather the development of party organization.[8] Encouraged by the anti-Gallican response to the XYZ Affair, Marshall was hopeful that the partisan passions of the moment would subside, and that intelligent men in positions of responsibility would redirect the nation on its proper course. (One senses that in his *History* he was lecturing President Jefferson along exactly such lines.)

But Marshall, the legitimist, was unable to explain the rejection of the Federalists in the election of 1800. Toward the end of his fifth volume, he chose to describe the accomplishments of the Federalist administrations, rather than the maturation of party opposition that placed Jefferson in the presidency. In doing so, Marshall conveniently escaped a problem which would have been as difficult to resolve in his normative scheme as it would have been injudicious to touch in the context of his struggles with the Jeffersonian administration.

Richard Hildreth, New Englander, abolitionist, and Whig, writing during the late 1840's and publishing during the early 1850's, was exempt from the political constraints that operated upon Marshall. Surprisingly enough, despite the lapse in time, Hildreth's history was more partisan than Marshall's. Indeed, in certain respects Jefferson's criticism that Marshall's *Life of Washington* was a Federalist tract applied even more to Hildreth. Whereas Marshall generally used discretion in his references to Jefferson as a party leader, Hildreth was more explicit. His description of Jefferson (who seemed to exemplify for Hildreth the worst traits of southern Republicanism) is so striking as to deserve quotation in full:

> Gifted by nature with a penetrating understanding, a lively fancy, and sensibilities quick and warm; endowed with powers of pleasing, joined to a desire to please, which made him, in the private circle when surrounded by friends and admirers, one of the most agreeable of men; exceedingly

8. *Ibid.,* 608, 605.

anxious to make a figure, yet far more desirous of applause than of power; fond of hypothesis, inclined to dogmatize, little disposed to argument or controversy, impatient of opposition, seeing every thing so highly colored by his feelings as to be quite incapable of candor or justice toward those who differed from him; adroit, supple, insinuating, and where he had an object to accomplish, understanding well how to flatter and to captivate; led by the warmth of his feelings to lay himself open to his friends, but toward the world at large cautious and shy; cast, both as to intellect and temperament, in a mold rather feminine than masculine, Jefferson had returned from France, strengthened and confirmed by his residence and associations there in those theoretical ideas of liberty and equality to which he had given utterance in the Declaration of Independence.[9]

To make certain that the reader perceived Jefferson more as the supple, devious, and feminine politician than as the author of the Declaration of Independence, Hildreth hurriedly added that "he was ever ready to allow even his most cherished theoretical principles to drop into silence the moment he found them in conflict with the popular current. To sympathize with popular passions seemed to be his test of patriotism; to sail before the wind as a popular favorite, the great object of his ambition; and it was under the character of a condescending friend of the people that he rose first to be the head of a party, and then the chief magistrate of the nation."[10]

Jefferson's course to the presidency, according to Hildreth, was tainted by duplicity at almost every critical juncture. While a member of Washington's cabinet, he had functioned as the "secret head of the opposition."[11] The two men who stood as obstacles to Jefferson's path to the presidency were John Adams and Alexander Hamilton. Adams was as forthright as Jefferson was devious, and as dedicated to principle as Jefferson was to applause. Although Adams aspired to the highest office in the land, "he still desired to be what he always had been, a leader, rather than a follower, rather to guide public opinion than merely to sail before it." Hamilton was less

9. Richard Hildreth, *The History of the United States of America*, 3 vols. (New York, 1851), IV, 291–292.
10. *Ibid.*, 293.
11. *Ibid.*, 455.

theoretical in his mental makeup than either Jefferson or Adams, but he was "a very sagatious observer of mankind" and had great practical talents. Finally, if Hamilton's partiality for the monarchic and aristocratic features of the British Constitution was ill-advised, his conclusion that the Union had more to fear from the states than from the executive power was clearly correct.[12]

The transparent partisanship, elitism, reverence for order, distaste for the emotions, and regard for practical intelligence embodied in these remarks suggest that Hildreth was a kind of crypto-Federalist. He was not far removed from Marshall, the Federalist steward with an abiding concern for order and legitimacy. But Hildreth was both less and more than this, as an examination of his interpretation of the first party system and the political economy should make clear.

Hildreth, like Marshall, discerned the beginning of an organized opposition party in the adverse reaction to Hamilton's fiscal program. By the first session of the Second Congress, the Federalists were no longer supporters of the Constitution but proponents of Hamiltonian finance. Antifederalists, dropping their objections to the Constitution, "subsided, for the most part, into opponents of Hamilton and his financial system." Although Hildreth used the term "political parties" to describe these divisions of allegiance, he was not constructing a theory of party development hinged on a conflict of simple economic interest as Beard subsequently did. By the time of the Third Congress, opposition to the funding system was "quite dropped" as "the basis of party rally," and in its stead there was substituted the "national antipathy to Great Britain."[13] Madison assumed the immediate lead of the party at this time, both because of his critical location in Congress; and because Jefferson had retired to Monticello for the time being. The issue which defined and organized a disparate opposition of "anti-Federalists, Republicans and Democrats"[14] was Madison's resolutions of January 3, 1794, calling

12. *Ibid.*, 295, 296, 293, 297.
13. *Ibid.*, 291, 459.
14. *Ibid.*, 450–451. The Democrats can be equated with the "French faction" which had been energized by the machinations of Edmond Genêt, *ibid.*, 416–425.

for discriminatory duties against nations with whom the United States did not have commercial treaties. The obvious target for this legislation was Great Britain, the object of broad popular hostility. Hildreth's interpretation contained some notable insights. His assertion that parties coalesced in the Third Congress is compatible with the findings of a recent computerized analysis by Mary Ryan.[15] He readily recognized, as have most scholars, that party antagonisms were inflamed by the press, which helped to enlarge the Republican opposition. He noted also that the Republicans were strengthened by support from the Democratic Societies, which were particularly powerful in swinging Pennsylvania out of the administration's orbit.[16] But he was sufficiently astute to dismiss as "impetuous" Theodore Sedgwick's broad contention that the societies had instigated the Whiskey Rebellion and formed the basis for most of the Republican opposition. The Republicans, Hildreth asserted, were willing to use the societies as allies against the administration, but they were not inclined to identify themselves with them.[17] Thus partisan opposition began in Congress over Hamilton's program; it congealed by organizing as a legislative party on the issue of foreign policy; and it became a more broadly-based party by covert connections with organizations that had already formed at the grass roots.

Hildreth's most intriguing passages on party formation had to do with the ideological distinctions (in the larger, holistic sense) between the two parties and the social and economic character of the popular support they aroused. Although his work by and large was a straightforward narrative of congressional proceedings, there were times

15. Mary P. Ryan, "Party Formation in the United States Congress, 1789–1796: A Quantitative Analysis," *William and Mary Quarterly*, 3d ser., XVII (1971), 523–542. Miss Ryan argued that the House of Representatives first felt the impact of the two-party system in a broad sense only with the second session of the Third Congress, but there is good evidence (including data presented by Ryan herself) that Madison's resolutions in the first session had such an effect.

16. Hildreth, *History*, IV, 425.

17. *Ibid.*, 507–512. Hildreth's interpretation of the relationship between the Congressional party and the societies was correct, judging from the debates in the House over Washington's condemnation of the societies. See *Annals of Congress* 3d Cong., 800–949.

when he took an analytical approach comparable to his other works on banking and political economy. In discussing the early division between the Federalists and the Republicans, for example, he distinguished between the natural aristocracy and the natural democracy from which political parties might naturally have arisen. Lawyers, judges, the clergy of the major denominations, merchants and capitalists, the large landed proprietors of the middle states, and the slaveholding planters of the South provided the logical components of the aristocracy. The natural democracy, on the other hand, was composed of the "great body of small land-holders, the mass of the free inhabitants, men who worked their farms with their own hands." Having made the distinction, Hildreth argued that "it would be a very great mistake to suppose that the line of separation between the political parties of the Union, either at this or any other period, at all coincided with the . . . natural aristocracy and a natural democracy." Parties emanated then, as always, from factions among the aristocracy, "the democracy chiefly making itself felt by the occasional unanimity with which it has thrown itself into the scale of one or other of such contending factions."[18]

The major factor that stimulated divisions among the national elite was the sectional tensions between southern opponents and northern supporters of the Federalist program. Hildreth ascribed this sectional rivalry in part to economic factors such as assumption and commercial policy, and in part to a lack of communication between the two regions. But the most pervasive source of regionalism in party politics was the different life styles of the North and the South.

The difference in northern and southern modes of life was apparent in Hildreth's tendency to describe southern Republicans and the southern-dominated "French faction" with adjectives such as "warm," "frenzied," "fanatic," "heated," "passionate," and similar terms suggestive of intemperance and irrationality which he associated with the subtropical ethos of the slave plantation. A dedicated abolitionist who wrote what has been called the forerunner of all sub-

18. Hildreth, *History*, IV, 347–348.

sequent antislavery novels,[19] Hildreth placed strong emphasis on the institution of slavery as a source of regional tensions in the first party system. He devoted some 20 pages to the debates over Hamilton's first report on the public credit, for example, but allocated 29 pages to the debate over slavery stimulated by Quaker petitions at roughly the same time—January and February, 1790.

It would be easy, but mistaken, to classify Hildreth as an impassioned abolitionist, a crypto-Federalist, and a parochial New Englander. To some degree he was all of these things, but a proper assessment of his anti-Republican bias and his emphasis on sectional conflict must be seen within the context of his larger social theory and his experiences in the South and in Latin America.

Unlike some abolitionists, Hildreth had firsthand knowledge of slavery. Mainly for reasons of health, he spent some time in Florida in 1834 and 1835, and he lived for three years in the West Indies and British Guiana in the early 1840's. During his stay in Guiana he wrote certain of his works on morals and political economy which helped to inform his interpretation of the Federalists and Republicans and which made his *History* much different from a standard Federalist treatment.[20] Hildreth did not show the concern for national legitimacy that characterized Marshall's writing, nor did he emphasize the church and the common law as buttresses of a conservative, orderly society as did the Federalists.[21] He actually condemned the common law, religious conservatism, and a rigidly hierarchical society along with slavery as being retrogressive and harmful to progress.

Hildreth was a Benthamite utilitarian, and only by recognizing this philosophical orientation can one appreciate the full meaning of his

19. Hildreth, *Memoirs of Archy Moore* (Boston, 1835), later called *The White Slave.*
20. Hildreth, *The Theory of Morals* (Boston, 1844); *A History of Banks* (Boston, 1837); *Banks, Banking and Paper Currencies* (Boston, 1840); *The Theory of Politics* (New York, 1854) was actually written ten years earlier. Hildreth also wrote a treatise on British colonial law. For a discussion of Hildreth's philosophical position see Martha M. Pingel, *An American Utilitarian: Richard Hildreth as a Philosopher* (New York, 1948).
21. This point was first made by Arthur M. Schlesinger, Jr., "The Problem of Richard Hildreth," *New England Quarterly,* XIII (1940), 223–245.

defense of the Federalists. It was a defense that actually anticipated the modern functionalists in delineating some of the social determinants of political organization. Hildreth assumed that labor was motivated by the expectation of tangible rewards such as wealth and distinction. He also recognized that political power was the product of individual talent (the force of will, intelligence, eloquence, and the like), the thirst for wealth and power, and collective, interest-oriented action. He believed that the closely associated properties of wealth and political power would be seized by a minority, for talent was unequally distributed. But he was also convinced that human society was dependent on a sense of benevolence that was present in all men, resulting from a contemplation of pain and pleasure in others. The rational rather than the religious or emotional component of man's intelligence was the spring of both self-interest and benevolence. Neither self-interest nor benevolence, or morality, was quantitatively static; it might be improved, and it was affected by a given economic and political system. A capitalist democracy in which as broad a segment of the population as possible was motivated by self-interest and an enlightened perception of the collective good was the best system yet developed. In such a system, policy would be formulated by talented leaders, but leaders who had risen through their superior abilities. Democracy, Hildreth believed, should be benevolently inclined toward the government to a sufficient degree to be aware of the necessity that certain duties must transcend selfish liberty or freedom from constraint.

Slavery was, of course, a violent negation of the principle of self-interest—the spring of labor and progress. Nor were the values of his political economy compatible with those of the aristocratic, privileged, slaveowning agricultural elite of the South that dominated the leadership of the Republican party. Whereas the Federalists represented rationality, order, and progress, the passionate and visionary Jefferson and the party that elected him to the presidency were profoundly prejudicial to the material and moral progress of the nation.

The ambiguities and internal contradictions in Hildreth's theory are of less interest to the student of party development than the uses to which it was put. The most intriguing of these uses was Hildreth's analysis of the causes of the Federalist defeat and decline.

Having delved minutely into the divisions within the Federalist party during the Adams administration, he concluded that the breakdown of party unity was a superficial rather than a fundamental cause of the downfall of the Federalists in the election of 1800. The Alien and Sedition Acts, the land tax, and the renewal of negotiations with France likewise contributed to Adams's defeat, "but, under any circumstances, it could not have been long deferred." The Federalists lost because they had been a numerical minority from the outset, and had maintained themselves in power only by superior energy, intelligence, practical skills, and the great prestige of Washington. It had been all along "an arduous and doubtful struggle." The Federalists embodied "the experience, the prudence, the practical wisdom, the discipline, the conservative reason and instincts of the country." The Jeffersonian opposition, a clear majority, expressed the nation's "hopes, wishes, theories, many of them enthusiastic and impracticable, more especially its passions, its sympathies and antipathies, its impatience of restraint."

Hildreth's sociopsychological impression was given additional force through a historically rooted regional analysis of party support: "The Federalists had their strength in those narrow districts where a concentrated population had produced and contributed to maintain that complexity of institutions and that reverence for social order, which, in proportion as men are brought into contiguity, become more absolutely necessaries of existence." The "ultra democratic" ideas of the Jeffersonian opposition obtained where population was dispersed, and where society was more immature and made "legal restraints the more irksome in proportion as their necessity was the less felt." Hildreth's analysis, faintly anticipatory of Frederick Jackson Turner and other Progressive historians, differed from Turner and Beard not only in the more comprehensive social and psychological dimensions of his hypothesis but also in the inclusion of the slaveholding planter not as an anomaly but as an integral part of the Republican opposition. Those regions in which the Republican party and democratic ideas triumphed over the Federalists were predominantly in the South and West—including both the undeveloped frontier and the long-settled southern tidewater. Hildreth took pains to point out that it was not simply a dispersed population but also the "despotic authority vested in individuals over families of slaves" that kept society in a state of immaturity.[22] Hildredth's fulminations about Jefferson and the elitist Virginians were rooted in his sense of a pervasive hypocrisy in the Jeffersonian stance of democracy comfortably afforded by a limited electorate and a slave labor force.

Hildreth exaggerated the Virginian commitment to slavery, and underemphasized the incidence of Federalism in the slaveholding tidewaters of Maryland and South Carolina. In doing so, he seemed more a partisan Federalist than Marshall. In an ironic way, this tendency in his writing validated his hypothesis, for the regional sources of partisan antagonisms discerned by Hildreth in the 1790's were coming to a fearsome climax during the ante-bellum period in which he wrote.

Jefferson once stated that the major difference between Federalists and Republicans was over theories of state rooted in Federalist fear and distrust of the people and Republican "cherishment" of the people.[23] Hildreth dismissed that notion as being ideologically in error. Charles Beard found it irrelevant to the sources of party development. In his two major works on party formation, *An Economic Interpretation of the Constitution* (1913) and *The Economic Origins of Jeffersonian Democracy* (1915),[24] Beard made it amply clear that the proper focus of analysis was not upon "pure political ethics" but "the dusty way of earthly strife and common economic endeavor. . . ."[25] The formulation and ratification of the Constitution and the

22. *History*, V, 415.
23. *The Writings of Thomas Jefferson*, ed. by Paul L. Ford, 10 vols. (New York, 1892–99), X, 227n.
24. Charles Beard, *An Economic Interpretation of the Constitution* (New York, 1913); *The Economic Origins of Jeffersonian Democracy* (New York, 1915).
25. *Economic Origins*, 3. Beard used this phrase (which he assured his readers was not a profane attack but the product of scholarly research) to describe the struggle over the Constitution, but the whole tendency of his study of party development was couched in that assumption.

resulting emergence of the first party system all grew out of a struggle between "capitalistic" and "agrarian" interests.

Beard's *An Economic Interpretation of the Constitution* is such a classic work as to require no summarization, but it is useful to stress that the triumph of commercial capital which he saw in the formulation of the Constitution directly set the stage not only for the struggle over ratification but also the aggregations of economic interests which shortly became institutionalized in the first party system. The audacious thrust by the forces of personality in the Convention, the unrepresentative victory of the Federalists over the Antifederalists in the state ratifying conventions, the aggressive financial program of Hamilton, the pro-British diplomacy of Washington's administration that culminated in Jay's Treaty, all formed an unbroken thread of capitalistic policy. Likewise, the battle of the Antifederalists against the Constitution, the formation of opposition in the administration and in Congress under Jefferson and Madison, the violent resistance to the whiskey excise, the widespread protest against the Jay Treaty, and ultimately the triumph of the Republicans in the election of 1800 manifested the increasingly enlivened and politically coherent resistance of the agrarian interest to that policy.

Beard's book represented a powerful departure from previous interpretations of the formation of the first party system for a number of reasons which have to be considered together. In no particular respect was his interpretation radically original. Both Marshall and Hildreth had noted the conflict between commercial and agrarian interests. Indeed, Beard quoted extensively from Marshall, whose comments on "the economic nature of the grievances on which the Republicans thrived" Beard approvingly endorsed as having "that remarkable clarity and precision which characterized his opinions from the bench. . . ."[26] Martin Van Buren contended that Hamilton's fiscal program was addressed to "the commercial, manufacturing, and trading classes . . . upon whom it, beyond all doubt, exerted a powerful influence. . . ." The Republicans, on the other hand, "forced into existence by Hamilton's obnoxious measures,

26. *Ibid.,* 237. See also Hildreth, *History,* IV, 350.

sprang chiefly from the landed interest" farthest removed from "the seductive influence of the money power. . . ."[27]

Nor was Beard the first to assert that there was a connection between the politics of the Constitution and the Federalist decade. Hildreth had much earlier contended that aristocratic planters and democratic farmers had united against the Constitution on the "common ground of pecuniary distress" because of a correct assumption that the Constitution was "the work of the creditor party, intended and likely to lead to a strict enforcement of contracts, both public and private." Jefferson and his "co-operators," not content with a "mere re-echo" of such grievances, "sought to infuse a new bitterness by dark charges of corruption and alarming insinuations of anti-Republican designs."[28] Beard went on to document Jefferson's charges, which both Hildreth and Marshall tended to dismiss out of hand. His probings into the security holdings of the delegates at the Constitutional Convention as well as the economic interests of members of Congress who passed Hamilton's fiscal program added a powerful dimension to his analysis. In an article in the *American Historical Review* published before the appearance of *The Economic Origins of Jeffersonian Democracy* he took pains to inform his readers of the exact methodology he employed "to eliminate all bias which might have led to oversights in particular cases."[29] Yet even such seemingly scientific techniques of quantitative analysis were far from original with Beard. Orin G. Libby had previously analyzed voting behavior in the ratifying conventions, in the Federal Congresses, and in the national elections.[30] Further, as will be shown below, Libby insisted on a definition of party that was much more compatible with that used by modern political scientists than did Beard.

But if Marshall and Hildreth noted the conflict between commer-

27. Martin Van Buren, *Inquiry into the Origin and Course of Political Parties in the United States* (New York, 1867), 170, 180–181.

28. Hildreth, *History*, IV, 350.

29. Beard, "Some Economic Origins of Jeffersonian Democracy," *American Historical Review*, XIX (Oct. 1912–July 1914), 287.

30. Orin G. Libby, *Geographical Distribution of the Vote on the Constitution* (Madison, Wisc., 1894).

cial and agrarian interests, they did not use that tension as a focal point of their analysis as did Beard. Van Buren, who often sounds "Beardian," saw fit to concentrate on the Jeffersonian contention that the Federalists perverted the Constitution while implementing it, and that the Republicans were the true Constitutionalists—a position which Beard noted and rejected as partisan nonsense. If Hildreth saw a connection between the Antifederalists and the Republicans, it did not possess the neat symmetry of Beard's subsumation of discrete events within a general interpretation of historical change. And if Libby had employed the technique of quantitative analysis, Beard's conclusions were more suited to the era.

It was the timely contribution of Beard to attack corporate aggrandizement by desanctifying the Constitution and the Federalist giants who formed the first links in a chain of capitalistic oppression of the agrarian populace that bound the late eighteenth to the early twentieth century. Beard's interpretation was methodologically compelling because of its empirical base, intellectually pleasing because of its symmetry, and ideologically palatable because of its timeliness. Its impact was extraordinary, and persists today in some popular texts on the history of political parties.[31]

While Beard's hypothesis regarding party development rested upon axioms set forth in his study of the Constitution, his most detailed exposition was contained in *The Economic Origins of Jeffersonian Democracy*—a book which was at once more and less satisfying than *An Economic Interpretation of the Constitution*. Contrasted with the latter, his treatment of the Federalist decade was more complex, less pegged to the rigid dichotomy of personalty and realty, and less distracted by the moral dimension of "the contest between the capitalist and the democratic pioneer."[32] Where Beard referred to a bifurcation of interest, it was usually in the more comprehensive and flexible terms of capitalistic and agrarian interests. He was not dissuaded from undertaking a detailed analysis of the party affiliations

31. The most striking example is Wilfred E. Binkley, *American Political Parties: Their Natural History* (New York, 1943, 1945, 1958, 1962).
32. Beard used this phrase of Frederick Jackson Turner's to open his book.

of Convention members, despite the fact that of the thirty-seven who could be categorized, twelve, or roughly one-third, became Republicans by his own count. While contending that almost half the members of the first House were security holders with a personal interest in funding the national debt, and that Jefferson's charge that Hamilton's fiscal program would not have passed without the support of those individuals was correct, Beard stated that "the charge of mere corruption must fall to the ground." He noted that "quite a number of security holders voted *against* assumption and contrary to their personal interest. . . . It was a clear case of a collision of economic interests: fluid capital versus agrarianism. The representation of one interest was as legitimate as the other. . . ."[33]

Beard's analysis of Republican ideology was likewise reasonably open-minded. In the discussion of the ideology as articulated by John Taylor and Jefferson, Beard contended that democracy and equality were no part of Taylor's argument against the Federalist policies and that "notwithstanding his generous use of the phrase 'popular rule,' Jefferson was as anxious as any Federalist to guard against 'the tyranny of majorities.' "[34] Neither Jefferson nor his party considered universal manhood suffrage as "an essential element of Republican faith." Virginia and North Carolina were among the last states to "surrender the dominion of the landed class," erected on property qualifications for the vote. Beard went on to contend that the states dominated by Republicans were "no more enamored of an equalitarian political democracy" than those dominated by the Federalists.[35]

Beard concluded furthermore that Jefferson while President did not pursue a consistently agrarian policy. In power, Jefferson, Gallatin, and others "deliberately adopted a policy of manipulating the government funds in such a way as to build up Republican moneyed machines in order to resist the force of the Federalist interests and provide competitors that would give the Republicans the power in the economic world which they so earnestly desired."[36] Jefferson, in

33. Beard, *Economic Origins,* 193–195.
34. *Ibid.,* 205, 459.
35. *Ibid.,* 463.
36. *Ibid.,* 446.

short, had compromised with capitalistic interests for pragmatic political purposes.

But if *Economic Origins* was a better history than *An Economic Interpretation* because of these qualities, it was in many respects a less satisfying work. Beard repeatedly insisted upon the capitalistic-agrarian conflict as the major source of partisan antagonisms and party organization despite the anomalies which he explicitly admitted or tacitly included. He was unable to explain the Republicanism of the wealthy New Hampshire merchant John Langdon, for example, except for a lame quote from Langdon's biographer contending that the merchant courted popularity "with the zeal of a lover and the constancy of a martyr."[37] In the structure of the book there was an implicit admission of another more general and consequential anomaly in the treatment of the Adams administration. Having followed a strict chronological pattern in tracing Federalist policies through the Washington administration, Beard abruptly shifted from an analysis of behavior to an examination of ideology in two chapters on the political economy of John Adams and John Taylor. The doctrines of both men supported his thesis. But the circumstances of Adams's election by a large agrarian constituency and the policies adopted during the administration, which hardly pleased the Hamiltonians and pro-British capitalists within the Federalist party, remained largely untouched.[38]

37. *Ibid.*, 48.
38. Manning J. Dauer dealt with this anomaly from a Beardian point of view. In an admirable study, *The Adams Federalists* (Baltimore, 1953), Dauer accepted Beard's fundamental proposition that the first party system was the product of a tension between agrarian and commercial interests, but he distinguished between the self-sufficient agrarian who formed the backbone of the Republicans and the commercially oriented agrarian who produced surpluses for markets at home and abroad. The latter group constituted the basis of Federalist agrarian support, claimed Adams rather than Hamilton as its leader, and drifted from the Federalist party during the split between Adams and Hamilton and in the early years of Jefferson's presidency. Eschewing the rigid dichotomies set forth by Beard, Dauer calculated that geographic and economic factors accounted for the election of 360 of 424 seats for which elections were held from the Fourth through the Seventh Congresses, but that religious and cultural factors such as the influence of the Congregational Church in New England accounted for many of the other elections. *Ibid.*, 31–32.

The difficulty Beard encountered was essentially philosophical. The economic determinism which formed the foundation of his interpretation contains the implicit assumption that men were influenced not only by economic motives, but that they also were rationally capable of pursuing them. Such controlling assumptions were sufficient to provide a plausible explanation of the career of a Hamilton, but less so that of a Jefferson or an Adams. Beard faltered as well when explaining the obvious acceleration of partisanship at the time of the Jay Treaty. Although he described the treaty as "another battle in the long campaign begun with the adoption of the Constitution,"[39] his analysis of the economics of the treaty disclosed fewer tensions between capitalism and agriculture than did his examination of Hamilton's program, which by Beard's own admission aroused less general opposition.

It was ironic that Marshall's contemporaneous sense of the sources of partisanship and Hildreth's utilitarian moralism should have posed fewer interpretive problems than Beard encountered. Marshall's concern for legitimacy was a powerful explanatory tool—whatever its objective validity—in that opposition was defined qua opposition. Hildreth's utilitarian posture allowed even greater flexibility. Lapses from rationality and benevolence were endemic in the history of mankind, and that an individual should fail to perceive his own self-interest or fail to have a sufficient sense of the collective good was perfectly understandable in the context of a halting progress toward moral enlightenment.

But perhaps the greatest limitation of Beard's analysis was his specific treatment of the organization of political parties. Because he addressed himself to the sources of a political party—the Jeffersonian Republicans—because he chose to focus his analysis on the provocations offered by the Federalists in implementing their procapitalist program, and because he used quantitative analysis not only in the examination of security holdings but also roll calls, it was incumbent upon him to work for a degree of precision in his definition of party comparable to that of Libby and others who had written on the subject before him. Yet very early in *Economic Origins* he de-

39. Beard, *Economic Origins*, 276.

voted a considerable amount of space to a refutation of the contentions of Libby and Bassett that the Federalist-Antifederalist struggle terminated with the adoption of the Constitution, and that the Federalist-Republican division was the result of different motivating forces. In doing so, Beard took strong exception to Libby's definition of party and the quantitative methods he used in the early Congresses to arrive at the conclusion that the two-party system did not emerge until Adams's administration. When that system emerged, according to Libby, it was the result of the disaffection produced by the Alien and Sedition Acts—measures as political as Beard's hypothesis was economic in nature. Libby insisted that a party could not come into existence until three conditions had been met: the party had to have been activated by issues of more than transitory or local importance; its members had to be sufficiently "intelligent" (one might read politically conscious) to vote together with some consistency on all measures and in those elections considered important by the party; and the party had to have a body of leadership. Beard, admitting that "it is not often useful to quarrel over niceties in terms," insisted that Libby's definition of party was too limiting to embrace a political party "in any age or any country. . . ."[40] That Beard's protestation had some substance cannot be denied. Yet clearly he chose to define parties as loose aggregations of interests during the entire Federalist period in order to better substantiate his hypothesis.

As a consequence, there were segments of Beard's work that were less illuminating than Marshall's or Hildreth's regarding the specific process of party formation. That this should have been the case was in one respect highly ironic: while Marshall, and to a degree even Hildreth, wrote before the political party had become an accepted fixture in American political life, Beard was unencumbered by any suspicion that party might be viewed as an illegitimate perversion of the commonweal.

As suggested at the outset of this essay, the analysis of the germination of the first party system was a complicated process for a number of reasons: the novelty of the institution; the conceptual difficulties

40. *Ibid.,* 19.

in defining party as distinguished from factions and interest groups; and the federal character of the American political system, among others. Part of this conceptual disorder might be reduced—though hardly eliminated—by separating substantive and structural approaches to party development. The two approaches, of course, were never completely distinct, but it is clear that Beard and earlier historians were more concerned with the issues and accents of partisan conflict and the kinds of popular support it engendered than with the organizational structure of the political party as an institution.[41]

The substantive approach to party politics naturally emphasized ideology and conflict. The structural approach, on the other hand, by focusing on party organization, tended to stress the role of the party as a mechanism for the resolution of conflict. There is, of course, no intrinsic reason why this should be so in the abstract, but within the context of American political experience the classic function of the political party has been to minimize ideological discord, to overcome antagonisms between class and region—in a word, to do precisely what the founding fathers assumed political combinations would *not* do. That much recent scholarship on the emergence of the first party system has been preoccupied with the formation of office-holding institutional structures is consonant with two current developments: the "end-of-ideology" atmosphere of the two decades following the Second World War; and the increasing awareness of behavioral techniques of ancillary disciplines such as political science.

The major emphasis of the structural approach was upon a party organization sufficient to mobilize the electorate, to capture political office, and to control public policy. In the words of William Nisbet Chambers, a political scientist who has provided one of the more insightful analyses of early party formation, a party must have a structure involving, among other things, a stable relationship between leaders (from the national to local levels) and followers in the elec-

41. There is another analytical distinction to be introduced below between "structuralists" and "functionalists" which is less distinct, but nonetheless useful. Suffice to say at this point that "structuralists" were concerned with the function of the political party in a more limited context than the "functionalists" described below.

torate.[42] Stability was a key term in this connection between active party leaders and the electorate. The factional systems that characterized the colonial and Revolutionary eras had both leaders and followers, but factions proved to be both unstable and impermanent. Thus, the continuity of political alignments from the struggle over the Constitution into the 1790's insisted upon by Beard was a question of some consequence from a structural angle of vision. Second, according to Chambers, parties performed a number of critical functions: nominating candidates, electioneering, shaping opinion, mediating among groups, managing government, and—in the American federal system—supplying connections between the branches of government. Parties also had certain other characteristics which helped define them: "range, density and stability of support"; the kinds of interests which align behind a party (a matter given strenuous emphasis by Beard, as we have seen); and the sorts of ideological commitments associated with a party—sometimes of such intensity as to produce virtually blind loyalty.[43]

The literature reflecting the structural approach was so voluminous that only a short sketch of its major tendencies, conclusions, and limitations can be included here. This brief examination will focus on works dealing specifically with the origins of the first party system.

Two of the more perceptive and innovative historians who ad-

42. William Nisbet Chambers, *Political Parties in a New Nation* (New York, 1963), 45.

43. *Ibid.,* 46–48. Chambers's definition, it will be noticed readily, included elements we have associated with the substantive approach to party—particularly the association of interest groups and ideology with party. But the structural approach stressed organization and function much more than ideology. The very ordering of Chambers's descriptive qualities suggests such a priority, as does the tendency of recent historians to view the partisan fervor of the 1790's as a kind of aberration both wondrous and absurd. See Cecelia Kenyon, "Men of Little Faith: The Anti-Federalists on the Nature of Representative Government," *William and Mary Quarterly,* 3d ser., XIII (1955), 3–43; Marshall Smelser, "The Federalist Period as an Age of Passion," *American Quarterly,* X (1958), 391–419; Smelser, "The Jacobin Phrenzy: The Menace of Monarchism, Plutocracy and Anglophilia," *Review of Politics,* XXI (1959), 239–258; John R. Howe, "Republican Thought and the Political Violence of the 1790's," *American Quarterly,* XIX (1967), 147–165; Linda Kerber, *Federalists in Dissent: Imagery and Ideology in Jeffersonian America* (Ithaca, 1970).

dressed themselves to the problem of the structure of party development were Joseph Charles and Noble Cunningham, Jr.[44] Charles's
work *The Origins of the American Party System* (written in 1942 and
published in 1956) began the departure from Beard and his imitators
such as Claude Bowers. Cunningham, in his *The Jeffersonian Republicans: The Formation of Party Organization* (1957), did exactly
what the subtitle of his book promised—he fixed more precisely the
timing and organizational structure of the Republican party system.
Both historians, but particularly Cunningham, attended closely to
the specifics of party organization in Congress and at the grass
roots. Both used an elementary quantitative analysis of roll calls to
locate the emergence of parties in the Congress—a technique which
has been used by historians with increasing sophistication.[45] By asking
different questions, and by using different techniques of analysis than
had been used by the Beardians, they reached conclusions that either
discredited or sharply modified most of Beard's generalizations.

Neither Charles nor Cunningham discovered a significant continuity of ideological alignments between the struggle over the Consti-

44. Joseph Charles, *The Origins of the American Party System* (Williamsburg, 1956). The first publication was in a series of articles in the *William
and Mary Quarterly* in 1955. References here are to the Harper Torchbook
edition (New York, 1961); Noble Cunningham, Jr., *The Jeffersonian Republicans: The Formation of Party Organization* (Chapel Hill, 1957). In a
sequel, Cunningham traced the party operations of the Republicans in office:
The Jeffersonian Republicans in Power: Party Operations, 1801–1809 (Chapel
Hill, 1963).

45. Cunningham's technique of roll-call analysis was somewhat different
from that of Charles, however. Charles and Cunningham both selected
measures considered to be tests of partisan affiliation without any systematic
explanation of how those measures were determined. In a sense both fell into
the trap which Beard noted Orin Libby had encountered; it was not always
possible to determine what was or was not an administration measure. Charles
indicated he chose measures "of national importance or those which members
of the House felt to embody some important principle of government . . ."
(*Origins*, 93). Cunningham chose 36 measures involving roll calls in the first
session of the Second Congress, eliminating repetitious insignificant roll calls
such as "private bills of no national significance and votes on minor questions
on which there was little division" (*Jeffersonian Republicans*, 270). Cunningham's analysis hinged on the extent to which each member agreed or disagreed with the position of Madison, the acknowledged leader of the Republican opposition in the House at this time. The limitations of both Cunningham's
and Charles's methodology will be discussed below.

tution and the division between the Federalists and the Republicans. By scrutinizing roll calls, they argued that the congressional opposition coalesced later in time than the Beardians had contended, and in Charles's words in response to issues that had to do with "abstract republicanism" rather than finance.[46] By examining closely the structure of party leadership, Charles concluded that the Federalists achieved a party unity under the brilliant, but in Charles's view almost demonically centralizing, leadership of Hamilton—a unity that was more superficial than real. The early congressional opposition was led not by Jefferson, the agrarian, but by Madison—a less congenial symbol for the Beardian dichotomy because of Madison's early nationalism and neomercantilism. Charles stressed that the extension of party organization from the national capital to the states and the grass roots was stimulated much more by Jay's Treaty than by Hamilton's fiscal program.[47]

Cunningham's more meticulous and objective study corroborated in impressive detail much of what Charles had argued the decade before, while at the same time modifying and extending Charles's structural analysis. Cunningham arrived at the following conclusions: that the Republican opposition coalesced first in the Federal Congress under the leadership of Madison; that party organization was from the top down rather than from the bottom up;[48] and that full-scale party organization down to the grass roots occurred unevenly during the late 1790's in response to Jay's Treaty and the undeclared war with France rather than Hamiltonian finance.

Cunningham noted also the improvement in Republican party

46. Charles, *Origins*, 95–96, 35.
47. *Ibid.*, 83, 122.
48. Cunningham was more emphatic than Charles about this point. In the process of condemning Washington for refusing to recognize the legitimacy of an opposition, Charles suggested that the Republicans were often forced into illicit, or at least surreptitious, modes of protest, as the Whiskey Rebellion and Fries's "Insurrection" in 1790 would suggest. Also, Charles's statement that Jefferson did not create a party, while not wholly out of line with Cunningham's argument, was not strictly compatible with it. It was Charles's contention that "a widespread popular movement recognized and claimed him [Jefferson] as its leader." *Origins*, 90. Cunningham perceived Jefferson as much more active after the passage of the Alien and Sedition Acts. *Jeffersonian Republicans*, 96–97, and ch. 3, passim.

machinery: the creation of township and county committees; the formation of state caucuses; the drawing of tickets; legislative actions to improve the party's fortunes by substituting a general ticket for district tickets in the choice of presidential electors; and the incessant pamphlet and newspaper barrage. Cunningham's state-by-state analysis of Republican party machinery disclosed that Pennsylvania and New York were well ahead of the other states—even Virginia, the center of the congressional party. It was only the serious challenge of the Federalists in Virginia which prompted such leaders as Jefferson, Madison, and Monroe to improve upon their informal but effective personal connections in the manipulation of Virginia's partisan politics. Federalist challenges in other states produced comparable though less uniformly successful organizational efforts.[49]

Cunningham's research makes it apparent that generalizations about party organization cannot be made without taking into account local and regional differences. The more research that was done on the development of state and regional party organizations, the more it became apparent that the major thrusts of Beard's argument—continuity of alignments from the late 1780's into the 1790's, and the capitalist-agrarian tension built into those alignments—required serious modification.[50]

Harry Ammon, for example, described multiple shifts in partisan

49. *Ibid.,* ch. 7.
50. State and regional histories of political parties, particularly the Jeffersonian Republicans, appeared periodically during the century, but in the past two decades the level of detailed analysis and methodological sophistication increased markedly. Some earlier works were William A. Robinson, *Jeffersonian Democracy in New England* (New Haven, 1916); Anson E. Morse, *The Federalist Party in Massachusetts to the Year 1800* (Princeton, 1909); John Wolfe, *Jeffersonian Democracy in South Carolina* (Chapel Hill, 1940); Delbert H. Gilpatrick, *Jeffersonian Democracy in North Carolina* (New York, 1931); Harry M. Tinkcom, *The Republicans and Federalists in Pennsylvania, 1790–1801* (Harrisburg, Pa., 1950). Many of these works were detailed and useful, particularly that of Tinkcom, but a comparison of Gilpatrick's *Jeffersonian Democracy in North Carolina* with Alfred Young's *The Democratic-Republicans of New York* (Chapel Hill, 1967) illuminated the increasing concern with questions such as constituency characteristics, partisan connections, and the achievement and timing of organizational cohesion and ideological coherence.

alignments in Virginia between 1787 and the 1790's—particularly in the alteration of Virginians who supported the Constitution and subsequently moved over to the Republican opposition. Paul Goodman, in a convincing study of the Republicans in Massachusetts, contended that the party in that state lacked continuity with earlier partisan conflicts during the colonial and Revolutionary periods. The same situation seems to have obtained by and large in New Jersey—according to Carl Prince—who described the pre-Constitutional alignments there as a kind of chaotic local factionalism.[51]

The pattern was not always uniform, however. Alfred Young, in a meticulously comprehensive study of the emergence of the Republican party in New York, began his examination in 1763 and discerned a clear connection between political organizations of the Revolutionary and Federal eras. The New York Republican party "was built around the nucleus of George Clinton's Anti-Federalists who in the Revolution had been the leaders of the popular Whigs."[52] Piecing together the works of Robert L. Brunhouse and Harry M. Tinkcom, it is evident that there was a substantial degree of organizational continuity in the partisan politics of Pennsylvania as the radical Constitutionalists of the Revolutionary era became Jeffersonians and their conservative opponents emerged as the Federalists.[53]

After Forrest McDonald's trenchant critique of Beard's analysis of the formulation and ratification of the Constitution,[54] it was apparent that Beard's other imperative—the tension between capitalist and agrarian interests—required even greater modification. In states where there seemed to be little continuity between Constitutional and post-Constitutional partisan politics, the capitalist-agrarian dualism often proved quite irrelevant. Paul Goodman was unequivocal on this

51. Harry Ammon, "The Jeffersonian Republicans in Virginia: An Interpretation," *Virginia Magazine of History and Biography*, LXXI (1963), 153–167; Paul Goodman, *The Democratic Republicans of Massachusetts* (Cambridge, Mass., 1964), xi; Carl Prince, *New Jersey's Jeffersonian Republicans* (Chapel Hill, 1967), 7.

52. Young, *Democratic-Republicans of New York*, 567.

53. Robert L. Brunhouse, *Counter-Revolution in Pennsylvania* (Harrisburg, Pa., 1942); Tinkcom, *Republicans and Federalists in Pennsylvania*.

54. Forrest McDonald, *We The People* (Chicago, 1958).

score: "The social sources of party were far more complex and less homogeneous than Beard suggested." Massachusetts Republicans "united a diverse coalition of urban and rural folk, merchants and farmers, artisans and professionals, speculators and squatters, deists and Calvinists."[55] John Munroe demonstrated that agrarian Delaware was Federalist, while commercial Delaware became Republican.[56] Even where there was a continuity of sorts between the state and national parties of the 1780's and 1790's, Beard's dichotomy did not hold up with the consistency requisite for its acceptance as a determinative scheme. Alfred Young showed that the mechanic class of urban New York tended to identify with the merchant interest and to support both the Constitution and Hamilton's fiscal system, while certain wealthy New Yorkers such as the Livingstons defected to the Republicans.[57] The radical Constitutionalist ranks in Pennsylvania included merchants and speculators such as Charles Pettit, while the Jeffersonian Republicans of Philadelphia successfully advanced John Swanwick—a merchant who had served as Robert Morris's assistant in the Bank of North America—against the Federalist stalwart, Thomas Fitzsimmons, in the election to the Fourth Congress.

Recent analysis of the national political leadership in the House of Representatives has failed to substantiate Beard's agrarian-capitalist dichotomy. Paul Goodman, in an examination of the social status of more than 250 members of the House during the Fourth through Sixth Congresses, estimated that most congressmen in both parties were professionals (judges, lawyers, doctors, teachers and ministers) —59 percent for the Federalists and 42 percent for the Republicans.[58] The Republicans actually had a larger percentage of commercial and manufacturing representatives than did the Federalists (22 percent as contrasted with 20 percent), and while there were more agrarians in the Republican party than in the Federalists (35 percent to 20

55. Goodman, *Democratic Republicans of Massachusetts,* xi.
56. John Munroe, *Federalist Delaware, 1775–1815* (New Brunswick, N.J., 1954).
57. Alfred Young, "The Mechanics and the Jeffersonians: New York, 1789–1801," *Labor History* (1964), 247–276.
58. Paul Goodman, "Social Status of Party Leadership: The House of Representatives, 1797–1804," *William and Mary Quarterly,* 3d ser., XXV (1968), 471.

percent), it was clear that a heavy proportion of the agricultural representation was from the landed gentry of the South.[59]

Conventional wisdom has presumed that the Federalists were successful at the outset because of the bold leadership of Hamilton and the magisterial influence of Washington, but that the party faltered because of Hamilton's commercialism and Anglophilia, and was doomed to extinction because of its elitist ideology in an agrarian and increasingly democratic nation. Unable to descend to the mean business of electioneering, split by that internecine strife inherent in a court party of "notables," the Federalists lost control of the presidency, never to regain it, just one term after party organization began to touch the grass roots.

A number of recent studies dealing with the Federalists, while not entirely discarding the notion of Federalist debility, helped to recast the image of that party. Stephen Kurtz, in his study *The Presidency of John Adams,* showed that even the Hamiltonian Federalists organized protest meetings to generate petitions to Congress in support of the Washington position regarding the Jay Treaty, and that Adams made genuine efforts to establish contact with the populace before the election of 1800.[60] Lisle A. Rose's work on the Federalist party in the South, while endorsing the traditional view of the Federalists as an elitist party in many respects, noted that Federalist activity at the grass roots in Virginia and Georgia actually preceded and provoked Republican party organization.[61]

Federalist efforts toward the establishment of a popular organizational base are more fully documented in two fine recent studies: David Fischer, *Revolution of American Conservatism,* and James Banner, *To the Hartford Convention.*[62] Neither work attempted to recast Federalist leadership as democrats. Fischer, nonetheless, dis-

59. *Ibid.,* 470–471.
60. Stephen Kurtz, *The Presidency of John Adams* (Philadelphia, 1957), 59, 73, 393, 397–399.
61. Lisle A. Rose, *Prologue to Democracy: The Federalists in the South 1789–1800* (Lexington, Ky., 1968), 81–82.
62. David Fischer, *Revolution of American Conservatism: The Federalist Party in the Era of Jeffersonian Democracy* (New York, 1965); James Banner, *To the Hartford Convention: The Federalists and the Origins of Party Politics in Massachusetts, 1789–1815* (New York, 1970).

tinguished between those "old school" Federalists who left politics in disgust after the elevation of the Republicans and the "young Federalists" who took their places. Far from retiring from the field, the latter adopted the techniques of the Republicans in organizing electoral tickets and mustering popular support. Thus they sustained the Federalist opposition as a viable force well after the election of Jefferson—at least in the North, and especially New England. Banner, while also admitting the parochial, corporate, ethically homogeneous, hierarchical, and traditional ideological elements of the central Federalists' persuasion,[63] tended to go even further than Fischer in arguing that the Federalists remained in the partisan fray. Even the "old school" gentlemen who hardly cherished the democratic process attempted with varying success to cope with the Republicans through use of the press and electioneering, and thereby served as "a bridge between the decorous deference politics of colonial America and the more modern and aggressive politics of the new generation. . . . Resisting the twin snares of apathy and amateurism, they set the stage for Federalist ventures in organized popular politics."[64]

There were Federalists in all states, but they survived as a reasonably vital force almost exclusively in the North after Jefferson's election. As Rose pointed out, the Federalist notables in South Carolina gave up after 1800. That this should have been the case was intelligible in terms of the earliest beginnings of the party system in the Congress as outlined by Mary P. Ryan. Her analysis of voting clusters in the first four Congresses provided a striking demonstration of the increasing sophistication of historians using quantification to examine the first party system.[65] It was her contention that from the very first session of the First Congress two clusters of congressmen and senators formed (not so much over Hamilton's system or other financial measures as over the question of the location of the national capital, it should be noted), and that these clusters were overwhelmingly sectional in character. The membership of the two factions,

---

63. Banner, *To the Hartford Convention*, ch. 1.
64. *Ibid.*, 138.
65. Ryan, "Party Formation in the United States Congress."

becoming the Federalist and Republican parties, remained remarkably constant over time. Although the sharpness of the sectional contours softened somewhat as the legislative parties enlarged, and as an increasing variety of issues became the stuff of partisan controversy, the parties were still overwhelmingly sectional: in the second session of the fourth House the middle states were evenly split between the two parties, while there were eighteen Federalists and four Republicans from New England and thirty-one Republicans and six Federalists from the South.[66]

Paul Goodman's data on the social sources of congressional leadership also disclosed notable differences between the North and the South. The differences between Federalists and Republicans in the North pointed toward lively competition between the political establishment and socially inferior outsiders, while the differences between southern congressmen in the two parties seemed much less significant. In another essay on the first party system published at about the same time, Goodman postulated that viable two-party systems arose only in states where certain conditions existed conducive to a contest for power, including the existence of a differentiated and mobile society that prompted a spirit of competition. Such societies were more prevalent in the North, where erosion of the politics of deference was a central element in the growth of viable two-party systems. Federalism in South Carolina was an exception as long as the Federalist tidewater elite of South Carolina was challenged during the 1790's by Jeffersonian farmers in the interior, but after the victory of the Jeffersonians in 1800, the Republicans were able to turn the state into a virtual one-party regime. This occurred both because of control of electoral machinery and patronage by the Republicans and because of a stabilization of the social order with the growth of plantation cotton culture and the consequent reconciliation of tidewater and interior elites.[67]

66. *Ibid.*, 533.
67. Paul Goodman, "The First American Party System," in William Nisbet Chambers and Walter D. Burnham, eds., *The American Party Systems: States of Political Development* (New York, 1967), 56–89.

Both Goodman and Ryan, in resorting to quantitative techniques of collective biography and cluster bloc analysis, stressed sectional differences, but the questions they posed and the hypotheses they offered seemed to point in opposite directions. Analyzing the conditions that make for viable two-party systems on the state level, Goodman showed that a challenge of the establishment from Republican outsiders in the North, where old patterns of deference had eroded, posed an unanswered question why Republicans from New England and the middle states in Congress should have "made common cause with their social superiors to the South."[68] The implication of his findings was that there was little relationship between the sources of two-party systems in the states and in the Congress. Ryan, looking strictly at the formation of legislative parties in the Congress, stressed their rapid development and conjectured that pressures from the bottom up such as the Whiskey Rebellion may have brought the first party system into full bloom.[69] The implication of her hypothesis was that there was a direct relationship between party formations on the state and national levels. But if the common cause of the southern elitists and the socially inferior northern Republicans was grounded in popular protest, the alliance was incongruous, to say the least.

In short, while post-Beardian structural analysis has disclosed the weakness of simplistic dualism, it revealed also a complicated tapestry of political alignments that not only removed the comfortable conceptual coherence of Beard's interpretation but seemed to defy any sensible generalizations.

Some efforts were made by both historians and social scientists to remedy this void during the last decade by employing the functional concepts of party formation developed by political scientists and sociologists. This approach essentially had two dimensions. One was a descriptive analysis of the characteristics of party formation within a comparative historical context. The other was a more properly func-

68. Goodman, "The First American Party System," passim; "Social Status of Party Leadership," 474.
69. Ryan, "Party Formation in the United States Congress," 541–542.

tional avenue wherein the appearance of political parties was analyzed in the context of the problems of political development, or
modernization, particularly in the emergent nations of the recent past.
Many of the questions raised by functionalists had obvious relevance
for the interpretation of the first American party system.

The question whether the first party system originated in Congress
and then extended to the grass roots was a matter of considerable
significance, for example, when considered in the framework provided by Maurice Duverger. In his book *Political Parties,* published
in 1955,[70] Duverger distinguished between "internally" and "externally" created parties. Internally created parties were those which
cohered first in the national legislature, and then expanded into the
electorate as a consequence of enlargement of the suffrage. Such
parties have been customary in Western parliamentary democracies,
and were characterized by a relatively low level of party discipline
and a somewhat broad consensus. Because they were establishmen-
tarian, internally created parties were able to contain conflict within
manageable bounds. External parties were those stimulated by forces
and organizations outside the political establishment such as trade
unions and societies of intellectuals who desired to challenge the
ruling order.[71] Seen in this general framework, the stress laid by
Cunningham and recent historians on the congressional origins of the
first party system tended to place that system within the rather conservative Western parliamentary tradition. The thesis of Beard that
the Republican party was an extension of Antifederalism implied, if
it did not explicitly express, the other notion of a counterthrust of
the unrepresented populace challenging the legitimacy of the Federalist regime.[72]

70. Maurice Duverger, *Political Parties* (New York, 1955). See especially
xxiii–xxxvii.

71. The Socialist parties of the late nineteenth century were examples of
externally created parties which, as the history of such parties in Western
Europe testified, generally offered a sharper challenge of the status quo. The
external parties tended also to be more disciplined and to have more coherent
and uncompromising ideologies.

72. Another example of the Republican party as an "externally" created
force can be seen in William Miller, "First Fruits of Republican Organiza-

The extension of internally created legislative parties beyond the confines of government into the constituencies may occur as a consequence of the legislative party's having to organize electoral support for its continuance in office. But there is no guarantee that this will take place. Joseph LaPalombara and Myron Weiner suggested that the emergence of parties in developing countries—a category that naturally included the early national era of the United States—was often linked with crisis situations involving challenges of the legitimacy of established authority, demands for participation in the political process by energized elements of the population, and efforts to achieve national integration in a polity previously segmented along ethnic or linguistic or geographic lines.[73] "The political party is both a manifestation and a condition of the thrust to modernity," they argued. While the term "modernization" was somewhat elusive, the speculation of LaPalombara and Weiner that a certain level of communication was necessary in a given society if people were to band together in political organizations seemed persuasive. So, too, was their stress on secularization in education, urbanization, and the shift from a subsistence economy to a money economy as factors contributing to political modernization.[74]

LaPalombara and Weiner also raised the question whether in developing political systems parties tended simply to reflect the socioeconomic pressures upon the governmental process, or whether the form a party system took had a determinative and sustained influence upon the character of the political institutions of the nation. If the latter proposition was accepted (as it was by LaPalombara and Weiner),[75] it followed that the capacity of a society to cope with the various crises mentioned above might depend upon the sort of party

tion: Political Aspects of the Congressional Election of 1794," *Pennsylvania Magazine of History and Biography*, 63 (1939), 118–143. Miller argued that the Republican party was simply the "interstate chain of Democratic Societies" (119). Cunningham rejected this as unwarranted from the documentation, *Jeffersonian Republicans*, 64n.

73. Joseph LaPalombara and Myron Weiner, eds., *Political Parties and Political Development* (Princeton, 1966), 14–15.

74. *Ibid.*, 30, 20–21.

75. *Ibid.*, 399–400.

system adopted by the polity. If an emerging nation had a multiple party system in which parties were organized along intransigent ideological lines and the habit of resolving conflict was not well established, the nation might succumb to territorial divisions or internal conflict between economic classes. If, on the other hand, the prevailing tendency was toward a two-party system in which conflicts were mediated or subsumed by the parties themselves, the party system might be a crucial factor in the maintenance of political stability. In the emerging nations of the twentieth century, a one-party system often identified with the leadership that managed independence from colonial rule has been a recurring phenomenon. The "party of the revolution," or the "party of national liberation," frequently claimed that it was the sole instrument of legitimacy, and accordingly suppressed opposition parties. A viable system was one which was able to withstand the transfer of power from one group or party to another. The existence of a party system might help immeasurably to surmount such a crisis.[76]

With such functional characteristics in mind, it was anachronistic to condemn Washington and the Federalists for failing to recognize the legitimacy of the Republican opposition. Joseph Charles's statement that Washington "is to be blamed, not for allying himself with a party, but for not knowing that he had done so, and for denouncing those opposed to his party as opposed to the government,"[77] failed to take into account the general tendency of national establishments in emerging nations to treat opposition as seditious.[78] The deep suspicion of the Republicans that the Federalists were Tories who were attempting to restore monarchy, or a semblance of it, was the other side of a crisis over legitimacy. Likewise, if the problem of national integration was an important factor in party formation, as most functionalists stressed, the strongly regional complexion of the first party system became more comprehensible. Historians scoffed at Jefferson's

76. *Ibid.*, 401–402, 407–412.
77. *Origins of the American Party System*, 44.
78. In the United States this tendency persisted even into the Jeffersonian era. See Leonard Levy, *Freedom of Speech and Press in Early American History: Legacy of Suppression* (Cambridge, Mass., 1960).

claim that the election of 1800 was a political revolution in view of his failure to dismantle the Federalist program, but viewed from a functional perspective which clearly revealed the difficulty of achieving a peaceful transfer of power, Jefferson's claim becomes more credible. To the extent that a two-party system contributed to that transfer, we may hypothesize with LaPalombara and Weiner that the particular form a party system assumes may have enduring impact on the political institutions of a nation.

During the 1960's a number of students of the first party system incorporated concepts used by functionalists. Seymour Martin Lipset, a sociologist with a keen interest in historical antecedents of contemporary institutions, discussed the problems of the establishment and legitimation of national authority, the achievement of national integration, and the formulation of a national identity in terms of these concepts. Using comparative analysis in a far-ranging fashion, Lipset found some comparisons between the Federalists and "patron parties in Africa that are national but which represent a linking of local notables rather than an organization designed to mobilize the common people." The efforts of both the Federalists and the Republicans to suppress organized opposition "clearly indicate that in many ways our early political officials resembled those heads of new states in the twentieth century who view criticism of themselves as tantamount to an attack on the nation itself."[79]

While Lipset gave only passing attention to the first party system, William Nisbet Chambers made that system a central concern. A political scientist informed by functional concepts, Chambers wrote some highly influential works on early American party development, most notably his previously mentioned book *Political Parties in a New Nation* and a subsequent essay, "Parties and Nation-Building in America," which was included in the volume edited by LaPalombara and Weiner.[80] Consonant with the theme of the volume, Chambers

79. Seymour Martin Lipset, *The First New Nation* (New York, 1963), 37, 49.

80. William Nisbet Chambers, "Political Parties and Nation-Building in America," LaPalombara and Weiner, eds., *Political Parties and Political Development*, 79–106.

contended that the United States—the first polity to throw off colonial rule and reconstitute itself as an independent nation—was characterized by certain preconditions for party organization that make it a veritable laboratory for the analysis of party systems in emergent nations. It had, among other things, a differentiated, pluralistic society productive of conflicting interests that could energize party competition, and a tradition of popular involvement in the political process dating back to the colonial era which made for a desire to create the political party as a mechanism for the articulation of various interests. Pre-Constitutional political activity did not, however, produce political organizations with the range and density of support as well as the coherent ideologies requisite for the true political party.[81] It was the creation of a national locus for party development in the Constitution that completed the preconditions for the first party system. These preconditions were energized by Hamilton's comprehensive, coherent, and intricate financial program—in actuality a program of nation building. Opposition to Hamilton's program was inevitable, but the result was a viable two-party system which channeled grievances within generally accepted norms. That system overcame the various crises of popular participation and national integration. "No group perhaps got all it wanted, but all important groups had some means to express their demands; and serious dysfunction was avoided."[82]

The advantages of functional analysis logically entail deficiencies. The achievement of conceptual consistency necessarily discards those anomalies to which the historian is more alert. Recent investigations of the Federalists, for example, made them much more than a party of notables in Lipset's terms. It also seemed that Chambers found more modern characteristics in the first party system than actually existed. His analysis endowed that system with more rationalization, more coherence, more resolution of conflict, than the turbulent political history of the 1790's warranted. Indeed, the argument may be

81. Chambers's analysis of pre-party politics is more fully discussed in his previous book *Political Parties in a New Nation*, ch. 1.
82. "Parties and Nation-Building in America," 92–93.

advanced that parties often did the opposite of what historians assumed they were supposed to do. Far from smoothing the edges of ideological discord, they intensified it, and within the federal government, parties did little to by-pass the checks against efficient use of power built into the Constitution.[83]

Of the three crises affecting party formation stressed by functionalists—legitimation, participation, and integration—the last seems to have been the most important in the United States. Federalist leadership was an authentic extension of the leadership of the Revolution, particularly in the person of Washington. As Paul Goodman pointed out, voters were energized rather than enfranchised during the 1790's. Indeed, as Richard McCormick suggested, participation crises in American history have occurred when there were sharp fall-offs, not increases, in voter participation, such as during the presidency of Monroe.[84] But as Goodman again contended, parties tended to sharpen the definition of conflicting interests, and in the process regional antagonisms were exacerbated. "Frustrated Virginians became exploited planters and Southerners; disappointed Massachusetts men became aggrieved merchants and Easterners."[85] Nor was the problem resolved with the election of Jefferson. The multiple presidential candidacies from the various sections of the Union before the

83. See Richard Hofstadter, *The Idea of a Party System* (Berkeley and Los Angeles, 1969), for an articulate summation of the pervasive aversion to the very concept of an organized political party. Morton Grodzins, "Political Parties and the Crisis of Succession in the United States: The Case of 1800," LaPalombara and Weiner, eds., *Political Parties and Political Development,* 303–327, concluded that political parties were not responsible for the peaceful transfer of power in that crucial election; "If anything, they made the peaceful succession more, rather than less, difficult" (304). James Sterling Young's innovative study, *The Washington Community, 1800–1828* (New York, 1966) contained a persuasive argument that Republican party organization did little to bridge the gap between the executive and legislative branches.

84. Goodman, "The First American Party System," 63–64; and Richard McCormick, "Political Development and the Second Party System," Chambers and Burnham, eds., *American Party Systems,* 90–116. It is McCormick's contention that presidential elections were the most important factors in consolidating the two-party system.

85. Goodman, "The First American Party System," 63–64.

advent of the second party system, the inability of that system to over-come sectional antagonisms, and finally the breakup of the Union in the Civil War all testified to the persistence of the problem of integration.

As LaPalombara and Weiner suggested, there were really two types of integration problems. One had to do with territorial integrity and the willingness of the populace to place national over parochial concerns. A second problem, related to the first but analytically distinct, was the "regularization of structures and processes whereby the discrete elements in a given national territory are brought into meaningful participation in the political system."[86] Applying these two aspects of integration to the first party system, the Constitution might be said to have accomplished the second, or "process integration," by creating the national arena stressed so strongly by Chambers and others, while the emergence of political parties was closely connected with both, but perhaps mostly with the first problem of "national integration." It is worth stressing that despite the oft-noted undemocratic aspects of the Constitution, representation in the House was extraordinarily sensitive to constituent interests. After the first reapportionment, which enlarged the House to 105 members in 1792, there was one representative for every 33,000 persons—a ratio much more akin to today's state legislature than to the Federal Congress. The number of adult white males in a congressional constituency was strikingly small: New York had 10 congressmen representing some 67,000 white adult males, and Virginia had 19 congressmen for fewer than 90,000 white adult males. Even with a relatively broad franchise, less than 2,000 voters cast their votes in New York's third district (Westchester and Richmond counties) when Philip Van Cortlandt won the seat by a margin of 20 votes in 1794.[87] To the extent that voters were alert to the behavior of their representatives in Congress,

---

86. LaPalombara and Weiner, eds., *Political Parties and Political Development*, 413.
87. The figures are from the first census and tabulations in Young, *Democratic-Republicans of New York*, 591. I have used Young's ratio of four-fifths of the total adult white males sixteen years and over to arrive at the Virginia figure.

members of the House had to be highly attuned to the mood of their constituencies.[88]

But if the congressional constituency of the 1790's resembled today's state electoral district, the nation as a whole, given conditions of travel and communication at that time, was substantially larger than the United States in the twentieth century. Antifederalist literature sedulously stressed that "this extensive country," "this immense extent of territory," "this immense continent," could never be gathered into an "uncompounded republick."[89] How could such a dispersed population be "all reduced to the same standard of morals, of habits, and of laws?" asked James Winthrop. George Clinton emphasized that the "dissimilitude of interest, morals, and politics" in the Union would produce an "unkindred legislature . . . a house divided against itself."[90]

These were not simply rhetorical caveats of provincial bosses. The warnings were sincere; they struck a responsive chord among the people, and they prompted thoughtful Federalist retorts. It was Madison's argument in *Federalist* Number Ten that an extended republic would provide the necessary security against oppressive majority factions precisely because it would have a house divided against itself. While their conclusions were opposite, both the advocates and the opponents of the Constitution were thinking of partisan politics within the context of what functionalists have termed a crisis of integration.

88. That Van Cortlandt was a marginal Republican rather than a core member of the Republican bloc in terms of his voting record in Congress testifies to this proposition. Indeed, there was a direct relationship between the margin of victory at the polls and the partisan posture of the New York congressmen during the Fourth Congress. Another example of the relationship between a representative and his constituency was the case of Thomas Tredwell, who was a core member of the Republican bloc in the Third Congress when elected from the first district (Long Island), but was resoundingly defeated by a vote of 1109–298 when he moved to the Federalist seventh district in northeastern New York. *Ibid.*, 592.

89. Richard Henry Lee, *Letters of a Federal Farmer,* Letter II; George Clinton, *Cato,* III; George Mason, speech in the Virginia ratifying convention; James Winthrop, *Agrippa,* IV.

90. Winthrop, *Agrippa,* IV; Clinton, *Cato,* III.

The assumptions of the Antifederalists were strangely akin to those of the more conservative and provincial high Federalists (excluding, of course, Madison), for both assumed that a republic should be homogeneous. The two groups differed, of course, in the means whereby they would achieve it. The Antifederalists would restrict the size of the republic, while the conservative Federalists would rely upon a continuation of the politics of deference. Both were astonishingly bad prognosticators, for the Antifederalists quickly perceived that the national government could indeed respond to the manifold constituent pressures of an extended republic, while the high Federalists encountered greater challenges in their home districts and found fewer allies in the national elite than they had reason to expect. Madison was the shrewdest analyst of all, but even his forecast momentarily fell wide of the mark. There is good reason to believe that Madison never anticipated the two-party system he helped to create because the Virginian, perhaps more than any other individual—certainly more than Hamilton or Jefferson—was alert to the pre-Constitutional partisan politics of the Continental Congress. He had served during three critical years in that Congress, and had kept in constant touch with congressional proceedings after he was ineligible for reappointment under the Articles of Confederation.

Madison's schooling in national politics confirmed his belief in the existence of multiple factions—one might substitute the term "legislative parties," for that had been the situation in the Continental Congress. Cluster bloc analysis of the roll calls of the Continental Congress in the general mode that Mary Ryan used for the first four Federal Congresses reveals that delegates tended to form in regional groupings corresponding to the three colonial sections—New England, the middle colonies, and the South.[91] Nor were these legislative

91. The bloc analysis I have done for the Continental Congress differs in some respects from that of Miss Ryan, but is comparable in that virtually all issues productive of dissent were taken into consideration. Both Charles and Dauer used highly selective samples, and Cunningham was equally selective in that he analyzed only the first session of the Second Congress and further assumed that the posture of Madison serves as an index of the position of the opposition party. While this is a plausible assumption, it is open to question, both from Ryan's conclusions and from my own analysis of the

parties formless and chaotic. Voting configurations in many sessions of the Continental Congress and the very early sessions of the House of Representatives were so similar that an observer unaware of the reconstitution of the national government might assume that the House was simply an enlarged and more representative Continental Congress. That this should have been so is perfectly comprehensible in terms of the persistence of parochial loyalties, the problem of integration in an emergent nation, and the marked continuity of issues and the legislative leadership during the 1780's and the 1790's.

There were constant problems of national policy that were shunted more than transformed by the Constitution. The struggle over the public debt did not originate with Hamilton's program; almost every aspect of that program was anticipated by the fiscal reforms proposed by Robert Morris when he was superintendent of finance during the early 1780's. The location of the national capital, the management of the West, and the formulation of policy toward France and England were only a few of the issues that perplexed and divided members of the Continental Congress just as they continued to perplex and divide the Federal Congresses.

Nor were these problems unfamiliar to a large percentage of the members of the Senate and the House during the Federal period. Virtually one-half of the senators in the First Congress and a significant number of the more influential members of the House of Representatives had served in the Continental Congress. Men in the first House such as Livermore, Gerry, Partridge, Sedgwick, Huntington, Sherman, Wadsworth, Floyd, Boudinot, Clymer, Fitzsimmons, Vining, Carroll, Bland, Madison, Ashe, Bloodworth, Williamson, Huger, and Baldwin had already experienced the national concerns and parochial antagonisms that characterized the proceedings of the Continental Congress.

Considered in this light, the first party system—forming in the

---

Federal Congresses. She noted that Madison did not score particularly high in terms of party loyalty, and I have found that while Madison's position increasingly coincided with the opposition, he clearly lagged behind his fellow Virginians during the First Congress in opposing the incipient Federalist party.

Regional Distribution of Voting Blocs* in the Continental and Federal Congresses

Congress	Region**	Bloc (Legislative Party) Membership***			
		East	Middle	South	Independent
Continental	NE	6			6
Congress	M		9		1
1783	S		3	7	1
Continental	NE	10			
Congress	M	6			2
1786	S			15	
First	NE	14			3
House	M	5	8	3	2
(1789–91)	S	1	6	19	6
		(Federalist)		(Republican)	
Fourth	NE	27		5	2
House	M	12		14	4
(1795–97)	S	6		39	2

* Refers to 66.7% agreement or more between all pairs of delegates on non-repetitive roll calls on which there was at least 10% disagreement in the entire Congress. Two classes of membership are included: core members who had 66.7% agreement with all other members of the core, and marginal members who had 66.7% agreement with at least half of the core membership. Marginal members constituted roughly 30% of the membership of an average bloc, and tended to come from outside the region in which the legislative party had its major strength.

** NE: N.H., Vt., Mass., R.I., Conn.
M: N.Y., N.J., Pa., Del.
S: Md., Va., N.C., S.C., Ga., Ky., Tenn.

*** Some members appear in two blocs because of close relationship between the blocs. Madison, for example, was a core member of the Middle bloc and a marginal member of the Southern bloc in the first House. For purposes of simplification, two minor intersectional blocs have been excluded—one in the 1783 session of the Continental Congress and one in the first House. The members have been included among the Independents.

national legislature, as structuralists have agreed—was probably in a state of germination before the passage of the Constitution in the sense that a tradition of concerted action by national legislators had already begun. Ironically, Beard may have actually underestimated how deeply the roots of the party system were planted in the Revolutionary era.[92]

92. The works of Merrill Jensen, *The New Nation* (New York, 1950), and Gordon Wood, *The Creation of the American Republic* (Chapel Hill, 1969),

The continuities of membership and the configurations illustrated in the table prove nothing conclusively, but they do suggest a few hypotheses that deserve further exploration. First, the national legislature subsumed two kinds of polarities that lent themselves to party formation: regional tensions and ideological tensions of a more complicated nature that brought together socioeconomic and political grievances. The regional contest was played out largely by Virginia and Massachusetts, each with its own satellites, because of their size and weight in the House. (Virginia and Kentucky alone accounted for 17 of the 40 core members of the Republican party in the fourth House.) The ideological tensions were partly the product of regional differences in manners, habits, interests, morals, politics, and laws given such stress by the Antifederalists; they were also partly the product of strains between popular and deferential styles of politics.

Second, the party system that emerged in the national legislature was significantly distinct from the party battles that were fought in the states, or at least within most of them. It is incongruous, to say the least, that Virginia should have provided the major leadership for Republicans who were challenging the status quo in the more differentiated states. What sort of coherence existed in the alliance between elitists such as Charles Pinckney of South Carolina and backwoods democrats from Pennsylvania such as John Smilie? Conversely, why was it that John Adams was unable to win the support of the Federalist-dominated legislature of South Carolina in 1796? That state's electoral vote was given to Thomas Pinckney and Thomas Jefferson.

Considering the tendency toward a multiple-party system and the

---

are highly competent treatments of the Revolutionary and Confederation eras that have clear implications for party formulation, some of which are not inconsistent with Beard's conclusions. Jackson Turner Main's *The Antifederalists* (Chapel Hill, 1961) and his forthcoming study of partisan politics in Revolutionary legislatures are also valuable contributions that will help locate the sources of the first party system. Probably the most provocative treatment in this regard is Staughton Lynd, *Class Conflict, Slavery and the Constitution* (Indianapolis, 1967). Lynd may make too much of the issue of slavery, but the book contains significant insights into the strains between North and South as well as the critical role of the West in national politics preceding and following the Constitution.

disjunction between national and state politics, the question may be raised: How did a two-party system arise at all? That it did may be the consequence of two more factors that may be suggested as yet other hypotheses. There was one general issue that could energize the diverse parts of an extended polity, barring radical innovations in the use of central power. That issue was foreign policy. The key question on that issue was what America's posture toward Britain and France should be, in terms of both practical diplomacy and the ideological impact of the French Revolution within the United States. Most structuralists were in agreement on this point, but it should be added that it was foreign policy—specifically the Jay-Gardoqui negotiations—that split the Continental Congress in an unprecedented fashion in 1786. That this should have been the case was not surprising, simply because most of the actions of the national government were involved with foreign, not domestic, concerns. It is necessary to remind ourselves that the national government was "at a distance and out of sight," as James Sterling Young has stressed.[93]

There were exceptions to the rule of the remoteness of government which also helped to account for the first party system—exceptions which also were rooted in the era of the Revolution. Certain areas, notably Philadelphia, the capital during the partisan decade of the nineties, as well as the region from New York City to the Potomac felt a more proximate influence from the national capital. It was in this vital core region that a third middle force in national politics materialized during the early 1780's and in the first House. Madison himself belonged to a middle block from Pennsylvania, Maryland, and Virginia during the First Congress when the question of the location of 'the national capital dominated partisan politics. It was in this middle region that the most dynamic growth could have been anticipated from the development of the emerging West, from an expanded carrying trade, and from the servicing of the public debt. Further, it was this border region between the North and the South that had the most to lose from the division that was predicted from all sides.

At the same time, it was in the middle region—above all, Pennsyl-

93. Young, *Washington Community,* especially ch. 1.

vania—that the greatest congruence occurred between national and state party politics. This had been true even during the Confederation era; when the more radical Constitutionalist party of Pennsylvania dominated the Pennsylvania assembly, the congressional delegation generally aligned with the New England bloc. When their conservative opponents were in power, however, this congressional delegation either aligned with the South or, as was more frequently the case, established a third force with southern support and decidedly nationalist leanings.[94]

The passage of the Constitution meant that both parties could be represented in the Congress at the same time, and the impact of this innovation in "process integration" was most immediately felt in the middle states. (Note the laggard development of two-party representation in both New England and the South in the table.) Another demonstration of the convergence of national and state politics was that popular protest against national measures centered in Pennsylvania. Both the Whiskey Rebellion and Fries's Insurrection occurred in that state. Whether the party system helped more to resolve than to trigger such crises is open to question.

By recognizing the strains which were imposed upon the integration process by such major issues as Hamilton's fiscal program, the location of the national capital, the reapportionment of the House, the Jay Treaty and its aftermath, it is possible to see how a broadly based two-party system emerged in a polity that should have produced a congeries of congressional parties. But the precise nature of that system still eludes us. There are valid elements in Beard's emphasis on the antagonism between capitalists and agrarians; clearly, party politics were partly the product of social tensions associated with the growth of more differentiated societies in many of the states; and there was a relatively healthy tradition of popular participation and sophisticated political experience within the United States that was necessary for the growth of political parties. There were also competing libertarian and corporate ideological commitments that

94. See H. J. Henderson, "Constitutionalists and Republicans in the Continental Congress," *Pennsylvania History*, XXXVI (1969), 119–144.

made possible the institutionalization of broad and strangely diverse interests that were embedded in the first party system. But unless the manifold forces that were arraigned against each other are more sharply defined, and unless the modes of communication that brought those forces together are more closely scrutinized, the explanation of the growth and the disintegration of the first party system will remain incomplete.

BIBLIOGRAPHY

MARY-JO KLINE

The Writings of Richard B. Morris

READERS unfamiliar with Richard Brandon Morris's career may
be surprised by the range of topics represented in this bibliography.
But his students and friends will not be. They well know that he has
been constitutionally incapable of limiting his interests or containing
his enthusiasms about books and people. And therein lies the key to
his personality as well as his intellect. His character no less than his
mind is kaleidoscopic, and numberless students have benefited from
his capacity to share their diverse scholarly passions, and to adapt himself to their differing personalities, political persuasions, and research
goals. Conservative Republicans, avowed Marxists, Orthodox Jews,
and adherents to evangelical Protestant sects were among the students
who chose him as their mentor at Columbia. Their work forced Professor Morris to familiarize himself with the demographic characteristics of New England and New Amsterdam, Russia's diplomacy under
Catherine the Great, and the machinations of the Mohawk Nation
under Chief Joseph Brant. Good fortune brought many of us to Professor Morris's door at Fayerweather Hall: no one else had the patience and intellectual versatility to put up with us. This bibliography
of his writings should serve to illustrate that versatility and that
abiding interest in people.

A brief word about the arrangement of his bibliography is in order
because of its extraordinary breadth. Books and pamphlets have been

375

broken down into categories representing the type of publication each represents; i.e., monographs, textbooks, compendia, etc. Within this organization, it seemed wise to order essays in a topical arrangement. Although these topical headings are broad in nature, they may be helpful in locating Professor Morris's writings down through the years. The essays span more than half a century, from "Alexander Hamilton as a Hebraist," published in May, 1920, to "The Power to Make Wars," published in April, 1972. Certain writings defied any rational categorization and have been listed at the end of the bibliography.

Although every effort was exerted to make the bibliography as complete as possible, there are bound to be some omissions. Because Professor Morris was unaware of the preparation of this book and bibliography, it was impossible to draw upon his infallible memory for reference. Fortunately, many gaps were filled in by his family (especially by his son, Professor Jeffrey B. Morris of the College of the City of New York), by his associates on the staff of *The John Jay Papers* (Dr. Carol Berkin and Miss Ene Sirvet), and by colleagues who were kind enough to furnish lists of little-publicized writings that otherwise might have gone unnoticed. Whatever the political or scholarly leanings of Professor Morris's students, we all absorbed a fine sense of conspiracy from the foremost expert on European espionage during the American Revolution.

Two categories of writings have been omitted by intention: book reviews and prefaces to others' writings. Without Dr. Morris's assistance no complete lists of reviews and prefaces could be compiled; an incomplete listing would at best seem capricious. It must be remembered, however, that the influence of a scholar is felt in many ways, and that through scores of book reviews Richard Morris has had a subtle but real impact on the literature of his field. A case in point is his reviews of William Wirt Blume's edition of the *Transactions* of the Michigan Supreme Court, in which Professor Morris presented his theories on the obligation and limitations of editors of court records. In other reviews he made significant comments on historical methods, substantive issues, and research opportunities. Anyone wishing to explore fully the contributions of Richard B. Morris to early American historiography would have to cull—from dozens of newspapers, public periodicals, and scholarly journals—the myriad reviews and review-essays that reveal in a variety of ways the workings of the Morris mind. So too with his prefaces, introductions, letters to the editor of the *New York Times,* and countless other fugitive pieces.

One last qualification must be made as to the "authoritative" nature of this bibliography: only published materials to which a reader might have ready access have been included. Many of Professor Morris's most interesting offerings have not been recorded in this way. Several papers delivered at scholarly conferences have gone unpublished. Nor was it considered appropriate to list press releases, even though his contributions in this area cover important matters, such as the electoral college (December, 1960) and the campaign funds of Richard M. Nixon (October 5, 1952). Those of us privileged to have been his correspondents during his travels abroad can testify that his letters from Paris, Berlin, Kabul, and Tehran deserve a place in the next edition of *A Treasury of Great Reporting.*

Professor Morris himself would be the first to admit that he is as much at home with the spoken as the written word. But there seems to be no appropriate way to list televised lectures or interviews. (The latter would have been highlighted by the remarks he made upon release from the Westchester County jail after his arrest for thwarting the destruction of historic trees in Mount Vernon.) Nor was there any way to describe materials such as his testimony for the Javits-Stennis bill before the United States Senate in March, 1972.

It would have been equally difficult to catalog those contributions which have been "felt" rather than recorded on paper or television tape. Professor Morris's scholarly influence is far broader than even this bibliography can possibly reveal. His work as editor of the Anglo-American Legal History Series and as secretary to the Legal History Committee of the American Historical Association will be remembered as well as his own essays in the field. Without scholars like Richard B. Morris, the area of "labor history" would have waited much longer to receive recognition as a distinct and valid scholarly activity. Every

author who has contributed to the New American Nation Series can
testify to his uncanny ability as a literary mentor and demanding editor. The archives of New York City have held his concern and interest
from the days of the W.P.A. in the 1930's through his appointment
to Mayor John Lindsay's commission on municipal archives in the
1960's.

One omission from this bibliography will disappoint Professor
Morris as deeply as it does his colleagues: *The John Jay Papers.* The
first volume of this important series will be published shortly, but it
could not be included here. It is especially appropriate that the Jay
Papers project will occupy Professor Morris in the first years of his
retirement, for John Jay and the editor of his papers resemble each
other in certain essential attitudes. Although Professor Morris, a short
ebullient native of the Bronx, might be surprised to hear himself compared to the tall, reserved, aristocratic Chief Justice, the views of these
two New Yorkers are remarkably similar. Richard B. Morris, like John
Jay, followed a career determined by a profound love for the developing American republic, and by a passionate concern for the moral
values and legal system guiding this nation. That love and that concern
are the themes basic to the diverse publications listed below.

Books and Pamphlets: Monographic Works and Collected Essays

The American Revolution, A Short History, 1763–1783. New York, 1955.
The American Revolution Reconsidered. New York, 1967. (The sub-
      stance of these essays comprised the Anson G. Phelps Lectures in
      Early American History at New York University, 1966. Two of the
      essays are revised and enlarged versions of earlier contributions to
      the *William and Mary Quarterly.*)
Early American Court Records: A Publication Program. New York, 1940.
      (Also published in the *New York University Law Quarterly Review,*
      XVIII [January, 1941], 210–245.)
The Emerging Nations and the American Revolution. New York, 1970.
*Fair Trial: Fourteen Who Stood Accused from Anne Hutchinson to Alger
      Hiss.* Rev. ed., New York, 1967. (Originally published New York,
      1952.)
Government and Labor in Early America. New York, 1965. (Originally
      published New York, 1946.)

Handbook of Civilian Protection, with Louis L. Snyder and J. E. Wisan. New York, 1942.

Historiography of America, 1600–1800, as Represented in the Publications of Columbia University Press. New York, 1933.

James DeLancey of New York: A Monograph. New York, 1939.

John Jay, the Nation, and the Court. Boston, 1967. (The substance of these essays comprised the Gaspar Bacon Lectures on the Constitution of the United States at Boston University, 1965.)

The Making of a Nation: 1775–1789, with the editors of *Life.* New York, 1963. (*The Life History of the United States,* II.)

The New World: Prehistory to 1774, with the editors of *Life.* New York, 1963. (*The Life History of the United States,* I.)

The Peacemakers: The Great Powers and American Independence. New York, 1970. (Originally published New York, 1965.)

Studies in the History of American Law, with Special Reference to the Seventeenth and Eighteenth Centuries. 2d ed., Philadelphia, 1959. (Originally published New York, 1930.)

Textbooks and Reference Volumes

America: A History of the People, with William Greenleaf and Robert H. Ferrell. Chicago, 1971.

Ancient and Medieval Times: From the Earliest Records to the Opening of the French Revolution. Part I of "Civilization in Europe," with J. Salwyn Schapiro. Rev. and enl. ed., Boston, 1937. (Originally published Boston, 1928. 2d ed., Boston, 1930.)

Encyclopedia of American History. Rev. and enl. ed., New York, 1970. (Originally published New York, 1953. Rev. eds., New York, 1961, 1965.)

Four Hundred Notable Americans. New York, 1965. (Originally published as the biographical section of the *Encyclopedia of American History,* rev. ed., 1961.)

A Guide to the Principal Sources for Early American History (1600–1800) in the City of New York, with Evarts B. Greene. 2d ed., New York, 1953. (Originally published New York, 1929.)

Harper Encyclopedia of the Modern World, with Graham W. Irwin. New York, 1970. (Published in Britain as *An Encyclopedia of the Modern World: A Concise Reference History from 1760 to the Present,* London, 1970.)

U.S.A.: The History of a Nation, with William Greenleaf. 2 vols. Chicago, 1969.

Compendia and Edited Books

Alexander Hamilton and the Founding of the Nation. New York, 1969. (Originally published New York, 1957.)

The American Revolution, 1763–1783: A Bicentennial Collection. New York and Columbia, S.C., 1970.

Basic Documents in American History. Rev. ed., New York, 1965. (Originally published Princeton, 1956.)

Basic Documents on the Confederation and Constitution. New York, 1970.

Basic Ideas of Alexander Hamilton. New York, 1965. (Originally published New York, 1957.)

The Era of the American Revolution: Studies Inscribed to Evarts Boutell Greene. Gloucester, Mass., 1971. (Originally published New York, 1939; also, New York, 1965.)

Great Presidential Decisions: State Papers That Changed the Course of History. New York, 1966. (Originally published Philadelphia, 1960. Rev. ed., Philadelphia, 1965.)

History in the First Person, with Louis Snyder. Harrisburg, 1951.

Proceedings of the Maryland Court of Appeals, 1695–1729, with Carroll T. Bond. Washington, 1933.

Select Cases of the Mayor's Court of New York City, 1674–1784. Washington, 1935.

Significant Documents in United States History. New York, 1969.

The Spirit of Seventy-Six: The Story of the American Revolution as Told by Participants, with Henry Steele Commager. 1-vol. ed., New York, 1967. (Originally published in 2 vols., Indianapolis, 1958. Excerpts from the introduction published as "Telling the Story of the Revolution," *Saturday Review,* XLI [December 27, 1958], 9 ff.)

They Saw It Happen: Eyewitness Reports of Great Events, with Louis Snyder. Harrisburg, 1951.

A Treasury of Great Reporting: "Literature under Pressure" from the Sixteenth Century to Our Own Time, with Louis Snyder, 2d ed., New York, 1962. (Originally published Harrisburg, 1949.)

Trevelyan, Sir George Otto. *The American Revolution.* Arr. for 1 vol. London, 1966.

Voices from America's Past, with James L. Woodress. 3 vols. St. Louis, 1963. (Originally published as separate pamphlets, St. Louis, 1961– 1962. The individual pamphlets, as arranged in the 3-vol. compilation, are:

The Beginnings of America, 1607–1763. 1961.

The Times That Tried Men's Souls, 1770–1783. 1961.

The Age of Washington, 1783–1801. 1961.

The Jeffersonians, 1801–1829. 1961.

Jacksonian Democracy, 1829–1848. 1961.

The Westward Movement, 1832–1889. 1961.

A House Divided: The Civil War, 1850–1865. 1961.

The Shaping of Modern America, 1865–1914. 1962.

Expanding Horizons: America Joins the World Powers, 1867–1914. 1962.
Democracy on Trial: The First World War, 1914–1920. 1962.
Boom and Bust: The Twenties and Thirties, 1920–1939. 1962.
Global Conflict: The United States in World War II, 1937–1946. 1962.
The Cold War, 1946–1961. St. Louis, 1962.
Turbulent Times: America in the Nuclear Age, 1946–1962. 1962).

Juvenile Literature

The First Book Edition of the Star-Spangled Banner. New York, 1961.
The First Book of the American Revolution. New York, 1956.
The First Book of the Constitution. New York, 1958.
The First Book of the Founding of the Republic. New York, 1968.
The First Book of the Indian Wars. New York, 1959.
The First Book of the War of 1812. New York, 1961.

Articles: The New Nation: Its History and Its Historians

"Alexander Hamilton and His Message for Our Times," University of Hawaii *Occasional Papers*, No. 65, Honolulu, 1957.
"Benjamin Franklin's Grand Design: The Albany Plan of Union Might Have Made the Revolution Unnecessary," *American Heritage*, VII (February, 1956), 106–109.
"Class Struggle and the American Revolution," *William and Mary Quarterly*, 3d ser., XIX (January, 1962), 3–29.
"Clues to the Washington Paradox," *New York Times Magazine*, February 22, 1959, 12 ff.
"The Confederation Period and the American Historian," *William and Mary Quarterly*, 3d ser., XIII (April, 1956), 139–156.
"The Ghost of Captain Kidd," *New York History*, XIX (July, 1938), 280–297.
"Insurrection in Massachusetts," in *America in Crisis: Fourteen Crucial Episodes in American History*, ed. by Daniel Aaron, New York, 1952, 21–49.
"The Jay Papers I: Mission to Spain," *American Heritage*, XIX (February, 1968), 8–21.
"The Jay Papers II: The Forging of the Nation," *American Heritage*, XX (December, 1968), 24 ff.
"The Jay Papers III: The Trials of Chief Justice Jay," *American Heritage*, XX (June, 1969), 80–90.
"John Peter Zenger, Instrument and Symbol of the Struggle for a Free Press," *American Heritage*, V (January, 1953), 26–27.

"The Revolution's Caine Mutiny," *American Heritage,* XI (April, 1960), 10–13.

"Seven Who Set Our Destiny," *New York Times Magazine,* February 19, 1961, 9 ff.

"The Spacious Empire of Lawrence Henry Gipson," *William and Mary Quarterly,* 3d ser., XXIV (April, 1967), 169–189.

"Spotlight on the Plowmen of the Jersies," New Jersey Historical Society *Proceedings,* LXVII (April, 1949), 106–123.

"Then and There the Child Independence Was Born," *American Heritage,* XIII (February, 1962), 36 ff.

"Washington and Hamilton: A Great Collaboration," American Philosophical Society *Proceedings,* CII (April, 1958), 107–116.

"Zealot for Right," *New York Times Magazine,* June 7, 1959, 19–22.

Articles: Labor and Economic History

"American Labor History Prior to the Civil War: Sources and Opportunities for Research," *Labor History,* I (Fall, 1960), 308–318.

"Andrew Jackson, Strikebreaker," *American Historical Review,* LV (October, 1949), 54–68.

"The Course of Peonage in a Slave State," *Political Science Quarterly,* LXV (June, 1950), 238–263.

"Criminal Conspiracy and Early Labor Combinations in New York," *Political Science Quarterly,* LII (March, 1937), 51–85.

"Jackson was No FDR," *Labor and Nation,* V (May–June, 1949), 38–40.

"Labor and Mercantilism in the Revolutionary Era," in *The Era of the American Revolution: Studies Inscribed to Evarts Boutell Greene,* 76–139.

"Labor Controls in Maryland in the Nineteenth Century," *Journal of Southern History,* XIV (August, 1948), 385–400.

"Labor Militancy in the Old South," *Labor and Nation,* IV (May–June, 1948), 32–36.

"The Measure of Bondage in the Slave States," *Mississippi Valley Historical Review,* XLI (September, 1954), 219–240.

"100 Years of Income Outgo," *New York Times Magazine,* August 5, 1962, 55.

"The Organization of Production during the Colonial Period," in *The Growth of the American Economy,* ed. by Harold F. Williamson, New York, 1951, 60–82. (Originally published New York, 1944.)

"The Regulation of Wages in Early Massachusetts," with Jonathan Grossman, *New England Quarterly,* XI (October, 1938), 470–500.

"White Bondage in Ante-bellum South Carolina," *South Carolina Historical and Genealogical Magazine,* XLIX (October, 1948), 191–207.

Articles: Legal History and Constitutional Issues

"The Courts, the Law, and Social History," in *Essays in Honor of Felix Frankfurter,* ed. by Morris D. Forkosch, New York, 1966, 408–422.

"Current Statesmen's Papers Publication Programs: An Appraisal from the Point of View of the Legal Historian," *American Journal of Legal History,* XI (April, 1967), 95–106.

"Entail," in *Encyclopaedia of the Social Sciences,* V, 553–556. 15 vols. New York, 1930–1935.

"*Fair Trial* Revisited," Association of the Bar of the City of New York *Record,* XXV (November, 1970), 556–565.

"Freedom of Expression: Its Past and Its Future," *New York History,* XXXI (April, 1950), 115–135.

"Freehold," in *Encyclopaedia of the Social Sciences,* VI, 461–464.

"Judicial Supremacy and the Inferior Courts in the American Colonies," *Political Science Quarterly,* LV (September, 1940), 429–434.

"Legalism versus Revolutionary Doctrine in New England," *New England Quarterly,* IV (April, 1931), 195–215.

"Massachusetts and the Common Law: The Declaration of 1646," *American Historical Review,* XXI (April, 1926), 443–453.

"The Present Validity of Eighteenth-Century Doctrines of the State," in *The Present-Day Relevance of Eighteenth-Century Thought,* ed. by Roger P. McCutcheon, Washington, 1956. (Paper presented at the Annual Meeting of the American Council of Learned Societies, January 26–27, 1956.)

"Primogeniture and Entailed Estates in America," *Columbia Law Review,* XXVII (January, 1927), 24–71.

"The Sources of Early American Law: Colonial Period," *West Virginia Law Quarterly and The Bar,* XL (April, 1934), 212–223.

Articles: Historical Materials

"Adventures in the Reference Room," *Wilson Library Bulletin,* XLI (January, 1967), 492–501. (A paper delivered at a meeting of the Cooperative Reference Services Committee, July 13, 1966.)

"The Challenge of Historical Materials," *The American Archivist,* IV (April, 1941), 91–116.

"The Federal Archives of New York City: Opportunities for Historical Research," *American Historical Review,* XLII (January, 1937), 256–272.

"The Gouverneur Morris Collection," *Columbia Library Columns,* V (November, 1955), 26–31.

"John Jay Comes Back to Columbia," Columbia University Graduate Faculties *Newsletter,* February, 1960.

"The Needs for Regional Depositories for Federal Records," *The American Archivist,* VI (April, 1943), 115–122.

"Putting the John Jay Papers to Work," *Columbia Library Columns,* IX (May, 1960), 3–7.

"The Salzer Collection of Mayor's Court Papers," *Columbia Library Columns,* VII (May, 1958), 14–20. (Summarized, with the same title, in *American Journal of Legal History,* II [October, 1958], 313–314.)

Articles: Modern History and Government

"The French Revolution Is Still an Issue," *New York Times Magazine,* January 28, 1962, 8 ff.

"Hits on the Hustings," *New York Times Magazine,* April 24, 1960, 98.

"Is the Eagle Un-American?," *New York Times Magazine,* February 14, 1960, 30 ff.

"Is Uncle Sam Obsolete?," *New York Times Magazine,* April 12, 1959, 28.

"Last Address: White House," *New York Times Magazine,* November 20, 1960, 118 ff.

"The Metropolis of the State," in *History of the State of New York,* ed. by Alexander C. Flick, X, 173–214. 10 vols. in 5. Port Washington, N.Y., 1962. (Originally published in 10 vols., New York, 1937.)

"The Muddled Problem of the Succession," *New York Times Magazine,* December 15, 1963, 11 ff.

"Our Friendly Quarrel with France," *New York Times Magazine,* April 29, 1962, 12 ff.

"The Power to Make Wars," *New York Times,* April 1, 1972, 43.

"The Presidency: Ten Fateful Decisions," *New York Times Magazine,* December 4, 1960, 23 ff.

"A Presidential Sense of Humor," *New York Times Magazine,* April 30, 1961, 47 ff.

" 'Rendezvous with Destiny'—F.D.R. in His Own Words," *New York Times Magazine,* April 10, 1960, 12 ff.

"Where Success Begins: Rags to Riches—Myth and Reality," *Saturday Review,* XXXVI (November 21, 1953), 15 ff.

Articles: The Jewish Tradition in America

"Alexander Hamilton as a Hebraist," *The American Hebrew,* May 7, 1920.

"Civil Liberties and the Jewish Tradition in Early America," American

Jewish Historical Society *Publications,* XLVI (September, 1956), 20–39.

"The Jewish Interests of Matthew Arnold, a Centenary Study," *The American Hebrew,* December 22, 1922.

"The Jewish Interests of Roger Williams," *The American Hebrew,* December 9, 1921.

"The Jewish Tradition at the Birth of America," with Louis J. Newman, *The American Hebrew,* September 30, 1921.

"Robert Ingersoll: His Warfare with the 'Jewish God,' " with Louis J. Newman, *The Jewish Tribune and Hebrew Standard,* September 5, 1924.

Miscellaneous Writings

"Alexander Hamilton: A Study in Courage," script for the radio series "The American Story," New York, 1957.

"Back in Stock, or an Editor Tells All," *The City College Alumnus,* February, 1950.

"Henry Hudson," script for the radio series "The American Story," New York, 1955.

"Historian Views Johnson," interview in *The Christian Science Monitor,* May 25, 1965, 3.

"The Role of Personality in College Teaching," in *Excellence in Teaching: Informal Talks to Faculty Members, Fiftieth Anniversary, University of Hawaii, 1907–1957,* Honolulu, 1957, 29–32.

"The View from the Top of Fayerweather," in *Freedom and Reform: Essays in Honor of Henry Steele Commager,* ed. by Harold M. Hyman and Leonard W. Levy, New York, 1967, 1–5.

Jewish Historical Society Publications, XLVI (September 1956), 20–39.

"The Jewish Interest of Matthew Arnold, a Centenary Study," The Menorah Journal, December 22.

"The Blood Libel in Christian Writing," The American Review, D.C., 1951.

"The Jewish Tradition and the Birth of America," with Louis Finkelstein, The American Historical Review XX, 15 ff.

"Robert Ingersoll's Romance with the Jewish God," with Louis J. Newman, Theodore Tribune and Hebrew Standard, Corpus $1795.

Miscellaneous Writings

"Alexander Hamilton: A Study in Courage", script for the radio series "The American Story," New York 1954.

Book as Stock or as Editor," WGAR, The City College Alumnus, February, 1956.

Henry Hudson, narrator of the radio series, "The American Story," New York, 1955.

"Mordecai Manuel Johnson," interview in The Christian Science Monitor, May 25, 1953.

"The Role of Personality in College Teaching," in Expansion in Teaching: Inaugural Talks to Faculty Members, Billiot Hancock, University of Rhode Island, 1956–1957, Honolulu, 1957, 29–32.

"The View from the Top of Psychology," in Poems and stations, same volume of Henry Stage Company, ed. by Harold M. Hyman and Leonard W. Levy, New York, 1967, 1–8.

Notes on Contributors

GEORGE ATHAN BILLIAS (A.B., Bates, 1948; M.A., Columbia, 1949; Ph.D., Columbia, 1958) is Professor of American History at Clark University. He has written, edited, or co-edited, among other works: *Massachusetts Land Bankers of 1740: General John Glover and His Marblehead Mariners; Law and Authority in Colonial America; George Washington's Generals; George Washington's Opponents;* and *American History: Retrospect and Prospect.*

PATRICIA U. BONOMI (B.A., University of California at Los Angeles, 1948; M.A., New York University, 1963; Ph.D., Columbia, 1970) is Associate Professor of History at New York University, where she teaches early American history. She is the author of *A Factious People: Politics and Society in Colonial New York.*

H. JAMES HENDERSON (A.B., Boston University, 1950; M.A., Columbia, 1957; Ph.D., Columbia, 1962) is Professor of History at Oklahoma State University, where he teaches early American history. He is the author of articles and essays on the politics of the American Revolution, including an essay in Stephen Kurtz and James Huston, eds., *Essays on the American Revolution.* His book on the partisan politics of the Continental Congress will be published in 1973.

HERBERT ALAN JOHNSON (B.A., Columbia, 1955; L.L.B., New York Law School, 1960; M.A., Columbia, 1961; Ph.D., Columbia, 1965) is Editor of the Papers of John Marshall at the Institute of Early American History and Culture and a Lecturer in History at the College of William and Mary. He is a specialist in early American legal history, with particular emphasis upon colonial New York. He wrote *The Law Merchant and Negotiable Instruments in Colonial New York, 1664–1730.*

MILTON M. KLEIN (B.S.S., City College of New York, 1937; M.S., City

387

College, 1939; Ph.D., Columbia, 1954) is Professor of History at the University of Tennessee. His articles on early American history have appeared in the *William and Mary Quarterly, New York History, South Atlantic Quarterly, Huntington Library Quarterly,* and *The Historian;* and he has edited *The Independent Reflector,* published in the John Harvard Library series.

MARY-JO KLINE (B.A., Barnard, 1961; M.A., Columbia, 1963; Ph.D., Columbia, 1970) is Associate Editor of the John Jay Papers, Columbia University. Her specialty is American political history in the Revolutionary and early national periods. Her book *Alexander Hamilton: A Biography in His Own Words* will be published by Harper & Row late in 1973.

MICHAEL KRAUS (B.S.S., City College of New York, 1923; Ph.D., Columbia, 1928) is Professor Emeritus of History at City College of New York. He has written *Intercolonial Aspects of American Culture on the Eve of the Revolution; The Atlantic Civilization: 18th Century Origins; The Writing of American History; The United States to 1865; Immigration: the American Mosaic; The North Atlantic Civilization;* and has co-authored *Prescott* (with William Charvat), and *Family Album for Americans* (with Vera Kraus).

RICHARD B. MORRIS (B.A., City College of New York, 1924; M.A., Columbia, 1925; Ph.D., Columbia, 1930; L.H.D., Hebrew Union, 1963) taught at CCNY from 1937 to 1949. Since 1946 he has been at Columbia University, where from 1959 he has held the Gouverneur Morris chair in American history. He has served also as a visiting professor at Princeton University, the University of Hawaii, and the Free University of Berlin. His voluminous publications include *Studies in the History of Early American Law; Government and Labor in Early America; The Peacemakers; The American Revolution Reconsidered; John Jay, the Nation and the Court; The Encyclopedia of American History;* and co-editorship of "The New American Nation" series.

EMIL OBERHOLZER (B.A., Bard, 1948; M.A., Columbia, 1949; Ph.D., Columbia, 1954) is a free-lance translator, editor, and researcher who specializes in Anglo-American church history. He has taught at City College of New York and Hunter College. He is the author of *Delinquent Saints: Disciplinary Action in the Early Congregational Churches of Massachusetts* and is now writing a biography of Agnes Maude Royden.

ALDEN T. VAUGHAN (B.A., Amherst, 1950; M.A., Columbia, 1956, 1958; Ph.D., Columbia, 1964) is Professor of History at Columbia, where he specializes in American colonial history. His publications include *New England Frontier: Puritans and Indians, 1620–1675; Chronicles of the American Revolution; America Before the Revolution, 1725–1775; The Puritan Tradition in America, 1620–1730;* and a bibliography of *The American Colonies in the Seventeenth Century.*

HARRY M. WARD (B.A., William Jewell, 1951; M.A., Columbia, 1954; Ph.D., Columbia, 1960) is Associate Professor of History at the University of Richmond, where he teaches American colonial and Revolutionary War history. He has written *Department of War, 1781–95; United Colonies of New England, 1643–90; "Unite or Die": Intercolony Relations, 1690–1763;* and *Statism in Plymouth Colony.*

JOHN J. WATERS (A.B., Manhattan College, 1957; A.M., Notre Dame, 1959; Ph.D., Columbia, 1965) is Associate Professor of History at the University of Rochester. His special interests include ethnicity, family politics, and leadership dynamics in colonial America; he has written on these topics in the *Journal of Social History,* the *William and Mary Quarterly,* and the *History of Childhood Quarterly.* His book *The Otis Family in Provincial and Revolutionary Massachusetts* received the 1968 Jamestown Foundation Award of the Institute of Early American History and Culture.

PHILIP L. WHITE (B.A., Baldwin-Wallace, 1947; M.A., Columbia, 1949; Ph.D., Columbia, 1954) is Associate Professor of History at the University of Texas at Austin, where he teaches graduate and advanced undergraduate courses on the period of the American Revolution. His major publications are *The Beekmans of New York in Politics and Commerce, 1647–1877,* and *The Beekman Mercantile Papers* (3 vols.).

Index

73 74 75 10 9 8 7 6 5 4 3 2 1